The Encyclopaedia of Celtic Myth and Legend

The Encyclopaedia of Celtic Myth and Legend

A DEFINITIVE SOURCEBOOK OF MAGIC, VISION, AND LORE

Compiled, edited and translated by
John and Caitlín Matthews

THE LYONS PRESS
GUILFORD, CONNECTICUT
AN IMPRINT OF THE GLOBE PEQUOT PRESS

The Lyons Press is an imprint of The Globe Pequot Press.
www.LyonsPress.com

10 8 6 4 2 1 3 5 7 9

Printed in the United States of America

ISBN 1-59228-302-0

First published in 2002 by Rider,
an imprint of Ebury Press, Random House,
20 Vauxhall Bridge Road, London SW1 V 2SA
www.randomhouse.co.uk

The Library of Congress Cataloging-in-Publication Data is available on file.

Contents

Acknowledgments   viii

Introduction: The Bright Knowledge   1

Invasions

1. Selections from The Book of Invasions (*Lebor Gabála Erenn*)   11
2. The First Battle of Moytura (*Cath Mag Tuiread Cong*)   17
3. The Second Battle of Moytura (*Cath Mag Tuiread*)   44

Conceptions and Births

4. The Conception of Conchobor (*Compert Conchobor*)   67
5. The Birth of Cormac (*Compert Cormaic mac Airt*)   72
6. The Birth of Noidiu Nae-Mbreathach (*Compert Noidiu*)   77

Cattle Raids

7. The Cattle Raid of Flidais (*Táin Bó Flidais*)   83
8. The Morrigan's Cow-Raid (*Táin Bó Regamma*)   87
9. The Cattle Raid of Cooley (*Táin Bó Cuailgne*)   91

Voyages

10. The Voyage of Bran, son of Febal (*Imram Brainn mac Febal*)   113
11. The Voyage of Máel Dúin (*Imram Máel Dúin*)   123

Hero Tales

12. The Boyhood Deeds of Cú Chulainn (*Compert Con Cú Chulainn*)   153
13. Six Tales of Mongán: Conception of Mongán (*Compert Mongán*), The Pursuit of Dubh-Lacha of the White Arms (*Toruigheacht Duibhe Lacha Laimh-ghile*), The Death of Fothad Airgdech (*Aided Fothaid Airgdig*), The Alms of Mongán (*Scél Mongán*), The Telling of Mongán's Frenzy (*Tucait Baile Mongán*), The Curse upon Mongán's Lineage (from the *Yellow Book of Lecan*)   166

Dreams and Visions

14. The Dream of Oengus (*Aislinge Oenguso*)   189
15. The Sick-Bed of Cú Chulainn (*Serglige Con Cú Chulainn*)   195

Battles

16. The Battle of Findchorad (*Cath Findchorad*)   221
17. The Battle of Mag Mucrama (*Cath Maige Mucrama*)   230

Wisdom and Lore

18. Fingen's Nightwatch (*Airne Fíngein*) 245
19. Selections from Cormac's *Glossary* (*Sanas Cormaic*) 256

Sieges, Burnings and Curses

20. The Destruction of Dind Rig (*Orgain Denna Rig*) 275
21. The Siege of Howth (*Talland Etair*) 281
22. The Destruction of Da Derga's Hostel (*Togail Bruidne da Derga*) 289
23. The Debility of the Ulstermen (*Ces Noínden Ulad*) 325

Love and Longing

24. The Story of Baile of the Clear Voice (*Scel Baili Binnberlaig*) 331
25. Trystan and Essyllt (*Ystori Trystan*) 334
26. The Noble Youth (*Y Melwas*) 340

Wooings

27. The Wooing of Emer (*Tochmarc Emer*) 345
28. Wooing of Luaine and the Death of Athirne (*Tochmarc Luaine agus Aidedh Aithairne Andso*) 369

Adventures

29. The Adventure of Eachdach's Sons (*Echtra mac nEchach Muigmedóin*) 379
30. The Adventures of Connla (*Echtra Connla*) 385

Feasts and Visitations

31. Bricriu's Feast (*Fled Bricriu*) 391
32. The Excuse of Guile's Daughter (*Ceasacht Inghine Guile*) 426

Exiles

33. The Exile of Conall Corc (*Longes Chonaill Corc*) 437
34. The Exile of the Sons of Uisliu (*Longes mac nUislenn*) 444

Deaths

35. The Death of Conchobar mac Nessa (*Aided Conchobar meic Nessa*) 457
36. The Death of Conn Cetchathach (*Aided Conn Cetchathach*) 461
37. The Death of Cú Chulainn (*Brislech mór Maige Muirthemne*) 468

Appendix: The Story List 476

Glossary 484
Bibliography 494
Thematic Index 500

To All the Keepers of Wisdom and Story

Acknowledgments

Thanks to Irene Dalichow for her invaluable assistance in providing the translation of the German commentaries to the *Táin Bó Flidais*. To the staff of the Bodleian Library and the Taylorian Institute for their patience in dealing with our queries. To Ari Berk and Claudio Crow Quinero for enthusiastic support throughout the long genesis of this book.

Introduction:
The Bright Knowledge

> What has preserved the wise lore of the men in Ireland? The
> common memory of the elders, transmission from ear to ear and
> the chanting of poets, amplified by the letter's law, invigorated by
> the law of nature: these are the three rocks upon which the law of
> the whole world is supported.
>
> from *Senchas Mór*

Among the Irish, the transmission of wisdom and story was called 'the
bright knowledge' or *gléfisa*. That bright knowledge was symbolic of a
great treasury of learning, knowledge and wisdom, a candle that was
eternally renewed as the light passed from recipient to recipient so that
a brighter light might illumine the world. Originally that light was
passed by oral recitation, illuminating memory; latterly, it became
written down, when it was subject to loss or forgetfulness. For when
stories and lore pass out of memory, they are no longer animated by the
heart nor part of everyday life.

Celtic scholarship is still a young skill – barely a hundred and sixty
years old. A great quantity of source material still lies untranslated in
manuscript or inaccessibly shrouded in learned editions. In this
collection, we have striven to bring together the most notable mythic
traditions from source material, without any retelling and with many
new translations. Our criterion has been to include mythic sources,
rather than draw upon folk-lore: a decision that has helped limit what
might have become a huge range of encyclopaedic volumes to one
volume.

The bulk of this collection is drawn from Irish sources, chiefly because
that is where most of the material can be found. Wales has a vast store
of poetic richness but we have chosen to concentrate upon the mythic
and story traditions, which are less well represented in print. Scotland,
Cornwall and Britanny alike have much hagiological literature and many
folk traditions, but they lack the texts of deep myth. While there are

indeed chronicles in these languages, these make for dull reading, so we have chosen to mine the mythic deposits instead.

It is often thought that the myths and legends of the Celtic countries should somehow be available in one place in a convenient volume or two. The reality is somewhat wide of this expectation. The material we have assembled here has been gathered from a vast series of sources, many of them very fragmentary, some bound into the backs of other manuscripts, some patched together with the help of younger, less fragmentary texts. We have not garnered these sources without the help of the brilliant and ground-breaking scholars who preceded us, for many another scholar has been in the quarry before us and painstakingly pieced together references, sources and texts to help create a more complete picture.

We often forget that such patchwork underlies established mythological traditions such as those of Greece, as a glance at the source-lists for Robert Graves' *Greek Myths* will testify: these derive from a similarly fragmentary set of Classical writers, references, poems and stories – many of these remembered tales which later writers have polished and set, to become standardised in our remembrance. Similarly, in Irish myth, the sources are not to be found in one convenient place nor are they from one partricular time.

Myth is a sacred process by which the remembered past is incorporated into the living present. In an alchemical process not dissimilar to the stratifications of geological rock deposit or archaeological evidence, early memory elides into present recall by a series of changes, embedding certain key notions that remain in consciousness as exemplars, guides and inspirations. These monolithic deposits, like notable rock-features that draw the eye in a dynamic landscape, have power to evoke strong connection with the ancestral continuum. Indeed, the importance of story to the Celts can scarcely be overestimated. Story was literally the stuff of life, providing information and wisdom as well as entertainment for the long dark nights, in ways that would otherwise have been lost forever.

The Irish created for themselves a mythic meta-history blend of spirits and ancestors. Like all peoples with an oral memory, they continually recreate themselves, now, as then, by association with those long gone, with heroes, kings and otherworldly beings to make sense of where they are at the present moment. We see this most clearly at the point of interchange between pagan and Christian Ireland, when the long-held memories begin to be transmitted, where Christian clerics interview long-dead ancestors, interrogating them about their stories before passing onto the statutory baptism that will render the deceased storyteller part of the living sacred continuum. This urgent necessity to enshrine ancient remembrances into the ongoing tradition is found in the way that even otherworldly beings proclaim the coming of Christ and his missionaries. Thus, the much loved stories of gods, mermaids, faery women, poets, heroes, lovers and honoured kings, become legitimately enshrined within chronicles, histories and other accounts, transcribed by monks who would not allow their witness to fade. These scribes, by associating all Irish ancestors with the descendants of Noah, incorporated the myths that we have today into a great family of witnesses that goes on and on.

We should say a word about the placement and arrangement of material. We have avoided any attempt at a mythic chronology of a Hesiodian order but preferred to utilise the story titles by which Irish poets made their living. These story-genres are well introduced in an eleventh century allegorical text called *Airecc Menman Uraird maic Coise* in which the poet Urard mac Coise (who lived about 990 CE) went to ask the help of King Domnall mac Muirchertach against raiders who had despoiled his home. Domnall asked the poet to tell him a story and Urard accordingly asked him what kind of story he would like. 'Name them all, so that I can make my choice,' demanded Domnall. Then Urard listed the prime story genres, including the *gnáthscéla* or common stories, the *tánai* or cattleraids, the *echtrai* or adventures, the *coimperta* or conception and birth stories, the *catha* or battles, the *togla* or plunderings, the *fesa* or feasts, the *buili* or madnesses, the *tochmarca* or wooings, the *aithid* or elopements, the *tomadmann* or floods, the *fisi* or visions, the *serca* or love-stories, *slúgaid* or hostings, the *tochomlada* of invasions and the *orcni* or destructions. To these titles we have added other traditional genres, such as the *immrama* (voyages) and *forbassa* (sieges), as well as creating a section to contain wise sayings or *feasa*.

We are aware that the Welsh material does not strictly fall into these categories, but we have lodged them together with the Irish in, we hope, a companionable way. We have been scrupulous in not including any text previously appearing in the companion volume to this one, *The Encyclopaedia of Celtic Wisdom*. Much of the material in this volume appears for a general English readership for the first time.

At the end of his list, Urard adds a fictitious and provocative title that includes himself and his own circumstances: *Orgain Cathrach mail*

Milscothaig maic Anma Airmiten maic Sochoisc Scohuide maic Ollaman Airchetail maic Dána Dligedaig maic Lugdach Ildánaig maic Rúaid Rofesa maic Creidme In Spirda naím Athar sceo Maic or 'The Destruction of the Citadel of Mael Milscothach, son of Reverend Soul, son of Discipline of Society, son of Professor of Poetry, son of Regular Verse, son of Lugaid of the Many Arts, son of Strength of Wisdom, son of Faith in the Holy Spirit, the Father and the Son.' King Domnall is so taken with this astoundingly jaw-breaking title that he demands to know that story instantly, and Urard is able to dramatically present his case and get the help he desires.

This extract not only demonstrates the wit and pride of the professional Irish poet, but also the breadth and versatility of the poet's repertoire. We should remember that these stories were held in memory, not written down, a qualification of only the highest poets, as the *Book of Leinster* says, 'To the highest four grades of poet are assigned 250 prime stories and 100 secondary stories, suitable to be told before kings and nobles.'

Bardic training indeed included the learning by heart of a vast repertoire. The basic curriculum of the Bardic Schools (in Ireland anyway) has been assembled from various sources by Eugene O'Curry in *Manners and Customs of the Ancient Irish* and Patrick Joyce in *A Social History of Ancient Ireland*. It consisted of the following:

1st Year: 50 Oghams or Alphabets. Elementary Grammar. 20 Tales.
2nd Year: 50 Oghams. 6 Easy lessons in Philosophy. Some specified
      poems. 30 Tales.
3rd Year: 50 Oghams. 6 Minor lessons of Philosophy. Certain specified
      poems. Grammar. 40 poems.
4th Year: The *Bretha Nemed* or Law of Privileges. 20 Poems of the
      species called *Eman*. 50 Tales.
5th Year: Grammar. 60 Tales.
6th Year: The Secret Language of the Poets. 48 Poems of the species
      called *Nuath*. 70 or 80 Tales.
7th Year: *Brosnacha*. (Miscellanies.) The Laws of Bardism.
8th Year: Prosody. Glosses (the meaning of obscure words). *Teinm
      Laeghdha. Imbas Forosnai. Dichetal Do Chennibh*. (Divinatory Skills.)
      Dindsenchus. (Topographical Stories).
9th Year: A specified number of compositions of the kind called *Sennat,
      Luasca, Nena, Eochraid, Sruith* and *Duili Feda*. To master 175 tales in
      this three-year period.

10th Year: A further number of the compositions listed above.

11th Year: 100 of the compositions known as *Anamuin*.

12th Year: 120 Cetals or orations. The Four Arts of Poetry.
   During the 3 Years to master 175 tales in all, along with the 175 of
   the *Anruth*, 350 Tales in all.

The sheer scope of learning possible to someone following this discipline, or indeed that mentioned by Caesar, has been assessed by R.A.S. Macalister, who writes:

> Suppose that the pupils were allowed two months' annual holiday, which is probably liberal: in other words, let us for arithmetical convenience keep them at school, 300 working days in a solar year. Then, if they learn no more than ten lines of poetry in a day, they will have acquired a total of 3000 by the end of the year, and in twenty years they will be masters of 60,000 lines. This is considerably more than twice the length of the two Homeric epics. Even if they learned only one line *per diem*, they would have assimilated matter roughly equal in amount to the first ten books of the *Iliad*: if they enlarged their daily task to thirty-five or forty lines, they would in the end possess, stored in memory, matter equal in extent to the prodigious *Mahabarata*.

For the fullest description of a Bardic School in operation we have to turn to a text written in 1722: *The Memoirs of the Marquis of Clanricarde*. Although the text is late, and concerns different aspects of the bardic education, it has been recognised as carrying an authentic charge of that tradition.

> It was . . . necessary that the place should be in the solitary recess of a garden or within a sept or enclosure far out of the reach of any noise, which an intercourse of people might otherwise occasion. The structure was a snug, low hut, and beds in it at convenient distances, each within a small apartment without much furniture of any kind, save only a table, some seats, and a conveniency for clothes to hang upon. No windows to let in the day, nor any light at all used but that of candles, and these brought in at a proper season only . . . The professors . . . gave a subject suitable to the capacity of each class . . . The said subject . . . having been given

over night, they worked it apart each by himself upon his own bed, the whole next day in the dark, till at a certain hour in the night, lights being brought in, they committed it to writing . . . The reason of laying the study aforesaid in the dark was doubtless to avoid then distraction which light and the variety of objects represented thereby . . . This being prevented, the faculties of the soul occupied themselves solely upon the subject in hand . . . Yet the course was long and tedious, as we find, and it was six or seven years before a mastery or the last degree was confirmed. . . .

Where possible, we have included whole texts or stories, but reasons of space have limited us to selecting representative passages from some of the longer ones, such as the *Táin Bó Cuailgne*. The reader will notice the extremely condensed nature of some of the stories, as if the storyteller or copyist assumed knowledge of incidents, relationships and other connections in his readership. This may well have been so, for the oral memory of heroic and mythic characters remains well-known even in Ireland and Wales today in a way that is less obvious within England. We should also remember that the embellishments of an oral storyteller were part and parcel of oral relation, not of transcribed traditions, and that the copyist was working with the exigencies of a limited amount of vellum: a fact that we tend to forget in these days of paper and printing.

With the new translations we have provided here, we have attempted to bring to light unfamiliar material previously unavailable to the general reader, with preceding notes to help contextualise the characters and happenings of the text, without bogging the reader down in linguistic and historical footnotes. Where there is cross-connection between texts or characters we have striven to point this out. We wish that we could have translated more and provided more up to date translations than some of the nineteenth and twentieth editions printed here, but this has not been possible. Translating from old and middle Irish or medieval Welsh is not for the faint-hearted! The language and expressions are frequently tortuous, recondite and bewildering. To present translations of sense and metaphorical cogency has been our aim.

Many early Irish translators often upkept their academic rigour by literal translations which do not serve the reader. Others have, irritatingly, avoided any treatment of the invocations of druids and poets as too difficult (which they often are!) or too silly to waste time on (which they are certainly not!). Their attempts to translate the Irish second person singular has often led to some Biblical-sounding prose in English, while their sometimes literal adherence to Irish word-order can make for an impenetrable thicket of pseudo-Irishisms. However, there are many outstanding brilliancies in the older translations we have chosen, notably the work of Whitley Stokes, Myles Dillon, Kuno Meyer and Mary Dobbs. These and many others have upheld standards of clear communication and impeccable scholarship that are nothing less than miraculously admirable, considering the difficulty of the sources.

The collection is intended, first and foremost, for general readers and those who feel a fascination for the Celtic world. However, we hope that students and Celtic researchers will also make use of it. To this end we have kept critical apparatus, notes and amendments to the minimum. We have deleted the frequent question marks, brackets and elisions which dot the pages of many of these translations, preferring to make the text as smooth as possible and referring scholars in need of more precise notation to the original sources, details of which are provided at the back of the book. We have also kept our own amendments to the minimum, preferring to include necessary glosses either in the text itself or in the brief introductory paragraphs which preface each text rather than as footnotes. Certain aspects of our editorial method should be mentioned for the sake of clarity.

Many of the texts contain different spellings of names – sometimes there are even variants within the same text! We have mostly let these stand as they were written in keeping with long-standing tradition.

Missing or inserted words are indicated by round brackets ( ) for those in the original edited versions texts and square brackets [ ] for those inserted by ourselves.

Certain of the older translations are very literal, and do not always read as smoothly as one might wish; however we have made only infrequent changes to remove the occasional repetitions from the track of the story. Again, we have in general let these stand as they are as an essential aspect of the writers who first set these stories down.

We have amended the layout of the stories in certain areas, occasionally paragraphing the longer passages of description where these became tedious to the eye. Many of the texts run passages of dialogue together into blocks and we have set these in modern style.

Occasionally the poems which are an integral part of the style of these texts have been rendered as prose; we have tried to put them back into more poetic form by breaking the text into lines.

We have provided a full bibliography for those who would like to explore these stories in yet more detail, as well as giving a brief thematic glossary to support the reader, noting major characters and their relationships to each other, as well as giving pronunciation tips on the names.

Our Celtic heritage has been scattered in many places. The bringing together of its lore has been our lifetimes' work, not solely that it might be read, but that it might also be lived and practised, that it might inspire and bring honour to everyday lives. We hope that those who are seeking for the bright knowledge will be able to illumine their own candle here, and that they may, in turn, pass on the *gléfisa* to their descendants.

Caitlín and John Matthews

Oxford

September, 2001

INVASIONS

1. Selections from The Book of Invasions

(Lebor Gabála Erenn)

Translated by R.A.S. Macallister

Reading through the texts which make up the several versions of the *Lebor Gabála Erenn* (literally *'The Book of the Takings of Ireland'*) is somewhat like wading through a bog – one is just as likely to get sucked down as illuminated by the huge, sprawling, contradictory mass of MSS which were faithfully and exhaustively edited by R.A.S. Macallister between 1938 and 1956. The five volumes which make up the work contain several recensions of each text, with poetic fragments thrown in for luck. The main manuscript sources, some fifteen variations of five actual versions, are contained in the collections of the Royal Irish Academy and Trinity College, Dublin. They date from the twelfth century to the fifteenth century.

Trying to make sense of all this richness of material is by no means easy, yet the texts are important enough to make the effort if one is to understand the mythic history of Ireland.

Much of the text was almost certainly adapted (if not actually re-written) by Christian clerics who expunged references to paganism and associated them with those of Biblical origin. Thus we find the curious suggestion that the first settlers in Ireland were descended from Noah – an idea which has given rise to a vast amount of speculation involving, among other things, the so-called 'lost' tribe of Israel. Everything is dated to the number of years before and after 'The Flood', which despite its Biblical association, may indeed refer to an historical disaster, felt even as far away from the East as Ireland. More work needs do be done in order to date the events described. But since we are in mythic time anyway in most of these stories, matters of dating are ultimately less important than the imaginative account of the proto-history of the country.

This aside, what we do find in the *Lebor Gabála* is an account of successive waves of people arriving on the shores of Ireland and meeting with resistance, which, in time, they overcome. Thus we hear for the first time of the great tribes of ancient Ireland – the Fomorians, the Fir Bolg and the Children of Nemed, and learn of their leaders, Cessair, Partholon and Nemed. Each group will be referred back to again and again in the stories collected here, forming a deep, mythic substrata for all that follows.

We have included three extracts here, which have been edited from the many cross-over versions collected by Macallister to make for smooth reading. The reason for their inclusion here is the way in which they set the scene for the early epics of the first and second battles of Moytura (pp. 17–64) which follow them. While we cannot attempt anything like a chronology, the invasion stories do follow a natural order, and paint an extraordinary picture of a time that was so ancient it had already become mythologised by the scribes and poets who first told these tales.

The Tuan mac Carell mentioned at the end of the Partholon extract is the same ageless, reincarnating hero whose story we included in *The Encyclopaedia of Celtic Wisdom*, pp. 93–98.

1. Cessair

Let us cease [at this point] from the stories of the Gaedil, that we may tell of the seven peoples who took Ireland before them. Cessair daughter of Bith son of Noe [Noah] took it, forty days before the Flood. Partholon son of Sera, three hundred years after the Flood. Nemed son of Agnoman of the Greeks of Scythia, at the end of thirty years after Partholon. The Fir Bolg thereafter. The Fir Domnann thereafter. The Gailioin thereafter. The Tuatha dé Danann thereafter. [The sons of Mil thereafter as Fintan said.] Now, who (was the first who) took Ireland after the creation of the world? This is what the Book of Druim Snechta says, that Banba was the name of the first woman who found Ireland before the Flood, and that from her Ireland is called 'Banba'. With thrice fifty maidens she came, and with three men. Ladra, one of the three men, he [was] the first dead man of Ireland at that time: from him is named Ard Ladrann. Forty years were they in the island: thereafter a disease came upon them, so that they all died in one week. Afterward Ireland was for two hundred years without a living person and thereafter came the Flood. A year and forty days was Ireland under the Flood. At the end of three hundred years thereafter, Partholon took Ireland: he dwelt there five hundred and fifty years, till the Cynocephali drave him out, and there escaped (survived) not one of his children alive. For thirty years after that there was not a man living in Ireland.

Thereafter Cessair daughter of Bith son of Noe took it, forty days before the Flood. This is the reason for her coming, fleeing from the Flood: for Noe said unto them: Rise, said he, [and go] to the western edge of the world: perchance the Flood may not reach it.

Thereafter, on Tuesday, dated the fifteenth, she set forth from the island of Meroe upon the river Nile in Egypt. She was ten years in Egypt. Twenty days had she upon the surface of the Caspian Sea. Twelve days had she on the Caspian Sea till she reached the Cimmerian Sea. One day had she in Asia Minor, to the Torrian Sea. A sailing of twenty days had she to the Alpine Mountain: for a space of nine days had she thence to Spain. A sailing of nine days had she from Spain to Ireland. On the fifth day of the month, on Saturday (she landed).

The crew of three ships arrived at Dun na mBarc in the territory of Corco Duibne. Two of the ships were wrecked. Cessair with the crew of her ship escaped, fifty women and three men: Bith son of Noe, of whom is Sliab Betha (named) – there was he buried, in the great stone-heap of Sliab Betha; Ladra the pilot, of whom is Ard Ladrand – he was the first dead man who went under the soil of Ireland; Fintan son of Bochra, of whom is 'Fintan's Grave' over Tul Tuinde. Cessair died in Cul Cessrach in Connachta, with her fifty maidens.

2. Partholon

Now Ireland was waste (thereafter), for a space of three hundred years, till Partholon son of Sera son of Sru came to it. He is the first who took Ireland after the Flood, on a Tuesday, on the fourteenth of the moon, in Inber Scene [. . .] Of the progeny of Magog son of Iafeth was he: in the sixtieth year of the age of Abraham Partholon took Ireland.

Four chieftains strong came with Partholon: himself, and Laiglinne his son, from whom is Loch Laiglinne in Ui mac Uais of Breg [named]; Slanga and Rudraige, the two other sons of Partholon, from whom are Sliab Slanga and Loch Rudraige [named]. When the grave of Rudraige was a-digging, the lake there burst forth over the land.

Seven years had Partholon in Ireland when the first man of his people died, to wit Fea, from whom is Mag Fea [named]; for there was he buried, in Mag Fea.

In the third year thereafter, the first battle of Ireland, which Partholon won in Slemna of Mag Itha against Cichol Clapperleg of the Fomoria. Men with single arms and single legs they were, who joined the battle with him. [. . .]

Partholon died, [along with] five thousand men and four thousand women, of a week's plague on the kalends of May. On a Monday plague took them, and the plague killed them all except one man, Tuan son of Starn son of Sera nephew of Partholon: and God fashioned him in many forms, and that man survived alone from the time of Partholon to the time of Findian and of Colum Cille. So he narrated to them the 'Takings of Ireland' from the time of Cessair. And that is Tuan son of Cairell son of Muiredach Muffiderg.

It was the four sons of Partholon who made the first division of Ireland in the beginning, Er, Orba, Fergna, Feron. There were four men, namesakes to them, among the sons of Mil, but they were not the same. From Ath Cliath of Laigen to Ailech Neit, is the division of Er. From Ath Cliath to the island of Ard Nemid, is the division of Orba. From Ailech to Ath Cliath of Medraige, is the division of Feron. From that Ath Cliath to Ailech Neit, is the division of Fergna. So that in that manner they first divided Ireland.

Partholon had the four oxen, that is the first cattle of Ireland. Of his company was Brea son of Senboth, by whom were a house, a flesh (cauldron), and duelling first made in Ireland. Of his company was Samailiath, by whom were ale-drinking and suretyship first made in Ireland. Of his company was Beoir, by whom a guest house was first made in Ireland.

So those are the tidings of the first Taking of Ireland after the Flood.

3. Nemeð anð the taking of Connaing's Tower

Now Ireland was deserted thereafter for thirty years after Partholon, till Nemed, son of Agnoman son of Paim son of Tait son of Sera son of Sru son of Esru son of Baath son of Rifath Scot came to it. For of the progeny of Rifath Scot is every Taking that took Ireland, except Cessair. At Sru son of Esru the relationship of Partholon and Nemed and the

Fir Bolg and the Tuatha dé Danann and the sons of Mil of Spain unite. And each of these peoples had the Scotic language: this is evident from the story that when Ith son of Breogan came into Ireland, and he and the Tuatha De Danann conversed, it is through Scotic he conversed with them and they with him: and they said that they were of the seed of Rifath. Others say that Nemed was of the seed of the son whom Partholon left in the East, namely, of the seed of Agla son of Partholon.

He came out of Scythia westward, voyaging on the Caspian Sea, till he came in his wandering to the great ocean in the north. His tally was thirty-four ships, with thirty in each ship. There appeared to them a tower of gold on the sea, and they all went to capture it. When the sea was full it would come over that tower and when it was at ebb much of it would be exposed. Such was the greed for the gold that took hold of them that they did not perceive the sea raging around them; so that the eddy took their ships from them except one boat, which carried Nemed and his three sons together with him: and it is they who protected the women. Nemed was a year and a half thereafter a-wandering, till they came to Ireland. [. . .]

Nemed won three battles against the Fomoire: the battle of Ros Fraechain in Connachta, where fell Gand and Sengand, the two kings of the Fomoire; and the battle of Murbolg in Dal Riada, where fell Stam son of Nemed at the hands of Conann son of Faebar in Lethet Lachtmaige in Murbolg of Dal Riata: and the battle of Cnamros in Laigen, where a slaughter of the men of Ireland fell, including Artoat son of Nemed and Beoan son of Starn son of Nemed, at the hands of the same. And those battles were broken before Nemed.

There was [at that time] a great oppression upon the children of Nemed at the hands of the Fomoire at that time, after the death of Nemed, namely at the hands of Morc [Crom?] son of Deled and of Conaing son of Faebar, who was in the Tower of Conaing: and that is Torinis Cetne [Tory Island] today, over against Ireland in the north-west. In it was the great fleet of the Fomoire. This was the oppression: they made a sheeplend of Ireland, and none would dare to let smoke be seen from a house in Ireland by day, at that time: also two thirds of their corn, their milk, and their progeny to be brought to them in taxation. The men of Ireland had to convey this every Samain night to the Fomoire, to Mag Cetne. And this is why it is called Mag Cetne, for the frequency with which they had to convey the tribute thither: as though they should say, Is it to the Same Plain (Mag Cetne) that the tribute will be borne this time.

Wrath and vexation took hold on the men of Ireland for the heaviness of the tax, and so the men of Ireland went to fight against the Fomoire. There were three warriors whom they brought with them, Semeon son of Iarbonel the Soothsayer son of Nemed, and Erglan son of Beoan son of Starn son of Nemed, and Fergus Redside son of Nemed.

Thirty thousand on sea, and thirty thousand on land, that was the tally of the host. And they captured the tower, and Conaing and his family fell at their hands. But after the capture Morc son of Deled appeared with the manpower of three-score ships; so that a joint slaughter, what with Fomoire and Children of Nemed, fell on the shore. Everyone who was not slain was drowned, for they perceived not the sea coming up over them, and none fled from the other, so strenuous was the fight and the battle. In the end only one ship escaped, in which were thirty warriors. They went away from Ireland, fleeing from the sickness and the tax.

Here follow the names of the thirty warriors who escaped, of the seed of Nemed, from the capture of Conainn's Tower. Erglan, Mathach, Artach, Beoan, Bethach, Britan, Baad, Ibad, Bechad, Bronal, Pal, Gortigern, Grenan, Glassan, Ceran, Gabran, Semeon Fortach, Goseen, Guilliuc, Caman, Griman, Taman, Tuirriue, Glas, Feb, Feran, Gam, Dam, Ding, Dial. Those are the names of the thirty men, who escaped from the capture of Conainn's Tower, and of them was Ireland taken again.

2. The First Battle of Moytura

(Cath Mag Tuiread Cong)

Translated by J. Fraser

This text, together with 'The Second Battle of Moytura' (*Mag Tuiread*) which follows it, form a cornerstone of Irish epic material. The first battle, which describes the wanderings of the legendary Fir Bolg and Tuatha dé Danann and their arrival in Ireland, their struggle for possession of the land and the eventual peace between them, appears in a single manuscript: H.2.17, now in the Library of Trinity College, Dublin. Several of the pages are severely damaged, with resultant gaps in the text – however, sufficient has survived to make it readable. The narrative is a powerful one, rich in vivid, savage battle scenes which display a wonderful command of language. Internal evidence, and some contradictions in the text such as when the warrior Aengaba dies in one scene and is resuscitated in the next, suggest that the work was compiled from several sources, not always expertly.

Both stories belong to the genre of Invasion stories, of which the cental source is the *Lebor Gabála Erenn* (*The Book of the Taking of Ireland*), extracts from which procede this story on pp. 11–16. Whether there is any historic truth in these stories remains questionable. It may well be that they preserve memories of strictly local affrays in which raiders from across the seas in Britain or Norway sought to expand their territories. What is important is the number of references to the early gods of Ireland, such as Dagda and Lugh Samildanach and Nuada of the Silver Hand. These texts stand at an important junction in the succession of the mythological texts relating to Ireland. They look forward to the reappearance in later stories of the gods who are still semi-human characters here, and they refer back to the mythological past.

The MS begins abruptly in the middle of a discussion between the poet Fintan and the survivors of the taking of Connaing's Tower, suggesting that the beginning of the story has been lost. However, we can fill in this from the brief reference in the Nemed section of the *Lebor Gabála* as well as learning something of the origins of the aboriginal people encountered by the wandering Children of Nemed.

The Fomorians (Fomoire) are described as a prehistoric tribe whose virtually demonic nature sets them apart from the incoming groups. The origins of their name is lost in an Indo-European past, though recent suggestions have indicated a root in the Celtic word for 'sea' – suggesting that they may have come from outside Ireland originally. The wanderings of the Tuatha dé Danann (the Tribe of Danu or Ana) take them to Greece and Spain, a course which may well refer back to one of the actual routes by which the Celtic peoples arrived in Britain and Ireland in the third century BCE. The Dananns themselves later became identified with the *sídhe* or faery peoples of Ireland, and were referred to as 'The Ever-living Ones' and 'The people of the *sídhe*'.

J. Fraser's translation captures all the fury and swiftness of the narrative. We have made no changes or omissions to this but have reproduced it as it appeared originally, in *Eriu* VIII (1915) pp. 1–63.

Mag Tuiread itself is a plain in the north-west of the province of Connacht.

'Children of powerful Nemed
what is the cause of your assembling?
What has brought you here –
contest, conflict, or combat?'

'What has brought us from our homes,
wise Fintan, is this: we suffer
at the hands of the Fomorians of Ireland
by reason of the greatness of the tribute.'

'Whatever be the tribute, on whomsoever
and wheresoever imposed, it is in our power
either to bear it or to escape from it.

'There is among you a party, quarrelsome,
though few in all the land, that do[es] more
to ruin it than the tribute of the Fomorians.

'Depart if you feel the time is ripe,
glorious sons of Nemed;

do not suffer wrong, remain not here,
but go far hence.'

'Is that your advice to us, wise Fintan?'

'It is,' said Fintan, 'and I have yet more counsel for you: you must not go by one route or in one direction, for a fleet cannot be brought together without outbreak of fighting; a large number means quarrelling, strangers provoke challenge, and an armed host conflict. You do not find it easy to live together in any one spot in Ireland, and it would not be any easier for your hosts in seeking new homes.

'Depart from this land, children of Nemed;
leave Ireland, and escape the violence of your enemies.
Stay here no longer, pay no more tribute.
Your sons or your grandsons will
recover the land from which you are now fleeing.

'You shall travel to the land of the Greeks –
'tis no lying tale I tell –
and though you set out in thousands,
your strength will not be found
sufficient in the East.

'The children of steadfast Beothach
shall leave you and go towards the cold North,
the children of Semeon to the East.
Though you feel it strange, depart.'

So they parted from each other, Fintan and the famous children of Nemed. Beothach, son of Iarbonel, remained, with his ten men and their wives, in Ireland, according to the poet:

'Iarbonel's son, Beothach of the clear-spoken judgements,
remained in Ireland. His children went far eastward,
to the north-west of Lochlann.'

Astonishing is the ignorance shown by those who would have it that Tait, son of Tabarn, was sole king over the children of Nemed, for he was yet unborn. He was born in the East, and never came to Ireland.

Immense was the fleet, eager the gathering – considering from how few sprang the great company that set out from Ireland, for only thirty men had escaped at the taking of Conaing's Tower, and of these a third remained with Beothach in Ireland. The remaining twenty must have multiplied greatly, for the number of ships that were now leaving Ireland was ten thousand, one hundred and forty.

Those dear friends, then, separated, and sad and sorrowful was the little remnant that remained in Ireland [. . .]

[Apparently the next page, which is illegible in the original MS, describes the wanderings of the third of the chieftains to escape the taking of Conaing's Tower. The remainder of the page must then describe the arrival of the Tuatha in Ireland.]

[. . .] the mysteries of wizardry, the knowledge, learning, and prophetic powers, the mastery of arms and skill in cunning feats, the travels and wanderings of the sons of Ibath, for it happened that those tales that had all gone abroad from one place came to be told. A different narrative is necessary for each race. Touching the children of Semeon, son of Starn. A storm had driven them from their course till they came to the dry strands of Thrace and the sandy shores of Greece, and there they settled. Thereupon the inhabitants and the champions of the land visited them, and made a compact of peace and concord with them. Territory was apportioned them, but on the sea-shore, on the distant borders, on cold rough stretches and rugged rocks, on the hill-sides and mountain slopes, on inhospitable heights and in deep ravines, on broken land and ground unfit for cultivation. But the strangers transported a great quantity of soil to the smooth, bare rocks, and made them into smiling clover-covered plains.

When the chiefs and powerful men of the land saw the smooth, broad and grassy fields, and the wide expanses of fruitful cultivated land, they would expel the occupants, and give them in exchange wild, rugged regions, hard stony lands infested with poisonous serpents. However, they tamed and cultivated the ground, and made it into good fruitful fields, smooth and broad like all their land that was taken from them.

But in the meantime the children of Nemed increased and multiplied till they numbered many thousands. The tribute grew heavier and their labour harder till they, now a powerful company, resolved secretly to make wide curved boats of the well-woven bags they used for carrying soil, and to sail for Ireland.

Two hundred years had passed since the taking of Conaing's Tower till the return of the children of Semeon to Ireland. It was at the same time that the famous warlike children of Israel were leaving Egypt in search of the happy land of promise, while the descendants of Gaidel Glas moved up from the south after the escape of the people of God and the drowning of Pharaoh, and came to cold, rugged Scythia.

During the two hundred years after the taking of Conaing's Tower the children of Semeon multiplied till they numbered many thousands, forming strong bold hosts. On account of the severity of the labour and the heaviness of the bondage imposed on them they determined to flee from persecution, endeavoured to escape and make their way to Ireland.

They made boats of their sacks, and stole some of the vessels, boats, and galleys of the soldiers of the Greeks. The lords and leaders, heads, chiefs and champions of that fleet were the five sons of Dela, according to the poet:

'To noble Ireland there set out
the five sons of Dela son of Loth the impetuous,
Rudraige, Genann, Gann, Slainge of the spears, and Sengann.'

They made off at nightfall, and manned their ships in the harbour where they had first landed. Slainge, the elder of the company, who was judge among his brothers, harangued them as follows:

'Now is the time for exertion, care, and watchfulness;
fierce and grey with foam is the sea;
each fair fleet sets forth to escape from intolerable wrong;
the tyranny of the Greeks is unaccustomed;
the plains of salmon-bearing Ireland we must strive to win.

'Give heed to and observe the wrong and injustice you suffer. You have in us five good men to lead the fleet, each of us a match for a hundred.'

'That is true,' his followers replied. 'Let us make the people of this land pay in full for the servitude and the heavy tribute they imposed on us.' And so they killed every one of the Greeks worth killing that they got hold of, and wasted the neighbouring land and made a devastating incursion over it and burnt it. They then brought their plunder and spoil to the place where their ships and galleys were and the smooth, black-prowed boats they had made of their sacks and bags, that is, to Traig Tresgad.

One thousand one hundred and thirty was the number of ships that put out, according to the poet:

'One thousand one hundred and thirty ships –
that, without falsehood, is the number
that accompanied Genann and his people from the East.

'Numerous, indeed, were the Fir Bolg
when they left Greece, a stout company
that set out vigorously on their voyage,
but not in a fleet built of wood.

'On Wednesday they put out to the West
over the wide Tyrrhenian sea,
and after a period of a full year and three days
they arrived in Spain.

'From there to noble Ireland
they made a speedy voyage;
all may proclaim it,
they took a period of thirteen days.'

So they came to Spain. They asked of their seers and druids for information and direction concerning the winds which should next carry them to Ireland. They sailed onwards before a south-west wind till they saw Ireland in the distance. But at that point the wind rose high and strong, and its violence drove huge waves against the sides of the ships; and the fleet separated into three great divisions, the Gaileoin, the Fir Bolg and the Fir Domnann. Slainge put to shore at Inber Slainge in the fifth of the Gaileoin; Rudraige landed at Tracht Rudraige in Ulster; and Genann in Inber Domnann. The wind freshened, and the storm drove Gann and Sengann till they put in at Inber Douglas, where Corcamruad and Corcabaisginn meet.

There they landed, and this is the first place to which sheep were brought in Ireland, and Sheep's Height is its name.

It was on Saturday, the first day of August that Slainge put into Inber Slainge; Gann and Genann put into Inber Domnann on Friday; and Rudraige and Sengann at Tracht Rudraige on Tuesday. The latter were anxious as to whether the Fir Bolg had reached Ireland or not, and sent messengers all over Ireland to gather all of them that had arrived in Ireland to one place, that is, the Stronghold of the Kings in Tara. All of them assembled there. 'We give thanks to the gods,' said they, 'for our return to thee, Ireland. Let the country be divided equitably between us. Bring hither the wise Fintan, and let Ireland be divided according to his decision.'

It was then that Fintan made five portions of Ireland. From Inber Colptha to Comar Tri nUisce was given to Slainge, son of Dela, and his thousand men; Gann's portion was from Comar Tri nUisce to Belach Conglais, Sengann's from Belach Conglais to Limerick. Gann and Sengann, thus, had the two Munsters; Genann was put over Connacht, and Rudraige over Ulster. The poet describes the division thus:

> 'On Saturday, an omen of prosperity,
> Slainge reached lofty Ireland;
> his bold career began at Inber Slainge.

> 'At dark Inber Douglas the two ships
> of Sengann and Gann touched the glorious land.
> Rudraige and prosperous Genann landed on Friday.
> These were all of them, and they were the five kings.

> 'From Inber Colptha to Comar Tri nUisce
> Fintan made one division; that was the portion
> of Slainge of the spears. His host was a thousand men.

> 'From Comar Tri nUisce to famous Belach Conglais
> was the fifth of wound-dealing Gann.
> He had a following of a thousand men.

> 'To Sengann, methinks was given
> from Belach to Limerick. He was at the head
> Of a thousand men when strife threatened.

> 'Genann was undisputed king of Connacht to the Maigue.
> Heroic Rudraige was king of Ulster;
> his were two thousand men in the hour of battle.

> 'Rudraige and Sengann of the spears were, it is certain,
> the chiefs of the Fir Bolg.
> The Gaileon followed glorious Slainge.
> A good king were he that had a more numerous host.'

They entered Ireland from the south, as God saw fitting. The wives of these five chiefs were Auaist, Liben, Cnucha, Edar, and Fuat, as the poet says:

> 'Fuat was the wife of Slainge as you hold,
> Edar of the warrior Gann,

Auaist of Sengann of the spears,
Cnucha of fair Genann.

'Liben was the wife of Rudraige the Red –
they made a pleasant company on a visit.
However, as for Rudraige, the feat-performing king,
I have heard that his wife was Fuat.'

The Fir Bolg then occupied Ireland, and were masters of it for thirty
years.

As for the Tuatha dé Danann, they prospered till their fame went
abroad over the lands of the earth. They had a god of wizardry of their
own, Eochaid Ollathir, called the Great Dagda, for he was an excellent
god. They had bold, hardy chiefs, and men proficient in every art; and
they determined to go to Ireland. Then set out those daring chiefs,
representing the military prowess of the world, and the skill and
learning of Europe. They came from the northern islands to Dobur and
Irrdobur, to S [. . .] and Genann's well. There they stayed for four years,
and at their coming to Ireland Nuada, son of Echtach, was king over
them.

   Then those warriors gathered their fleets to one place – till they had
three hundred ships under way. Thereupon their seers, Cairbre, Aed,
and Edan asked the chiefs of the host in which ship they should sail,
recommending that of Fiachra. The chiefs approved and went on
board. Then they all set sail, and after three years and three days and
three nights landed at wide Tracht Mugha in Ulster on Monday of the
first week in May.

   Now, on the arrival of the Tuatha dé Danann in Ireland, a vision was
revealed in a dream to Eochaid, son of Erc, high king of Ireland. He
pondered over it with much anxiety, being filled with wonder and
perplexity. He told his wizard, Cesard, that he had seen a vision. 'What
was the vision?' asked Cesard. 'I saw a great flock of black birds,' said the
king, 'coming from the depths of the Ocean. They settled over all of us,
and fought with the people of Ireland. They brought confusion on us,
and destroyed us. One of us, methought, struck the noblest of the birds
and cut off one of its wings. And now, Cesard, employ your skill and
knowledge, and tell us the meaning of the vision.' Cesard did so, and
by means of ritual and the use of his science the meaning of the king's
vision was revealed to him; and he said:

'I have tidings for you: warriors
are coming across the sea,
a thousand heroes covering the ocean;
speckled ships will press in upon us;
all kinds of death they announce,
a people skilled in every art, a magic spell;
an evil spirit will come upon you, signs
to lead you astray;
they will be victorious in every stress.'

'That,' said Eochaid, 'is a prophecy of the coming to Ireland of enemies from far distant countries.'

As for the Tuatha dé Danann, they all arrived in Ireland, and immediately broke and burnt all their ships and boats. Then they proceeded to the Red Hills of Rian in Brefne in the east of Connacht, where they halted and encamped. And at last their hearts and minds were filled with contentment that they had attained to the land of their ancestors.

Now it was reported to the Fir Bolg that that company had arrived in Ireland. That was the most handsome and delightful company, the fairest of form, the most distinguished in their equipment and apparel, and their skill in music and playing, the most gifted in mind and temperament that ever came to Ireland. That too was the company that was bravest and inspired most horror and fear and dread, for the Tuatha dé excelled all the peoples of the world in their proficiency in every art.

'It is a great disadvantage to us,' said the Fir Bolg, 'that we should have no knowledge or report of where yon host came from, or where they mean to settle. Let Sreng set out to visit them, for he is big and fierce, and bold to spy on hosts and interview strangers, and uncouth and terrifying to behold.' Thereupon Sreng rose, and took his strong hooked reddish-brown shield, his two thick-shafted javelins, his death-dealing sword, his fine four-cornered helmet and his heavy iron club; and went on his way to the Hill of Rain.

The Tuatha dé saw a huge fearsome man approaching them. 'Here comes a man all alone,' they said. 'It is for information he comes. Let us send some one to speak with him.'

Then Bres, son of Elatha, went out from the camp to inspect him and parley with him. He carried with him his shield and his sword, and his two great spears. The two men drew near to each other till they were within speaking distance. Each looked keenly at the other without speaking a word. Each was astonished at the other's weapons and appearance; Sreng wondered at the great spears he saw, and rested his shield on the ground before him, so that it protected his face. Bres, too, kept silent and held his shield before him. Then they greeted each other, for they spoke the same language – their origin being the same – and explained to each other as follows who they and their ancestors were:

> 'My flesh and my tongue were gladdened
> at your pleasant cheerful language,
> as you recounted the genealogies
> from Nemed downwards.
> By origin our two peoples are as brothers;
> our race and kin are descended from Semeon.
>
> 'This is the proper time to bear it in mind,
> if we are, in flesh and blood,
> of the same distinguished race as you.
> Humble your pride, let your hearts draw nigher,
> be mindful of your brotherhood,
> prevent the destruction of your own men.
>
> 'High is our temper, lordly our pride
> and fierce against our foes; you shall not abate it.
> Should our peoples meet, it will be
> a gathering where many will be crushed;
> let him who will bring entertainment,
> 'tis not he that will amuse them.'

'Remove your shield from before your body and face,' said Bres, 'that I may be able to give the Tuatha dé an account of your appearance.'

'I will do so,' said Sreng, 'for it was for fear of that sharp spear you carry that I placed my shield between us.' Then he raised his shield.

'Strange and venomous,' said Bres, 'are those spears, if the weapons of all of you resemble them. Show me your weapons.'

'I will,' said Sreng; and he thereupon unfastened and uncovered his thick-shafted javelins. 'What do you think of these weapons?' he said.

'I see,' said Bres, 'huge weapons, broad-pointed, stout and heavy, mighty and keen-edged.

'Woe to him whom they should smite,
woe to him at whom they shall be flung,
against whom they shall be cast;
they will be instruments of oppression.
Death is in their mighty blows,
destruction in but one descent of them;
wounds are their hard plying;
overwhelming is the horror of them.

'What do you call them?' said Bres.

'Battle javelins are these,' said Sreng.

'They are good weapons,' said Bres, 'bruised bodies they mean, gushing gore, broken bones and shattered shields, sure scars and present plague. Death and eternal blemish they deal, sharp, foe-like, and deadly are your weapons, and there is fury for fratricide in the hearts of the hosts whose weapons they are. Let us make a compact and covenant.'

They did so. Each came nigh to the other, and Bres asked: 'Where did you spend last night, Sreng?'

'At the hallowed heart of Ireland, in the Rath of the kings in Tara, where are the kings and princes of the Fir Bolg, and Eochaid, High-king of Ireland. And you, whence come you?'

'From the hill, from the crowded capacious camp yonder on the mountain-slope where are the Tuatha dé and Nuada, their king, who came from the north of the world in a cloud of mist and a magic shower to Ireland and the land of the west.' (However, he did not believe that it was thus they came.)

It was then Sreng said: 'I have a long journey, and it is time for me to go.'

'Go then,' said Bres, 'and here is one of the two spears I brought with me. Take it as a specimen of the weapons of the Tuatha dé.'

Sreng gave one of his javelins to Bres as a specimen of the weapons of the Fir Bolg. 'Tell the Fir Bolg,' said Bres, 'that they must give my people either battle or half of Ireland.'

'On my word,' said Sreng, 'I should prefer to give you half of Ireland than to face your weapons.' They parted in peace, after making a compact of friendship with each other.

Sreng went on his way to Tara. He was asked for tidings of the people he had gone to parley with; and he told his story. 'Stout are their soldiers,' he said, 'manly and masterful their men, bloody and battle-sure their heroes, very great and strong their shields, very sharp and hard of shaft their spears, and hard and broad their blades. Hard it is to fight with them; 'tis better to make a fair division of the land, and to give them half of Ireland as they desire.'

'We will not grant that, indeed,' said the Fir Bolg, 'for if we do, the land will all be theirs.'

Bres reached his camp, and was asked for a description of the man he had gone to parley with, and of his weapons. 'A big, powerful, fierce man,' he said, 'with vast, wonderful weapons, truculent and hardy withal, without awe or fear of any man.'

The Tuatha dé said to each other: 'Let us not stay here, but go to the west of Ireland, to some strong place, and there let us face whomsoever comes.' So the host travelled westward over plains and inlets till they came to Mag Nia, and to the end of Black Hill, which is called Sliabh Belgadain. On their arrival there they said: 'This is an excellent place, strong and impregnable. From here let us wage our wars, and make our raids, here let us devise our battles and hostings.' Their camping there is mentioned by the poet in the lines:

'From the Hill of Belgadain to the Mountain-lofty
is the mountain round which we wage our contests.
From its summit the Tuatha dé laid hold of Ireland.'

It was then that Badb and Macha and Mórrígan went to the Knoll of the Taking of the Hostages, and to the Hill of Summoning of Hosts at Tara, and sent forth magic showers of sorcery and compact clouds of mist and a furious rain of fire, with a downpour of red blood from the air on the warriors' heads; and they allowed the Fir Bolg neither rest nor stay for three days and nights. 'A poor thing,' said the Fir Bolg, 'is the sorcery of our sorcerers that they cannot protect us from the sorcery of the Tuatha dé.'

'But we will protect you,' said Fathach, Gnathach, Ingnathach, and Cesard, the sorcerers of the Fir Bolg; and they stayed the sorcery of the Tuatha dé.

Thereupon the Fir Bolg gathered, and their armies and hosts came to one place of meeting. There met the provincial kings of Ireland. First came Sreng and Serene and Sithbrugh the three sons of Sengann, with the people of the provinces of Curói. There came too Esca, Econn, and Cirb with the hosts of Conchobar's province; the four sons of Gann with the hosts of the province of Eochaid son of Luchta; the

four sons of Slainge with the army of the province of the Gaileoin; and
Eochaid, the high-king, with the hosts of Connacht. The Fir Bolg,
numbering eleven battalions, then marched to the entrance of Mag
Nia. The Tuatha dé, with seven battalions, took up their position at the
western end of the plain. It was then that Nuada proposed to the
Tuatha dé to send envoys to the Fir Bolg: 'They must surrender the half
of Ireland, and we shall divide the land between us.'

'Who are to be our envoys?' the people asked.

'Our poets,' said the king, meaning Cairbre, Ai, and Edan.

So they set out and came to the tent of Eochaid [mac Erc], the high-
king. After they had been presented with gifts, they were asked the
reason of their coming. 'This is why we are come,' they said, 'to request
the dividing of the land between us, an equitable halving of Ireland.'

'Do the nobles of the Fir Bolg hear that?' said Eochaid.

'We do,' they replied, 'but we shall not grant their request till
doomsday.'

'Then,' said the poets, 'when do you mean to give battle?'

'Some delay is called for,' said the Fir Bolg nobles, 'for we shall have
to prepare our spears, to mend our mail, to shape our helmets, to
sharpen our swords, and to make suitable attire.'

There were brought to them men to arrange those things. 'Provide,'
said they, 'shields for a tenth, swords for a fifth, and spears for a third
part. You must each furnish what we require on either side.'

'We,' said the envoys of the Tuatha dé to the Fir Bolg, 'shall have to
make your spears, and you must make our javelins.'

The Tuatha dé were then given hospitality till that was done.
(However, though it is said here that the Fir Bolg had no spears, such
had been made for Rindal, grandfather of their present king.) So they
arranged an armistice till the weapons arrived, till their equipment was
ready, and they were prepared for battle.

Their druids went back to the Tuatha dé and told their story from
beginning to end, how the Fir Bolg would not share the land with them,
and refused them favour or friendship. The news filled the Tuatha dé
with consternation.

Thereupon Ruad with twenty-seven of the sons of courageous Mil
sped westwards to the end of Mag Nia to offer a hurling contest to the
Tuatha dé. An equal number came out to meet them. The match
began. They dealt many a blow on legs and arms, till their bones were
broken and bruised, and fell outstretched on the turf, and the match

ended. The Cairn of the Match is the name of the cairn where they met, and Glen Carne Aillem the place where they are buried.

Ruad turned eastward, and told his tale to Eochaid. The king was glad of the killing of the Tuatha dé's young soldiers, and said to Fathach, 'Go to the west, and ask of the nobles of the Tuatha dé how the battle is to be fought to-morrow – whether it is to be for one day or for several.'

The poet went and put the question to the nobles of the Tuatha dé, that is, Nuada, the Dagda and Bres. 'What we propose,' they said, 'is to fight them with equal numbers on both sides.'

Fathach went back, and reported to the Fir Bolg the choice of the Tuatha dé. The Fir Bolg were depressed, for they disliked the choice of the Tuatha dé. They decided to send for Fintan to see if he could give them some counsel. Fintan came to them.

The Fir Bolg had entrenched a great fort. (It was called the Fort of the Packs, from the packs of dogs that preyed on the bodies of the dead after the battle, or the Fort of the Blood Pools, from the pools of gore that surrounded the wounded when the people came to see them.) They made a Well of Healing to heal their warriors from their wounds. This was filled with herbs. Another entrenched fort was made by the Tuatha dé. (It was called the Fort of the Onsets, from the onsets directed out of the battle.) They dug a Well of Healing to heal their wounds.

When these works had been finished, Cirb asked: 'Whence come ye, and whither go ye [now that the peace between us is ended]? The care of tomorrow's battle be yours. I will lead the attack with Mogarn and his son Ruad, Laige and his father Senach.'

'We will meet them with four battalions,' was the reply.

Six weeks of the summer, half the quarter, had gone on the appointed day of battle. The hosts rose on that day with the first glimmer of sunlight. The painted, perfectly wrought shields were hoisted on the backs of brave warriors, the tough, seasoned spears and battle-javelins were grasped in the right hands of heroes, together with the bright swords that made the duels dazzle with light as the shining sunbeams shimmered on the swords' graven groves. Thus the firm, close-packed companies, moved by the compelling passion of their courageous commanders, advanced towards Mag Nia to give battle to the Tuatha dé.

It was then that the Fir Bolg poet, Fathach, went forward in front of them to describe their fury and spread the report of it. He had raised up and planted firmly in the midst of the plain a pillar of stone, against which he rested. This was the first pillar set up in the plain, and Fathach's Pillar was its name thenceforth. Then Fathach in utter anguish wept floods of fervent, melancholy tears, and said:

'With what pomp they advance!
On Mag Nia they marshal with dauntless might.
'Tis the Tuatha dé that advance,
and the Fir Bolg of the decorated blades.

'The Red Badb will thank them
for the battle-combats I look on.
Many will be their gashed bodies
in the east after their visit to Mag Tured.
[Desolate] will be the host after parting
with the warriors I speak of.
Many a head shall be severed
with vigour and with pomp.'

The Tuatha formed a compact, well-armed host, marshalled by fighting warriors and provided with deadly weapons and stout shields. Every one of them pressed on his neighbour with the edge of his shield, the shaft of his spear, or the hilt of his sword, so closely that they wounded each other. The Dagda began the attack on the enemy by cutting his way through them to the west, clearing a path for a hundred and fifty. At the same time Cirb made an onslaught on the Tuatha dé, and devastated their ranks, clearing a path for a hundred and fifty through them. The battle continued in a series of combats and duels, till in the space of one day great numbers were destroyed. A duel took place between Aidleo of the Tuatha dé and Nertchu of the Fir Bolg. The glued seams of their shields were torn, their swords wrenched from their hilts, and the rivets of their spears loosened. Aidleo fell at the hands of Nertchu.

By the close of the day the Tuatha dé were defeated and returned to their camp. The Fir Bolg did not pursue them across the battlefield but returned in good spirits to their own camp. They each brought with them into the presence of their king a stone and a head, and made a great cairn of them. The Tuatha dé set up a stone pillar called the Pillar of Aidleo, after the first of them to be killed. Their physicians then assembled. The Fir Bolg too had their physicians brought to them.

They brought healing herbs with them, and crushed and scattered them on the surface of the water in the well, so that the precious healing waters became thick and green. Their wounded were put into the well, and immediately came out whole.

Next morning Eochaid, the high-king, went to the well all alone to wash his hands. As he was doing so, he saw above him three handsome, haughty armed men. They challenged him to combat.

'Give me time,' said the king, 'to go to fetch my weapons.'

'We will allow not a moment's delay for that; the combat must be now.'

While the king was in this difficulty, a young active man appeared between him and his enemies, and turning to the latter, said: 'You shall have combat from me in place of the king.'

They raised their hands simultaneously, and fought till all four fell together. The Fir Bolg came up after the struggle was over. They saw the dead men, and the king told them how they had come upon him, and how the solitary champion had fought with them in his stead. The Fir Bolg brought each man a stone to the well for him, and built a great cairn over him. The Champion's Cairn is the name of the cairn, and the hill is called the Hill of the Three. The strangers were Oll, Forus, and Fir, three physicians, brothers of Diancecht, and they had come to spy upon the physicians of the Fir Bolg, when they came upon Eochaid alone washing his face.

The battalions of the Tuatha dé were straightway drawn up in the plain to the east; and the Fir Bolg came into the plain against them from the west. The chiefs who went out in front of the Tuatha dé on that day were Ogma, Midir, Bodb Derg, Diancecht, and Aengaba of Norway. The women, Badb, Macha, Mórrígan and Danann offered to accompany them. Against them came of the Fir Bolg, Mella, Ese, Ferb, and Faebur, all sons of Slainge. Strong, mighty blows were dealt by the battalions on either side, and the bosses of shields were broken as they vigorously parried the blows, while the men-at-arms showed their fury, and the warriors their courage. Their spears were twisted by the continual smiting; in the hand-to-hand combats the swords broke on splintered bones; the fearsome battle-cries of the veterans were drowned in the multitude of shouts.

Briskly the young men turned about for the number of the exploits around them on every side. The warriors blenched at the clashing of swords, at the height of the heaving, and the fury of the fall. Well-timed was the warding there, and gallant the guarding, and rapid the rending blows. Nemed, Badrai's son, approached the flank of the Fir Bolg. Then men closed round him, and in the conflict Eochaid's son, Slainge the Fair, made towards him. The two warriors attacked each other. There was straining of spears and shivering of swords and shattering of shields and battering of bodies. However, Nemed fell at the hands of Slainge; they dug his grave and erected a pillar for him, and the Stone of Nemed is its name to this day. Four sons of Slainge, son of Dela, urged the fight against the Tuatha dé. On the side of the Tuatha dé the four sons of Cencal battled with them. They harassed each other till the sons of Cencal fell before the sons of Slainge. The latter were then set on by the five sons of Lodan the Swift, and the five sons of Lodan fell at their hands. Aengaba of Norway began to mow down the enemy and confuse their ranks. Ruad heard this, and rushed into the fray. The three sons of Dolad met him, and he wreaked his anger on them and they fell before him. From another quarter of the battle the three sons of Telle met him, and were slain by him in the same way. Lamh Redolam and Cosar Conaire were killed by Slainge the Fair by the side of the lake. Of those seventeen the gravestones were planted by the side of the lake, for they had been driven back as far as the lake.

Ruad and Aengaba of Norway met; they raised their shields against each other, and kept wounding each other till Aengaba had twenty-four wounds inflicted on him by Ruad. In the end Ruad cut off his head, and after that went on fighting till nightfall. [However, Aengaba is resuscitated later on.]

Ogma, son of Ethliu, made an attack on the host, and his track was marked by pools of crimson blood. From the east side Cirb entered the fray and made an onslaught on the hosts, and three hundred of the Tuatha dé fell before him.

When night fell the Fir Bolg were driven across the battlefield. However, they brought each a head and a stone to Eochaid their king. 'Is it you that have been beaten today?' said the king.

'Yes,' said Cirb, 'but that will not profit them.'

Next day it was the turn of Sreng, Semne, and Sithbrug, along with Cirb, to lead the Fir Bolg. They rose early in the morning. A flashing penthouse of shields and a thick forest of javelins they made over them, and the battle-props then moved forward. The Tuatha dé saw the Fir Bolg approaching them in that fashion across the plain from the east.

'With how much pomp,' they said, 'do those battle-props enter the plain and draw towards us.'

The Tuatha dé asked who should lead them on that day. 'I will,' said the Dagda, 'for in me you have an excellent god'; and, thereupon, he went forth with his sons and brothers. The Fir Bolg had firmly stationed their props and columns, and marshalled their battalions on the level of Mag Nia (which, henceforth, was called Mag Tured, the Plain of Props). Each side then sprang at the other. Sreng, son of Sengann, began to dislodge the hosts of the enemy. The Dagda set to breaking the battalions and harrying the hosts and dislodging divisions and forcing them from their positions. Cirb, son of Buan, entered the fray from the east and slaughtered brave men and spirited soldiers. The Dagda heard Cirb's onset, and Cirb heard the Dagda's battering blows. They sprang each at the other. Furious was the fight as the good swords fenced, heroic the heroes as they steadied the infantry, and answered the onslaughts. At last Cirb fell before the Dagda's battering blows.

Sreng, Sengann's son, was pressing back the hosts from their places when he came on three sons of Cairbre Cas of the Tuatha dé, and the three sons of Ordan. Cairbre's sons with their three columns fell before the sons of Ordan, as Sreng drove in the hosts. The enemy fell before him on every side, and the fury of the combat grew behind him.

After the fall of Cirb the Fir Bolg were driven into their camp. The Tuatha dé did not pursue them across the battlefield, but they took with them a head and a stone pillar apiece including the head of Cirb, which was burried in the Cairn of Cirb's Head.

The Fir Bolg were neither happy nor cheerful that night, and as for the Tuatha dé, they were sad and dispirited. But during the same night Fintan came with his sons to join the Fir Bolg, and this made them all glad, for valiant were both he and they.

In this cheerful mood the morning found them. The signals of their chiefs roused them on the spacious slopes of their camping ground, and they began to hearten each other to meet danger and peril. Eochaid, the high-king, with his son, Slainge the Fair, and the soldiers and chiefs of Connaught, came forth to join them. Sengann's three sons with the hosts of Curoi's province, took their place at one side of the line. The four sons of Gann with the warriors of Eochaid's province marched to the centre of the same army. Buan's sons Esca and Egconn ranged themselves with the men of Conchobar's province on the other wing. The four sons of Slainge with the host of the Gaileoin brought up the rear of the army. Round Eochaid, the high-king, they made a fold of valour of battle-scarred, blood-becrimsoned braves, and juggling jousters, and the world's trustiest troops. The thirteen sons of Fintan, men proven in courageous endurance of conflict, were brought to where the king was.

A flaming mass was the battle on that day, full of changing colours, many feats and gory hands, of sword-play and single combats, of spears and cruel swords and javelins; fierce it was and pitiless and terrible, hard-packed and close-knit, furious and far-flung, ebbing and flowing with many adventures. The Fir Bolg, in the order told, marched boldly and victoriously straight westwards to the end of Mag Tured till they came to the firm pillars and props of valour between themselves and the Tuatha dé.

The passionate Tuatha dé made an impetuous, furious charge in close-knit companies with their venomous weapons; and they formed one mighty gory phalanx under the shelter of red-rimmed, emblazoned, plated, strong shields. The warriors began the conflict. The flanks and the wings of the van were filled with grey-haired veterans swift to wound; aged men were stationed to assist and attend on the movements of those veterans; and next to those steady, venomous fighters were placed young men under arms. The champions and serving men were posted in the rear of the youths. Their seers and wise men stationed themselves on pillars and points of vantage, plying their sorcery, while the poets took count of the feats and wrote down tales of them.

As for Nuada, he was in the centre of the fight. Round him gathered his princes and supporting warriors, with the twelve sons of Gabran from Scythia, his body-guard. They were Tolc, Trenfer, Trenmiled, Garb, Glacedh, Gruasailt Duirdri, Fonnam, Foirisem, Teidm, Tinnargain and Tescad. He would have no joy of life on whom they made a gory wound. ('Twas they that killed the sons of Fintan, and the sons of Fintan killed them.) Thus they delivered their assault after fastening their bodies to rough-edged stones with clasps of iron; and made their way to the place appointed for the battle. At that moment Fathach, the poet of the Fir Bolg, came to his own pillar, and as he surveyed the armies to the cast and west, said:

> 'Swiftly advance the hosts
> marshalling on Mag Nia
> their resistless might;

tis the Tuatha dé that advance
and the Fir Bolg of the speckled swords.

'Methinks the Fir Bolg will lose
some of their brothers there –
many will be the bodies and heads
and gashed flanks on the plain.

'But though they fall on every side,
fierce and keen will be their onset;
though they fall, they will make
others to fall, and heroes will be laid low
by their impetuous valour.

'Thou hast subdued the Fir Bolg;
they will fall there by the side
of their shields and their blades;
I will not trust to the strength
of any one so long as I shall be
in stormy Ireland.

'I am Fathach, the poet; strongly
has sorrow vanquished me, and now,
that the Fir Bolg are gone,
I shall surrender to the swift advance of disaster.'

The furies and monsters and hags of doom cried aloud so that their
voices were heard in the rocks and waterfalls and in the hollows of the
earth. It was like the fearful agonising cry on the last dreadful day when
the human race will part from all in this world. In the van of the Tuatha
dé advanced the Dagda, Ogma, Alla, Bres, and Delbaeth, the five sons
of Elatha, together with Bres, grandson of Net, the Fomorian, Aengus,
Aed, Cermad the Fair, Midir, Bodb Derg, Sigmall Abartach, Nuada the
high-king, Brian, Iuchar and Iucharba, the three sons of Turenn
Bigrenn, Cu, Cian and Cethenn, the three sons of Cainte, Goibnenn
the Smith, Lucraidh the Joiner, Credne the Craftsman, Diancecht the
Physician, Aengaba of Norway; the three queens, Ere, Fotla and Banba,
and the three sorceresses, Badb, Macha and Mórrígan, with Bechuille
and Danann their two foster-mothers.

They fixed their pillars in the ground to prevent any one fleeing till
the stones should flee. They lunged at each other with their keen sharp

spears, till the stout shafts were twisted through the quivering of the victims on their points. The edges of the swords turned on the lime-covered shields. The curved blades were tempered in boiling pools of blood in the thighs of warriors. Loud was the singing of the lances as they cleft the shields, loud the noise and din of the fighters as they battered bodies and broke bones in the rear. Boiling streams of blood took the sight from the grey eyes of resolute warriors.

It was then that Bres made an onset on the Fir Bolg army, and killed one hundred and fifty of them. He struck nine blows on the shield of Eochaid the high-king, and Eochaid, in his turn, dealt him nine wounds. Sengann's son, Sreng, turned his face to the army of the Tuatha dé, and slew one hundred and fifty of them. He struck nine blows on the shield of the high-king Nuada, and Nuada dealt him nine wounds.

Each dealt dire blows of doom, making great gory wounds on the flesh of the other, till under their grooved blades shields and spears, heads and helmets broke like the brittle branches hacked with hatchets wielded by the stout arms of woodsmen. Heroes swayed to this side and that, each circling the other as they sought opportunity for a blow. The battle champions rose again over the rims of their emblazoned shields. Their courage grew, and the valiant virulent men became steadfast as an arch. Their hands shot up with their swords, and they fenced swiftly about the heads of warriors, hacking their helmets. For a moment they thrust back the ranks of the enemy from their places, and at the sight of them the hosts wavered like the water flung far over its sides by a kettle through excess of boiling, or the flood that, like a waterfall, an army splashes up over a river's banks, making it passable for their troops behind them.

So a suitable space was cleared for the chiefs; the heroes yielded them their places, and agile combatants their stations; warriors were dislodged by them, and the serving-men fled for horror of them. To them was left the battle. Heavily the earth was trodden under their feet till the hard turf grew soft beneath them. Each of them inflicted thirty wounds on the other. Sreng dealt a blow with his sword at Nuada, and, cutting away the rim of his shield, severed his right arm at the shoulder; and the king's arm with a third of his shield fell to the ground. It was then that the high-king called aloud for help, and Aengaba of Norway, hearing him, entered the fray to protect him.

Fierce and furious was the attack Aengaba and Sreng made on each other. Each inflicted on his opponent an equal number of wounds, but they were not comparable as an exchange, for the broad blade of Sreng's lance and his stout spear-shaft dealt deeper, deadlier wounds.

As soon as the Dagda heard the music of the swords in the battle-stress, he hastened to the place of conflict with deliberate bounds, like the rush of a great waterfall. Sreng declined a contest with the two warriors; and though Aengaba of Norway did not fall there, it was from the violence of that conflict that he afterwards died. The Dagda came and stood over Nuada, and, after the Tuatha dé had taken counsel, he brought fifty soldiers, with their physicians. They carried Nuada from the field. His hand was raised in the king's stead on the fold of valour, a fold of stones surrounding the king, and on it the blood of Nuada's hand trickled.

The Tuatha dé maintained the conflict keenly and stoutly, after their king was gone. Bres made his way into the ranks of the Fir Bolg to avenge his king, and came to the spot where Eochaid was urging the battle, and fortifying his fighters and exhorting his heroes and encouraging his captains and arranging his combats. Each of them then made for his opponent, and wounds were inflicted where they were undefended. Before the fierceness of their fury and the weight of their blows, soldiers were thrown into confusion. At last Bres was slain by Eochaid; and the Dagda, Ogma, Alla and Delbaeth attacked the latter to avenge their brother.

Eochaid was urging the fight, collecting and encouraging his captains, making close and compact the ranks of the soldiery, holding his fighting men firm and steadfast. The four brothers, in their search for Eochaid, drove the hosts before them to the place where they heard him urging the fight. Mella, Ese, Ferb and Faebur, sons of Slainge, met them and each struck at the other's shield. Their swords clashed and the conflict grew, and the edges of the curved blades cut gory wounds. The four sons of Slainge fell before the other four; and the Gravestones of Slainge's sons is the name of the place where they were buried.

The four sons of Gann then entered the fray. Against them advanced Goibnenn the Smith, Lucraid the Joiner, Dian Cecht and Aengaba of Norway. Horrible was the noise made by the deadly weapons in the champions' hands. Those combatants maintained the fight till the four sons of Gann were slain; and the Mound of the Sons of Gann is the name of the place where they were buried.

So Bedg, Redg and Rinne, the three sons of Ordan, set on the Tuatha dé, and the ranks shook before their onset. The three sons of Cainte met them, but they wearied of the fray; and the Mound of the Wizards is the place where they were buried.

Brian, Iuchar and Iucharba, the three sons of Turenn Bigrenn, set on the Fir Bolg host. They were opposed by two sons of Buan, and Cairbre son of Den. The sons of Buan were overcome by the sons of Turenn Bigrenn, and the Gravestones of Buan are the gravestones that cover them, and Cairbre's tomb is beside the gravestones.

Eochaid and his son, Slainge the Fair, now joined in the fray, and destroyed innumerable companies of the Tuatha dé. 'Our best men,' said Eochaid, 'have been destroyed, our people slaughtered, and it befits us to acquit us valorously.' So they made their way across the battlefield once again, and mowed down men and slaughtered soldiers and hacked hosts, and confused the ranks with their onsets. After this long-continued effort Eochaid was overcome by great weariness and excess of thirst. 'Bring Sreng to me,' he said. That was done. 'You and Slainge the Fair,' said Eochaid, 'must maintain the fight till I go in search of a drink, and to bathe my face, for I cannot endure this consuming thirst.'

'It shall be maintained right well,' said Slainge, 'though we are but few to wage it in your absence.'

Eochaid then went out of the battle with a guard of one hundred of his soldiers. The Tuatha dé followed them, and shouted at them.

But Slainge the Fair advanced to meet the host, and offered them battle, and prevented them from following the high-king. He was attacked by powerful Lugaid son of Nuada, and the two fought a cruel, fierce, strenuous fight, in which there were wounds and bruises and gory gashing. As soon as the rest saw that Slainge was prevailing they gave their support to Lugaid. Lugaid and Slainge fell together; and Lugaid's Grave is the place where Lugaid was buried, and Slainge's Mound the mound where they buried Slainge.

When the Tuatha dé wizards saw how the king of Ireland was suffering from a burning thirst, they hid from him all the streams and rivers of Ireland till he came to the strand of Eothail. Three sons of Nemed, son of Badrai, followed him, with a hundred and fifty men. They fought on the strand, and a number fell on either side. Eochaid and the sons of Nemed met in combat. Venomous in battle were the sons of Nemed, and tried in fighting against odds was Eochaid. They fought till their bodies were torn and their chests cut open with the mighty onslaughts. Irresistible was the king's onset as he ceaselessly cut

down his opponents, till he and the three sons of Nemed fell. Eochaid's
Cairn is the cairn where Eochaid was buried (it is also called the Cairn
of Eothail), and the Gravestones of the Sons of Nemed are at the
western end of the strand.

As for Sreng, son of Sengann, he continued fighting for a day and a
night after his fellows, till in the end neither side was capable of
attacking the other. Their swift blows had grown feeble through all the
slaughter and their spirits had fallen through all their ills, and their
courage faint through the vastness of their disasters; and so they parted.
The Tuatha dé retired to the fastness of Cenn Slebe and to the sloping
Glen of Blood, and to the Mound of Tears. There the Dagda said:

> 'Soldiers slain without measure,
> many a wound on heroes;
> cruel swords have torn your bodies.
> The Fir Bolg have overcome you
> [. . .] about their lands.'

'What have been your losses in this last battle?' said Nuada to the
Dagda. The Dagda told him in these words:

> 'I will tell, noble Nuada,
> the tales of the dread battle,
> and, after that, its calamities
> and disasters I will tell,
> O son of Echtach.

> 'In it fell our nobles before
> the violence of the Fir Bolg;
> so great are our losses
> that few know of them.

> 'Bres, son of Elatha,
> a warrior like a tower,
> attacked the ranks of the Fir Bolg,
> a glorious fight, and killed
> one hundred and fifty of them.

> 'He dealt nine blows –
> savage was the deed –
> on the broad shield of Eochaid,
> and Eochaid dealt Bres nine blows.

'Huge Sreng came
and slew three hundred of our host.
He dealt nine blows
on your shield, Nuada.

'You, Nuada, coolly dealt
Sreng nine mighty blows,
but Sreng cut off your right arm,
impetuous hero, at the shoulder.

'You raised a loud cry for help,
and he of Norway came up.
Sreng and Aengaba fought with a will
a well-contested fight of clashing weapons.

'As Aengaba cried for help,
I came up speedily; when I arrived,
still unweary, Sreng refused
a contest with both of us.
Mella, Ese, Ferb and blood-red Faebur
fell before us in the same battle.

'The four sons of Gann fell
at the hands of Goibnenn the Smith,
of Aengaba of the exploits,
of Lucraidh and of Diancecht.

'Bedg and Rinde and Redg,
the three sons of Ordan of the crafts,
were slain surely by the fair sons of Cainte.

'Eochaid and his son, Slainge the Fair,
slew in the battle a great number
of the heroes of the Tuatha dé.

'In the battle thirst overcame king Eochaid,
and he got not the draught he sought
till he came to the Strand of Eothail.

'The three sons of Nemid
overtook him on the silent strand,
and there they fought
till they all fell together.

'Lugaid, Nuada's son, methinks
was slain by Slainge the Fair;
and Slainge, though so fierce before,
was killed in fighting with the Tuatha dé.

'Brian, Iucharba and Iuchar,
the three sons of Turenn Bigrenn,
slew Esca and Econn and Airbe.

'After that 'twas Sreng that ruled the fight –
and many were those that changed colour –
for three days, but neither he nor we
turned in the struggle.

'Weary were we now on either side,
and we resolved to separate.
Each man's combats, as I heard,
so shall I exactly tell of.'

Sad and weary, wounded and full of heavy reproaches were the Fir Bolg
that night. Each one buried his kinsfolk and relatives, his friends and
familiars and foster-brothers; and then were raised mounds over the brave
men, and gravestones over the warriors, and tombs over the soldiers, and
hills over the heroes. After that Sreng, Semne and Sithbrug, the sons of
Sengann, called a meeting for council and deliberation to which three
hundred assembled. They considered what it was their interest to do,
whether they should leave Ireland, or offer regular battle, or undertake to
share the land with the Tuatha dé. They decided to offer the Tuatha dé
battle, and Sreng said:

'Resistance is destruction for men;
we resolutely gave battle;
there was clashing of hard swords;
the strong plying of spears
on the sides of noble warriors,
and the breaking of buckler on shield;
full of trouble are the plains of Ireland;
disaster we found about its woods,
the loss of many good men.'

They took up their strong, hooked shields, their venomous spears and
their sharp swords with blue blades. Thus equipped they made a keen,

murderous charge, a wild fiery company, with their spears close-pressed in the onset, cutting their way in a flaming fire of fury to meet any hardship and any tribulation. It was then that Sreng challenged Nuada to single combat, as they had fought in the previous battle. Nuada faced him bravely and boldly as if he had been whole, and said: 'If single combat on fair terms be what you seek, fasten your right hand, as I have lost mine; only so can our combat be fair.'

'If you have lost your hand, that lays me under no obligations,' said Sreng, 'for our first combat was on fair terms. We ourselves so took up the quarrel.'

The Tuatha dé took counsel, and their decision was to offer Sreng his choice of the provinces of Ireland, while a compact of peace, goodwill, and friendship should be made between the two peoples. And so they make peace, and Sreng chooses the province of Connacht. The Fir Bolg gathered round him from every side, and stubbornly and triumphantly took possession of the province against the Tuatha dé. The Tuatha dé made Bres their king, and he was high-king for seven years. He died after taking a drink while hunting in Sliab Gam, and Nuada, his missing hand having been replaced, became king of Ireland. And that is the story of the battle of Mag Tured Cunga.

This was written in the Plain of Eithne, the Goblin's daughter, by Cormac O'Cuirnin for his companion Sean O'Glaimhin. Painful to us is his deserting us when he goes from us on a journey.

3. The Second Battle of Moytura

(Cath Mag Tuiread)

Translated by Whitley Stokes

This text is one of the best known of the so-called 'Mythological Cycle' of tales dating from the eighth to fifteenth centuries. Not exactly a sequel to the 'First Battle of Mag Tuiread', it concentrates more on the Tuatha dé Danaan and the great Lug Samildanach (Many Skilled). There are many famous references in this story, including the passage at the beginning which lists the four sacred treasures of the Tuatha dé, the four cities from which they came and their four guardians. Nothing more is told of these places or people, but the four magical objects re-occur in several stories and influenced the later traditions of the Grail in medieval Arthurian literature.

The episode of Nuada's loss of his hand, and its replacement by the magical surgeon Dian Cecht, is another classic reference. As is the wonderful scene where Lug comes to Tara and begs admittance, listing his many skills, until he is at last allowed in because he is the only man who had *all* of these abilities. This is later paralleled in the description of the attributes which the warriors taking part in the battle can bring to the affray. The Tuatha dé use magic to overcome their enemies, helped by the many-gifted Lug and the healing skills of Dian Cecht who revives their dead.

Indeed there are so many of these references because the text itself is really a miscellany of tales pulled together by the author under the single heading. We have split up the text more here than in Whitley Stokes' original, as an indicator where the various episodes are joined on to the main theme of the battle. Nearly all the characters, though they are treated as semi-divine warriors here, are in fact gods, and as such they later appear in countless stories and poems. Here we see them at an early stage of their development.

The original MS is in Trinity College, Dublin and dates from the twelfth century. It was edited by Whitley Stokes in *Révue Celtique* XII (1891) pp. 52–130, 306–308. The final poems, uttered by the Mórrígan were not translated by Stokes. The first, 'Mórrígan's Prophecy' is translated here by Caitlín Matthews; the second is fragmentary and breaks off in Stokes' edition.

The Tuatha dé Danann lived in the Northern isles of the world, learning lore and magic and druidism and wizardry and cunning, until they surpassed the sages of the arts of heathendom. There were four cities in which they learned lore and science and diabolic arts, to wit Falais and Gorias, Murias and Findias. Out of Falias was brought the Stone of Fal, which was in Tara. It used to roar under every king that would take the realm of Ireland. Out of Gorias was brought the Spear that Lug had. No battle was ever won against it or him who held it in his hand. Out of Findias was brought the Sword of Nuada. When it was drawn from its deadly sheath, no one ever escaped from it, and it was irresistible. Out of Murias was brought the Dagda's Cauldron. No company ever went from it unthankful. Four wizards (there were) in those four cities. Morfesa was in Falias: Esras was in Gorias: Uscias was in Findias: Semias was in Murias. Those are the four poets of whom the Tuatha dé learnt lore and science.

Now the Tuatha dé Danann made an alliance with the Fomorians, and Balor grandson of Net gave his daughter Ethne to Cian son of Diancecht, and she brought forth the gifted child, Lug.

The Tuatha dé came with a great fleet to Ireland to take it from the Fir Bolg. They burnt their ships at once on reaching the district of Corcu Belgatan (that is, Connemara today), so that they should not think of retreating to them; and the smoke and the mist that came from the vessels filled the neighbouring land and air. Therefore it was conceived that they had arrived in clouds of mist.

The first battle of Moytura was fought between them and the Fir Bolg; and the Fir Bolg were routed, and a hundred thousand of them were slain, including their king Eochaid son of Ere.

In that battle, moreover, Nuada's hand was stricken off – it was Sreng son of Sengann that struck it off him – so Diancecht the leech put on him a hand of silver with the motion of every hand; and Credne the brazier helped the leech.

Now the Tuatha dé Danann lost many men in the battle, including Edleo son of Alla, and Ernmas and Fiachra and Turill Bicreo.

But such of the Fir Bolg as escaped from the battle went in flight to the Fomorians, and settled in Arran and in Islay and in Mann and Rathlin.

A contention as to the sovereignty of the men of Ireland arose between the Tuatha dé and their women; because Nuada, after his hand had been stricken off, was disqualified to be king. They said that it would be fitter for them to bestow the kingdom on Bres son of Elotha, on their own adopted son; and that giving the kingdom to him would bind the alliance of the Fomorians to them. For his father, Elotha son of Delbaeth, was king of the Fomorians.

Now the conception of Bres came to pass in this way:

Eru, Delbaeth's daughter, a woman of the Tuatha dé, was one day looking at the sea and the land from the house of Maeth Seeni, and she beheld the sea in perfect calm as if it were a level board. And as she was there she saw a vessel of silver on the sea. Its size she deemed great, but its shape was not clear to her. And the stream of the wave bore it to land. Then she saw that in it was a man of fairest form. Golden-yellow hair was on him as far as his two shoulders. A mantle with bands of golden thread was around him. His shirt had trimmings of golden thread. On his breast was a brooch of gold, with the sheen of a precious stone therein. He carried two white silver spears, and in them two smooth riveted shafts of bronze. Five circlets of gold adorned his neck, and he was girded with a golden-hilted sword with inlayings of silver and studs of gold.

The man said to her: 'Is this the time that our lying with thee will be easy?'

'I have not made a tryst with thee, verily,' said the woman. But they stretched themselves down together. The woman wept when the man would rise.

'Why weepest thou?' said he.

'I have two things for which I should lament,' said the woman. 'Parting from thee now that we have met. And the fair youths of the Tuatha dé Danann have been entreating me in vain, and my desire is for thee since thou hast possessed me.'

'Thy anxiety from these two things shall be taken away,' said he. He drew his golden ring from his middle-finger, and put it into her hand, and told her that she should not part with it, by sale or by gift, save to one whose finger it should fit.

'I have another sorrow,' said the woman. 'I know not who hath come to me.'

'Thou shalt not be ignorant of that,' said he. 'Elotha son of Delbaeth, king of the Fomorians, hath come to thee. And of our meeting thou shalt bear a son, and no name shall be given him save Eochaid Bres, that is Eochaid the beautiful; for every beautiful thing that is seen in Ireland, whether plain or fortress or ale or torch or woman or man or steed, will be judged in comparison with that boy, so that men say of it then "it is a bres."'

After that the man went back again by the way he had come, and the woman went to her house, and to her was given the famous conception.

She brought forth the boy, and he was named, as Elotha had said, Eochaid Bres. When a week after the woman's lying-in was complete the boy had a fortnight's growth; and he maintained that increase till the end of his first seven years, when he reached a growth of fourteen years. Because of the contest which took place among the Tuatha dé the sovereignty of Ireland was given to the boy; and he gave seven hostages to Ireland's champions, that is, to her chiefs, to guarantee the restoring of the sovereignty if his own misdeeds should give cause. His mother afterwards bestowed land upon him, and on the land he had a stronghold built, called Dun Brese; and it was the Dagda that built that fortress.

Now when Bres had assumed the kingship, the Fomorians – Indech son of Dea Domnann, and Elotha, son of Delbaeth, and Tethra, three Fomorian kings – laid tribute upon Ireland, so that there was not a smoke from a roof in Ireland that was not under tribute to them. The champions were also reduced to their service; to wit, Ogma had to carry a bundle of firewood, and the Dagda became a rath-builder, and had to dig the trenches about Rath Brese.

The Dagda became weary of the work, and he used to meet in the house an idle blind man named Cridenbel, whose mouth was out of his breast. Cridenbel thought his own ration small and the Dagda's large. Whereupon he said: 'O Dagda! of thy honour let the three best bits of thy ration be given to me!'

So the Dagda used to give them to him every night. Large, however, were the lampooner's bits, the size of a good pig. But those three bits were a third of the Dagda's ration. The Dagda's health was the worse for that.

One day, then, as the Dagda was in the trench digging a rath, he saw the Mac Oc [Aengus] coming to him.

'That is good, O Dagda,' says the Mac Oc.

'Even so,' said the Dagda.

'What makes thee look so ill?' said the Mac Oc.

'I have cause for it,' said the Dagda; 'every evening Cridenbel the lampooner demands the three best bits of my portion.'

'I have a counsel for thee,' said the Mac Oc. He put his hand into his purse, took out three crowns of gold, and gave them to him.

'Put these three gold pieces into the three bits which thou give at close of day to Cridenbel,' said the Mac Oc. 'These bits will then be the goodliest on thy dish; and the gold will turn in his belly so that he will die thereof, and the judgment of Bres thereon will be wrong. Men will say to the king: 'The Dagda has killed Cridenbel by means of a deadly herb which he gave him." Then the king will order thee to be slain. But thou shalt say to him: "What thou utterest, O king of the warriors of the Fene, is not a prince's truth. For I was watched by Cridenbel when I was at my work, and he used to say to me 'Give me, O Dagda, the three best bits of thy portion. Bad is my housekeeping tonight.' So I should have perished thereby had not the three gold coins which I found today helped me. I put them in my ration. I then gave it to Cridenbel, for the gold was the best thing that was before me. Hence, then, the gold is inside Cridenbel, and he died of it."' The Dagda followed this advice, and was called before the king.

'It is clear,' said the king. 'Let the lampooner's belly be cut open to know if the gold be found therein. If it be not found, thou shalt die. If, however, it be found, thou shalt have life.'

After that they cut open the lampooner's belly, and the three coins of gold were found in his stomach, so the Dagda was saved. Then the Dagda went to his work on the following morning, and to him came the Mac Oc and said: 'Thou wilt soon finish thy work, but thou shalt not seek reward till the cattle of Ireland are brought to thee, and of them choose a heifer black-maned.'

Thereafter the Dagda brought his work to an end, and Bres asked him what he would take as a reward for his labour. The Dagda answered: 'I charge thee,' said he, 'to gather the cattle of Ireland into one place.' The king did this as the Dagda asked, and the Dagda chose of them the heifer which the Mac Oc had told him to choose. That seemed weakness to Bres: he thought that the Dagda would have chosen somewhat more.

Now Nuada was in his sickness, and Diancecht put on him a hand of silver with the motion of every hand therein. That seemed evil to his son Miach. Miach went to the hand which had been replaced by Diancecht, and he said 'joint to joint of it and sinew to sinew,' and he healed Nuada in thrice three days and nights. The first seventy-two hours he put it against his side, and it became covered with skin. The second seventy-two hours he put it on his breast (. . . .) That cure seemed evil to Diancecht. He flung a sword on the crown of his son's head and cut the skin down to the flesh. The lad healed the wound by means of his skill. Diancecht smote him again and cut the flesh till he reached the bone. The lad healed this by the same means. He struck him a third blow and came to the membrane of his brain. The lad healed this also by the same means. Then he struck the fourth blow and cut out the brain, so that Miach died, and Diancecht said that the leech himself could not heal him of that blow.

Thereafter Miach was buried by Diancecht, and herbs three hundred and sixty-five, according to the number of his joints and sinews, grew through the grave. Then Airmed opened her mantle and separated those herbs according to their properties. But Diancecht came to her, and he confused the herbs, so that no one knows their proper cures unless the Holy Spirit should teach them afterwards. And Diancecht said 'If Miach be not, Airmed shall remain.'

So Bres held the sovereignty as it had been conferred upon him. But the chiefs of the Tuatha dé murmured greatly against him, for their knives were not greased by him, and however often they visited him their breaths did not smell of ale. Moreover, they saw not their poets nor their bards nor their lampooners nor their harpers nor their pipers nor their jugglers nor their fools amusing them in the household. They did not go to the contests of their athletes. They saw not their champions proving their prowess at the king's court, save only one man, Ogma son of Ethliu. This was the duty which he had, to bring fuel to the fortress. He used to carry a bundle every day from the Clew Bay islands. And because he was weak from want of food, the sea would sweep away from him two-thirds of his bundle. So he could only carry one third, and yet he had to supply the host from day to day. Neither service nor taxes were paid by the tribes, and the treasures of the tribe were not delivered by the act of the whole tribe.

Once upon a time there came a-guesting to Bres's house, Cairbre son of Etain, poet of the Tuatha dé. He entered a cabin narrow, black, dark, wherein there was neither fire nor furniture nor bed. Three small cakes, and they dry, were brought to him on a little dish. On the morrow he arose and he was not thankful. As he went across the enclosure, he said:

> 'Without food quickly on a dish:
> Without a cow's milk whereon a calf grows:
> Without a man's abode in the gloom of night:
> Without paying a company of story-tellers,
> Let that be Bres's condition.
> Let there be no increase in Bres.'

Now that was true. Nought save decay was on Bres from that hour. That is the first satire that was ever made in Ireland.

Now after that the Tuatha dé went together to have speech with their fosterson, Bres son of Elotha, and demanded of him their sureties. He gave them the restitution of the realm, and he was not well-pleased with them for that. He begged to be allowed to remain till the end of seven years. 'That shall be granted,' said the same assembly; 'but thou shalt remain on the same security. Every fruit that comes to thy hand, both house and land and gold and silver, cows and food, and freedom from rent and taxes until then.'

'Ye shall have as ye say,' said Bres.

This is why they were asked for the delay: that he might gather the champions of the fairy-mound, the Fomorians, to seize the tribes by force. Grievous to him seemed his expulsion from his kingdom.

Then he went to his mother and asked her whence was his race.

'I am certain of that,' said she; and she went on to the hill whence she had seen the vessel of silver in the sea. She then went down to the strand, and gave him the ring which had been left with her for him, and he put it round his middle-finger, and it fitted him. For the sake of no one had she formerly given it up, either by sale or gift. Until that day there was none whom it suited.

Then they went forward till they reached the land of the Fomorians. They came to a great plain with many assemblies therein. They advanced to the fairest of these assemblies. Tidings were demanded of them there. They replied that they were of the men of Ireland. They were then asked whether they had hounds; for at that time it was the custom, when a body of men went to an assembly, to challenge them to a friendly contest. 'We have hounds,' said Bres. Then the hounds had a coursing match, and the hounds of the Tuatha dé were swifter than the hounds of the Fomorians. Then they were asked whether they had steeds for a horse-race. They answered, 'We have'; and their steeds were swifter than the steeds of the Fomorians. They were then asked whether they had any one who was good at sword-play. None was found save Bres alone. So when he set his hand to the sword, his father recognised the ring on his finger and inquired who was the hero. His mother answered on his behalf and told the king that Bres was a son of his. Then she related to him the whole story even as we have recounted it.

His father was sorrowful over him. Said the father: 'What need has brought thee out of the land wherein thou didst rule?'

Bres replied: 'Nothing has brought me save my own injustice and arrogance. I stript them of their jewels and treasures and their own food. Neither tribute nor taxes had been taken from them up to that time.'

'That is bad,' said the father. 'Better were their prosperity than their kingship. Better their prayers than their curses. Why hast thou come hither?'

'I have come to ask you for champions,' said he. 'I would take that land by force.'

'Thou shouldst not gain it by injustice if thou didst not gain it by justice,' said the father.

'Then what counsel hast thou for me?' said Bres.

Thereafter he sent Bres to the champion, to Balor grandson of Net, the king of the Isles, and to Indech son of Dea Domnannii the king of the Fomorians; and these assembled all the troops from Lochlann westwards unto Ireland, to impose their tribute and their rule by force on the Tuatha dé, so that they made one bridge of vessels from the Foreigners' Isles to Erin. Never came to Ireland an army more horrible or fearful than that host of the Fomorians. Men from Scythia of Lochlann and men out of the Western Isles were rivals in that expedition.

Now as to the Tuatha dé, this is what they were doing. After Bres, Nuada was again in sovereignty over the Tuatha dé. At that time he held a mighty feast at Tara for them. Now there was a a certain warrior on his way to Tara, whose name was Lug Samildanach. And there were then two door-keepers at Tara, namely Gamal son of Figal and Camall son of Riagall. When one of these was on duty he saw a strange company coming towards him. A young warrior fair and shapely, with a king's trappings, was in the forefront of that band. They told the door-keeper to announce their arrival at Tara. The door-keeper asked: 'Who is there?'

'Here there is Lug Lamfada (i.e., Lug Long-Arm) son of Cialu son of Diancecht and of Ethne daughter of Balor. Foster-son, he, of Tailltiu daughter of Magmor king of Spain and of Eochaid the Rough son of Duach.'

The door-keeper asked of Lug Samildanach: 'What art dost thou practise?' said he; 'for no one without an art enters Tara.'

'Question me,' said he: 'I am a wright.'

The door-keeper answered: 'We need thee not. We have a wright already, even Luchta son of Luachaid.'

He said: 'Question me, O door-keeper! I am a smith.'

The door-keeper answered him: 'We have a smith already, Colum Cualleinech of the three new processes.'

He said: 'Question me: I am a champion.'

The door-keeper answered: 'We need thee not. We have a champion already, Ogma son of Ethliu.'

He said again: 'Question me: I am a harper.'

'We need thee not. We have a harper already, Abcan son of Bicelmos whom the Tuatha dé Danann chose in the fairy-mounds.'

Said he: 'Question me: I am a hero.'

The door-keeper answered: 'We need thee not. We have a hero already, even Bresal Etarlam son of Eochaid Baethlam.'

Then he said: 'Question me, O door-keeper! I am a poet and I am a historian.'

'We need thee not. We have already a poet and historian, even En son of Ethaman.'

He said, 'Question me: I am a sorcerer.'

'We need thee not. We have sorcerers already. Many are our wizards and our folk of might.'

He said: 'Question me: I am a leech.'

'We need thee not. We have for a leech Diancecht.'

'Question me,' said he; 'I am a cupbearer.'

'We need thee not. We have cupbearers already, even Delt and Drucht and Daithe, Tae and Talom and Trog, Glei and Glan and Glesi.'

He said: 'Question me: I am a good brazier.'

'We need thee not. We have a brazier already, Credne Cerd.'

He said again, 'Ask the king,' said he, 'whether he has a single man who possesses all these arts, and if he has I will not enter Tara.'

Then the door-keeper went into the palace and declared all to the king. 'A warrior has come before the enclosure,' said he. 'His name is Samildanach (many-gifted), and all the arts which thy household practise he himself possesses, so that he is the man of each and every art.'

The king said then that the chess-boards of Tara should be taken to Samildanach, and he won all the stakes, so that then he made the Cro of Lug [i.e. enclosed him]. But if chess was invented at the epoch of the Trojan war, it had not reached Ireland then, for the battle of Moytura and the destruction of Troy occurred at the same time.

Then that was related to Nuada. 'Let him into the enclosure,' says he; 'for never before has man like him entered this fortress.'

Then the door-keeper let Lug pass him, and he entered the fortress and sat down in the sage's seat, for he was a sage in every art.

Then the great flag-stone, to move which required the effort of fourscore yoke of oxen, Ogma hurled through the house, so that it lay on the outside of Tara. This was a challenge to Lug. But Lug cast it back, so that it lay in the centre of the palace; and he put the piece which it had carried away into the side of the palace and made it whole.

'Let a harp be played for us,' said the company. So the warrior played a sleep-strain for the hosts and for the king the first night. He cast them into sleep from that hour to the same time on the following day. He played a wail-strain, so that they were crying and lamenting. He played a laugh-strain, so that they were in merriment and joyance.

Now Nuada, when he beheld the warrior's many powers, considered whether Samildanach could put away from them the bondage which they suffered from the Fomorians. So they held a council concerning the warrior. The decision to which Nuada came was to change seats with the warrior. So Samildanach went to the king's seat, and the king rose up before him till thirteen days had ended. Then on the morrow he met with the two brothers, Dagda and Ogma, on Grellach Dollaid. And his brothers Goibniu and Diancecht were summoned to them. A full year were they in that secret converse, wherefore Grellach Dollaid is called Amrun of the Tuatha dé Danann.

Thereafter the wizards of Ireland were summoned to them, and their medical men and charioteers and smiths and farmers and lawyers. They held speech with them in secret. Then Nuada enquired of the sorcerer whose name was Mathgen, what power he could wield? He answered that through his contrivance he would cast the mountains of

Ireland on the Fomorians, and roll their summits against the ground. And he declared to them that the twelve chief mountains of the land of Erin would support the Tuatha dé Danann, in battling for them, to wit, Sliab League, and Denna Mad and the Mourne Mountains, and Bri Ruri and Sliab Bladma, and Sliab Snechtai, Sliab Mis and Blai-sliab and Nevin and Sliab Maccu, Belgadan and Segais and Cruachan Aigle.

Then he asked the cupbearer what power he could wield. He answered that he would bring the twelve chief lochs of Ireland before the Fomorians, and that they would not find water therein, whatever thirst might seize them. These are those lochs: Derg Loch, Loch Luimnigh, Loch Corrib, Loch Ree, Loch Mask, Strangford Loch, Belfast Loch, Loch Neagh, Loch Foyle, Loch Gara, Loch Reag, Marloch. They would betake themselves to the twelve chief rivers of Ireland – Bush, Boyne, Baa, Nem, Lee, Shannon, Moy, Sligo, Erne, Finn, Liffey, Suir; and they will all be hidden from the Fomorians, so that they will not find a drop therein. Drink shall be provided for the men of Ireland, though they bide in the battle to the end of seven years.

Then said Figol son of Mamos, their druid: 'I will cause three showers of fire to pour on the faces of the Fomorian host, and I will take out of them two-thirds of their valor and their bravery and their strength, and I will bind their urine in their own bodies and in the bodies of their horses. Every breath that the men of Ireland shall exhale will be an increase of valour and bravery and strength to them. Though they bide in the battle till the end of seven years, they will not be weary in any wise.'

Said the Dagda: 'The power which ye boast I shall wield it all by myself. It is thou art the Dagda (good hand), with everyone': wherefore thenceforward the name 'Dagda' adhered to him. Then they separated from the council, agreeing to meet again that day three years.

Now when the provision of the battle had then been settled, Lug and Dagda and Ogma went to the three Gods of Danu, and these gave Lug the plan of the battle; and for seven years they were preparing for it and making their weapons.

The Dagda had a house in Glenn Etin in the north, and he had to meet a woman in Glenn Etin a year from that day, about Samhain (Hallowe'en) before the battle. The river Unius of Connacht roars to the south of it. He beheld the woman in Unius in Corann, washing herself, with one of her two feet at Allod Echae (i.e., Echumech), to the south of the water, and the other at Loscuinn, to the north of the water.

Nine loosened tresses were on her head. The Dagda conversed with her, and they made a union. 'The Bed of the Couple' is the name of the place thenceforward. The woman that is here mentioned is the Mórrígu. Then she told the Dagda that the Fomorians would land at Mag Seetne, and that he should summon Erin's men of art to meet her at the Ford of Unius, and that she would go into Seetne to destroy Indech son of Dea Domnann, the king of the Fomorians, and would deprive him of the blood of his heart and the kidneys of his valour. Afterwards she gave two handfuls of that blood to the hosts that were waiting at the Ford of Unius. 'Ford of Destruction' became its name, because of that destruction of the king. Then that was done by the wizards, and they chanted spells on the hosts of the Fomorians.

This was a week before Samhain, and each of them separated from the other until all the men of Ireland came together on Samhain. Six times thirty hundred was their number, that is, twice thirty hundred in every third.

Then Lug sent the Dagda to spy out the Fomorians and to delay them until the men of Ireland should come to the battle. So the Dagda went to the camp of the Fomorians and asked them for a truce of battle. This was granted to him as he asked. Porridge was then made for him by the Fomorians, and this was done to mock him, for great was his love for porridge. They filled for him the king's cauldron, five fists deep, into which went four-score gallons of new milk and the like quantity of meal and fat. Goats and sheep and swine were put into it, and they were all boiled together with the porridge. They were spilt for him into a hole in the ground, and Indech told him that he would be put to death unless he consumed it all; he should eat his fill so that he might not reproach the Fomorians with inhospitality.

Then the Dagda took his ladle, and it was big enough for a man and woman to lie on the middle of it. These then were the bits that were in it, halves of salted swine and a quarter of lard. 'Good food this,' said the Dagda (. . . .)

At the end of the meal he put his curved finger over the bottom of the hole on mould and gravel. Sleep came upon him then after eating his porridge. Bigger than a house-cauldron was his belly, and the Fomorians laughed at it. Then he went away from them to the strand of Eba. Not easy was it for the hero to move along owing to the bigness of his belly. Unseemly was his apparel. A cape to the hollow of his two elbows. A dun tunic around him, as far as the swelling of his rump. It was, moreover, long-breasted, with a hole in the peak. Two brogues on him of horse-hide, with the hair outside. Behind him a wheeled fork to carry which required the effort of eight men, so that its track after him was enough for the boundary-ditch of a province. Wherefore it is called 'The Track of the Dagda's Club'.

Then the Fomorians marched till they reached Scetne. The men of Ireland were in Mag Aurfolaig. These two hosts were threatening battle. 'The men of Ireland venture to offer battle to us,' said Bres son of Elotha to Indech son of Dea Domnann. 'I will fight anon,' said Indech, 'so that their bones will be small unless they pay their tributes.'

Because of Lug's knowledge the men of Ireland had made a resolution not to let him go into the battle. So his nine fosterers were left to protect him, Tollus-dam and Ech-dam, and Eru, Rechtaid the white and Fosad and Fedlimid, Ibor and Scibar and Minn. They feared an early death for the hero owing to the multitude of his arts. Therefore they did not let him forth to the fight.

The chiefs of the Tuatha dé Danann were gathered round Lug. And he asked his smith, Goibniu, what power he wielded for them.

'Not hard to tell,' said he. 'Though the men of Erin bide in the battle to the end of seven years, for every spear that parts from its shaft, or sword that shall break therein, I will provide a new weapon in its place. No spear-point which my hand shall forge,' said he, 'shall make a missing cast. No skin which it pierces shall taste life afterwards. That has not been done by Dolb the smith of the Fomorians.'

'And thou, O Diancecht,' said Lug, 'what power canst thou wield?'

'Not hard to tell,' said he. 'Every man who shall be wounded there, unless his head be cut off, or the membrane of his brain or his spinal marrow be severed, I will make quite whole in the battle on the morrow.'

'And thou, O Credne,' said Lug to his brazier, 'what is thy power in the battle?'

'Not hard to tell,' said Credne. 'Rivets for their spears, and hilts for their swords, and bosses and rims for their shields, I will supply them all.'

'And thou, O Luchta,' said Lug to his wright, 'what service wilt thou render in the battle?'

'Not hard to tell,' said Luchta. 'All the shields and javelin shafts they require, I will supply them all.'

'And thou, O Ogma,' said Lug to his champion, 'what is thy power in the battle?'

'Not hard to tell,' said he. 'I will repel the king and three enneads of his friends, and capture up to a third of his men.' (. . . .)

'And ye, O sorcerers,' said Lug, 'what power will you wield?'

'Not hard to tell,' said the sorcerers. 'We shall fill them with fear when they have been overthrown by our craft, till their heroes are slain, and deprive them of two thirds of their might, with constraint on their urine.'

'And ye, O cupbearers,' said Lug, 'what power?'

'Not hard to tell,' said the cupbearers. 'We will bring a strong thirst upon them, and they shall not find drink to quench it.'

'And ye, O druids,' said Lug, 'what power?'

'Not hard to tell,' said the druids. 'We will bring showers of fire on the faces of the Fomorians, so that they cannot look upwards, and so that the warriors who are contending with them may slay them by their might.'

'And thou, O Cairbre son of Etain,' said Lug to his poet, 'what power canst thou wield in the battle?'

'Not hard to tell,' said Cairbre. 'I will make a satire on them. And I will satirise them and shame them, so that through the spell of my art they will not resist warriors.'

'And ye, O Be-culle and O Danann,' said Lug to his two witches, 'what power can ye wield in the battle?'

'Not hard to tell,' said they. 'We will enchant the trees and the stones and the sods of the earth, so that they shall become a host under arms against them, and shall rout them in flight with horror and trembling.'

'And thou, O Dagda,' said Lug, 'what power canst thou wield on the Fomorian host in the battle?'

'Not hard to tell,' said the Dagda. 'I will take the side of the men of Erin both in mutual smiting and destruction and wizardry. Under my club the bones of the Fomorians will be as many as hailstones under the feet of herds of horses where you meet on the battlefield of Moytura.'

So thus Lug spoke with every one of them in turn; and he strengthened and addressed his army, so that each man of them had the spirit of a king or a mighty lord. Now every day a battle was fought between the tribe of the Fomorians and the Tuatha dé, save only that kings or princes were not delivering it, but only keen and haughty folk.

Now the Fomorians marvelled at a certain thing which was revealed to them in the battle. Their spears and their swords were blunted and broken and such of their men as were slain did not return on the morrow.

But it was not so with the Tuatha dé. For though their weapons were blunted and broken to-day, they were renewed on the morrow, because Goibniu the smith was in the forge making swords and spears and javelins. For he would make those weapons by three turns. Then Luchta the wright would make the spearshafts by three chippings, and the third chipping was a finish and would set them in the ring of the spear. When the spearheads were stuck in the side of the forge he would throw the rings with the shafts, and it was needless to set them again. Then Credne the brazier would make the rivets by three turns, and would cast the rings of the spears to them; and thus they used to cleave together.

This then is what was used to put fire into the warriors who were slain, so that they were swifter on the morrow. Because Diancecht and his two sons, Octriuil and Miach, and his daughter Airmed sang spells over the well named Slane. Now their mortally wounded men were cast into it as soon as they were slain. They were alive when they came out. Their mortally wounded became whole through the might of the incantation of the four leeches who were about the well. Now that was harmful to the Fomorians, so they sent a man of them to spy out the battle and the actions of the Tuatha dé, namely Ruadan son of Bres and of Brigit the Dagda's daughter. For he was a son and a grandson of the Tuatha dé. Then he related to the Fomorians the work of the smith and the wright and the brazier and the four leeches who were around the well. He was sent again to kill one of the artisans, that is Goibniu. From him he begged a spear, its rivets from the brazier and its shaft from the wright. So all was given to him as he asked. There was a woman there grinding the weapons, Cron mother of Panlug; she it is that ground Ruadan's spear. Now the spear was given to Ruadan by a chief, wherefore the name 'a chief's spear' is still given to weavers' beams in Erin.

Now after the spear had been given to him, Ruadan turned and wounded Goibniu. But Goibniu plucked out the spear and cast it at Ruadan, so that it went through him, and he died in the presence of his father in the assembly of the Fomorians. Then Brig came and bewailed her son. She shrieked at first, she cried at last. So that then for the first time crying and shrieking were heard in Erin. Now it was that Brig who invented a whistle for signalling at night.

Then Goibniu went into the well, and he became whole. There was a warrior with the Fomorians, Octriallach son of Indech son of Dea Domnann, son of the Fomorian king. He told the Fomorians that each man of them should bring a stone of the stones of Drowes to cast into the well of Slane in Achad Abla to the west of Moytura, to the east of Loch Arboch. So they went, and a stone for each man was cast into the well. Wherefore the cairn thus made is called Octriallach's Cairn. But another name for that well is Loch Luibe, for Diancecht put into it one of every herb (*lub*) that grew in Erin.

Now when the great battle came, the Fomorians marched out of their camp, and formed themselves into strong battalions. Not a chief nor man of prowess of them was without a hauberk against his skin, a helmet on his head, a broad spear in his right hand, a heavy sharp sword on his belt, a firm shield on his shoulder. To attack the Fomorian host on that day was 'striking a head against a cliff,' was 'a hand in a serpent's nest,' was 'a face up to fire'. These were the kings and chiefs that were heartening the host of the Fomorians, namely, Balor son of Dot son of Net, Bres son of Elotha, Tuiri Tortbuillech son of Lobos, Goll and Irgoll Loscennlomm son of Lommnglunech, Indech son of Dea Domnann the king of the Fomorians, Octriallach son of Indech, Omna and Bagna, Elotha son of Delbaeth.

On the other side the Tuatha dé Danann arose and left their nine comrades keeping Lug, and they marched to the battle. When the battle began, Lug escaped from his guardians with his charioteer, so that it was he who was in front of the hosts of the Tuatha dé. Then a keen and cruel battle was fought between the tribe of the Fomorians and the men of Ireland. Lug was heartening the men of Ireland that they should fight the battle fervently, so that they should not be any longer in bondage. For it seems better for them to find death in protecting their fatherland than to bide under bondage and tribute as they had been (. . . .)

The hosts uttered a great shout as they entered the battle. Then they came together and each of them began to smite the other. Many fine men fell there. Great the slaughter and the grave-lying that was there. Pride and shame were there side by side. There was anger and indignation. Abundant was the stream of blood there over the white skin of young warriors mangled by hands of eager men. Harsh was the noise of the heroes and the champions mutually fending their spears and their shields and their bodies when the others were smiting them with spears and with swords. Harsh, moreover, was the thunder that was there throughout the battle, the shouting of the warriors and the clashing of the shields, the flashing and whistling of the glaives and the ivory-hilted swords, the rattling and jingling of the quivers, the sound and winging of the darts and the javelins, and the crashing of the weapons. The ends of their fingers and of their feet almost met in the mutual blows, and owing to the slipperiness of the blood under the feet of the soldiers, they would fall from their upright posture and beat their heads together as they sat. The battle was a gory, ghastly mêlée, and the river Unsenn rushed with corpses.

Then Nuada Silver-Hand and Macha, daughter of Ernmass, fell by Balor grandson of Net. And Cassmael fell by Octriallach son of Indech. Lug and Balor of the Piercing Eye met in the battle. An evil eye had Balor the Fomorian. That eye was never opened save only on a battlefield. Four men used to lift up the lid of the eye with a polished handle which passed through its lid. If an army looked at that eye, though they were many thousands in number, they could not resist a few warriors. It had a poisonous power. Once when his father's druids were concocting charms, he came and looked out of the window, and the fume of the concoction came under it, so that the poison of the concoction afterwards penetrated the eye that looked. He and Lug met. 'Lift up mine eyelid, my lad,' said Balor, 'that I may see the babbler who is conversing with me.'

The lid was raised from Balor's eye. Then Lug cast a sling-stone at him, which carried the eye through his head while his own army looked on. And the sling-stone fell on the host of the Fomorians, and thrice nine of them died beside it, so that the crowns of their heads came against the breast of Indech son of Dea Domnann, and a gush of blood sprang over his lips. Said Indech: 'Let Loch Halfgreen my poet be summoned to me!' Half-green was he from the ground to the crown of his head.

Loch went to the king. 'Make known to me,' said Indech, 'who has flung this cast on me.'

Then the Mórrígu, daughter of Ernmass, came, and heartened the Tuatha dé to fight the battle fiercely and fervently. Thereafter the battle became a rout, and the Fomorians were beaten back to the sea. The champion Ogma son of Ethliu, and Indech son of Dea Domnann the king of the Fomorians, fell in single combat. Loch Half-green besought Lug for quarter. 'Give me my three wishes,' said Lug.

'Thou shalt have them,' said Loch. 'Till Doom I will ward off from Ireland all plundering by the Fomorians, and, at the end of the world, every ailment.' So Loch was spared. Then he sang to the Gael the 'decree of fastening'.

Loch said that he would bestow names on Lug's nine chariots because of the quarter that had been given him. So Lug told him to name them.

[Here the original MSS lists all the chariots, charioteers and their equipment]

'What is the number of the slain?' said Lug to Loch.

'I know not the number of peasants and rabble. As to the number of Fomorian lords and nobles and champions and kings' sons and over-kings, I know, even five thousand three score and three men: two thousand and three fifties: four score thousand and nine times five: eight score and eight: four score and seven: four score and six: eight score and five: two and forty including Net's grandson. That is the number of the slain of the Fomorian overkings and high nobles who fell in the battle. Howbeit, as to the number of peasants and common people and rabble, and folk of every art besides who came in company with the great army – for every champion and every high chieftain and every overking of the Fomorians came with his host to the battle, so that all fell there, both his freemen and his slaves – we reckon only a few of the servants of the overkings. This then is the number that I have reckoned of these as I beheld: seven hundred, seven score and seven men (. . .) together with Sab Uanchennach son of Cairbre Cole, son was he of a servant of Indech son of Dea Domnann, that is, a son of a servant of the Fomorian king. As to what fell besides of 'half-men' and of those who reached not the heart of the battle, these are in no wise numbered till we number stars of heaven, sand of sea, flakes of snow, dew on lawn, hailstones, grass under feet of herds, and Manannan mac Lir's horses (waves) in a sea-storm.'

Thereafter Lug and his comrades found Bres son of Elotha unguarded. He said: 'It is better to give me quarter than to slay me.'

'What then will follow from that?' said Lug.

'If I be spared,' says Bres, 'the cows of Erin will always be in milk.'

'I will set this forth to our wise men,' said Lug.

So Lug went to Maeltne Mor-brethach, and said to him: 'Shall Bres have quarter for giving constant milk to the cows of Erin?'

'He shall not have quarter,' said Maeltne; 'he has no power over their age or their offspring, though he can milk them so long as they are alive.'

Lug said to Bres: 'That does not save thee: thou hast no power over their age and their offspring, though thou canst milk them. Is there aught else that will save thee, O Bres?' said Lug.

'There is in truth. Tell thy lawyer that for sparing me the men of Ireland shall reap a harvest in every quarter of the year.'

Said Lug to Maeltne: 'Shall Bres be spared for giving the men of Ireland a harvest of corn every quarter?'

'This has suited us,' saith Maeltne: 'the spring for ploughing and sowing, and the beginning of summer for the end of the strength of corn, and the beginning of autumn for the end of the ripeness of corn and for reaping it. Winter for consuming it.'

'That does not rescue thee,' said Lug to Bres; 'but less than that rescues thee.'

'What?' said Bres.

'How shall the men of Ireland plough? How shall they sow? How shall they reap? After making known these three things thou wilt be spared.'

'Tell them,' said Bres, 'that their ploughing be on a Tuesday, their casting seed into the field be on a Tuesday, their reaping on a Tuesday.'

So through that stratagem Bres was let go free.

In that fight, then, Ogma the champion found Orna the sword of Tethra, a king of the Fomorians. Ogma unsheathed the sword and cleansed it. Then the sword related whatsoever had been done by it; for it was the custom of swords at that time, when unsheathed, to set forth the deeds that had been done by them. And therefore swords are entitled to the tribute of cleansing them after they have been unsheathed. Hence, also, charms are preserved in swords thenceforward. Now the reason why demons used to speak from weapons at that time was because weapons were worshipped by human beings at that epoch, and the weapons were among the safeguards of that time (. . . .)

Now Lug and the Dagda and Ogma pursued the Fomorians, for they had carried off the Dagda's harper, whose name was Uaitne. Then they reached the banqueting-house in which were Bres son of Elotha and Elotha son of Delbaeth. There hung the harp on the wall. That is the harp in which the Dagda had bound the melodies so that they sounded not until by his call he summoned them forth; when he said this below:

> Come Daurdabla!
> Come Coir-cetharchuir!
> Come summer, Come winter!
> Mouths of harps and bags and pipes!

Now that harp had two names, Daur-da-bla, 'Oak of two greens' and Coir-cethar-chuir, 'Four-angled music'.

Then the harp went forth from the wall, and killed nine men, and came to the Dagda. And he played for them the three things whereby harpers are distinguished, to wit, sleep-strain and smile-strain and wail-strain. He played wail-strain to them, so that their tearful women wept.

He played smile-strain to them, so their women and children laughed. He played sleep-strain to them, and the company fell asleep. Through that sleep the three of them escaped unhurt from the Fomorians though these desired to slay them.

Then the Dagda brought with him the heifer which had been given to him for his labour. For when she called her calf all the cattle in Ireland which the Fomorians had taken as their tribute, grazed.

Now after the battle was won and the corpses cleared away, the Mórrígu, daughter of Ernmas, proceeded to proclaim that battle and the mighty victory which had taken place, to the royal heights of Ireland and to its fairy hosts and its chief waters and its rivermouths. And hence it is that Badb (i.e., the Mórrígu) also describes high deeds. 'Hast thou any tale?' said every one to her then. And she replied:

> Peace high as heaven,
> heaven to the earth,
> earth under heaven,
> strength in everyone.
>
> Cup's great fullness,
> fullness of honey,
> mead til satiety,
> summer in winter.
>
> Spear reliant on shield,
> shield reliant on host,
> host upon occasion for battle.
>
> Grazing for sheep,
> wood grown like antlers,
> weapons forever departing,
> mast upon the trees,
> bough low bending,
> bending with increase.
>
> Wealth for a son,
> a son strongly-necked;
> yoke of a bull,
> a bull from a praise-song.

Refrain for a tree,
wood for a fire,

fire for the asking,
rock from the soil,
woven into victories;
Boyne for hostel,
hostel of resonant extent.

Green growth after spring,
autumn increase of horses,
a company for the land,
land with trade to its furthest shore:
may it be mighty-forested, perpetually-sovereign!

Peace high as heaven,
life eternally.

Then, moreover, she was prophesying the end of the world, and fore-
telling every evil that would be therein, and every disease and every
vengeance. Wherefore then she sang this lay below:

I shall not see a world that will be dear to me.
Summer without flowers,
Kine will be without milk,
Women without modesty,
Men without valour,
Captures without a king
Woods without mast,
Sea without produce,
Wrong judgments of old men,
False precedents of lawyers,
Every man a betrayer,
Every boy a reaver.
Son will enter his father's bed,
Father will enter his son's bed,
Every one will be his brother's brother-in-law,
An evil time!
Son will deceive his father,
Daughter will deceive her mother. . . .

CONCEPTIONS
AND BIRTHS

4. The Conception of Conchobor

(Compert Conchobor)

Translated by Kuno Meyer

There are several versions of this story, including a brief mention in the *Yellow Book of Lecan*, where Conchobor is the son of Cathbad, and a longer version in the *Book of Leinster* where he is the son of Fachtna Fathach, a gigantic king of Ulster. The most detailed version is the one printed here, edited from Stow MS 992 in the British Museum. There is some confusion at the beginning, where it is clear that Cathbad is leading one group of Fiana while another, nameless, Fenian leads a second group. The two parties clash and fight before agreeing to join forces and attack Nessa's twelve tutors. The motive for this seems not to exist. The Fiana were given to going forth on 'training expeditions' called *fianaigecht*, and this story seems to begin with an example of this. Nessa then undertakes a *fianaigecht* of her own to seek revenge on the killers.

The idea of giving birth after drinking water which contained a worm or worms is found elsewhere in a text called *Cophur na Muccide* in which two worms are swallowed by two cows which later give birth, respectively, to the famous bull, Dond Cuailnge, the Brown Bull, the object of the famous Cattle Raid of Cuailgne, (pp. 91–110) and the cow Findbennach Ai, the White Bull belonging to Queen Maeve of Connaught. In other versions of the story Fachtna's brother, Fergus mac Róich, marries Ness and becomes king. Ness' prevention of the birth of her child until an auspicious date is also found in the story of the birth of Cormac (see below pp. 72–76).

There was a king over Ulster, called Eochu Salbuide mac Loich. A daughter was born to him, called Ness, daughter of Eochu Salbuide, and twelve tutors took her in fostership. Assa was her name at first, for she was of good manners and gentle to educate. This was the time that a certain [unnamed] Fenian knight from the southern part of Ulster went on a Fenian expedition through Erinn, with three times nine men. Cathbad, the illustrious druid [also went forth at this time]. He was endowed with great knowledge and druidical skill and bodily strength, and his origin was from Ulster, though he was absent from there.

Now, Cathbad came into a wilderness with *his* three times nine men. They [the two bands of Fianna] then begin to fight, until they grow weary, and at last they make a covenant, for they would all have fallen together unless they made it, as they had equal numbers. Thereupon Cathbad with his people, and the other Fenian knight with his people went into Ulster, and killed the twelve tutors of the maiden – for they were all in one house feasting. And none of them escaped but the maiden only, and it was not known who had wrought the slaughter. The maiden then went with great wailing to her father. The father said it was not possible to avenge her, as it was not known who wrought the slaughter.

Now the maiden was angry and wroth at this. She then went on a Fenian expedition with three times nine men to avenge her tutors. She destroyed and plundered every single district. Till then her name was Assa, for she was gentle. But Nihassa was her name after that, because of the greatness of her prowess and valour. It was her custom to ask news of Fenian knights from every stranger that she met, to see whether she would find out the name of the man that wrought the slaughter.

Once upon a time, she was in a wilderness, and her people were preparing their food. Then she went forth alone on quest into the wilderness as she was wont to go on quest in every wilderness that she came into. As she was there, she saw a clear beautiful spring in the midst of the wilderness. Thereupon she went into the spring to bathe, and left her weapons and her dress on the land.

Now Cathbad came on quest to the same wilderness, and he reached the spring where the maiden was bathing. Cathbad then went between the maiden and her dress and her weapons, and he bared his sword over the head of the maiden.

'Now spare me,' cried the maiden.

'Grant my three requests,' said Cathbad.

'Thou shalt have them,' said the maiden.

'For this I have determined,' said Cathbad, 'that thou must be under my protection, and there must be peace and covenant between us, and thou must be my only wife as long as thou livest.'

'It is better for me than to be killed by thee, and my weapons gone,' said the maiden.

Then they and their people unite in one place. At a propitious hour Cathbad then proceeds to Ulster and to the father of the maiden, who makes them welcome and gives them land, namely Raith Cathbaid in the country of the Picts, near the river called Conchobor in Crich Rois.

Now, at a certain hour in the night, a prodigious thirst fell upon Cathbad. Then Ness went through the whole fort to seek a drink for him. She went to the river Conchobor and strained the water in the cup through her veil, and then brought it to Cathbad.

'Let a light be kindled,' said Cathbad, 'that we may see the water.'

Then there were two worms in the water. Cathbad bared his sword over the head of the woman with intent to kill her.

'Drink thyself, then,' said Cathbad, 'what thou wouldst have me drink, or thou wilt be killed, if thou drink not the water.'

Then the woman drinks of the water twice, and she drinks a worm at either draught. Thereupon the woman grew pregnant for as long a time as every woman is pregnant, and some say that it was by the worms that she was pregnant. But Fachtna Fathach was the leman of the maiden, and he caused this pregnancy instead of Cathbad, the noble druid.

Now Cathbad on a time went to talk with the king Fachtna Fathach, the son of Rudraige, and they came to Mag Inis. The pangs of childbirth came upon the woman on her journey.

'O would it were be in thy power,' said Cathbad, 'O wife, not to bring forth the child that is in thy womb till to-morrow, for thy son would then be king of Ulster, or of all Erinn, and his name will last in Erinn for ever, for it is (. . .) of the same day that the illustrious child will be born whose glory and power has spread over the world, namely Jesus Christ, the son of God everlasting.'

'I will do so,' said Ness, 'if it do not come out through my side, it shall not come out any other way until that time arrive.'

Thereupon Ness went to the meadow that was on the bank of the river Conchobor. There she sat her down on a flagstone that was on the brink of the river. So there came the pangs of childbirth upon her. Then Cathbad spoke this poem prophesying the birth of Conchobor, and he said this here below:

'O Ness, thou art in peril.

'Let everyone rise at thy birth-giving,

Not . . . to soothe thee.
Beautiful is the colour of thy hands,
O daughter of Eochu Buide.
Be not sorrowful, O wife,
A head of hundreds and of the hosts
Of the world will he be, thy son.

'The same propitious hour
To him and to the king of the world.
Everyone will praise hint
For ever to the day of judgment.
The same night he will be born,
Heroes will not defy him,
As hostage he will not be taken,
He and Christ.

'In the plain of Inis thou wilt bear him,
Upon the flagstone in the meadow.
Glorious will be his story,
He will be the king of grace,
He will be the hound of Ulster,
Who will take pledges of knights.
Awful will be the disgrace
When he falls . . .

'Conchobor his name,
Whoso will call him.
His weapons will be red,
He will excel in many routs.
There he will find his death,
In avenging the pitiable god.
Clear will be the track of his sword
Over the slanting plain of Laim.

'He will be no son to Cathbad,
The beautiful active man.
Yet by me he is beloved
Because . . . useful to me.
He will be a son of Fachtna Fathach,
As Scathach knows,
He will often take hostages

From the north and from the south.'

Then the maiden gave birth to the child that was in her womb, namely the glorious illustrious child and the promised son whose fame spread over Erinn, and the stone still remains on which he was born, to wit, to the west of Airgdig. Thus the boy was born, with a worm in either of his hands. Then he went head over heels towards the river Conchobor, and the river went over his back, until Cathbad seized him, and he was called after the name of the river, namely Conchobor mac Fachtna. Cathbad took the boy in his bosom, and gave thanks for him and prophesied to him, so that it was then he uttered this song:

'Welcome the stranger that has come here,
As they have told you,
He will be the gracious lord,
The son of noble Cathbad.
The son of noble Cathbad,
And of Ness, the strong,
Above every man.
My son and my grandson.

'My son and my grandson,
The ornament of the world of men.
He will be a king of grace above others
He will be a poet, he will be just.

'He will be a poet, he will be just,
He will be the head of warriors over the sea,
My beloved bird from the heavens,
My kitten, my head.'

The boy was then reared by Cathbad, so that therefore he was called Conchobor the son of Cathbad. Afterwards Conchobor assumed the kingship of Ulster in right of his mother and his father, for Fachtna Fathach the son of Rudraige, the king of Erinn, was his father, and it is he that begat Conchobor in Cathbad's stead. And through the strength of the valour and of the druidical knowledge of that man Cathbad, was the battle of Forgarach and Ilgarach gained upon Ailill and Medb at the cattlespoil of Cuainge from the province of Ulster.

5. The Birth of Cormac

(Compert Cormaic mac Airt)

Translated by Caitlín Matthews

This conception story is from a text called *Scéla Eogain,* and is interwoven with the *Cath Mag Mucrama.* It tells of the conception of Cormac mac Art, the Irish Solomon. It begins with a comparison conception, that of Eóghan Mór's son, Fiachu, with Art's son, Cormac, who are both conceived before the Battle of Mag Mucrama. The druid, Olc Aiche, whose name means 'drinks the field', creates a fivefold magical protection or *caim* that ensures Cormac's safety. Cormac's rearing among wolves after the death of his father Art is nothing short of miraculous: when he is restored to his kindred, he is acclaimed like a young Dalai Lama, so enthusiastic are the people to greet him. He gives a judgment of such wisdom that he is recognised, even by Lugaid mac Conn, his uncle, who relinquishes the kingship of Tara to his nephew. We read more about Lugaid mac Conn, the King who cedes place to Cormac, in the 'Battle of Mag Mucrama' pp. 230–242.

Our translation is from Ms Laud 610, as edited by Kuno Meyer.

When Eóghan Mór went off to the Battle of Mucrama, he passed the night in the house of Tréth moccu Creccai. Tréth had a beautiful daughter by the name of Moncha. Eóghan commanded that the girl should sleep with him and she was given to him. Up until this time, he had fathered no child, but it was from this union that Moncha bore him a famous son, after Eóghan Mór's death in the battle against Mac Conn.

Fiachu Muillethan was the name of the boy born of that union. He was called Muillethan or Broad-Crowned because a druid said to Moncha while she was in labour, 'If the birth of your boy were tomorrow, he would surpass all other sons, and his own descendants would be kings.' Hearing this, Moncha went and sat on a stone in the bed of the Suir river at Raphae. Because his head was pressed against the stone, his name became Fiachu Broad-Crown, son of Eóghan Mór. Had the boy been born on the previous day when Moncha's labour had begun, the druid prophesied that the child would became the greatest jester in Ireland. And it was for this reason that she delayed his birth to the following day, and so he is called Muillethan because of the way that the crown of his head was pressed out of shape against the stone. It is because of Fiachu's parentage that it is a crime for any of the Eoghanacht clan to kill any of the Crecraige people.

In just such a way, Art son of Conn also had no offspring until he slept with Achtan, daughter of the smith-druid, Olc Aiche, the night before the battle of Mag Mucrama. Achtan was the mother of Cormac mac Art mac Conn. He was the same Cormac who succeeded to the kingship after Mac Conn mac Lugith, at the age of thirty.

When Art came from Tara to the battle he was about a hundred and fifty warriors ahead of the main host when he came to Ache, where Achtan, daughter of Olc Aiche, was before him at the milking place. She was the most lovely woman in Ireland. Olc Aiche had fifty milking places about Aiche, the region of which had been named after him. Each of these milking points provided his sustenance, for his drink was made up of the milkings of a hundred cows, and at each place, the vessel holding that milk had to be ready waiting for him.

As Art arrived, Achtan had just filled her father's milk churn. One of Art's companions asked the girt for a drink.

'Who is it asking?' she said.

'Art mac Conn, king of Ireland,' said the man.

'All right, then one of you must carry it,' she said.

Two men were unable to lift it, but Achtan herself lifted and poured it out for them.

'What a wonderful thing it would be if only you would give yourself to the king,' said one of the company.

'In such matters I have no power,' said the girl. 'Wait and see what my father thinks about it.'

Olc Aiche came, 'Where is my drink?' he demanded. Achtan filled the churn with new milk for him.

'This is my drinking vessel, but it is clear to me that this is not the same milk. Where is my drink?' he asked. 'This is not it!'

The girl told him everything.

'And what did Art say to you?'

'He said it would be a good thing if I gave myself entirely to him.'

Her father said, 'It would indeed be better.'

'That would be my desire,' said Achtan, 'as long as you also thought it good.'

'Good will come of it,' said Olc Aiche, 'for the child that you bear him will be the only son he will have, and from that boy will be the kingship of Ireland forever. Set food before the king: fifty oxen, fifty boars, a hundred and fifty loaves, fifty vats of wine. Bring fifty bridles and fifty cow-halters; and ask for tokens from the king's own regalia to be given to you.'

All these things were given to Art the next day and also Achtan herself accompanied by fifty girls. The food was distributed by Art. A tent was erected around them, and the girl slept with Art. She reported her father's words and asked for tokens that she might keep. Art gave her his sword, his golden thumb-ring and his festival clothes, before they sadly said goodbye to each other. And the girl was carrying Cormac, grandson of Conn in her womb.

Art then went to the battle. After her nine months were over, Olc Aiche's daughter gave birth to a son called Cormac. For Olc Aiche had said of him, 'You will truly bear a *mac ngor* or warm-hearted son,' from which he was called 'Cor-mac.' At his birth, the druid-smith, Olc Aiche, placed five protective circles about Cormac, protecting him against wounding, drowning, fire, enchantment, wolves and every evil chance.

Not long afterwards, Achtan was asleep in the grass when, without her knowledge, a wolf-bitch came and took the boy from her. And the wolf-bitch suckled the baby at her own teats, but Achtan had no idea where Cormac had gone. In that region there lived Luigne Fer Trí, a famous trapper who would lay snares for animals. He came upon a wolf-litter and there he captured a boy who ran with the wolves. Luigne Fer Trí took the cubs and raised them for a year. When Achtan learned of this, she went to Luigne Fer Trí and told him what had happened to the boy.

'Go away and hide the boy,' said the trapper, 'or else you will be put to death if Lugaid mac Conn finds out about this.'

So Achtan went immediately that night with her son to the north of Ireland to find Fiachna Cassán, Art's own foster-father. As she crossed a mountain in the middle of the night, the wolves of Ireland attacked her and tried to take her son away by force, howling all about her. But on that mountain was a herd of wild horses who came about them and protected them. This is why the mountain is named Slíabh Conachla [Mountain of the Horse-Band] in east Luigne.

Finally, she came northwards to Art's foster-father. He was at the well washing himself, overwhelmed with sorrow over the death of Art.

'It is not right to grieve so much,' said Achtan to him.

'Who are you?' Fiachna asked her,

And after she had told him the whole story, he put his arms about her neck and wept over the boy until he was wet with tears. A frame of yew-wood was made about the boy with a purple covering so that the hands of the people who swarmed to welcome the child might not kill him.

The boy was raised by his foster-kindred until he was thirty years old. On the advice of Olc Aiche's druidic omens, he came to Tara on an auspicious day, with his father's sword at his side, and wearing the old thumb-ring and his father's festival clothes. These fitted him perfectly.

As that tall, straight fellow came alone to Tara, he observed something: outside Tara was a man trying to appease a crying woman. Cormac came up behind the man, drawing his sword.

'You've no right to draw a sword on me, for I am Lugaid mac Conn's steward, Nechtan.'

'Give me what I ask,' said Cormac.

'Very well,' said the steward.

'I need food, security and a promise of silence about me.'

'You will have it,' said the steward.

'Tell me why the woman is crying?' asked Cormac.

'She's crying about the king's judgement, since it doesn't please her. Because her sheep cropped the queen's field of woad-plants, they are to be forfeit to the queen.'

'One sheep-shearing would surely be a fairer judgement! The man who so judged, never before gave false judgement,' said Cormac. 'Let me see him.'

The steward reported these words to Lugaid mac Conn in Tara.

Lugaid said to his steward, 'Go to him. He is the one who will succeed me. If there is a true descendant of Art in Ireland, then he is the one. Let him be under my protection. Since I uttered that judgement, the kingship is no longer mine. I will leave Tara in his care. My term of kingship is over for it is thirty years since my accession.'

The young man came and was welcomed by Lugaid mac Conn, who

rose before him.

'Not so!' said Cormac, 'I shall not be king as long as you live.'

But Lugaid mac Conn raised his knee [honouring Cormac], saying, 'This was only my house until your term of kingship.'

Mac Conn summoned his retinue and mercenaries, giving them the order, 'Let us go back to Munster, to our own heritage. Tara belongs to each king in turn.'

Then Mac Conn and his son Macniá, and his four sons Dau, Trían, Eochu and Lugith, set out.

Cormac asked, 'How is it possible for you to leave the green of your royal rule? Speak a judgement.'

'Not so,' said Lugaid mac Conn, 'it is for you to speak in judgement, since it is the beginning of your lordship.'

'If that is your will,' said Cormac.

'I am indeed taking my leave,' said Lugaid mac Conn.

Then Cormac said, 'I will [take the kingship.']

6. The Birth of Noidiu Nae-Mbreathach

(Compert Noidiu)

Translated by Caitlín Matthews

The precocity of children and their utterances is a notable theme in Celtic literature. The epitome of the wonder-child who is born knowing everything is seen in the Welsh Taliesin. The boy in this following fragment is Noidiu of the Nine Pronouncements. According to a triad, there were three who spoke immediately after birth: Aímac Ollaman, Morann mac Cairpre and Noidiu Noibrethach. Their stories are all within *The Yellow Book of Lecan*. Aí mac Ollaman was the poet of the Tuatha dé Danaan whose birth was heralded by a great wind that shook the house: a druid prophesied that the child in its mother's womb would be a prodigious infant. The story of Morann mac Cairpre or mac Maine, the great judge, is told in *Encyclopaedia of Celtic Wisdom*, p. 269. Born in a caul, he is rejected by his father who sends his mother to drown the boy in the sea, but she is prevented by a faery man. The caul removes itself from him and folds itself into a collar when he is dipped in the sea and when nine waves have gone over him, after which the baby sings a poetic invocation praising the creator of the world.

Noidiu had the reputation of being a great judge whose pronouncements became precedents in law. Noidiu is really a title rather than a personal name, meaning 'baby'. In this fragment, the baby utters nine pronouncements or judgemental aphorisms; his gestation is also lengthened ninefold. The Celtic obsession with ninefold matters revolves around the mystical three times three, a tripling of the already lucky three. The mother's unnatural reaction to her child in this story is similar to that of Morann's father: the infant's unusual ability to speak fits it for exposure rather than survival. But it is the baby who has the last word here! The line marked * below is obscure and may refer to the fact that Fingel doesn't have a known husband who would give her baby his name and title: because he is born outside a socially-recognised partnership, Noidiu is literally a no-one. The following line 'to every cow her calf', is actually later pronounced over the book that St Columba copied from his patron's psalter, St Finnian of Moville, who appropriates the copy, in an early dispute about copyright. Our translation is from Margaret Dobbs' edition from the fourteenth-century *Yellow Book of Lecan*.

These are the words of Noidiu of the Nine Pronouncements, son of Fingel, daughter of Daire mac Dedu, and of a hero who came from the sea. Now Fingel was confined against any risk of conception since there was a prophecy by Daire's druids that Daire would only live until his daughter bore a son: a true prophecy. Fingel was playing ball with the daughter of Noide mac Noimall by the water's edge when she saw a spirit emerge from the sea who made love to her. It was said that she was pregnant for nine years and nine months. Then the boy was born and Daire, his grandfather, promptly died. As soon as he was born, the boy uttered nine pronouncements.

'Cast him to the ground,' cried his mother.

'No, mother,' said the baby, 'put something under me.'

'Kill him quick!' said his mother. 'He spoke!'

'No, mother, to every tongue belongs its own proverb. It's fine that I use my own tongue.'

'We must kill him!' said his mother.

'No, mother. Those who give life must also feed it. To every being belongs its own food.'

'Feed yourself then!' said the mother.

'No, mother. Babies can't feed themselves.'

'You should be taken to your father,' she said.

'No, mother; every son belongs to his mother.'

'You've already made a meal of me while in the womb.'

'No, mother. I am not entitled to be born.'

**You didn't think about the fact that his cow goes with him and her calf with me.'

'No, mother. To every cow her calf. Let the calf be left with its mother.'

'Take him away somewhere!' said the mother.

'No, mother. Every cow's calf has its own family. The breast is my family.'

'Take him to the king!' said the mother.

'True, mother. Every good thing belongs to the king but any sea-treasure belongs the one who owns the land. My mother and myself are but flotsam.'

'Take up the boy and take him with you to rear,' said the mother to her nurse.

'No, mother. To every criminal his crime. Long before I sentence you, you die.'

And Fingel died at that moment. Because of this, no son has the right to judge his mother.

CATTLE RAIDS

7. The Cattle Raid of Flidais

(Táin Bó Flidais)

Translated by Caitlín Matthews

Táin Bó Flidais or 'The Cattle Raid of Flidais' is seen as one of the prequels to *Táin Bó Cuailgne*, (pp. 91–110) although it speaks of the 'exiles of Ulster' which implies that this story takes place after the death of Deirdriu and the Sons of Usliu, (pp. 444–453) for whom Fergus agreed to stand guarantor. After their ambush and murder, Fergus left Ulster to live with Ulster's natural enemies, Ailill and Medb of Connacht.

The Flidais of the title is the wife of Ailill Finn, a local king of what is now Co. Mayo, but she is a much more ancient figure. She has many of the qualities attributed to the Cailleach Beare: many husbands, a voracious sexual appetite and, according the *Coir Anman* 295, she is the mistress of stags and the owner of a herd of supernatural cattle. We hear little about her in this story, except for the healing power of her mantle.

Fergus mac Roích, her lover, whose name derives from the proto-Celtic *virogustus* 'best of men' and his surname, 'son of the Great Horse,' is a remarkable man in every respect. According to the *Scéla Conchobar mac Nessa* (LL 106a) Fergus mac Roích was a gigantic 'heptad tall'. The measurement between his one eye and the other was seven fists (42 inches) and the water from washing his hair filled a bushel bowl. His penis was seven fists long and his scrotum was the size of a bushel bag. Seven women were needed to satisfy his lust unless Flidais was with him. His food was seven vats of ale, seven pigs, seven deer and his strength was as seven men. Fergus' proverbial virility passed into nineteenth century oral tradition and caused the people of the Boyne Valley to refer to the pillar stone of Fál on the Hill of Tara as *bod Fheargais* – 'the penis of Fergus'.

Our translation of Fergus' affair with Flidais is from the twelfth century *Leabhar Laighnech* of Trinity College, Dublin, from the edition of J.

Corhais. This text, confusingly, has two Ailills in it. Ailill Finn is the husband of Flidais and Ailill mac Mátach is the King of Connacht, husband of Queen Medb. The latter says he will come with Fergus but doesn't, compounding this failure of diplomacy by sending Fergus himself, with all his Ultonian bluster to deliver an offer Ailill Finn can't refuse: let me in to be as your guest or give me some cattle to go away. Ailill Finn's niggardly hospitality is the excuse that Fergus needs to provoke a conflict. Dubthach Dóeltenga or 'the Back-Biter' is the same riotous and evil-tongued Ultonian hero who kills Conchobor's own son Maine in the *Táin Bó Cuailgne*, and who subsequently goes into exile after the death of Naoisi and the Sons of Usniu. At the end of the story, another Ultonian trouble-maker, Bricriu the satirist, uses the rough of his tongue to provoke a complete recovery in the warriors wounded by Ailill Finn. There are inconsistencies, such as the fact that the storyteller has forgotten that Ailill was severely wounded and is not among the number of the Connacht men! The last sentence really does not explain why this story is one of the prequels of the *Táin Bó Cuailgne*, unless you count one cattle-raid as a good excuse for the next!

Because this text is very terse, we have put the odd auxiliary word or clause in brackets to clarify the meaning implied by the narrative or character. The original tenses shuttle between present and past with great rapidity, but we have retained the past narrative tense for readability.

Flidais the wife of Ailill Finn, lived in Kerry. She loved Fergus mac Roích because of the great deeds that were told about him. Every week, the messengers that she sent out went busily to and fro between herself and Fergus. When Fergus arrived in Connacht he revealed this state of affairs to Ailill mac Mátach, King of Connacht.

'What am I going to do about this business so that I bring no shame upon your name or that of your country?' Fergus asked the king.

'Yes, what indeed?' said Ailill. 'My wife Queen Medb and myself will put our heads together and see which of us should go to Ailill Finn and get some help. But because someone should go there is no reason why you yourself should not be a member of the [diplomatic!] party. The better will the gift be! [if such an honourable man as you are with us.]

And so Fergus began his journey. Thirty men went with Fergus and Dubthach (Dóeltenga) until they arrived at Áth Fénnai in the north of Kerry. There they made for the fort where they were welcomed.

'Tell us why you have come?' asked Ailill Finn.

'Why, to stay with you,' said Fergus. 'You see, there is a dispute between ourselves and Ailill mac Mátach.'

'Then you may not stay with me,' replied Ailill Finn. 'If it had been any of your followers, then he would have been welcome, but as for you – I am told that my wife is in love with you.'

'Give us cattle then as a gift for we are in great want (of food.)'

'You'll get no such thing from me, said Ailill, '(better that) you stay as my guests.'

And that night, they were brought an ox and some bacon, with a supply of beer (exactly) proportionate to the food.

'I'm hardly going to use up your food,' Fergus said (provokingly), '(just) because I don't get a gift from you.'

'Leave this fortress at once!' Ailill said.

'I'll tell what you will have then,' replied Fergus. 'We won't lay siege to you.' And they set out.

Fergus (called back to the fortress), 'I need a single man to come to the ford at the gate of the fortress.'

'You will have neither denial nor any (championly) substitute, upon my honour,' swore Ailill, 'I will go myself.'

'Which of us will confront him, Dubthach?' Fergus asked (his companion.)

'In my opinion, it should be myself who comes against him,' answered Dubthach.

Then Dubthach went into the ford towards his opponent. He flung his spear towards Ailill and it penetrated both his legs. Then Ailill threw his spear at Dubthach, driving the shaft into him.

Fergus the Dextrous One himself stepped out to attack. As he did so, Ailill Finn cast his spear through him and he fell down.

Flidais came running from the fortress. She threw her cloak over the three of them, healing them. Fergus' company fled and Ailill Finn ['s men?] chased after them. Twenty of Fergus' company were killed in bloody massacre. Eight alone escaped to Cruachan to tell what had happened.

Ailill mac Mátach and Medb raised the nobility of Connacht and, with the exiles of Ulster (to reinforce them), they went into the kingdom of Kerry to Áth Fénnai with their army. Meanwhile, the warriors (who had fought over) Flidais (and) who had been severely wounded were brought into the fortress.

Ailill Finn was invited to parley with Ailill and Medb outside the fortress, but he said, 'I will not go! The conceit and baseness of that man out there is beyond everything!'

The (wounded) warriors (i.e. Fergus, Dubthach and one unnamed other) were brought away from the fortress into the camp of Ailill mac Mátach. They spent a whole week on the border besieging the fortress, (during which) a hundred and forty warriors from the nobility of Connacht were killed.

'You did not journey from us under a lucky sign, Fergus,' said King Ailill mac Mátach.

'That was not lawfully said,' said Bricriu, (ironically) 'since nobody fell at *our* hands. Each one of these (men) was a pillar in battle (by himself), let alone the three of them (having fallen.) Great indeed are these pillars if they are to be exposed to the dogs and scavengers of the air!'

As he spoke these words, the three (wounded men) raised themselves and, completely naked, lifted the gate of the fortress (off its hinges) into the middle of the castle itself and the army of Connacht stormed into the stronghold after them, killing seven hundred warriors, among them Ailill Finn and thirty of his sons, along with Amalgaid Múad, Eochach Muinmedain, Corpore Cromm, Ailill of Brefne, the three Oengus Bodbgnai, the three Echaids of Irrus, the seven Br
esléns of Aí, and the fifty Domnalls.

Then they brought Flidais from the fortress and whatever animals could be taken, which was a hundred cows in milk, a hundred and forty oxen, and another three thousand head of stock besides.

After this, Flidais lived with Fergus mac Roích. Every seventh day, Flidais would deliver provisions to the men of Ireland for their nourishment [from the takings of this raid.] Then she moved with Fergus to Táin in his own country and he gained power within the ruling of Ulster. It was there that she died at Tráig Baili. And this is why the Táin Bó Flidais belongs to the prequels (or fore-stories) of the Táin Bó Cuailgne.

8. The Mórrígan's Cow-Raid

(Táin Bó Regamma)

Translated by A.H. Leahy

This is one of several stories – including 'Froech's Cattle-Raid' and 'The Cattle-Raid of Flidais' (pp. 83–86) which are considered as preludes to the great Cattle-Raid of Cooley (*Táin Bó Cuailgne*, pp. 91–110). Here Cú Chulainn hears a cry at night which draws him out and triggers a meeting with the Mórrígan, an aspect of the ancient Celtic triple goddess of battles – the others being Badb and Macha. The ensuing dialogue is fascinating and sets up the animosity between the hero and the goddess, who predicts the way that she will defeat him at the battle of the Ford; Cú Chulainn responding with his own prophetic boasts of how he will slaughter a vast number of warriors who are sent against him. (See the *Táin Bó Cuailgne* for the outcome of this encounter.) The strange and bizarrely-named beings who accompany the Mórrígan are straight out of the wildest reaches of the Celtic imagination.

There are two versions of the story, one in the *Yellow Book of Lecan* and the other in Egerton 1782. Leahy's translation is based in that edited by Windisch in *Irische Texte* II, (Leipzig 1880–1905) who combined both of these versions. The title of the piece, *Táin Bó Regamma*, seems to have nothing to do with the story and Windisch suggests Táin bó Mórrígana, 'The Mórrígan's Cow-Raid', which we have adopted here. We have retained the actual title of the manuscript version for the sake of clarity.

When Cú Chulainn lay in his sleep at Dun Imrid there he heard a cry from the north; it came straight towards him; the cry was dire, and most terrifying to him. And he awaked in the midst of his sleep, so that he fell, with the fall of a heavy load, out of his couch, to the ground on the eastern side of his house. He went out thereupon without his weapons, so that he was on the lawns before his house, but his wife brought out, as she followed behind him, his arms and his clothing. Then he saw Laeg in his harnessed chariot, coming from Ferta Laig, from the north, and 'What brings thee here?' said Cú Chulainn.

'A cry,' said Laeg, 'that I heard sounding over the plains.'

'On what side was it?' said Cú Chulainn.

'From the north-west it seemed,' said Laeg, 'that is, across the great road of Caill Cuan.'

'Let us follow after to know [more] of it,' said Cú Chulainn.

They went out thereupon till they came to Ath da Ferta. When they were there, straightway they heard the rattle of a chariot from the quarter the loamy district of Culgaire. Then they saw the chariot come before them, and one red horse in it. The horse was one footed, and the pole of the chariot passed through the body of the horse, till a wedge went through it, to make it fast on its forehead. A red woman was in the chariot, and a red mantle about her, she had two red eye-brows, and the mantle fell between the two *ferta* [poles] of her chariot behind till it struck upon the ground behind her. A great man was beside her chariot, a red cloak was upon him, and a forked staff of hazel at his back, he drove a cow in front of him.

'That cow is not joyful at being driven by you!' said Cú Chulainn.

'The cow does not belong to you,' said the woman, 'she is not the cow of any friend or acquaintance of yours.'

'The cows of Ulster,' said Cú Chulainn, 'are my proper (care).'

'Dost thou give a decision about the cow?' said the woman; 'the task is too great to which thy hand is set, O Cú Chulainn.'

'Why is it the woman who answers me?' said Cú Chulainn, 'why was it not the man?'

'It was not the man whom you addressed,' said the woman.

'Ay,' said Cú Chulainn, '(I did address him) though thyself hath answered for him!'

"h-Uar-gaeth-sceo-luachair-sceo is his name,' [cold wind who rushes around] said she.

'Alas! his name is a wondrous one,' said Cú Chulainn. 'Let it be thyself who answers, since the man answers not. What is thine own name?' said Cú Chulainn.

'The woman to whom thou speakest,' said the man, 'is Faebor-begbeoil-cuimdiuir-folt-seenbgairit-sceo-uath.' [Littlemouthed-edgedequally-smallhair-shortsplinter-muchclamour]

'Do ye make a fool of me?' cried Cú Chulainn, and on that he sprang into her chariot: he set his two feet on her two shoulders thereupon, and his spear on the top of her head.

'Play not sharp weapons on me!'

'Name thyself then by thy true name!' said Cú Chulainn.

'Depart then from me!' said she: 'I am a female satirist in truth,' she said, 'and he is Daire mac Fiachna from Cuainge: I have brought the cow as fee for a master-poem.'

'Let me hear the poem then,' said Cú Chulainn.

'Only remove thyself from me,' said the woman; 'it is none the better for thee that thou shakest it over my head.'

Thereon he left her until he was between the two poles (*ferta*) of her chariot, and she sang to him: [. . .]

Cú Chulainn threw a spring at her chariot, and he saw not the horse, nor the woman, nor the chariot, nor the man, nor the cow.

Then he saw that she had become a black bird upon a branch near to him. 'A dangerous woman thou art,' said Cú Chulainn.

'Henceforward,' said the woman, 'this clay-land shall be called *dolluid* (of evil,)' and it has been the Grellach Dolluid over since.

'If only I had known it was you,' said Cú Chulainn, 'not thus should we have separated!'

'What thou hast done,' said she, 'shall be evil to thee from it!'

'Thou hast no power against me,' said Cú Chulainn.

'I have power indeed,' said the woman; 'it is at the guarding of thy death that I am; and I shall be,' said she. 'I brought this cow out of the fairy-mound of Cruachan, that she might breed by the Black Bull of Cuainge, that is the Bull of Daire mac Fiachna. It is up to that time that thou art in life, so long as the calf which is in this cow's body is a yearling; and it is this that shall lead to the *Táin Bó Cuailgne*.'

'I shall myself be all the more glorious for that Tain,' said Cú Chulainn: 'I shall slay their warriors: I shall break their great hosts: I shall be survivor of the Tain!'

'In what way canst thou do this?' said the woman, 'for when thou art in combat against a man of equal strength (to thee), equally rich in victories, thine equal in feats, equally fierce, equally untiring, equally noble, equally brave, equally great with thee, I will be an eel, and I will draw a noose about thy feet in the ford, so that it will be a great unequal war for thee.'

'I swear to the god that the Ulstermen swear by,' said Cú Chulainn,

'I will break thee against a green stone of the ford; and thou shalt have no healing from me, if thou leavest me not.'

'I will in truth be a grey wolf against thee,' said she, 'and I will strip a stripe [of flesh] from thee, from thy right (hand) till it extends to thy left.'

'I will beat thee from me,' said he, 'with the spear, till thy left or thy right eye bursts from thy head, and thou shalt never have healing from me, if thou leavest me not.'

'I shall in truth,' she said, 'be for thee as a white heifer with red ears, and I will go into a lake near to the ford in which thou art in combat against a man who is thine equal in feats, and one hundred white, red-eared cows shall be behind me and "truth of men" shall on that day be tested; and they shall take thy head from thee.'

'I will cast at thee with a cast of my sling,' said Cú Chulainn, 'so as to break either thy left or thy right leg from under thee; and thou shalt have no help from me if thou leavest me not.'

They separated, and Cú Chulainn went back again to Dun Imrid, and the Mórrígan with her cow to the fairy mound of Cruachan; so that this tale is a prelude to the *Táin Bó Cuailgne*.

9. The Cattle Raid of Cooley

(Táin Bó Cuailgne)

Translated by Caitlín Matthews

The *Táin Bó Cuailgne* describes one of the most notable incidents in Irish legend. It concerns the campaign led by Medb of Connacht to take the Brown Bull of Cooley in Ulster. But the timing of this raid is disadvantageous to the Ultonian warriors who are suffering the debility brought upon them by the curse of Macha (see p. 325.) Only Cú Chulainn is able to hold the pass single-handedly until the Ultonians recover. This long text resembles the Homeric *Iliad*, with descriptions of the combats and overthrows of Cú Chulainn. In this extract, which comes nearly half-way into the story, we hear how the Mórrígan herself comes to the hero and how he calls his fate upon himself by refusing her attentions. When the Goddess of Battle and Victory visits, it is perhaps good to show interest! But, as we see from p. 468, the goddess gets her prey in the end. Along with Mórrígan, her sisters Némain, Goddess of Vengeance, and Badb, Goddess of the Slain, also make their appearance here as battle is joined.

Up to this point, Queen Medb has been offering her champions inducements of land and property as well as the hand of her daughter, Finnabair, in order to inspire her men into defeating Cú Chulainn, but to no avail, since he defeats and kills all whom he encounters. Cruel and compromising conflicts of honour arise throughout the *Táin*, where Cú Chulainn's foster-kindred and friends are prevailed upon to act as Medb's champions, the most heart-rending being that combat between the hero and his friend, Ferdia. But in this episode, he fights another of his fellow-pupils, Lóch, who was with him in Alba, learning warcraft from the female warrior, Scathach. As they fight, the Mórrígan choses this moment to attack him, shapeshifting as she does so.

What with Medb's determination to break the normal rules of fair play

– one combatant to attack another at one time, no night ambushes and so on – and the magical shapeshifting of the Mórrígan, the unending combats take their toll of even Cú Chulainn's great strength, and he is visited by his spiritual patron and, some sources say, real father, the god Lugh. The hero has been actively defending Ulster from November till February without sleep, until he receives the help of the *sí*, the people of the faery.

While Cú Chulainn sleeps, the youths of Ulster, who are immune from the debility affecting its grown-up warriors, come to his rescue and in a poignant attempt to defeat Connacht, fall to their deaths in combat. After his healing at the hands of Lug, Cú Chulainn is reinvigorated and there follows a detailed description of the arming of his scythed chariot and of the hero's famous *ríastra* or battle distortion, whereby Cú Chulainn and his charioteer become agents of Badb, the Goddess of Vengeance, making their own spoil-heap for her crows and ravens to gnaw upon. As Cú Chulainn and Laeg, dressed in his raven-feather cloak, make their circuit of the battlefield, we can see them as the agents of Badb, the taker of the slain: they certainly leave her rich pickings to feast upon!

Cú Chulainn is also supported by his foster-father, Fergus, who is fighting on the side of Connacht since his exile from Ulster after the betrayal of Deirdriu and Naosi. He speaks for fair play throughout the story, but this extract ends with him and the rulers of Connacht irritably squabbling, in very poetical language, about how Cú Chulainn can be overcome and whether Fergus and the Ultonian exiles in his company can really be trusted.

It is impossible to reproduce the whole text of the *Táin* here for reasons of space but we give a connected cross-section that reveals the nature of the story and the supernatural manner in which the gods influence and aid the combat. We are aware throughout of the scribe or copyist's presence, making comment and interpreting for the reader, such as when he defines 'the gods and ungods' as the powerful people and the farming people, respectively. This is clearly a medieval inter-polation, not necessarily how the ancient Irish would have understood these terms. Our translation is taken from the oldest recension of the story, from the *Book of Leinster*, working from the Irish edition of Cecile O'Rahilly. The portions in square brackets indicate tentative translations of obscure text. Clarifying matter about relationships or names is given in round brackets. The final death of Cú Chulainn and the revenge of the Mórrígan are told in 'The Death of Cú Chulainn', pp. 468–475.

1. The dialogue of Cú Chulainn and the Mórrígan

Cú Chulainn saw a woman of great beauty coming towards him, dressed in clothes of many colours.

'Who are you?' asked Cú Chulainn.

'The daughter of King Búan,' she said. 'I have come to you because I love your great fame, and I have brought my treasures and my cattle with me.'

'This is not a good time for you to come to us. We are in a bad way through hunger. It is not easy for me to engage with a woman when I am in this trouble.'

'Then I shall help you in it,' she said.

'It's not for a woman's body that I've come here!'

'Less easy will it be then when I come against you while you are fighting against your enemies. I shall take upon me the shape of an eel entangling your feet in the ford so that you shall fall.'

'Better that form than a king's daughter,' he said. 'I shall take you between my toes until your rib-bones split, and you will bear this hurt until words of blessing are said over you.'

'Then I shall drive the cattle over the ford to you while I take the form a grey she-wolf upon me.'

'And I shall cast a stone at you from my sling to dash the eye from your head, and you will bear this hurt until words of blessing are said over you.'

'Then I shall come to you in the form of a hornless red heifer before the cattle, and they will stampede around you at the fords and pools, and yet you will never see me before you.'

'And I shall cast a stone at you,' he said, 'so as to break the legs from under you, and you will bear this hurt until words of blessing are said over you.'

And then she left him.

He was a week at Ath nGreacha, where every day a man would fall at his hands.

2. The death of Lóch Mac Emonis

Then Lóch Mac Emonis was called and, like all the rest, he was promised the region of Mag Muirthemne in the pasture lands of Mag nAí, as well as the equipment of twelve warriors and a chariot worth seven female slaves. But he did not think it worthy to fight a mere boy.

He had a brother called Long Mac Ebonis. A similar inducement was offered to him: the maiden (Finnabair), clothes, chariot and land.

Long went to meet Cú Chulainn, who killed him; the body was brought back dead and laid down before his brother, Lóch.

Then Lóch said that if he only knew that it was a bearded man who had killed his brother, he would avenge his death by killing him.

'Take strong battle to him,' said Medb to her people, 'across the ford from the west, so that you can cross the river and break the rules of fair play where he's concerned.'

The warriors known as the Seven Maines, went ahead and saw him at the edge of the ford to the west. He was wearing his festival clothes. The women kept climbing upon the men's shoulders in order to see him.

Medb said, 'I regret that I cannot see the boy around whom they are gathering.'

Lethrend, Ailill's groom, said, 'It would bring no health to your mind to see him!'

She came to the ford then where he stood. 'Who is that man over there, Fergus?' asked Medb.

Fergus said,

> 'A boy who defends with sword and shield
> [the great horn at the waist of the ford;
> manfully and festively upholding the honour
> of a wounded Ulster which suffers
> the law that even kings cannot escape.
> The spear-shaft of Mag Muirthemne!
> The mace of Culainn's Hound!]'

Then Medb also climbed on to the men to get a glimpse of him. And it was then that the women informed Cú Chulainn that he was being laughed at in the camp because he was beardless, and that no proven hero had come against him yet, except untried boys. It would be wise to smear blackberry juice upon his chin. This he did in order to engage in combat with a grown man, with Lóch. Also he took a handful of grass and chanted a spell over it, so that everyone thought he had a beard on his chin.

'Why, we see that Cú Chulainn is bearded after all,' said the women, trying to provoke Lóch. 'Surely it must be right for a warrior to fight him!'

'I'll not fight with him until seven days have passed,' said Lóch.

'He cannot be left unchallenged for such a length of time,' exclaimed Medb. 'Let us send a band of warriors to come to him every night in case he can be surprised that way.'

And so they did. Every night, a new band of warriors went searching for him but he killed them all. These were the names of the bands that fell there: seven Conalls, seven Oengus's, seven Uargus's, seven Celtres, eight Fiacs, ten Ailills, ten Delbaeths and ten Tasachs. Such were his exploits that week at Ath nGrencha.

Medb then took counsel about how she should proceed against Cú Chulainn, for she was greatly troubled by the number of her host that had been so far killed. She decided that she would send some valiant, proud men to attack him en masse so that he might agree to parley with her. She had arranged a meeting with him the next day to institute a false truce and so capture him. She sent him a messenger asking him to come and meet with her, commanding that he should come unarmed, since she herself would be meeting him with only her women for company.

Traigthrén, the messenger, came to Cú Chulainn with Medb's message. Cú Chulainn gave his word that he would abide by the agreement.

'Tell me, in what manner do you go to parley with Medb tomorrow, Cú Chulainn,' asked Láeg, his charioteer.

'Why just as Medb asked!' replied Cú Chulainn.

'Many are her treacheries,' said the charioteer. 'She has some mischief up her sleeve!'

'What shall we do then?' said the hero.

'Tie your sword at your waist,' said the charioteer, 'so that you won't be surprised. A warrior without his weapons has no claim to his honour-price but is merely entitled to the compensation of someone who doesn't bear arms.'

'Let's do that then,' said Cú Chulainn.

The parley was at Ard Aignech, called Fochaird today.

Mebd arrived at the meeting, having prepared an ambush for Cú Chulainn. Fourteen of the bravest men of her household were among them: the two Glas Sinnas, sons of Briccride; the two Ardáns, sons of Licc; the two Glas Ognas, sons of Crond; with Drúcht, Delt, Dathen, Téa, Tascur, Tualangm Taur and Glese.

Cú Chulainn came out to meet her and the men sprang out at him, attacking in concert by throwing fourteen spears at him. Cú Chulainn dived for cover so that none of the spears so much as grazed his skin. Then he retaliated and killed all fourteen of them. These fourteen of Fochaird are also known as the men of Crónech for they were killed in Crónech at Fochaird.

Cú Chulainn said of this deed,

> 'Skilful my warrior exploit!
> Fearful blows I strike
> against a ghostly army.
> I take battle to many hosts,
> death-dealing destruction
> to the brave troops of Medb and Ailill.
> A cold-blooded treachery
> perpetrated by woman's mind
> requires good counsel, wisely taken,
> to combat courageous men
> and overcome them
> by heroic exploits!'

And that was how that exploit gave rise to the name, Fochaird, from this *fó cherd* or skilful deed of Cú Chulainn's at this place.

Cú Chulainn then came and found them (the Connacht host) setting up camp and he killed the two Daigres, the two Anles and the four men called Dúngaid Imlich. Then Medb began to provoke Lóch, saying, 'Great is the shame upon you that the man who murdered your brother is now slaughtering our troops, and here are you doing nothing to stop him! We're convinced that a bold, boastful boy like him yonder will be unable to stand against the vengeful anger of one like yourself, especially since the pair of you had the same teacher and fostermother in the arts of war.'

Then Lóch, seeing that that Cú Chulainn had a beard, made ready to attack him and avenge the death of his brother.

'Come further up the ford,' said Lóch, 'so that we shan't engage at the ford bloodied by Long's death.'

And as Cú Chulainn entered the ford, the men began to drive cattle across it.

'There will be little water here today,' predicted Gabrán, the poet. Which is why that place is known by the names Ath Darteisc (Ford of

Thirst) and Tír Mór Darteisc (Country of Great Thirst).

As the combatants met at the ford and began to fight, hammering blows upon each other, an eel came and wound itself three times around Cú Chulainn's feet so that he fell on his face across the ford. Lóch thrust at him with his sword until the ford ran red with his blood.

'This is a bad show in the face of the enemy!' exclaimed Fergus (Cú Chulainn's foster-father). 'One of you men incite him,' he said to his retainers, 'so that he doesn't fall without purpose.'

Then Bricriu Nemthenga mac Carbada (the satirist) got up and began to taunt Cú Chulainn. 'Your strength is spent against a weak adversary,' he said, 'especially now since the Ulstermen are on their way to you, released from their debility. It must be hard for you to demonstrate the hero's part before the men of Ireland and to fend off a doughty opponent with your weapons tangled in that way!'

Hearing that, Cú Chulainn rose up and struck at the eel so that its ribs were broken. At the same time, the cattle rushed eastwards through the army-camp, bearing away the tents upon their horns, frightened by the thunder-clash of the warriors' shields in the ford.

Then the she-wolf attacked him, driving the cattle westwards towards him. He cast a stone from his sling and struck the eye into the back of her head. Then she (the Mórrígan) took the form of a hornless red heifer who led the stampeding cattle into the streams and fords. Cú Chulainn said, 'I can't see the fords for the streams!' He cast a stone at the hornless red heifer and broke her leg.

Then Cú Chulainn chanted:

> 'Alone the beasts I'm guarding;
> neither letting them come nor go.
> Standing the chilly hours,
> alone against many people.
>
> 'Someone tell Conchobor,
> it's time to help me now.
> Mágach's sons take off their cattle
> and share them out between them.
>
> 'A single man can be defended,
> but no single log will catch alight.
> But bring two or three of them
> and their torches would blaze.

Many foes near overcome me,
in too many single combats.
I cannot fight such great warriors
as I stand here all alone.'

And then Cú Chulainn fulfilled the triple promise he had threatened
the Mórrígan with in the *Táin Bó Regamma*. (see p. 87) And he
overcame Lóch in the ford with (his spear) the *gáe bolga*, which (Laeg)
the charioteer had thrown to him from downstream. And, because
Lóch when he fought had skin like horn, Cú Chulainn pierced him
through the anus with his spear.

'Step away from me,' said Lóch.

As Cú Chulainn did so, Lóch fell on the other side of the ford.
Which is why that place is called Ath Traiged (the Dried-up Ford) in
Tír Mór.

Then the rules of fair play were subverted towards Cú Chulainn on
that day as five men came at the same time to attack him; they were two
called Crúaid, two Calads and one called Derothor. Cú Chulainn
singlehandedly killed them all. That place is now called Cóicsius
Focherda and Cóicsius Oengoirt. (The Five-fold Hero Feat or The
Five-fold Single-handed Field.) Or it maybe because Cú Chulainn had
been fifteen days in Focherd that it takes its name Cóicsius Focherda
(The Fortnight Feat) in the *Táin*. Cú Chulainn cast so many stones
from Delga against them that no living thing, neither man nor beast,
could get past him to the south between Delga and the sea.

3. The healing of the Mórrígan

While Cú Chulainn lay in great exhaustion, the Mórrígan came to him
in the shape of an old grandmother with one eye, milking a cow with
three teats. He asked her for a drink and she gave the milk of one teat.

'May she who gave me food be healthy!' said Cú Chulainn. 'May the
blessing of the gods and ungods be upon you!' – The powerful people
were their gods and the farming people were their ungods.

As he spoke, her head was healed. Then she gave him milk from the
second teat, and her eye was healed. As she gave him milk from the
third teat, so her leg was healed.

It is said that each time he said, 'Words of blessing upon you.'

'Ah, but you told me I should never receive healing from you!' said
the Mórrígan.

'If I'd known that it was yourself,' said Cú Chulainn, 'I'd never have healed you!'

In another version of the *Táin*, this tale is called *Ríamdrong Con Culainn for Tarthesc*. (The Overwhelming of Cú Chulainn Upon Tarthesc.)

Fergus then demanded guarantees that Cú Chulainn should receive fair play. And after that, they opposed him in single combat. He killed five men of the Cend Coriss clan which we now call Delgu Murthemne. Then he filled Fota in his field, Bó Mailce at his ford, Salach in his marsh, Muinne in his fort, Lúar in Lethbera and Fer Toíthle in Toíthe. The places where these men fell have been named after them and so remembered.

Cú Chulainn then killed Traid, Dorna, Derna, Col, Mebal and Eraise at Méthe and Cethe, this side of Ath Tíre Móir. These people were druids and their wives.

Then Medb sent out a hundred men from her own household to kill Cú Chulainn, but he killed them all at Ath Chéit Chúile. Then Medb exclaimed, 'It is criminal that our people should be killed!'

Which is how the places Glais Chró, Cuillenn Cind Dúin and Ath Céit Chúile were named. (The Bloody Stream, the House of the Holly Tip, and the Ford of the Hundred Retainers.)

4. The coming of Lug

The four provinces of Ireland set up camp at the place called Breslech Mór in Mag Muirthemne, sending their portion of the cattle and spoils ahead of them south towards Clithar Bó Ulad.

Cú Chulainn positioned himself upon the gravemound of Lerga nearby the host, where his charioteer, Laeg mac Ríangabra, made a fire for him that evening. Cú Chulainn could distantly see, over the leaders of the four provinces of Ireland, the glint of the setting sun through the evening clouds burning upon the bright gold of their weapons.

He was seized by anger and fury at the great number of the host and overwhelming multitude of his enemies. He took up his two spears, his shield and his sword. Shaking his shield, waving his spears and sword, he gave vent to the hero's cry from the depths of his throat. Then the bannogs and buccas and the beings of the valley and the demons of the air gave answer, inspired by the terror that his cry had pronounced. Némain (the war goddess) fell upon the army with frenzy, and the four provinces of Ireland made such a clamour with the ends of their own spears and weapons that a hundred warriors dropped dead of fear and terror in the middle of the camp that night.

But Laeg saw a lone man coming straight towards them out of the north-east acrosss the encampment of the Irishmen.

'What manner of man is that?' asked Cú Chulainn.

'A tall, fair man with curly yellow hair. He has a green mantle folded about him with a brooch of white silver fastening it. Against his skin, he wears a shirt of kingly satin with a panel of red gold in it reaching to his knees. He carries a black shield with a battle-boss of white bronze. A five-pointed spear is in his hand and a death-dealing javelin accompanies it. It is a wonder to see the the play, sport and great game he makes with them. But no-one stops him nor does he stop anyone, as if no-one could see him.'

'Truly said, my friend,' said Cú Chulainn, 'for this is one of my allies from the sí who has come to comfort me, for they well know my trouble as I stand alone across the four great provinces of Ireland because of the Cattle Taking of Cuailgne.'

And it was as Cú Chulainn had said. When the warrior reached the place when Cú Chulainn stood, he spoke comfortingly to him, 'Manfully done, Cú Chulainn!' he said.

'This has been no great thing,' replied Cú Chulainn.

'I shall give help to you,' said the warrior.

'Who are you?' asked Cú Chulainn.

'I am your father from out of the sí, Lug mac Ethlend.'

'My wounds are thick upon me. It is time enough that they were healed.'

'Sleep then for a while, Cú Chulainn,' said the warrior. 'While you sleep here upon the hill of Lerga for three days and three nights, I shall fight against the host myself.'

Then he sang to him a low resonant tune which sent him into a deep sleep until all the hero's wounds were clean again. Then Lug said,

> 'I, Lug, call you to hear:
> Arise, great son of Ulster,
> healing has been given to your wounds,
> inflicted by spiteful marauders,
> a great sheaf against a small one.
> This god will make a way;
> though a host will come inflicting injury,

help from the *sí* will free you,
[will save you from this pack of wolves,
defend you from the hostile pit.
A lone boy left on guard,
defending the doomed beasts.
A ghostly shape shall smite.]
No strength of life is in them;
wreak your blazing authority
with strength upon your poisonous foes.
Sweep your chariot through the valleys,
and so arise!'

Cú Chulainn slept for three days and three nights. It was good that he did since his need for sleep corresponded with his exhaustion. From the Monday after the feast of Samhain until the Wednesday after the feast of Imbolc, Cú Chulainn had had no sleep, except for brief naps at midday when he leant on his spear, head against his fist, and the spear against his knee, but continued hacking, cutting, smiting and slaughtering the four great provinces of Ireland.

Then the warrior from the *sí* strewed plants and healing herbs as well as curative invocations on to the gashes and many wounds of Cú Chulainn, so that he began to recover in his sleep without noticing it.

It was then that the Youth Troop came southwards from Emain Macha, three hundred kings' sons of Ulster, led by Fallamain, son of Conchobor. Three times they fought against the host (of Connacht), killing three times their own number, but the young men died too, all apart from Fallamain himself. Fallamain swore that he would not return to Emain Macha without carrying back the head of Ailill crowned with his golden circlet. But it was not a simple task before him, for the two sons of Beithe mac Báin, Ailill's fostermother and fosterfather, joined with him and wounded him, so that he died at their hands. And this was the Slaughter of Ulster's Youth Troop and the Death of Fallamain mac Conchobor.

Meanwhile, Cú Chulainn lay on the mound of Lerga in a healing coma for three days and three nights. Finally he rose from his sleep, passed his hand over his face and turned red from head to foot. His manly vigour rose up in him as if he were anticipating a festival, or a war-gathering, or a march, or an alehouse, or a feast or the inaugural assembly of all Ireland.

'How long have I been sleeping, warrior?' he asked.

'Three days and three nights,' answered the warrior.

'That bodes no good to me then,' said Cú Chulainn.

'Why is that?' asked the warrior.

'Because the host has gone unopposed all this time!' said Cú Chulainn.

'That is not so,' said the warrior.

'Tell me how that was so,' said Cú Chulainn.

'The Youth Troop came south from Emain Macha, a hundred and fifty Ulster kings' sons, led by Fallamain, Conchobor's son. While you slept for three days and three nights, they fought against the host three times. Three times their own number fell at their hands, and the young men themselves were all killed except Fallamain, and he swore that he would carry off Ailill's head complete with its golden circlet. But it was not easy for him and he himself was killed.'

'If only I had been in my rightful strength. If I had been, the Youth Troop would not have perished, nor would Fallamain mac Conchobor been killed!'

'Fight on, little Hound; there is no stain upon your reputation, no slight upon your courage!'

'Stay with us tonight, warrior,' implored Cú Chulainn, 'so that we can avenge the Youth Troop together.'

'I will not stay,' said the warrior, 'for whatever great exploits or courage a man performs in your company, the glory and fame of them will attach to you, not to him. And so I will not stay. But go bravely against the host all by yourself, for it is not with them that the power over your life lies at this time.'

5. The scythed chariot and the battle distortion

'What of the scythed chariot, master Laeg?' asked Cú Chulainn. 'Can you yoke it? Is all its equipment ready? If you have, then get it ready, but if anything's missing, leave it now.'

The charioteer rose up and put on his charioteer's battle armour. His battle-dress was like this: a smooth, soft tunic made of deerhide, light and airy, supple as skin in cut, so as not to hinder the movements of his arms. Over that he wore an overtunic of black raven's feathers which some say was made by Simon Magus for Darius, King of the Romans, and given by Darius to Conchobor, and by Conchobor to Cú Chulainn and by Cú Chulainn to Laeg. The charioteer donned his crested helmet, with its four-sided panels engraved with every colour and shape, which reached down to his shoulders: this suited him well and was no burden to wear. In order to distinguish himself from his master, he placed upon his brow a circlet of red burning gold, shaped over the anvil's edge. He took up the horse spancel and his decorated horse-stick in his right hand, while in his left he took the leading reins that controlled the horses' movement as he drove

Then he accoutered the horses in their iron battle armour, covering them from head to foot with spikes and spears, barbs and blades, so that every wheel of the chariot was studded with blades, and every corner and surface bristled with points so that the chariot tore to pieces whatever it struck.

Then he set a warding, breastplate charm upon the horses and upon his companion, so that they were invisible to everyone in the camp, while everyone remained visible to them. It was altogether good that he did so, for he would need the three great gifts of the charioteer's craft that day: leaping the gap, steering straight and using the horse-stick. So it was that the battle hero took his harness upon him, he who fenced Badb's enclosure with bodies, he, Cú Chulainn, son of Sualtaim. His battle-dress consisted of twenty-seven tunics, waxed, compacted and wadded together, tied with strings, cords and thongs close to his skin, so that he shouldn't unseat his senses and his understanding when the battle frenzy came upon him.

Over these he wore his hero's battle-belt of cowhide of stiff, well-tanned leather made from the best hides of seven yearling oxen, which covered him from narrow waist to the width of his armpits: this shielded him against the spears, javelins, points, lances and blows, so that they glanced aside from it as though they had struck stone, rock or horn. Then he put on his silk-smooth loin-guard with its gold-speckled border over the soft parts of his lower belly. Over this he wore a dark loin-guard of supple brown leather made from the well-softened parts of four yearling oxen, with the battle-belt to hold it in place. So it was that the kingly hero seized his warlike battle weapons.

These were the weapons of conflict that he had: eight short swords together with his flashing, ivory-hilted sword; eight small spears with his five-pronged spear; eight little darts with his special self-guided dart; eight shields along with his dark-red, curved shield into which a prize boar could fit with its edged, razor-sharp rim that would cut a hair against the current. Whenever the hero performed the edge-feat with the shield rim, he could cut as well with its edge as with a spear or sword.

Then he donned his crested battle-helmet which proclaimed battle, strife and slaughter from every inch and angle of it, a cry like the shout of a hundred warriors in full roar, so that it sounded like all the bannogs and buccas, and beings of the valley and demons of the air were wailing before, above and around him wherever he went, prophesying the letting of warriors' and champions' blood. He then enfolded himself in his concealing cloak made from material from Tír Tairngire (the otherworldly Land of Promise) which had been given him by his druidic foster-father.

Then the first battle distortion came upon Cú Chulainn, rendering him horrifyingly many-shaped, weird and unrecognisable. The flesh upon his body shook like a tree in a great wind or like a bulrush in a stream, every limb, joint, knuckle and organ of him. He leapt into a furious bout of contortion inside his skin, whereby his feet and shins and knees reversed themselves, and his heels, calves and ham-strings faced forward. The muscles within his calves showed on the front of his shins, and the balled knots of them were big as a warrior's fist. The sinews of his head stretched down to the nape of his neck, making a great, measureless ball as big as the head of a month-old child. His face and appearance hollowed in like a bowl. One eye was sucked in so deep that the beak of wild crane could scarcely have dug it out from the back of his skull. The other eye stood out from his cheek. His mouth was horribly distorted. One of his cheeks was drawn back to the jawbone so that his innards were visible. His lungs and liver beat in his mouth and throat. His lower and upper jaws gnashed together like a sword and shield. A stream of fiery foam-flakes the size of ram's fleeces streamed into his mouth from his throat. The beating of his heart sounded like baying of a bloodhound or like the attack of a lion falling upon bears.

There streamed from him the brands of Badb; poisonous cloud-drifts and sparks of fiery expulsions rained into the air above him, so fierce was his rage. The hair of his head curled like crooked red hawthorn thrust in to hedge a gap. If a kingly appletree laden with fruit had been shaken about his head, hardly one apple would have reached the ground but would have been impaled upon each separate spike of hair because of the way that it bristled from his scalp. The hero-radiance rose from his brow as broad as a warrior's fist and as long as his nose. He beat his shields together furiously, urging on his charioteer and casting sling-stones at the host. Then, high as the massive, strong, powerful length of a great ship's mast, rose a dark-stream of blood from the top of his skull, dissolving into a dense druidic mist – just as the smoke of a king's hostel hangs over the house at twilight on a winter's day when the king is expected.

After this distortion had contorted the hero, Cú Chulainn leapt into his scythed chariot, which bristled with iron-points, thin edges, hooks, steel prongs, and all the nails that were attached to the chariot on all its shafts, straps, loops and bindings. This was how the chariot was: made of a stream-lined framework, compact but convenient for heroic feats, straight as a die and fit for a hero. Eight sets of kingly weapons could fit into it, and its movement was swift as the swallow or the wind, fleet as a deer running over a level plain. It was drawn by two swift horses, spirited and reckless, with neat, prick-eared heads, firm-hoofed, roan-breasted, steady and sure, quick to be harnessed to the shafts of the splendid chariot. One horse was lithe and swift-leaping, ready for battle, with arching neck and hoofs that scattered sods of earth. The other horse had a curling mane, with thin, slender hoofs and hocks.

Then Cú Chulainn did the thunderfeat of a hundred deaths, the thunderfeat of two hundred deaths, the thunderfeat of three hundred deaths, the thunderfeat of four hundred deaths. But at the thunderfeat of five hundred deaths he stopped, for he considered that this was a commendable number to fall by him at this first assault, in his first attack against the four provinces of Ireland. And this was the way that he had come out to attack his enemies, driving his chariot in a circuit about the four great provinces of Ireland.

He drove his chariot so heavily that the iron wheels sank into the earth, casting up enough sods to build forts and ramparts. All about the circuit and ditch he had made with his chariot was a heap of rocks, stones and gravel that the wheels had thrown up. He had created this encircled wall of Badb around the four great provinces of Ireland so that none of them should escape from him nor sneak away until he had taken vengeance for the death of the Youth Troop of Ulster.

He went into the centre of their ranks, throwing up a great spoil heap of bodies three times around the main host. Then he launched the attack of an enemy upon his foes, so that they fell sole to sole, neck to headless neck, so dense was the carnage. He encircled them three times more, leaving a wall six corpses deep, with the soles of three upon the necks of three others, all around the camp, so that the name of this part of the *Táin* is called Sesrech Breslige, or the Sixfold Slaughter. It is one of three incalculable slaughters, of which the others are Imshlige Glennamnach and the Great Battle of Gáirech and Irgairech. But at Sesrach Breslige it was hounds, horses and men that fell together.

Other versions of the story relate that Lug mac Eithlend fought alongside Cú Chulainn in the battle of Sesrech Breslige.

The number of the slain is not known, nor is it possible to say how many footsoldiers fell. Of their leaders and captains, these alone have been reckoned: the two Crúaids, the two Calads, the two called Cír, the two Cíars, the two Ecells, the three Croms, the three Cauraths, the three Comirges, four called Feochar, four called Furacher, four called Cass, four called Fota, five Cauraths, five Cermans, five Cobthachs, six called Saxan, six called Dách, six Dáires, seven Rochairds, seven called Rónán, seven called Rúrthech, eight Roclads, eight called Rochtad, eight Rindachs, eight Cairpres, eight called Mulach, nine Diagiths, nine Dáires, nine called Dámach, ten Fiacs, ten called Fiacha and ten Fedelmids.

Cú Chulainn killed one hundred and fifty kings in that battle of Breslech Mór in Mag Murthemne, as well as innumerable hounds, horses, women, boys and children and commoners. There was not one man in three in all Ireland who escaped without his thighbone or the side of his head or one eye being injured or without some scar for the rest of his life.

After the battle against so many, neither Cú Chulainn nor his charioteer or horses, suffered one wound or scratch.

6. Cú Chulainn, the beautiful and terrible

The next morning, Cú Chulainn came out to survey the host and to show off his gentle and beautiful appearance to the women, matrons, girls and maidens, to the poets and men of the gift, for he did not feel that the dark, druidical guise under which he had previously appeared was entirely to his credit. So for that reason, he emerged today to display his gentle and beautiful self.

He was indeed fair to look upon, the youth who came to show himself to the hosts, Cú Chulainn mac Súaltaim. Three kinds of hair seemed to grow upon his head: it was dark near the scalp, blood red down the strands and tipped with gold at the ends. His hair was arranged into three ringlets in the hollow at the nape of his neck, each strand of hair falling like gold thread. The loose-flowing, bright-golden, splendid, long-tressed and beautifully coloured locks fell over his shoulders. Hundreds of crimson locks of fiery golden red surrounded his neck. His hair was woven with hundred plaits threaded with carbuncle gems. Four dimples shaded each cheek: a yellow one, a green one, a blue and a purple one. There were seven bright jewel-like pupils in each of his kingly eyes. He had seven toes on each foot and seven fingers on each hand, each with the grip of a hawk's talons or the claws of a gryphon in each digit.

He had put on his festival clothes that day, with a well-cut mantle of vivid purple, fringed and hung in five folds, which was clasped with a brooch of white silver decorated with gold inlay over his white breast, so that it drew the eyes of men like a lantern because of the blinding brilliance of its light. Next to his skin was a silken tunic of satin which fell to the top of the dark warrior's loin-guard made of red, kingly satin. He carried a shield of dark-red purple, with five concentric circles of gold upon it and a rim of white bronze. A gold-hilted, richly ornamented sword with a red-gold boss swung from his belt, ready for action. Beside him in the chariot was a tall, glimmer-edged spear along with his keen hungry javelin, rivetted with gold. In one hand, he grasped nine heads, while he held ten in the other, which he brandished at the armies. Such were the spoils of one night's fighting by Cú Chulainn.

The women of Connacht began climbing upon the soldiers and the women of Munster climbed up on to the shoulders of the men that they might better view the appearance of Cú Chulainn. But Medb hid her face for dread of him, under the curved shelter of a shield, not daring to show her face.

So it is that Dubthach Dóel Ulad spoke:

> 'If this is the contorted one,
> we'll have piles of dead.
> Screams we'll have in the courts,
> tales told in many lands.

> 'Many a gravestone lifted,
> many kingly deaths will ensue.
> Neither good nor benefit to battle
> against the solitary combatant.

> 'I see his intemperate shape:
> eight heads in his plunder-pile.
> I see the broken trophies:
> ten heads for his treasure.

> 'I see how the womenfolk strain

their faces above the slaughter.
I see how the great queen
shrinks from giving battle.

'If I were a battle-counsellor,
he'd be attacked from all sides.
We would shorten the life
of this contorted one.'

Then Fergus answered him like this:

'Take Dubhtach Chafer-Tongue away,
to the back of the host with him!
No good has he done since
the slaughter of maiden-boys.

'He made an infamous violence
killing Fiacha, Conchobor's son.
No better was his next deed:
the death of Coirpre mac Feidlimid.

'The kingship of Ulster is not his quarry,
this son of Lugaid mac Casruba.
But this is how he uses them:
the unkilled set at odds.

'Evil would it be to Ulster's exiles,
the death of our beardless youths.
If Ulster's host fell upon you,
they would claim back the herds.

'Ulster's curse of debility drags on
greatly before their recovery.

'Great stories will be told,
great queens will make moan,
men's bodies will be mangled,
great will be the slaughter!

'Corpses trampled under foot,
ravens gorged on raven-feast,
shields scattered on the slopes,
survivors will seek shelter.

'Blood of war-bands will be shed

by inhuman hosts.
Far have the exiles journeyed
out of Ulster's homely borders.

Ungrasping of the doom before you,
take Dubthach Chafer-Tongue away!'

And Fergus flung Dubthach from him and he landed on his nose next
those standing around. Then Ailill said,

'Do not contend, Fergus
about the cows and women of Ulster.
I predict a great slaughter
at the ford's gap.
Though they come one by one,
death clogs the ford every single day.'

Then Medb said,

'Rise up, Ailill,
with your three-ranked warband,
and guard the beasts.
That whelp of a boy
makes much bluster
in the gravely passes,
among the dark pools.
Courageous Fergus
and his brave Ulster exiles
will be compensated
when the battle is done,
with sorrow's easing
from the war poets.'

Then Fergus replied,

'Woman's counsel
should not be heeded.
Inflaming blossoms
that scorch kindred,
inflicting death and evil
upon relations.
Utterances that inflame

rather than sooth the fever.'

The poet, Gabrán, said,

> 'Don't waste words
>   upon servants and queens,
> bestowing on the women's side
>   the flavour of your sayings:
> so, twenty eyelids flutter!
>   What untoppled judge
> in this great cemetery
>   warrants your hatred?'

'Don't avoid your opponent,' said Fergus. 'Go and greet him in the ford!'

'Hear it, Ailill!' said Medb. Then Ailill said,

> 'Fergus knows well these great lands.
>   He grinds on at our household,
> but fails to lead the beasts.
>   But alongside which host
> will he lash the cattle?
>   He counsels destruction,
> but greater is his boastful babble.'

Then Fergus said,

> 'Do not do this, Medb!
>   greatly separated
> are the exiles who've served you
>   this many years.
> Don't scold those far from
>   their own country.'

(*The single combats go on, until Fergus, Cú Chulainn's own foster-father, is asked to fight against the hero. Although he first refuses, he is made drunk and enters the ford. Cú Chulainn retreats so that Fergus can honourably retreat back to his side. Finally, there is nothing for it but for Medb to send Cú Chulainn's own best friend, Ferdia, against him.*)

VOYAGES

10. The Voyage of Bran, Son of Febal

(Imram Brainn mac Febal)

Translated by Kuno Meyer

In this story Bran, the king of Ireland, is invited to the Land of Women by a faery woman with a magical silver branch. This theme of the visit to the Otherworld appears widely throughout Celtic literature. Pwyll visits Annwn in 'The Adventure of Pwyll' from the *Mabinogion*, as does Eochaid in 'The Wooing of Etain', and both Loeg and the eponymous hero in 'The Sick-Bed of Cú Chulainn' (pp. 195–218). In the text included here such a visit constitutes the main purpose of the story. In fact it is representative of a whole class of stories known as *imrama*, 'voyages; lit. 'rowings about'. These seem to have been widely known in other parts of Europe and influenced the later ecclesiastical stories such as the ninth-century 'Voyage of Brendan'. Indeed, there are evident signs of Christian interpolations in this story, as where Manannán describes the people of the Otherworld as being 'without sin' and delivers something of a sermon about the evils of believing in the gods! 'Imram Brainn' probably dates from the eighth century AD. It contains some of the most vivid descriptions of the Otherworld. The various place names in the poem: Plain of Silver, Emne, Silvery Land, Mag Rein, Mag Mon, Mag Mell, Ciuin, etc, are all names for the Otherworld. The story naturally reminds us of the *Odyssey*, and it has been suggested that the Irish knew Homer's great tale and copied it. It also describes the perils of travelling in the Otherworld for too long, for since time is different there, when Bran and his followers return to Ireland they find that far more time has passed than they thought – they have become memories. The great son predicted in the latter part of Manannán's poem is none other than Mongán, more of whose story is told here on pp. 166–186. Most of Bran's actual adventures are not described in the text, but perhaps we may guess that thay were not unlike those in the 'Voyage of Máel Dúin' (pp. 123–150).

It was fifty quatrains the woman from unknown lands sang on the floor of the house to Bran son of Febal, when the royal house was full of kings, who knew not whence the woman had come, since the ramparts were closed.

This is the beginning of the story. One day, in the neighbourhood of his stronghold, Bran went about alone, when he heard music behind him. As often as he looked back, still behind him the music was. At last he fell asleep at the music, such was its sweetness. When he awoke from his sleep, he saw close by him a branch of silver with white blossoms, nor was it easy to distinguish its bloom from the branch. Then Bran took the branch in his hand to his royal house. When the hosts were in the royal house, they saw a woman in strange raiment therein. It was then she sang the fifty quatrains to Bran, while the host heard her, and all beheld the woman.

And she said:

> A branch of the apple-tree from Emne
> I bring, like those one knows;
> Twigs of white silver are on it,
> Crystal brows with blossoms.
>
> There is a distant isle,
> Around which sea-horses glisten:
> A fair course against the white-swelling surge,
> Four pillars uphold it.
>
> A delight of the eyes, a glorious range,
> Is the plain on which the hosts hold games:
> Coracle contends against chariot
> In the southern Plain of White Silver.
>
> Pillars of white bronze under it
> Glittering through beautiful ages.
> Lovely land throughout the world's age,
> On which the many blossoms drop.
>
> An ancient tree there is with blossoms,
> On which birds call the canonical Hours.
> 'Tis in harmony it is their wont
> To call together every Hour.
>
> Splendours of every colour glisten
> Throughout the gentle-voiced plains.

Joy is known, ranked around music,
In southern White-Silver Plain.

Unknown is wailing or treachery
In the familiar cultivated land,
There is nothing rough or harsh,
But sweet music striking on the ear.

Without grief, without sorrow, without death,
Without any sickness, without debility,
That is the sign of Emne –
Uncommon is an equal marvel.

A beauty of a wondrous land,
Whose aspects are lovely,
Whose view is a fair country,
Incomparable is its haze.

Then if Silvery Land is seen,
On which dragonstones and crystals drop,
The sea washes the wave against the land,
Hair of crystal drops from its mane.

Wealth, treasures of every hue,
Are in Ciuin, a beauty of freshness,
Listening to sweet music,
Drinking the best of wine.

Golden chariots in Mag Rein,
Rising with the tide to the sun,
Chariots of silver in Mag Mon,
And of bronze without blemish.

Yellow golden steeds are on the sward there,
Other steeds with crimson hue,
Others with wool upon their backs
Of the hue of heaven all blue.

At sunrise there will come
A fair man illumining level lands;
He rides upon the fair sea-washed plain,
He stirs the ocean till it is blood.

A host will come across the clear sea,
To the land they show their rowing;
Then they row to the conspicuous stone,
From which arise a hundred strains.

It sings a strain unto the host
Through long ages, it is not sad,
Its music swells with choruses of hundreds
They look for neither decay nor death.

Many-shaped Emne by the sea,
Whether it be near, whether it be far,
In which are many thousands of variegated women,
Which the clear sea encircles.

If he has heard the voice of the music,
The chorus of the little birds from Imchiuin,
A small band of women will come from a height
To the plain of sport in which he is.

There will come happiness with health
To the land against which laughter peals,
Into Imchiuin at every season
Will come everlasting joy.

It is a day of lasting weather
That showers silver on the lands,
A pure white cliff on the range of the sea,
Which from the sun receives its heat.

The host race along Mag Mon,
A beautiful game, not feeble,
In the variegated land over a mass of beauty.
They look for neither decay nor death.

Listening to music at night,
And going into Ildathach,
A variegated land, splendour on a diadem of beauty,
Whence the white cloud glistens.

There are thrice fifty distant isles
In the ocean to the west of us;

Larger than Erin twice
Is each of them, or thrice.

A great birth will come after ages,
That will not be in a lofty place,
The son of a woman whose mate will not be known,
He will seize the rule of the many thousands.

A rule without beginning, without end,
He has created the world so that it is perfect,
Whose are earth and sea,
Woe to him that shall be under His un-will!

'Tis He that made the heavens,
Happy he that has a white heart,
He will purify hosts under pure water,
'Tis He that will heal your sicknesses.

Not to all of you is my speech,
Though its great marvel has been made known:
Let Bran hear from the crowd of the world
What of wisdom has been told to him.

Do not fall on a bed of sloth,
Let not thy intoxication overcome thee;
Begin a voyage across the clear sea,
If perchance thou mayst reach the land of women.

Thereupon the woman went from them, while they knew not whither she went. And she took her branch with her. The branch sprang from Bran's hand into the hand of the woman, nor was there strength in Bran's hand to hold the branch.

Then on the morrow Bran went upon the sea. The number of his men was three companies of nine. One of his foster-brothers and mates was set over each of the three companies of nine.

When he had been at sea two days and two nights, he saw a man in a chariot coming towards him over the sea. That man also sang thirty other quatrains to him, and made himself known to him, and said that he was Manannán son of Lir, and said that it was upon him to go to Ireland after long ages, and that a son would be born to him, Mongán son of Fiachna – that was the name which would be upon him.

So Manannán sang these thirty quatrains to Bran:

Bran deems it a marvellous beauty
In his coracle across the clear sea:
While to me in my chariot from afar
It is a flowery plain on which he rows about.

That which is a clear sea
For the prowed skiff in which Bran is,
That is a happy plain with profusion of flowers
To me from the chariot of two wheels.

Bran sees
The number of waves beating across the clear sea:
I myself see in Mag Mon
Rosy-coloured flowers without fault.

Sea-horses glisten in summer
As far as Bran has stretched his glance:
Rivers pour forth a stream of honey
In the land of Manannán son of Lir.

The sheen of the main, on which thou art,
The white hue of the sea, on which thou rowest,
Yellow and azure are spread out,
It is land, and is not rough.

Speckled salmon leap from the womb
Of the white sea, on which thou lookest:
They are calves, they are coloured lambs
With friendliness, without mutual slaughter.

Though but one chariot-rider is seen
In Mag Mell of many flowers,
There are many steeds on its surface,
Though them thou seest not.

The size of the plain, the number of the host
Colours glisten with pure glory,
A fair stream of silver, cloths of gold,
Afford a welcome with all abundance.

A beautiful game, most delightful,
They play sitting at the luxurious wine,

Men and gentle women under a bush,
Without sin, without crime.

Along the top of a wood has swum
Thy coracle across ridges,
There is a wood of beautiful fruit
Under the prow of thy little boat.

A wood with blossom and fruit,
On which is the vine's veritable fragrance,
A wood without decay, without defect,
On which are leaves of golden hue.

We are from the beginning of creation
Without old age, without consummation of earth,
Hence we expect not that there should be frailty;
Sin has not come to us.

An evil day when the Serpent went
To the father to his city!
She has perverted the times in this world,
So that there came decay which was not original.

By greed and lust he has slain us,
Through which he has ruined his noble race:
The withered body has gone to the fold of torment,
An everlasting abode of torture.

It is a law of pride in this world
To believe in the creatures, to forget God,
Overthrow by diseases, and old age,
Destruction of the soul through deception.

A noble salvation will come
From the King who has created us,
A white law will come over seas;
Besides being God, He will be man.

This shape, he on whom thou lookest,
Will come to thy parts;
'Tis mine to journey to her house,
To the woman in Moylinny,

For it is Manannán son of Lir, [who speaks]
From the chariot in the shape of a man;
Of his progeny will be a very short while,
A fair man in a body of white clay.

Manannán the descendant of Lir will be
A vigorous bedfellow to Caintigern:
He shall be called to his son in the beautiful world,
Fiachna will acknowledge him as his son.

He will delight the company of every fairy-mound,
He will be the darling of every goodly land,
He will make known secrets – a course of wisdom
In the world, without being feared.

He will be in the shape of every beast,
Both on the azure sea and on land,
He will be a dragon before hosts at the onset,
He will be a wolf in every great forest.

He will be a stag with horns of silver
In the land where chariots are driven,
He will be a speckled salmon in a full pool,
He will be a seal, he will be a fair-white swan.

He will be throughout long ages
A hundred years in fair kingship,
He will cut down battalions – a lasting grave
He will redden fields, a wheel around the track.

It will be about kings with a champion
That he will be known as a valiant hero,
Into the strongholds of a land on a height
I shall send an appointed end from Islay.

High shall I place him with princes,
He will be overcome by a son of error;
Manannán the son of Lir
Will be his father, his tutor.

He will be – his time will be short
Fifty years in this world:

A dragon-stone from the sea will kill him
In the fight at Senlabor.

He will ask a drink from Loch Lo,
While he looks at the stream of blood;
The white host will take him under a wheel of clouds
To the gathering where there is no sorrow.

Steadily then let Bran row,
Not far to the Land of Women,
Emne with many hues of hospitality
Thou wilt reach before the setting of the sun.

Thereupon Bran went from Manannán mac Lir. And he saw an island. He rowed round about it, and a large host was gaping and laughing. They were all looking at Bran and his people, but would not stay to converse with them. They continued to give forth gusts of laughter at them. Bran sent one of his people on the island. He ranged himself with the others, and was gaping at them like the other men of the island. Bran kept rowing round about the island. Whenever his man came past Bran, his comrades would address him. But he would not converse with them, but would only look at them and gape at them. The name of this island is the Island of Joy. Thereupon they left him there.

It was not long thereafter when they reached the Land of Women. They saw the leader of the women at the port. Said the chief of the women: 'Come hither on land, O Bran son of Febal! Welcome is thy coming!'

Bran did not venture to go on shore. The woman threw a ball of thread to Bran straight over his face. Bran put his hand on the ball, which adhered to his palm. The thread of the ball was in the woman's hand, and she pulled the coracle towards the port. Thereupon they went into a large house, in which was a bed for every couple, even thrice nine beds. The food that was put on every dish vanished not from them. It seemed a year to them that they were there – it chanced to be many years. No savour was wanting to them.

Home-sickness seized one of them, even Nechtan son of Collbran. Bran's kindred kept praying him that he should go to Erin with them. The woman said to them their going would make them rue. However, they went, and the woman said that none of them should touch the land, and that they should visit and take with them the man whom they had left in the Island of Joy.

Then they went until they arrived at a gathering at Srub Brain on the coast of Erin. The men asked of them who it was came over the sea. Said Bran: 'I am Bran the son of Febal.' One of the men said: 'We do not know such a one, though the "Voyage of Bran" is in our ancient stories.'

One of Bran's men sprang from them out of the coracle. As soon as he touched the earth of Ireland, forthwith he was a heap of ashes, as though he had been in the earth for many hundred years. 'Twas then that Bran sang this quatrain:

> For Collbran's son great was the folly
> To lift his hand against age,
> Without any one casting a wave of pure water
> Over Nechtan, Collbran's son.

Thereupon, to the people of the gathering Bran told all his wanderings from the beginning until that time. And he wrote these quatrains in ogam, and then bade them farewell. And from that hour his wanderings are not known.

11. The Voyage of Máel Dúin

(Imram Máel Dúin)

Translated by Whitley Stokes

This is without doubt the most famous of the *Imrama*, or 'Voyages' –
and justly so, for it presents a fantastic array of imagery and lore,
couched in the form of the voyage and the many adventures encountered
by the heroes. The present text dates from no earlier than the eleventh
century but it is undoubtedly based on a far earlier text or texts (once
again, as in so many of the stories reproduced here, there is ample
evidence of several versions which have been – not always expertly –
joined.) Here there are all the signs of the Christian scribe taking ancient,
pagan elements of the story and shaping them to his own use, making of
the whole a kind of parable and concentrating on elements which he was
able to reconcile with his own beliefs.

Despite this, the story still preserves a considerable amount of mythic
and legendary material, including some fine descriptions of the Otherworld, a visit of the Land of Women (cf. 'The Voyage of Bran' pp.
113–122), and encounters with various animals. The tradition of
animals as helpers is widely disseminated in Celtic myth and legend, and
probably dates back to the shamanic beliefs of the ancient world, where
helpful spirits in animal form are often encountered. 'The Voyage of
Máel Dúin' seems to have been viewed as a kind of handbook for the
soul's journey – it may have been seen in this way from earlier times;
certainly by the eleventh century, when this story was first written down,
it had all the signs of being a kind of Celtic Book of the Dead.

Whitley Stokes, the translator of this text, drew upon four manuscript
versions, dating from the eleventh to the fifteenth centuries. One of
these contains a long poetic version of the tale, which has been
translated elsewhere by Caitlín Matthews in *The Celtic Book of the Dead*
(1992). Of the supposed author, Aed the Fair, who describes himself as

'the chief sage (*ardecnaid*) of Ireland', nothing is known, but we can safely assume that he was a cleric, though probably not in holy orders. He seems to have had some knowledge of Classical literature, since the episode in chapters XXI and XXVIII recalls the Calypso episode in Homer's *Odyssey*. The fruits and nuts described in Ch XXIX may derive from references in the Roman historian Lucian's *Vera Historia*. However a very strong influence on the author seems to have been the ninth-century Latin romance *Perigrinatio sanci Brandini Abatis* (the Voyage of St Brendan), with which our story has many incidents in common.

The character named Biccne is probably the same as Bricriu Poison-Tongue – a troublesome character from the Conchobor cycle who is the central character in 'Bricriu's Feast' (pp. 391–425). The incident of the fairy woman who draws back the boat by throwing a *clew* (a kind of magical rope) appears also in 'The Voyage of Bran' (p. 121) and again in 'Togail Troi' from the *Book of Leinster*. Other parallels exist with the *Imram hua Corra,* from the *Book of Fermoy*, which also has the Miller of Hell (Ch XIV), the Island of Weeping (Ch XV); and the Island of Laughter (Ch XXXI) – but this is a much later text in every way, and heavily Christianised.

The name Torach (Ch XXXIII) refers to an actual island off the coast of Donegal, where there stood both a monastery and a church in which St Colomcille was especially venerated. The author's knowledge of this may well suggest that he was in some way attached to the place, or had at least visited it.

The Voyage of Máel Dúin's Boat

Three years and seven months was it wandering in the ocean.

There was a famous man of the Eóghanacht of Ninuss (that is, the Eóghanacht of the Arans): his name was Ailill of the Edge of Battle. A mighty soldier was he, and a hero-lord of his own tribe and kindred. And there was a young nun, the prioress of a church of nuns, with whom he met. Between them both there was a noble boy, Máel Dúin, son of Ailill, was he.

This is the way according to which Máel Dúin's conception and his birth came to pass.

Once upon a time the king of the Eóghanacht went on a raid into another district and province, and with him fared Ailill of the Edge of Battle. They unyoked and encamped on an upland therein. There was a church of nuns near to that upland, [even Kildare today]. At midnight, then, when every one had ceased from moving in the camp, Ailill went to the church. It was the hour that the (aforesaid) nun went to strike the bell for nocturn. Ailill caught her hand, and threw her down, and lay with her.

Said the woman to him: 'Unblessed is our state,' saith she, '(for) this is the time for my conceiving. Whence is thy race and what is thy name?'

Said the hero: 'Ailill of the Edge of Battle is my name, (and I am) of the Eóghanacht of Ninuss in Thomond.'

Then after ravaging and taking hostages, the king returned to his district, Ailill also being with him.

Soon after Ailill had reached his tribe, marauders of Leix slew him. They burned (the church named) Dubcluain upon him.

At the end of nine months the woman brought forth a boy, and gave him a name, Máel Dúin was he. The boy was afterwards taken secretly to her [female] friend, even to the king's queen; and by her Máel Dúin was reared; and she gave out that she was his mother.

Now the one foster-mother reared him and the king's three sons, in one cradle, and on one breast, and on one lap.

Beautiful, indeed, was his form; and it is doubtful if there hath been in flesh anyone as beautiful as he. So he grew up till he was a young warrior and fit to use weapons. Great, then, was his brightness and his gaiety and his playfulness. In his play he outwent all his comrades, both in throwing balls, in running, and leaping, and putting stones, and racing horses. He had, in sooth, the victory in each of those games.

One day, then, a certain [haughty] warrior grew envious against him, and he said in [a] transport [of] anger: 'Thou,' saith he, 'whose clan and kindred no one knows, whose mother and father no one knows, to vanquish us in every game, whether we contend with thee on land or on water, or on the draughtboard!'

So then Máel Dúin was silent, for till then he had thought that he was a son of the king and of the queen his foster-mother. Then he said to his foster-mother, 'I will not dine and I will not drink until thou tell me,' saith he, 'my mother and my father.'

'But,' saith she, 'why art thou inquiring after that? Do not take to heart the words of the haughty warriors. I am thy mother,' saith she. 'The love of the people of the earth for their sons is no greater than the love I bear to thee.'

'That may be,' saith he: 'nevertheless, make known my parents to me.'

So his foster-mother went with him, and delivered him into his (own) mother's hand; and thereafter he entreated his mother to declare his father to him.

'Silly,' saith she, 'is what thou art doing, for if thou shouldst know thy father thou hast no good of him, and thou wilt not be the gladder, for he died long ago.'

'"Tis the better for me to know it,' saith he, 'however it be.'

Then his mother told him the truth. 'Ailill of the Edge of Battle was thy father,' saith she – 'of the Eóghanacht of Ninuss.'

Then Máel Dúin went to his fatherland and to his own heritage, having his (three) foster-brothers with him; and beloved warriors were they. And then his kindred welcomed him, and bade him be of good cheer.

At a certain time afterwards there was a number of warriors in the graveyard of the church of Dubcluain, putting stones. So Máel Dúin's foot was planted on the scorched ruin of the church, and over it he was flinging the stone. A certain poison-tongued man of the community of the church, Briccne was his name – said to Máel Dúin: 'It were better,' saith he, 'to avenge the man who was burnt there than to cast stones over his bare burnt bones.'

'Who (was) that?' saith Máel Dúin.

'Ailill,' saith he, 'thine (own) father.'

'Who killed him?' asked Máel Dúin.

Briccne replied: 'Marauders of Leix,' saith he, 'and they destroyed him on this spot.'

Then Máel Dúin threw away the stone (which he was about to cast), and took his mantle round him, and his armour on him; and he was mournful thereat. And he asked the way to wend to Leix, and the guides told him that he could only go by sea.

So he went into the country of Corcomroe to seek a charm and a blessing of a wizard who dwelt there, to begin building a boat. (Nuca was the wizard's name, and it is from him that Boirenn Nuca is named.) He told Máel Dúin the day on which he should begin the boat, and the number of the crew that should go in her, to wit, seventeen men, or sixty according to others. And he (also) told him that no number greater or less than that should go; and he (lastly) told him the day he should set to sea.

Then Máel Dúin builds a three-skinned boat; and they who were to go in it in his company were ready. Germán was there and Diurán the Rhymer.

So then he went to sea on the day that the wizard had told him to set out. When they had gone a little from land, after hoisting the sail, then came into the harbour after them his three foster-brothers, the three sons of his foster-father and foster-mother; and they shouted to them to come back again to them to the end that they might go with them.

'Get you home,' saith Máel Dúin; 'for even though we should return (to land), only the number we have here shall go with me.'

'We will go after thee into the sea and be drowned therein, unless thou come unto us.'

Then the three of them cast themselves into the sea, and they swim far from land. When Máel Dúin saw that, he turned towards them so that they might not be drowned, and he brought them into his boat.

I

That day till vespers they were a-rowing, and the night after it till midnight, when they found two small bare islands, with two forts in them; and then they heard out of the forts the noise and outcry of the intoxication, and the [boasting of the] soldiers, [as they displayed their] trophies. And this was what one man said to the other: 'Stand off from me,' saith he, 'for I am a better hero than thou, for it is I that slew Ailill of the Edge of Battle, and burnt Dubcluain on him; and no evil hath hitherto been done to me therefor by his kindred; and *thou* hast never done the like of that!'

'We have the victory in our hands,' saith Germán and saith Diurán the Rhymer. 'God hath brought us direct, and God hath guided our barque. Let us go and wreck these two forts, since God hath revealed to us our enemies in them!'

As they were saying these words, a great wind came upon them, so that they were driven (over the sea, all) that night until morning. And even after morning they saw nor earth nor land, and they knew not whither they were going. Then said Máel Dúin: 'Leave the boat stilly, without rowing; and whither-soever it shall please God to bring it, [it shall be brought].'

Then they entered the great, endless ocean; and Máel Dúin afterwards said to his foster-brothers: 'Ye have caused this to us, casting yourselves upon us in the boat in spite of the word of the enchanter and wizard, who told us that on board the boat we should go only the number that we were before you came.'

They had no answer, save only to be silent for a little space.

II

Three days and three nights were they, and they found neither land nor ground. Then on the morning of the third day they heard a sound from the north-east. 'This is the voice of a wave against a shore,' said Máel Dúin.

Now when the day was bright they made towards land. As they were casting lots to see which of them should go on shore, there came a great swarm of ants, each of them the size of a foal, down to the strand towards them, and into the sea. What the ants desired was to eat the crew and their boat; so the sailors flee for three days and three nights; and they saw not land nor ground.

III

On the morning of the third day they heard the sound of a wave against the beach, and with the daylight they saw an island high and great; and terraces all round about it. Lower was each of them than the other, and there was a row of trees around it, and many great birds on these trees. And they were taking counsel as to who should go to explore the island and see whether the birds were gentle. 'I will go,' saith Máel Dúin. So Máel Dúin went, and warily searched the island, and found nothing evil therein. And they ate their fill of the birds, and brought some of them on board their boat.

IV

Three days thereafter, and three nights were they at sea. But on the morning of the fourth day they perceived another great island. Sandy was its soil. When they came to the shore of the island they saw therein a beast like a horse. The legs of a hound he had, with rough, sharp nails; and great was his joy at seeing them. And he was prancing before them, for he longed to devour them and their boat. 'He is not sorry to meet us,' saith Máel Dúin; 'let us go back from the island.' That was done; and when the beast perceived them fleeing, he went down to the strand and began digging up the beach with his sharp nails, and pelting them (with the pebbles), and they did not expect to escape from him.

V

Thereafter they rowed afar, and a great, flat island they see before them. Then to Germán fell an ill lot to go and look at that island. 'Both of us will go,' saith Diurán the Rhymer, 'and thou wilt come with me some other time into an island which it fills to my lot to explore.' So the two of them entered the island. Great was its size and its breadth, and they saw therein a long, great green, with vast hoofmarks of horses upon it. As large as the sail of a ship was the mark of the hoof of each horse. They saw, moreover, the shells of huge nuts like . . . and they saw there, also, great leavings of the plunder of many men. So they dreaded that which they saw, and they called their people to them to see what they beheld. They were afraid then, after seeing what they beheld, and they all, swiftly, hastily, went on board their boat.

When they had gone a little from land, they beheld (rushing) along the sea to the island a great multitude, which, after reaching the green of the island, held a horse-race. And swifter than the wind was each horse, and great was the shouting (of the multitude) and their outcry and noise. And then the strokes of their horse-rods at the meeting were heard by Máel Dúin, and he heard, moreover, what each of them was saying: 'Bring the grey steed!' 'Drive the dun horse there!' 'Bring the white horse!' 'My steed is faster!' 'My horse leaps better!' When the wanderers heard those words, they went away with all their might, for they felt sure it was a meeting of demons they beheld.

VI

A full week were they voyaging, in hunger and in thirst, when they discovered a great, high island with a great house therein on the seashore and a doorway out of the house into the plain of the island and another door (opening) into the sea, and against that door there was a valve of stone. That valve was pierced by an aperture, through which the seawaves were flinging the salmon into the midst of that house. Máel Dúin and his men entered that house, and therein they found no one. After this they beheld a testered bed for the chief of the house alone, and a bed for every three of his household, and food for three before every bed, and a vessel of glass with good liquor before every bed, and a cup of glass on every vessel. So they dined off that food and liquor, and they give thanks to Almighty God, who had helped them from the hunger.

VII

When they went from the island they were a long while voyaging, without food, hungrily, till they found (another) island, with a great cliff round it on every side, and therein was a long, narrow wood, and great was its length and its narrowness. When Máel Dúin reached that wood he took (from it) a rod in his hand as he passed it. Three days and three nights the rod remained in his hand, while the boat was under sail, coasting the cliff, and on the third day he found a cluster, of three apples at the end of the rod. For forty nights each of these apples sufficed them.

VIII

Thereafter then, they found another island, with a fence of stone around it. When they drew near it a huge beast sprang up in the island, and raced round about the island. To Máel Dúin it seemed swifter than the wind. And then it went to the height of the island and there it performed (the feat called) 'straightening of body', to wit, its head below and its feet above; and thus it used to be: it turned in its skin, that is, the flesh and the bones revolved, but the skin outside was unmoved. Or at another time the skin outside turned like a mill, the bones and the flesh remaining still.

When it had been for long in that wise, it sprang up again and raced round about the island as it had done at first. Then it returned to the same place; and that time the lower half of its skin was unmoved, and the other half above ran round and round like a millstone. That, then, was its practice when it was going round the island.

Máel Dúin and his people fled with all their might, and the beast perceived them fleeing, and it went into the beach to seize them, and began to smite them, and it casts and lashes after them with stones of the harbour. Now one of these stones came into their boat, and pierced through Máel Dúin's shield, and lodged in the keel of the curragh.

IX

Now, not long after that they found another lofty island, and it was delightful, and therein were many great animals like unto horses. Each of them would take a piece out of another's side, and carry it away with its skin and its flesh, so that out of their sides streams of crimson blood were breaking, and thereof the ground was full.

So they left that island swiftly, madly, hastily (and they were) sad, complaining, feeble; and they knew not whither in the world they were going and in what stead they should find aid or land or ground.

X

Now they came to another great island, after great weariness of hunger and thirst, and they sad and sighing, having lost all hope of aid. In that island were many trees: full fruited were they, with great golden apples upon them. Red short animals like swine were under those trees. Now they used to go to those trees and strike them with their hindlegs, so that the apples would fall from the trees, and then they would consume them. From dawn to sunset the animals did not appear at all, but they used to stay in the caverns of the ground. Round about that island many birds were swimming out on the waves. From matins to none, further and further they used to swim from the island. But from none to vespers nearer and nearer they used to come to the island, and arrive therein after sunset.

Then they used to strip off the apples and eat them. 'Let us go,' saith Máel Dúin, 'into the island wherein the birds are. Not harder for us (to do so) than for the birds.' One of the crew went to see the island, and he called his comrade to him on shore. Hot was the ground under their feet, and they could not dwell there for its warmth, because it was a fiery land, and the animals used to heat the ground above them.

On the first day they brought with them a few of the apples which they were eating in their boat. When the morning was bright the birds went from the island swimming to sea. With that the fiery animals were upraising their heads out of the caves, and kept eating the apples till sundown. When they were put back into their caves the birds use to come in place of them, to eat the apples. Then Máel Dúin went with his people, and they collected all the apples that were there that night. Alike did the apples forbid hunger and thirst from them. So then they filled their boat with the apples as seemed good to them, and went again to sea.

Now when those apples failed, and their hunger and thirst were great, and when their mouths and their noses were full of the stench of the sea, they sight an island which was not large, and therein (stood) a fort surrounded by a white, high rampart as if it were built of burnt lime, or as if it were all one rock of chalk. Great was its height from the sea: it all but reached the clouds. The fort was open wide. Round the rampart were great, snow-white houses. When they entered the largest of these they saw no one there, save a small cat which was in the midst of the house, playing on the four stone pillars that were there. It was leaping from each pillar to the other. It looked a little at the men, and did not stop itself from its play. After that they saw three rows on the wall of the house round about, from one doorpost to the other. A row there, first, of brooches of gold and of silver, with their pins in the wall, and a row of neck-torques of gold and of silver: like hoops of a vat was each of them. The third row (was) of great swords, with hilts of gold and of silver. The rooms were full of white quilts and shining garments. A roasted ox, moreover, and a flitch in the midst of the house, and great vessels with good intoxicating liquor.

'Hath this been left for us?' saith Máel Dúin to the cat. It looked at him suddenly and began to play again. Then Máel Dúin recognised that it was for them that the dinner had been left. So they dined and drank and slept. They put the leavings of the liquor into the pots, and stored up the leavings of the food. Now when they proposed to go, Máel Dúin's third foster-brother said: 'Shall I take with me a necklace of these necklaces?'

'Nay,' saith Máel Dúin, 'not without a guard is the house.'

Howbeit he took it as far as the middle of the enclosure. The cat followed them, and leapt through him (the foster-brother) like a fiery arrow, and burnt him so that he became ashes, and (then) went back till it was on its pillar. Then Máel Dúin soothed the cat with his words, and set the necklace in its place, and cleansed the ashes from the floor of the enclosure, and cast them on the shore of the sea.

Then they went on board their boat, praising and magnifying the lord.

XII

Early on the morning of the third day after that they espy another island, with a brazen palisade over the midst of it which divided the island in two, and they espy great flocks of sheep therein, even a black flock on this side of the fence and a white flock on the far side. And they saw a big man separating the flocks. When he used to fling a white sheep over the fence from this side to the black sheep it became black at once. So, when he used to cast a black sheep over the fence to the far side, it became white at once. The men were adread at seeing that.

'This were well for us (to do),' saith Máel Dúin: 'let us cast two rods into the island. If they change colour we (also) shall change if we land on it.'

So they flung a rod with black bark on the side wherein were the white sheep, and it became white at once. Then they flung a peeled, white rod on the side wherein were the black sheep, and it became black at once.

'Not fortunate was that experiment,' saith Máel Dúin, 'let us not land on the island. Doubtless our colour would not have fared better than the rods.'

They went back from the island in terror.

XIII

On the third day afterwards they perceived another island great and wide, with a herd of beautiful swine therein. Of these they kill a small pig. Then they were unable to carry it to be roasted, so they all came round it. They cooked it and bore it into their boat.

Then they see a great mountain in the island, and they proposed to go and view the island from it.

Now when Diurán the Rhymer and Germán went to visit the mountain they find before them, a broad river which was not deep. Into this river Germán dipt the handle of his spear, and at once it was consumed as if fire had burnt it. And (so) they went no further. Then, too, they saw, on the other side of the river, great hornless oxen lying down, and a huge man sitting by them. Germán after this struck his spear-shaft against his shield to frighten the oxen.

'Why dost thou frighten the silly calves?' saith that huge herdsman.

'Where are the dams of these calves?' saith Germán.

'They are on the other side of yonder mountain,' saith he.

Diurán and Germán return to their comrades, and tell them the tidings.

'We will not go at all,' saith Máel Dúin, 'into an island of which that is the news.'

So thence they (all) went [away].

XIV

Not long thereafter they found an island, with a great hideous mill wherein was a miller huge, [rough, barehanded, withered and hideous therein]. They asked him: 'What mill is this?'

['No mill] indeed,' saith he, '[why ask what ye cannot] know.'

'Nay,' say they.

'Half the corn of your country,' saith he, 'is ground here. Everything which is begrudged is ground in this mill.'

With that they see the heavy, countless loads on horses and human beings (going) to the mill and from it again; only that what was brought from it was carried westward. Again they asked: 'What is the name of this mill?'

'The mill of Inber Tre-cenand,' saith the miller.

When they heard and saw all these things they went on their way, into their boat.

XV

Now when they went from that island of the mill they found a large island, and a great multitude of human beings therein. Black were these, both in bodies and raiment. Fillets [were] round their heads, and they rested not from wailing. An unlucky lot fell to one of Máel Dúin's two foster-brothers to land on the island. When he went to the people who were wailing he at once became a comrade of theirs and began to weep along with them. Two were sent to bring him thence, and they did not recognise him amongst the others, (and) they themselves turned to lament. Then said Máel Dúin: 'Let four (of you),' saith he, 'go with your weapons, and bring ye the men perforce, and look not at the land nor the air, and put your garments round your noses and round your mouths, and breathe not the air of the land, and take not your eyes off your own men.'

The four went, and brought back with them perforce the other two. When they were asked what they had seen in the land, they would say: 'Verily, we know not,' say they; 'but what we saw (others doing) we did.'

Thereafter they came rapidly from the island.

XVI

Thereafter they come to another lofty island, wherein were four fences, which divided it into four parts. A fence of gold, first: another of silver: the third fence of brass: and the fourth of crystal. Kings in the fourth division, queens in another, warriors in another, maidens in the other. A maiden went to meet them, and brought them on land, and gave them food. They likened it to cheese; and whatever taste was pleasing to anyone he would find it therein. And she dealt (liquor) to them out of a little vessel, so that they slept in intoxication of three days and three nights. All this time the maiden was tending them. When they awoke on the third day they were in their boat at sea. Nowhere did they see their island or their maiden.

Then they rowed away.

XVII

Thereafter they found another island which was not large. Therein was a fortress with a brazen door and brazen fastenings, thereon. A bridge of glass (rose) by the portal. When they used to go up on the bridge they would fall down backwards. With that they espy a woman coming out from the fortress, with a pail in her hand. Out of the lower part of the bridge she lifts a slab of glass, and she filled the pail out of the fountain which flowed beneath the bridge, and went again into the fortress.

'A housekeeper comes for Máel Dúin!' saith Germán.

'[For] Máel Dúin indeed!' saith she, closing the door behind her.

After this they were striking the brazen fastenings and the brazen net that was before them, and then the sound which they made was a sweet and soothing music, which sent them to sleep till the morrow morning.

When they awoke they saw the same woman (coming) out of the fortress, with her pail in her hand, and she fills (it) under the same slab.

'But a housekeeper comes to meet Máel Dúin!' saith Germán.

'Marvellously valuable do I deem Máel Dúin!' saith she, shutting the enclosure after her.

The same melody lays them low then till the morrow.

Three days and three nights were they in that wise. On the fourth day thereafter the woman went to them. Beautiful, verily, came she there. She wore a white mantle, with a circlet of gold round her hair. Golden hair she had. Two sandals of silver on her rosy feet. A brooch of silver with studs of gold in her mantle, and a filmy, silken smock next her white skin.

'My welcome to thee, O Máel Dúin!' saith she; and she named each man (of the crew) apart, by his own name. 'It is long since your coming here hath been known and understood.'

Then she takes (them) with her into a great house that stood near the sea, and hauls up their boat on shore. Then they saw before them in the house a couch for Máel Dúin alone, and a couch for every three of his people. She brought them in one pannier food like unto cheese or *táth* [cheese made from sour milk curds]. She gave a share to every three. Every savour that each desired this he would find therein. There she tended Máel Dúin apart. And she filled her pail under the same slab, and dealt liquor to them. A turn for every three she had. Then she knew when they had enough. She rested from dealing to them.

'A fitting wife for Máel Dúin were this woman,' saith every man of his people.

Then she went away from them, with her one vessel and with her pail.

Said his people to Máel Dúin: 'Shall we say to her, would she, perchance, sleep with thee?'

'How would it hurt you,' saith he, 'to speak to her?'

She comes on the morrow. They said to her: 'Wilt thou show affection to Máel Dúin, and sleep with him? And why not stay here tonight?'

She said she knew not, and had never known what sin was. Then she went from them to her house; and, on the morrow, at the same hour, she comes [to further attend them]. And when they were drunken and sated, they say the same words to her.

'Tomorrow,' saith she, 'an answer concerning that will be given to you.' Then she went to her house, and they sleep on their couches. When they awoke, they were in their boat on a crag; and they saw not the island, nor the fortress, nor the lady, nor the place wherein they had been.

XVIII

As they went from that place they heard in the north-east a great cry and chant as it were a singing of psalms. That night and the next day till none they were rowing that they might know what cry or what chant they heard. They behold a high, mountainous island, full of birds, black and dun and speckled, shouting and speaking loudly.

They rowed a little from that island, and found another island which was not large. Therein were many trees, and on them many birds. And after that they saw in the island a man whose clothing was his hair. So they asked him who he was, and whence his kindred.

'Of the men of Ireland am I,' saith he. 'I went on my pilgrimage in a small boat, and when I had gone a little from land my boat split under me. I went again to land,' saith he; 'and I put under my feet a sod from my country, and on it I gat me up to sea. And the Lord established that sod for me in this place,' saith he, 'and God addeth a foot to its breadth every year from that to this, and [makes] a tree every year to grow therein. The birds which thou beholdest in the trees,' saith he, 'are the souls of my children and my kindred, both women and men, who are yonder awaiting Doomsday. Half a cake, and a slice of fish, and the liquor of the well God hath given me. That cometh to me daily,' saith he, 'by the ministry of angels. At the hour of none, moreover, another half cake and slice of fish come to every man yonder and to every woman, and the liquor of the well, as is enough for every one.'

When their three nights of guesting were complete, they bade (the pilgrim) farewell, and he said to them: 'Ye shall all,' saith he, 'reach your country save one man.

XX

On the third day after that they find another island, with a golden rampart around it and the [floor] of it white like down. They see therein a man, and this was his raiment, the hair of his own body. Then they asked him what sustenance he used. 'Verily,' saith he, 'there is here a fountain in this island. On Friday and on Wednesday whey or water is yielded by it. On Sundays, however, and on [the] feasts of martyrs good milk is yielded by it. But on the feasts of apostles, and of Mary and of John Baptist, and also on the hightides (of the year), it is ale and wine that are yielded by it.'

At none, then, there came to every male of there half a cake and a piece of fish; and they drank their fill of the liquor which was yielded to them out of the fountain of the island. And it cast them into a heavy sleep from that hour till the morrow.

When they had passed three nights of guesting, the cleric ordered them to go. So then they went forth on their way and afterwards bade him farewell.

XXI

Now when they had been long a-voyaging on the waves they saw far from them an island, and as they approached it, they heard the noise of the smiths smiting a mass (of iron) on the anvil with sledges, like the smiting of three or of four. Now when they had drawn nigh it they heard one man asking of another: 'Are they close at hand?' saith he.

'Yea,' saith the other.

'Who,' saith another man, 'are these ye say are coming there?'

'Little boys they seem in a little trough yonder,' saith he.

When Máel Dúin heard what the smiths said, he saith: 'Let us retreat,' saith he, 'and let us not turn the boat, but let her stern be foremost, so that they may not perceive that we are fleeing.'

Then they rowed away, with the boat stern-foremost. Again the same man who was biding in the forge asked: 'Are they now near the harbour?' saith he. 'They are at rest,' saith the watchman: 'they come not here and they go not there.'

Not long thereafter he asked again: 'What are they doing now?' saith he. 'I think,' saith the look-out-man, 'that they are running away; meseems they are further from the port now than they were some time ago.'

Then the smith came out of the forge, holding in the tongs a huge mass (of glowing iron), and he cast that mass after the boat into the sea; and all the sea boiled; but he did not reach the boat, for they fled with all their warriors' might, swiftly, hurriedly, forth into the great ocean.

XXII

After that they voyaged till they entered a sea that resembled green glass. Such was its purity that the gravel and the sand of the sea were clearly visible through it; and they saw no monsters nor beasts therein among the crags, but only the pure gravel and the green sand. For a long space of the day they were voyaging in that sea, and great was its splendour and its beauty.

XXIII

They afterwards put forth into another sea like a cloud, and it seemed to them that it would not support them or the boat. Then they beheld under the sea down below them roofed strongholds and a beautiful country. And they see a beast: huge, awful, monstrous, in a tree there, and a drove of herds and flocks round about the tree, and beside the tree an armed man, with shield and spear and sword. When he beheld yon huge beast that abode in the tree he goeth thence at once in flight. The beast stretched forth his neck out of the tree, and sets his head into the neck of the largest ox of the herd, and dragged it into the tree, and anon devours it in the twinkling of an eye. The flocks and the herdsman flee away at once; and when Máel Dúin and his people saw that, greater terror and fear seize them, for they supposed that they would never cross that sea without falling down through it, by reason of its tenuity like mist.

So after much danger, they pass over it.

XXIV

Thereafter they found another island, and up around it rose the sea, making vast cliffs (of water) all about it. As the people of that country perceived them, they set to screaming at them, and saying: 'It is they! It is they!' till they were out of breath. Then Máel Dúin and his men beheld many human beings, and great herds of cattle, and troops of horses, and many flocks of sheep. Then there was a woman pelting them from below with large nuts which remained (floating) on the waves above by them. Much of those nuts they gathered and took with them. (Then) they went back from the island, and thereat the screams ceased.

'Where are they now?' saith the man, who was coming after them [when he heard] the scream.

'They have gone away,' saith another band of them.

'They are not so,' saith another band.

Now it is likely that there was someone concerning whom they (the islanders) had a prophecy that he would ruin their country and expel them from their land.

XXV

They gat them to another island, wherein a strange thing was shewn to them, to wit, a great stream rose up out of the strand of the island and went, like a rainbow, over the whole island, and descended into the other strand of the island on the other side thereof. And they were going under it (the stream) below without being wet. And they were piercing (with their spears) the stream above; and (then) great, enormous salmon were tumbling from above out of the stream down upon the soil of the island. And all the island was full of the stench (of the fish), for there was no one who could finish gathering them because of their abundance.

From Sunday eventide to Monday forenoon that stream did not move, but remained at rest in its sea round about the island. Then they bring into one place the largest of the salmon, and they filled their boat with them, and went back from that island still on the ocean.

XXVI

Thereafter they voyaged till they found a great silver column. It had four sides, and the width of each of these sides was two oarstrokes of the boat, so that in its whole circumference there were eight oarstrokes of the boat. And not a single sod of earth was about it, but (only) the boundless ocean. And they saw not how its base was below, or – because of its height – how its summit was above. Out of its summit came a silvern net far away from it; and the boat went under sail through a mesh of that nets. And Diurán gave a blow of the edge of his spear over the mesh.

'Destroy not the net,' saith Máel Dúin, 'for what we see is the work of mighty men.'

'For the praise of God's name,' saith Diurán, 'I do this, so that my tidings may be the more believed; and provided I reach Ireland (this piece of the mesh) shall be oftered by me on the altar of Armagh.'

Two ounces and a half was its weight when [it was] measured (afterwards) in Armagh.

And then they heard a voice from the summit of yonder pillar, mighty, and clear, and distinct. But they knew not the tongue it spake, or the words it uttered.

XXVII

Then they see another island (standing) on a single pedestal, to wit, one foot supporting it. And they rowed round it to seek a way into it, and they found no way thereinto; but they saw down in the base of the pedestal a closed door under lock. They understood that that was the way by which the island was entered. And they saw a plow on the top of the island; but they held speech with no-one, and no-one held speech with them. They (then) go away back (to sea).

XXVIII

After that they came to a large island, and there was a great plain therein, and on this a great table-land, heatherless, but grassy and smooth. They saw in that island near the sea, a fortress, large, high and strong, and a great house therein adorned and with good couches. Seventeen grown-up girls were there, preparing a bath. And they (Máel Dúin and his men) landed on that island and sat on a hillock before the fort.

Máel Dúin said this: 'We are sure that yonder bath is getting ready for us.'

Now at the hour of none they beheld a rider on a race-horse (coming) to the fortress. A good, adorned horsecloth under her seat: she wore a hood, blue and she wore a bordered, purple mantle. Gloves with gold embroidery on her hands; and on her feet sandals. As she alighted, one of the girls at once took the horse. Then she entered the fortress and went into the bath. Then they saw that it was a woman that had alighted from the horse, and not long afterwards came one of the girls unto them.

'Welcome is your arrival!' saith she. 'Come into the fort: the queen invites you.' So they entered the fort and they all bathed. The queen sat on one side of the house, and her seventeen girls about her. Máel Dúin sat on the other side, over against the queen, with his seventeen men around him. Then a platter with good food thereon was brought to Máel Dúin, and along with it a vessel of glass, full of good liquor; and (there was) a platter for every three and a vessel for every three of his people.

When they had eaten their dinner the queen said this: 'How will the guests sleep?' saith she.

'As thou shalt say,' saith Máel Dúin.

['Come into this house here,'] saith she. 'Let each of you take his woman, even her who is over against him, and let him go into the chamber behind her.'

For there were seventeen canopied chambers in the house with good beds set. So the seventeen men and the seventeen grown-up girls slept together, and Máel Dúin slept with the queen. After this they slumbered till the morrow morning. Then after morning they arose (to depart).

'Stay here,' saith the queen, 'and age will not fall on you, but the age that ye have attained. And lasting life ye shall have always; and what came to you last night shall come to you every night without any labour. And be no longer awandering from island to island on the ocean!'

'Tell us,' saith Máel Dúin, 'how thou art here.'

'Not hard (to say) indeed,' she saith. 'There dwelt a good man in this island, the king of the island. To him I bore yon seventeen girls, and I was their mother. Then their father died, and left no heir. So I took the kingship of this island after him. Every day,' she saith, 'I go into the great plain there is in the island, to judge the folk and to decide (their disputes).'

'But why dost thou leave us today?' saith Máel Dúin.

'Unless I go,' she saith, 'what happened to us last night will not come to us (again). Only stay,' she saith, 'in your house, and ye need not labour. I will go to judge the folk for sake of you.'

So they abode in that island for the three months of winter; and it seemed to them that (those months) were three years.

'It is long we are here,' saith one of his people to Máel Dúin. 'Why do we not turn to our country?' saith he.

'What you say is not good,' saith Máel Dúin, 'for we shall not find in our own country aught better than that which we find here.'

(But) his people began to murmur greatly against Máel Dúin, and they said this: 'Great is the love which Máel Dúin hath for his woman. Let him, then, stay with her if he so desires,' saith the people. 'We will go to our country.'

'I will not stay after you,' saith Máel Dúin.

One day, then, the queen went to the judging whereunto she used to go every day. When she had gone they went on board their boat. Then she comes on her horse and flings a clew after them, and Máel Dúin catches it, and it clung to his hand. A thread of the clew was in her band, and she draws the boat unto her, by means of the thread, back to the harbour.

So then they stayed with her thrice three months. Then they came to (this) counsel. 'Of this we are sure, now,' saith his people, 'that great is Máel Dúin's love for his woman. Therefore he attends the clew that it may cleave to his hand and that we may be brought back to the fortress.'

'Let some one else attend the clew,' saith Máel Dúin, 'and if it clings to his hand, let his hand be cut off.'

So they went on board their boat. (The queen came and) flung the clew after them. Another man in the boat catches it, and it clings to his hand. Diurán cuts off his hand, and it fell, with the clew (into the sea). When she saw that, she at once began to wail and shriek, so that all the land was one cry, wail and shrieking. So in that wise they escaped from her, out of the island.

XIX

They were for a very long while afterwards driven about on the waves, till they found an island with trees upon it like willow or hazel. Thereon were marvellous fruits [and] great berries. So of these then they stript a little tree, and then they cast lots to see who should prove the fruit that had been on the tree. (The lot) fell to Máel Dúin. He squeezed some of the berries into a vessel and drank (the juice), and it cast him into a deep sleep from that hour to the same hour on the morrow. And they knew not whether he was alive or dead, with the red foam round his lips, till on the morrow he awoke.

(Then) he said to them, 'Gather ye this fruit, for great is its excellence.' So they gathered (it), and they mingled water with it, to moderate its power to intoxicate and send asleep. Then they gathered all there was of it, and were squeezing it, and filling (with its juice) all the vessels they had; and (then) they rowed away from that island.

XXX

Thereafter they landed on another large island. One of its two sides was a wood with yews and great oaks therein. The other side was a plain, with a little lake in it. Great herds of sheep were therein. They beheld there a small church and a fortress. They went to the church. An ancient grey cleric was in the church, and his hair clothed him altogether. Máel Dúin asked him: 'Whence art thou?' saith he.

'I am the fifteenth man of the community of Brenainn of Birr. We went on our pilgrimage into the ocean and came into this island. They have all died save me alone.' And then he showed them Brenainn's tablet which they (the monks) had taken with them on their pilgrimage. They all prostrated themselves to the tablet and Máel Dúin gave it a kiss.

Now saith the ancient man, 'Eat your fill of the sheep, and do not consume more than sufficeth you.'

So for a season they are fed there on the flesh of the fat sheep.

One day, then, as they were looking out from the island they see (what they take to be) a cloud coming towards them from the south-west. After a while, as they were still looking, they perceived that it was a bird; for they saw the pinions waving. Then it came into the island and alighted on a hill near the lake. Then they supposed, it would carry them in its talons out to sea. Now it brought with it a branch of a great tree. Bigger than one of the great oaks (was) the branch. Large twigs (grew) out of it, and a dense top was on it (covered) with fresh leaves. Heavy, abundant fruit it bore, red berries like unto grapes – only they were bigger. So (the wanderers) were in hiding, a-watching what the bird would do. Because of its weariness, it remained for a while at rest. (Then) it began to eat some of the fruit of the tree. So Máel Dúin went till he was at the edge of the bill on which the bird was, to see whether it would do him any evil, and it did none. All his people then went after him into that place.

'Let one of us go,' saith Máel Dúin, 'and gather some of the fruit of the branch which is before the bird.'

So one of them went, and he gathers a portion of the berries, and the bird blamed him not, and did not (even) look (at him) or make a movement. They, the eighteen men with their shields, went behind it, and it did no evil to them.

Now at the hour of none of the day they beheld two great eagles in the south-west, in the place whence the great bird had come, and they swooped down in front of the great bird. When they had been for a long while at rest, they begin to pick and strip off the lice that infested the upper and lower parts of the great bird's jaws, and its eyes and ears.

They (the two eagles) kept at this till vespers. Then the three of them began to eat the berries and the fruit of the branch. From the morrow morning till mid-day, they were picking, the same vermin out of all its body, and plucking the old feathers out of it, and picking out completely the old scales of the mange. At midday, however, they stripped the berries from the branch, and with their beaks they were breaking them against the stones, and then casting them into the lake, so that its foam upon it became red. After that the great bird went into the lake and remained washing himself therein nearly till the close of the day. After that he went out of the lake, and settled on another place in the same hill, lest the lice which had been taken out of him should come (again).

On the morrow morning the (two) birds with their bills still picked and sleeked the plumage (of the third), as if it were done with a comb. They kept at this till mid-day. Then they rested a little, and then they went away to the quarter whence they had come.

Howbeit the great bird remained behind them preening himself and shaking his pinions till the end of the third day. There at the hour of tierce on the third day he soared up and flew thrice round the island, and alighted for a little rest on the same hill. And afterwards he fared afar towards the quarter whence he had come. Swifter and stronger (was) his flight at that time than (it had been) before. Wherefore it was manifest to them all that this was his renewal from old age into youth, according to the word of the prophet, who saith, 'Thy youth shall be renewed like the eagle's.'

Then Diurán seeing that great marvel, said: 'Let us go into the lake to renew ourselves where the bird has been renewed.'

'Nay,' saith another, 'for the bird hath left his venom therein.'

'Thou sayest ill,' saith Diuran, 'I the first will go into it.'

Then he went in and bathes himself there, and plunged [his] lips into (the) water, and drank sups thereof. Passing strong were his eyes thereafter so long as he remained alive; and not a tooth of him fell (from his jaw), nor a hair from his head; and he never suffered weakness or infirmity from that time forth.

Thereafter they bade farewell to their ancient man; and of the sheep they took with them provision. They set their boat on the sea, and then they seek the ocean.

XXXI

They find another large island, with a great level plain therein. A great multitude were on that plain, playing and laughing without any cessation. Lots are cast by Máel Dúin and his men to see unto whom it should fall to enter the island and explore it. The lot fell on the third of Máel Dúin's foster-brothers. When he went he at once began to play and to laugh continually along with the islanders, as if he had been by them all his life. His comrades stayed for a long, long space expecting him, and he came not to them. So then they leave him.

XXXII

After that they sight another island, which was not large; and a fiery rampart was round about it; and that rampart used to revolve round the island. There was an open doorway in the side of that rampart. Now, whenever the doorway would come (in its revolution) opposite to them, they used to see (through it) the whole island, and all that was therein, and all its indwellers, even human beings beautiful, abundant, wearing adorned garments, and feasting with golden vessels in their hands. And the wanderers heard their ale-music. And for a long space were they seeing the marvel they beheld, and they deemed it delightful.

XXXIII

Not long after they had gone from that island they see far off among the waves a shape like a white bird. They turned the prow of the boat unto it southward, to perceive what they beheld. So when they had drawn near it in rowing they saw that it was a human being and that he was clothed only with the white hair of his body. He threw himself in prostrations on a broad rock.

When they had come to him, they entreat a blessing from him, and ask him whence he had gone to yonder rock.

'From Torach, verily,' saith he, 'I have come here, and in Torach was reared. Then it came to pass that I was cook therein; and I was an evil cook, for the food of the church wherein I was dwelling I used to sell for treasures and jewels for myself: so that my house became full of counterpanes and pillows and of raiment, both linen and wool of every colour, and of brazen pails and of small brazen *tellenna* [bowls], and of brooches of silver with pins of gold. Insomuch that unto my house there was nothing wanting of all that is hoarded by man; both golden books and book-satchells adorned with brass and gold. And I used to dig under the houses of the church and carry many treasures out of them.

'Great then was my pride and my haughtiness.

'Now one day I was told to dig a grave for the corpse of a peasant, which had been brought into the island. As I was (working) at that grave I heard from below me the voice out of the ground under my feet: "Do not dig up that place!" saith the voice. "Do not put the corpse of the sinner on me a holy pious person!"

'"(Be it) between me and God, I will put (it in)," say I, in my excessive haughtiness.

'"Even so," saith he, "if you put it on me," saith the holy man, "thou shalt perish on the third day hence, and thou shalt be an inhabitant of hell, and the corpse will not remain here."

'Said I to the ancient man: "What good wilt thou bestow upon me if I shall not bury the man above you?"

'"To abide in eternal life along with God," saith he.

'"How," say I, "shall I [believe] that?"

'"That is neither hard nor . . . for thee," saith he. "The grave thou art digging will now become full of sand. Thence it will be manifest to thee that thou wilt not be able to bury the man above me, (even) though thou triest."

'That word was not ended when the grave became full of the sand. So thereafter I buried the corpse in another place.

'Now at a certain time I set a new boat with tanned hide on the sea. I went on board my boat, and I was glad to look around me: and I left in my house nothing, from small to great, that was not brought by me, with my vats and goblets and with my dishes. While I was in that wise looking at the sea, and the sea was calm for me, great winds come upon me, and draw me into the main, so that I saw neither land nor soil. Here my boat became still, and thereafter it stirred not from one stead.

'As I looked round me on every side, I beheld on my right hand the man sitting upon the wave. Then he said to me: "Whither goest thou?" saith he.

'"Pleasant to me," say I, "is the direction in which I am gazing over the sea."

'"It would not be pleasant to thee, if thou knewest the band that surrounds thee."

'"What may this band be?" say I.

'Saith he to me: "So far as thy sight reaches over sea and up to the clouds is one crowd of demons all around thee, because of thy covetousness and thy pride and haughtiness, and because of thy theft and thine other evil deeds. Knowest thou," saith he, "why thy boat stops?"

'"Verily, I know not," say I.

'"Thy boat shall not go out of the place wherein it stands until thou do my will."

'"Mayhap I shall not endure it," say I.

'"Then thou wilt endure the pains of hell unless thou endure my will."

'He came towards me then, and lays his hand on me; and I promised to do his will.

'"Fling," saith he, "into the sea all the wealth that thou hast in the boat."

'"It is a pity,' say I, "that it should go to loss."

'"It shall in no wise go to loss. There will be one whom thou wilt profit."

(Then) I fling every thing into the sea, save a little wooden cup.

'"Go now," saith he to me, "and [before] the stead in which thy boat will pause stay therein." And then he gave me for provision a cup of whey-water and seven cakes.

'So I went,' saith the ancient man, 'in the direction that my boat and the wind carried me: for I had let go my oars and my rudder. As I was there then, tossing among the waves, I am cast upon this rock, and then I doubted whether the boat had stopped for I saw neither land nor soil here. And then I remembered what had been said, namely, to stay in the stead where my boat should stop. So I stood up and saw a little crag against which the wave beat. Then I set my foot on that little crag, and my boat escapes from me, and the crag lifted me up, and the waves withdrew. Seven years am I here,' saith he, '(living) on the seven cakes and on the cup of whey-water which was given me by the man who sent me from him. And I had no (provision) save only my cup of whey-water. This still remained there.

'After that I was in a three-days-fast,' saith he. 'Now after my three days, at the hour of none, an otter brought me a salmon out of the sea. I pondered in my mind that it was not possible for me to eat a raw salmon. I threw it again into the, sea,' saith he, 'and I was fasting for another space of three days. At the third none, then, I saw an otter bring the salmon to me again out of the sea, and another otter brought flaming firewood, and set it down, and blew with his breath, so that the fire blazed thereout. So I cooked the salmon, and for seven other years I lived in that wise. And every day,' saith he, 'a salmon used to come to me, with its fire, and the crag increaseth so that (now) it is large. And on that day seven years my salmon is not given me: (so) I remained again (fasting) for another space of three days.

'At the third none of the three days there half a cake of wheat and a piece of fish were cast up to me. Then my cup of whey-water escapes from me, and there came to me a cup of the same size filled with good liquor, which is on the crag here, and it is full every day. And neither wind, nor wet, nor heat, nor cold affects me in this place. Those are my narratives,' saith the ancient man.

Now when the hour of none arrived, half a cake and a piece of fish come to each of thern all, and in the cup which stood before the cleric on the rock was found their fill of good liquor. Thereafter said the ancient man to them:

'Ye will all reach your country, and the man that slew thy father, O Máel Dúin, you will find him in a fortress before you. And slay him not, but forgive him, because God hath saved you from manifold great perils, and ye, too, are men deserving of death.'

Then they bade farewell to the ancient man, and went on their accustomed way.

XXXIV

Now, after they had gone thence they come to an island with abundant cattle, and with oxen and kine and sheep. There were no houses nor forts therein, and so they eat the flesh of the sheep. Then said some of them, seeing a large falcon there: 'The falcon is like the falcons of Ireland!'

'That is saith true indeed,' say some of the others.

'Watch it,' saith Máel Dúin, 'and see how the bird will go from us.'

They saw that it flew from them to the south-east. So they rowed after the bird in the direction in which it had gone from them. They rowed that day till vespers. At nightfall they sight land like the land of Ireland. They row towards it. They find a small island, and it was from this very island that the wind had borne them into the ocean when they first went to sea.

Then they put their prow on shore, and they went to the fortress that was in the island, and they were listening. And the inhabitants of the fortress were then dining.

They heard some of them saying: 'It is well for us if we should not see Máel Dúin.'

'That Máel Dúin has been drowned,' saith another man of them.

'Mayhap it is he who will wake you out of your sleep,' saith another man.

'If he should come now,' saith another, 'what should we do?'

'O that were not hard (to say),' saith the chief of the house: 'great welcome to him if he should come, for he hath been for a long space in much tribulation.'

Thereat Máel Dúin strikes the clapper against the doorvalve.

'Who is there?' saith the doorkeeper.

'Mael Dúin is here,' saith he himself.

'Then open,' saith the chief: 'welcome is thy coming.'

So they entered the house, and great welcome is made to them, and new garments are given them. Then they declare all the marvels which God had revealed to them, according to the word of the sacred poet who saith: *Haec olim meminisse iuuabit.* [. . .]

Máel Dúin (then) went to his own district, and Diurán the Rhymer took the five half-ounces (of silver) which he had brought from the net, and laid them on the altar of Armagh, in triumph and in exultation at the miracles and great marvels which God had wrought for them. And they declared their adventures from beginning to end, and all the dangers and perils they had found on sea and land. Now Aed the Fair, chief sage of Ireland, arranged this story as it standeth here; and he did (so) for delighting the mind and for the [people] of Ireland after him.

HERO TALES

12. The Boyhood Deeds of Cú Chulainn

(Compert con Cú Chulainn)

Translated by Caitlín Matthews

'The Boyhood Deeds of Cú Chulainn' comes at the beginning of the epic known as the *Táin Bó Cuailgne,* or the 'Cattle Raid of Cooley'. Here, the main protagonists of the Connacht side, who have stolen the Brown Bull of Cuailgne belonging to the Ulster side, ask for further information about the formidable young champion who is single-handedly defeating their troops. Queen Medb and King Ailill of Connacht question Fergus, who is exiled in disgrace from Ulster. He is one of Cú Chulainn's foster-fathers, fully cognisant of the boy's history: he and his companion-exiles brief the rulers of Connacht about how prodigiously skilled is their opponent.

Their lively account gives the true flavour of the boastful nature of Celtic story relation. Indeed, these testimonies could well stand along-side the kind of inflated legends that often accompany sports personalities today. They could certainly hold their own with almost any teenage cartoon series or comic book heroes. Undefeated by bigger and more skilful boys, by the ghosts of the dead or by savage dogs, Cú Chulainn blags a ride with one of the top charioteers of Ulster in order to further demonstrate just how worthy he is to be accorded adult warrior status, even though is still under ten years old!

As we will can see from the later and more heroic extract of the *Táin* on p. 91 when the older Cú Chulainn defends Ulster single-handedly from Samhain to Imbolc (November to February), this is clearly a boy with a marked destiny for war, combat and battle. Medb and Ailill soon discover that these boyhood deeds turn into something much more destructive as the story wears on.

Our translation is taken from the earliest recension of the story, from the *Book of Leinster.* We have worked from the Irish edition of Cecile O'Rahilly.

1. Cú Chulainn and the boys

'Tell us about this Hound that you Ulstermen boast of. How old is that youth now?' asked Ailill.

'That's no problem,' replied Fergus. 'When he was five he went to play with the boys in Emain Macha. When he was six, he went to learn the weapon-skills of Scáthach and to woo Emer. When he was seven, he took up manly arms. Now he is seventeen years old.'

'So is he the most valourous of the Ulstermen?' asked Medb.

'More than any other, surely,' replied Fergus. 'You'll not meet a harder fighter than himself, nor a sharper, speedier spear-tip than his. No champion is fiercer, no raven more predatory. There's no-one of comparable age to equal even a third of his courage. No lion is more savage. No protecting shield-wall, no battle-hammer's swing, no marauder of hosts is his equal when it comes to stopping an army in its tracks.

'You'll find no-one of comparable age to Cú Chulainn in development, dress, ferocity, speech, voice, nobility, voice, appearance, power, hardness, deeds, courage, attack, rage, anger, victory, vengeance, violence, scouting, accuracy of aim, hunting, speed, audacity and temper, able to perform the trick of piercing nine men through on every spear-cast.'

'Is that all?' said Medb. 'Surely he has just the one body? He is vulnerable, capable of being captured. He is but the age of a virgin girl and his manly promise must be before him.'

'Not at all,' said Fergus. 'It's no wonder that he should have done that amazing trick today. When he was even younger than this his deeds were those of a man.'

Fergus told them, 'He was brought up by his father and mother in Airgthech on Mag Muirthemne, reared on the stories of the Emain boys. You know how a hundred and fifty boys are usually stationed there? This is the way that King Conchobor divides his royal reign: one third of the day he watches the boys at their sport, another third he plays *fidhchell* [a board game], and the rest of the time drinking beer until he falls into an inebriated sleep. Ah! though myself and my men have been exiled by him, I still hold that there is not an Irish warrior more marvellous than Conchobor!' Fergus concluded.

'Anyway, Cú Chulainn begged his mother to let him join the boys.

'"There's no way you're going there unless some of Ulster's warriors take you," she said. "That seems a very long time to wait," Cú Chulainn said. "Just point out to me the way to Emain."

'"It lies to the north, yonder," she said, "but it's a hard journey. Sliabh Fúaith lies between you and Emain."

'"Well, I'll just try and see anyway," said Cú Chulainn.

'So off he went with his little wooden shield, his toy spear, his hurley stick and ball. He just kept going by casting the spear ahead and catching it by the point before the end had time to pierce the ground. Then he approached the boys without first extracting a promise of protection from them. Now you see, that no-one usually came to the playing field without first making this sensible precaution, but Cú Chulainn didn't know that such a thing was a *geis* [forbidden] to them.

'"This boy's out to insult us," said Follomon mac Conchobair. "He's clearly of Ulster. Let's get him, lads!"

'And they each threw their spears at him, all a hundred and fifty of them, and they all stuck in his little wooden shield. Then they chucked their balls at him, and he caught every last one of them against his chest. Then they hurled their hurley sticks at him and he managed to ward them off so that they didn't injure him and stacked them up on his back.

'Then his battle-distortion came upon him. Each separate hair upon his head stood up in spikes as if the smith had hammered them there. You would have sworn that there was a glead of fire on every hair. Then he closed up one eye, small as a needle's eye, and opened the other until it was the size of mead-cup's bowl. He drew back his jaw to ear's stretch and his mouth rib-wide until his internal organs could be seen. And over his head the hero-light shone.

'He lay into those boys, knocking down fifty of them before they could reach the gates of Emain. Nine of them leapt past me and Conchobar as we played at fidhchell. Cú Chulainn jumped over the board in hot pursuit of them and Conchobar grabbed him by the forearm.

'"Those boys deserve better treatment than that," said Conchobar.

'"But Conchobar, sir, I was surely in the right!" he said. "I came all the way from my father and mother's house to play with them and they were unkind to me."

'"What's your name, lad?" asked Conchobar.

'"Sétanta, son of Sualtaim and of Deichtire, your sister. I really didn't expect to be picked on there."

'"But why were the boys not sworn to protect you before you played with them?" asked Conchobar.

'"I didn't know you needed to do that," said Cú Chulainn. "Will you promise to protect me against them?"

'"Of course," said Conchobar.

'But, you know, he just turned round and attacked the boys inside the house.

'"What have they done to you now?" asked Conchobar.

'"Let me make a promise to protect them," said Cú Chulainn.

'"I think that would be a good idea," said Conchobar, smiling.

'"Then I promise," said Cú Chulainn.

'And so they all went down the playing field, and the boys who'd been knocked out were got to their feet by their foster-mother and fathers.'

2. Cú Chualainn and the battlefield ghosts

'Another time, when Cú Chulainn was a boy, he never slept in Emain.

'"Why is it that you don't sleep?" Conchobar asked him.

'"I can't sleep unless my head and feet are as high as the other."

'So Conchobar arranged for a monolith to be set at his head and another at his feet, and between them they made a special bed for him.

'Now it chanced once that some man went to wake up Cú Chulainn and got his fist right on the forehead. It drove the man's forehead into his brain and knocked down one of the monoliths at the same time.'

'That was surely the fist of a warrior and the arm of a strong man indeed!' said Ailill.

'Yes! And from then onwards no-one dared wake him, but they left him till he woke by himself!' said Fergus. 'And it was because of this that I can tell you another tale.'

'Now there was a conflict between Ulster and Eógan mac Durthacht and all the Ulstermen had gone to battle against him and Cú Chulainn was left sleeping at home. Ulster suffered defeat, but Conchobar, Cúscraid Menn Macha and some others were left on the field. It was their groanings that wakened Cú Chulainn. Now he stretched so much that the two monoliths at his head and feet were smashed to bits. Bricriu here saw what had happened,' said Fergus. 'Then Cú Chulainn rose and I met him myself in front of the fort as I hobbled in badly wounded.'

'"Fergus, sir, welcome here!" he said, "Where's Conchobar?"

'"I've no idea," I told him.

'So he took himself off into the dark night and made for the battlefield. And there he saw this man with only half a skull left, carrying half of another man behind him on his back.

'"Help me, Cú Chulainn," he cried out. "I've been sore wounded and here I am carrying half of my brother on my shoulders. Help me carry me for a bit."

'"I will not, so!" he replied.

'And then the half-head threw his half-kin towards Cú Chulainn but he shrugged the body off. Then they wrestled and Cú Chulainn got thrown. As he lay there, stunned, he could hear the shrieks of the battle-crow hag feasting upon the slain, and he said to himself, "What kind of apprentice warrior am I to be deterred by a few ghosts?"

'And so he got to his feet, took up his hurley stick and smashed off his enemy's head and used it for a ball, driving it before him across the plain, calling out, "Is my master Conchobor on this field anywhere?"

'Conchobar gave a groan and Cú Chulainn struck out towards him, finding him wedged into a ditch so fast that earth hid him from view.

'"What are you doing upon the battlefield?" asked Conchobar. "Have you come to be scared witless by horrors?" But he lifted Conchobar from that ditch, I tell you. Not six of the strongest Ulstermen could have brought him out of there more courageously!

'"Scout ahead and make a fire for me yonder in that house," Conchobar asked him. And Cú Chulainn made up a roaring fire for him.

'"It would be good, it would surely save me from death, to have a roast-pig right now," said Conchobar.

'"I'll go get you one," said Cú Chulainn.

'And off he went and found a man squatting before a cooking-pit in the middle of the forest. He was holding his weapons in one hand and cooking the a pig with the other. He was some nasty piece of work, I can tell you, but Cú Chulainn attacked the ugly-looking sod and took his head and his pig as well. And so Conchobar got his roast pig.

'"Let's go to our own house now," said Conchobar.

'On the way they met Cúscraid mac Conchobair, bleeding from many wounds, and Cú Chulainn bore him home on his back. And so the three of them got back to Emain Macha.'

3. How Cú Chulainn received his manhood name

Conall Cernach took up the relation. 'Aye, we know that lad well, Fergus and I, all the more so because he is a foster-son of ours. Not long after the incident Fergus has just told you, the boy performed another thing.

'It was when Culainn the smith had made a feast for Conchobar and he asked him not to invite the whole court with him. His feast was a modest one, appropriate for one whose wealth was earned by his bare hands and his tongs rather than from his vast estates and cattle. So Conchobar set off with but fifty chariot-mounted warriors, the best and most famous of his heroes.

'Conchobar paid a visit to the playing field on his way. Such was his custom when passing, to drop in and say a few words to encourage them. There he saw Cú Chulainn playing ball against one hundred and fifty and beating the lot of them. Whenever the boys went to drive their balls into the hole, he would clog the hole with his own balls so that not a single one of theirs could go in. Whenever any of them tried to throw a ball into the hole, Cú Chulainn played being goal-keeper and none got in. When they wrestled, it was Cú Chulainn who could throw all one hundred and fifty of them, and yet not all of them together could get near enough to throw him. When they played at pulling off each other's clothes, he would strip them stark-naked while they didn't even manage to get the pin out of his cloak.

'Conchobar was astounded. He wondered aloud whether the boy's present deeds would be similarly impressive upon his reaching manhood. And everyone said that they certainly would. Conchobar then asked Cú Chulainn, "We're on our way to a feast to which you're invited. Come along!"

'"But I've not played hard enough yet, Conchobar, sir," the boy said. "I'll follow on afterwards."

'When Conchobar reached the feast, Culann asked him, "Were you expecting anyone else to follow you?"

'"No," Conchobar said, forgetting all about his prior agreement with his foster-son.

'"You see, I have a bloodhound that was brought from Spain," Culainn said. "I've got him restrained by three chains, with three men holding each of them. If no-one else is coming let him be unchained to guard our cattle and goods. Let the fortress be secured!"

'It was then that the boy turned up and the dog leapt at him. He was so absorbed with his playing that he continued throwing his ball and then cast his hurley stick after it so that it struck the ball in mid-air: a piece of well-judged throwing! Then he cast his toy spear after them and caught it before it could fall to earth. The dog got closer and closer, but it didn't stop him playing.

'Conchobar and his court were so horrified by this that they were petrified. They had already worked out that they couldn't reach him alive even had the fortress been unlocked. Now as the hound was almost upon the boy, he threw away his ball and hurley stick and tackled him with his bare hands. With one hand on the hound's throat and the other on the back of his head, he whacked the dog against the nearby monolith so that the hound's limbs flew in four directions. But some say that he threw his ball into the hound's gob and that the impact drove the guts out of him through his backside!

'The Ulstermen went as one man to fetch the boy, some leaping over the walls of the fortress and other running through the gate. They scooped him up and put him Conchobar's arms. There was uproar at the thought that the king's sister's son had almost been savaged and killed. Then Culainn himself came into the hall.

'"For the sake of your mother, I welcome you, lad. But, speaking for myself, I would rather I had not called this feast, for now my wealth is wasted and my work is worthless without that hound of mine. That dog was as a servant to me, one who maintained my life and honour, defending my goods and protecting my cattle, guarding my beasts whether in field or barn."

'"Don't worry yourself overmuch," said the boy. "I'll see that a whelp from the same litter is raised by me for you and until the pup grows up and is trained and ready, I myself will be the hound who will protect yourself and your beasts. I shall protect the whole of Mag Murthemne so that neither flock nor herd shall stray across it without my knowledge."

'"Then, let your name be Cú Chulainn," said Cathbad the druid.

'"I'm glad that this should be my name," said Cú Chulainn.

'So you see,' said Conall Cernach, 'it's no wonder that the one who did such a thing when he was only seven should have performed such brave deeds now that he is eighteen!'

4. The day that Cú Chulainn became a man

'Ah, but he did another great deed,' said Fiachu mac Fir Fhebe. 'Cathbad the druid was with his son Conchobar mac Nessa. There were about hundred men in their prime, learning druidic skills – that was the number the Cathbad would instruct normally. One of his students asked Cathbad to predict what kind of luck was available on that day. Cathbad told him that if any boy took up arms as a warrior on that day, his fame for brave deeds would be spread throughout Ireland and his name last forever.

'It so happened that Cú Chulainn heard this and went to Conchobar to ask for arms.

'"Who made this prediction for you?" he asked his foster-son.

'"The reverend Cathbad," replied Cú Chulainn.

'"Oh, I know him alright!" said Conchobar. And he gave his foster-son a spear and shield. And Cú Chulainn wielded them so vigorously that he broke them, going on to wreck the fifteen spare sets of weapons stored in the house that were kept to replace any broken arms or set aside against a boy taking up manly arms. So it was that Conchobar's own weapons were finally given to him and these didn't break. Cú Chulainn brandished them, blessing their kingly owner saying, "Great good upon the people and the nation over whom the owner of these weapons reigns!"

'Then Cathbad came over to them, asking, "Is the boy taking valour?"

'"He is," replied Conchobar to his father, Cathbad.

'"Such an undertaking is unlucky for the son of his mother," said Cathbad.

'"But wasn't it you who told him this prediction?"

'"It was not, so!" said Cathbad.

'"What's the meaning of this deception, you little pest?" Conchobar scowled at Cú Chulainn.

'"King of the Army, it's not a lie," Cú Chulainn said. "Cathbad predicted this good luck this morning when he sat with his students. I heard what he said from where I was on the south side of Emain, and then I came straight to you."

'"Oh yes, it's indeed a day of good fortune," said Cathbad, "But what you didn't hear is that it is also certain that whoever takes valour today will be not only famed and applauded but also short-lived!"

'"What magnificent luck!" cried Cú Chulainn. "As long as I'm famous, I'd be happy with only one day upon the earth."

'And so it was. But later on one of the students asked again, what good fortune was available on that day, and Cathbad told him, "Whoever mounts a chariot for the first time today will be famous in Ireland for all time."

'And again Cú Chulainn heard this and ran to Conchobar, asking, "Conchobar, sir; give me a chariot!"

'And Conchobar gave him one. Cú Chulainn appraisingly slapped between the two shafts and the chariot fell to pieces. So it was with twelve chariots: he smashed them all up. Finally, Conchobar's own chariot was given to him and it withstood his stringent test. Finally, he climbed up into the chariot with Conchobar's charioteer, Ibor, who turned the chariot about.

'"Alright, now! Get down! These are fine horses I have here!" said the charioteer.

'"I'm pretty fine too, boy," said Cú Chulainn. "Go once round Emain and I'll reward you."

'So the charioteer drove off and Cú Chulainn got him to keep on going so that he might run into the boys, "so that they can wish me well." Then he begged to go back over the road one more time. And when they'd arrived, Cú Chulainn said the charioteer, "Use the whip on them!"

'"Where shall we head?" asked Ibor.

'"As far as the road goes."

'So they came to Slíabh Fúait where they discovered Conall Cernach. It was his turn to guard the province that day. You see, every Ulster warrior takes his turn and spends a day at Slíabh Fúait so as to protect anyone who comes that way, whether he might be a poet full of verses or a warrior to offer challenge or battle, and so that any movements might be noticed and news brought to Emain.

'Wealth, victory and triumph to you!" Conall greeted them.

'Conall, why don't you go back to the fortress and leave me to watch now," said Cú Chulainn.

'"Well, I don't know," said Conall. "Fair enough if it were a poet needing protection, but it would be a different matter if you had to fight someone. It's a bit premature for you to do that now."

'"Perhaps that chance might not fall out today," said Cú Chulainn. "Anyway, let's go and check on the sand dunes by Loch Echtra. There's usually some warriors lodged there."

'"Very well then," said Conall, preparing to guard him.

'So off they went and Cú Chulainn cast a stone idly from his sling and broke the shaft of Conall Cernach's chariot.

'"Now why did you do that, lad?" asked Conall.

'"I was just testing my casting and my aim," said Cú Chulainn, innocently. "Isn't it forbidden for you Ulstermen to drive in a dangerously unroadworthy chariot like that? Go back to Emain, sir, and let me keep watch."

'"Alright then," the long-suffering Conall said. And Conall Cernach did not return to that spot.

'Cú Chulainn went on to Loch Echtra, but there was no-one there. Ibor told the boy that they should be returning to Emain to be in time for dinner.

'"Not yet," said Cú Chulainn. "Tell me, what's that mountain over there?"

'"Slíabh Monduirnd," said Ibor.

'"Let's go there then," said the boy.

'So off they went and when they'd reached it, he asked again, "What's that white cairn up there on the mountain top?"

'"It's called the White Cairn," replied Ibor.

'"And what's that plain over there?"

'"Mag mBreg," said Ibor.

'And then Ibor told him the name of each of the principle fortresses between Tara and Cennannas, along with their fields, fords, notable places and settlements, fortresses and defensible hills. He also showed him the fortress of the three sons of Nechta Scéne: Fóill, Fannall and Túachell.

'"Now are those the men who say that they've killed more Ulstermen than there are actually living now?" asked Cú Chulainn.

'"That's the very ones," said Ibor.

'"Let's go and see them," said the boy.

'"It'll be dangerous!" warned Ibor.

'"Well, it's not to avoid danger that we're going," responded Cú Chulainn.

'So off they went, unyoking their horses at the fork between the river and a bog on the south of Nechan Scéne's sons' fortress. Cú Chulainn threw the protective ogam-inscibed withy that was wound about the boundary monolith as far as his arm could throw it, right out into the river so that it floated downstream. This provocatively violated the geis that bound the sons of Nechta Scéne, who saw what had been done and out they came.

'Now after he had unwound the withy and thrown it into the river, Cú Chulainn had cast himself down to sleep at the boundary stone, having told Ibor, "Don't bother waking me for a few men; just wake me up for a lot."

'Now the charioteer was pretty frightened, I can tell you, and he harnessed horses to the chariot in readiness for a swift departure, pulling urgently at the rugs and skins underneath Cú Chulainn, but not daring to waken him more directly because of his previous warning.

'The sons of Nechta Scéne came upon them.

'"Who's this then?" one of them said.

'"A little boy has come out on a chariot-ride today," the charioteer told them.

'"Well, may his weapon-taking bring him neither wealth nor success. He cannot stay here on our land nor can the horses graze here much longer."

'"Their reins are already in my hand," said Ibor, uneasily. "You've got nothing against the boy that you need to be so unfriendly. Besides, the boy's asleep."

'"I'm not the boy here!" Cú Chulainn awoke. "Surely that's the boy yonder who comes picking a battle with a man."

'"It'll be a pleasure," said the warrior, grinning.

'"Please to step into the ford then," said Cú Chulainn.

'"Here's a fitting adventure for you," said Ibor. "Watch out for the man who comes against you. His name Fóill means Sly. If you don't get him on the first thrust, you'll never overcome him."

'"I swear by the gods of my people that he shan't play that trick again on any Ulsterman once the fury of my foster-father Conchobar's spear pierces him. An outlaw's fate and death upon him!"

'Then Cú Chulainn threw his spear towards Fóill and broke his back. He despoiled the body and took his head.

'"Watch out for the next man," said Ibor. "His name is Fannall or Swallow. He moves across water with the grace of a swan or swallow."

'"I swear that he won't have the opportunity to try that trick against Ulstermen ever again," said Cú Chulainn. "You yourself have seen how I manoeuvre over the pond at Emain!"

'They met head-on in the ford and Cú Chulainn killed him, took his property and took off his head.

'"Now, watch the next man," said Ibor. "He is called Túachell or Cunning for a good reason: weapons cannot wound him."

'"I have the many-headed, iron-tipped battle spear. That'll see him as full of holes as a sieve!" Cú Chulainn boasted.

'Then he threw the spear and knocked him down, and, wading into the ford, he cut off his head. He carried the head and spoils back to Ibor.

'As they finished harnessing up, they heard the keening of Nechta Scéne, their mother. But they bundled up the spoils and put the three heads upon the chariot, saying, "These'll be my tokens of triumph when I come to Emain. I'll not be parted from them."

'Then they set back off with their trophies and Cú Chulainn said to the charioteer, "You promised me a good blow in the chariot, and now we need it because of the fight and because of the pursuit following us."

'And so they drove on to Slíabh Fúait, so swiftly that, as they crossed Brega, the horses began to outstrip the wind and the birds themselves, at the urgings of Ibor. Cú Chulainn played at catching the stone from his sling before it could reach the ground as they went.

At Slíabh Fúait, they found a herd of deer ahead of them, "What kind of swift cattle are they?"

'"That's the wild deer," said Ibor.

'"Do you think the Ulstermen would prefer me to take them back alive or dead?"

'"Well, it would be considered marvellous if you could get them back alive," said Ibor. "There's not many can do that but there's not a one among them but could bring them back dead. Now you're not telling me you bring even one of them home alive?"

'"I can so!" Cú Chulainn asserted. "Use the horse-whip and drive the deer into the bog."

'The charioteer did this and the horses stuck fast in the bog. Cú Chulainn leapt out of the chariot and caught the nearest deer, the best stag in the herd. He whipped the horses through the bog and overcame the deer, tying it up between the two poles of the chariot.

'After that they saw a flock of swans.

'"Would the Ulstermen consider it better for me to bring these birds alive or dead?"

'"The most courageous and hardy bring them back alive."

'Cú Chulainn then threw a sling-shot at the birds, bringing down eight of them. Then he took up a big stone and struck twelve more. This he did on the return stroke.

'"Collect the birds for me," said Cú Chulainn to Ibor, "If I collect them, the deer will be upon you."

'"It's not going to be easy to do that,' said the charioteer. "The horses have got so wild, I can hardly pass them. And I can't get down over the iron wheels because of their sharpness, and I can't go past the stag behind because his antlers are so big they're crowding the space between the chariot poles."

'"Step upon his antlers, then!" commanded Cú Chulainn. "I swear by the Ulsterman's gods that I shall stare and hypnotise him so well that he won't stir his head or hurt you."

'So Ibor did that and Cú Chulainn fastened the reins and Ibor got the swans. Then Cú Chulainn tied the birds to the lashings of the chariot and it was like this that he returned to Emain with a wild stag behind his chariot, a flock of swans flying over it and three severed heads hanging from its sides.

'As they neared Emain, the watchman called out, "An armed chariot rider's coming this way. He'll be the death of every man in the fort unless naked women go out quick to meet him."

'Then the charioteer turned the left side of the chariot towards Emain which was geis for him to do and Cú Chulainn cried, "I swear by the gods of the Ulstermen that unless some man comes out to fight me, I shall let the blood of everyone within."

'"Send naked women out to meet him quickly," called Conchobar.

'Then the women of Emain came down, led by Mugain, wife of Conchobar mac Nessa, and they bared their breasts to Cú Chulainn.

'"We are the warriors who will come against you today," cried Mugain.

'And Cú Chulainn covered his face. Then the warriors of Emain seized him quickly and plunged him into a bath of cold water which burst with the heat of him. A second bath was brought and he was thrown into it and that was near boiled away. The third bath that he was put into was by that time temperate enough. Then he emerged and Mugain dressed him a blue cloak with a silver cloak-pin and a hooded tunic, and he sat beside Conchobar's knee, which forever after was his natural resting place.

'And it's no wonder that one who did that in his seventh year,' said Fiachu mac Fír Fhebe, 'should triumph over any odds and be triumphant now that his seventeenth year is complete this very day.'

13. Six Tales of Mongán

(Compert Mongán, Tóruigheacht Duibhe Lacha Láimh-ghile, Aided Fothaid Airgdig, Scel Mongán, Tucait Baile Mongán, and a story from the Yellow Book of Lecan)

Translated by Kuno Meyer and Eleanor Knott

The traditions about Mongán present a fascinating array of stories, ranging from high prophecy to low comedy. There was a sixth-century historical character called Mongán who was a leader of the Dál nAraide at Rathmore in Co. Antrim, but there the resemblance ends and we are totally in the land of legendary account. The Mongán stories reveal an interest in magical contests that the real Mongán might have thought unheroic, relying as many of them do upon poetic cunning and supernatural assistance.

The conception of Mongán comes about by a process of magical substitution that reminds us of Uther Pendragon's visit to Igraine in the Arthurian legend. Born to Caintigerna, the wife of Fiachna, Mongán is the cuckoo in the nest, passed off as Fiachna's son, but he is magically educated by his real father, Manannán mac Lír, an education that later stands him in good stead. The conception and death of Mongán are notable in that they are stories which vestigially survive in the Scottish ballad of the Great Selkie of Sule Skerry: a boy is conceived or fostered upon a mortal woman by an otherworldly being with the power to shapeshift, and who is later killed, while in the form of a seal, by that woman's mortal husband. The birth and death of Mongán are prophesied by Manannán mac Lír himself in the *Voyage of Bran*, see p. 120. Mongán's death is at the hands of Artur ap Bicior, a Briton to whom Mongán has just allowed an unpursued retreat. Artur picks up a stone and casts it at his head, killing Mongán, just as was prophesied.

The longest of the Mongán stories, 'The Pursuit of Dubh Lacha of the White Arms' relates a fuller version of his conception, though we have retained the preceding *compert* or conception story because it gives interesting detail. We hear about Mongán's education and then pass swiftly on to how he gets the worse half of the bargain with the King of Leinster. Much of this story has interesting echoes from the First Branch of the *Mabinogion* where Rhiannon uses her wiser wits to overcome her husband's opponents. Dubh-Lacha is a resourceful woman indeed. The story ends in low comedy with the King of Leinster's household being completely disrupted and with the poor man sleeping with, not the lovely queen he first thought of, but a very unpleasant looking hag. (For a modern version of this story see *Celtic Love* by Caitlín Matthews.)

In a further tale, *Aided Fothaid Airgdig*, we hear how Mongán contends with another poet, Forgoll, and has to pay him off for slighting the poet's knowledge. The dead hero, Cáilte, comes to Mongán's assistance with expert and firsthand information. We also learn here how the hero is really the reincarnation of Fionn mac Cumhaill. The Celtic peoples held that transmigration was possible: this usually entailed the soul moving from shape to shape, sometimes at death's juncture and sometimes not, but it did not always mean that human shapes were taken. Characters like Etain or Tuan mac Carill spent many years in animal shape before resuming human form. In this story we hear about another wife of Mongán's, Breóthigern.

In the 'Alms of Mongán', we see how the hero takes pity upon a poor scholar and enables him to gain a little wealth by sending him in turn to various of the sidhe mounds for hospitality. At the last one, the youth carefully takes only exactly what he has been permitted: a wise precaution, since faery goods have a way of proving troublesome if taken unadvisedly, as one of Máel Dúin's foster-brothers finds in the 'Voyage of Máel Dúin (p. 132).

The recital of 'Mongán's Frenzy' is really a story of intoxication. During a terrible storm, Mongán and his wife, Findtigern take shelter in what appears to be a sidhe mound, since time stretches, making one night as long as a year. Whatever it was about his adventures that Mongán originally recited, we shall never know – unless it is drawn from the ensuing tales gathered here – since the text is fragmentary.

In the 'Curse Upon Mongán's Lineage', we discover why Mongán is childless. The royal Ultonian poet, Eochu, rightly fears being poetically upstaged in wisdom by Mongán, who does indeed provoke the poet by questions about the local landscape. Unable to answer satisfactorily, Eochu takes refuge in cursing Mongán with childlessness. Finally we learn of Mongán's death in a brief statement from 'The Annals of Clonmacnoise'.

The main source for these texts is *The Voyage of Bran*, where they are translated by Kuno Meyer from a variety of sources. 'The Curse upon Mongán' story is translated from the *Yellow Book of Lecan* by Eleanor Knott, in *Eriu* 8 (1915–16).

1. The Conception of Mongán (Compert Mongán)

Fiachna Lurga, the father of Mongán, was sole king of the province [of Ulster]. He had a friend in Scotland, to wit, Aedán the son of Gabrán. A message went from him to Aedán. A message went from Aedán to him that he would come to his aid. He was in warfare against Saxons. A terrible warrior was brought by them for the death of Aedán in the battle. Then Fiachna went across. He left his queen at home.

While the hosts were fighting in Scotland, a noble-looking man went to his wife in his stronghold in Rathmore of Moylinny. At the time he went there were not many in the stronghold. He asked the woman to arrange a place of meeting. The woman said there were not in the world possessions or treasures, for which she would do anything to disgrace her husband's honour. He asked her whether she would do it to save her husband's life. She said that if she were to see him in danger and difficulty, she would help him with all that lay in her might. He said she should do it then 'for thy husband is in great danger. A terrible man has been brought against him on whom they cannot [. . .], and he will die by his hand. If we, I and thou, make love, thou wilt bear a son thereof. That son will be famous; he will be Mongán. I shall go to the battle which will be fought tomorrow at the third hour, so that I shall save him, and I shall vanquish the warrior before the eyes of the men of Scotland. And I shall tell thy husband our adventures, and that it is thou that hast sent me to his help.'

It was done thus. When army was drawn up against army, the hosts saw something – a noble-looking man before the army of Aedán and

Fiachna. He went towards Fiachna in particular, and told him the conversation with his wife the day before, and that he had promised to come to his help at that hour. Thereupon he went before the army towards the other, and vanquished the soldier. And the battle was routed before Aedán and Fiachna.

And Fiachna returned to his country. And the woman was pregnant and bore a son, even Mongán son of Fiachna. And he thanked his wife for what she had done for him, and she confessed all her adventures. So that this Mongán is a son of Manannán mac Lir, though he is called Mongán son of Fiachna. For when he went from her in the morning he left a quatrain with Mongán's mother, saying:

> 'I go home,
> The pale pure morning draws near:
> Moninnán son of Ler
> Is the name of him who came to thee.'

2. The Pursuit of Dubh-Lacha of the White Arms (Toruigheacht Duibhe Lacha Laimh-ghile)

Once upon a time Fiachna Finn, son of Baetán son of Murchertach, son of Muredach, son of Eóghan, son of Niall, went forth from Ireland, until he came to Lochlann, over which Eolgarg Mór son of Magar, was at that time king. There he found great respect and love and honour. And he was not long there, when a disease seized the king of Lochlann, who asked of his leeches and physicians what would help him. And they told him there was in the world nothing that would help him, save a red-eared shining-white cow, which was to be boiled for him. And the people of Lochlann searched for the cow, and there was found the single cow of Caillech Dub (Black Hag). Another cow was offered to her in its stead, but the hag refused. Then four were offered to her, one cow for every foot, and the hag would not accept any other condition but that Fiachna [himself] should become security. Now this was the hour and the time that messengers came for Fiachna Finn, the son of Baetán, and he went with those messengers, and took the kingship of Ulster, and was king for one year.

One day at the end of a year he heard cries of distress in in front of the fort, and he told (his men) to go and see who made those cries, and to let the person that made them into the house. And there was the hag from Lochlann come to demand her security. Fiachna knew her and bade her welcome and asked tidings of her.

'Evil tidings I have,' said the hag. 'The king of Lochlann has deceived me in the matter of the four kine that were promised to me for my cow.'

'I will give thee four kine on his behalf, O hag,' said Fiachna. But the hag said she would not take them.

'I will give twenty kine on his behalf,' said Fiachna.

'I shall not take them,' said the hag.

'I will give four times twenty kine,' said Fiachna, 'twenty kine for each cow.'

'By my word,' said the hag, 'if all the kine of the province of Ulster were given to me, I should not take them, until thou come thyself to make war upon the king of Lochlann. As I have come to thee from the east, so do thou come on a journey with me.'

Then Fiachna assembled the nobles of Ulster until he had ten equally large battalions, and went and announced battle to the men of Lochlann. And they were three days a-gathering unto the battle. And combat was made by the king of Lochlann on the men of Ireland. And three hundred warriors fell by Fiachna in the fight. And venomous sheep were let out of the king of Lochlann's tent against them, and on that day three hundred warriors fell by the sheep, and three hundred warriors fell on the second day, and three hundred on the third day. That was grievous to Fiachna, and he said: 'Sad is the journey on which we have come, for the purpose of having our people killed by the sheep. For if they had fallen in battle or in combat by the host of Lochlann, we should not deem their fall a disgrace, for they would avenge themselves. Give me,' saith he, 'my arms and my dress that I may myself go to fight against the sheep.'

'Do not say that, O King,' said they, 'for it is not meet that thou shouldst go to fight against them.'

'By my word,' said Fiachna, 'no more of the men of Ireland shall fall by them, till I myself go to fight against the sheep; and if I am destined to find death there, I shall find it, for it is impossible to avoid fate; and if not, the sheep will fall by me.'

As they were thus conversing, they saw a single tall warlike man coming towards them. He wore a green cloak of one colour, and a brooch of white silver in the cloak over his breast, and a satin shirt next his white skin. A circlet of gold around his hair, and two sandals of gold under his feet. And the warrior said: 'What reward wouldst thou give to him who would keep the sheep from thee?'

'By my word,' said Fiachna, '[whatever thou ask], provided I have it, I should give it.'

'Thou shalt have it (to give),' said the warrior, 'and I will tell thee the reward.'

'Say the sentence,' said Fiachna.

'I shall say it,' said he; 'give me that ring of gold on thy finger as a token for me, when I go to Ireland to thy wife to sleep with her.'

'By my word,' said Fiachna, 'I would not let one man of the men of Ireland fall on account of that condition.'

'It shall be none the worse for thee; for a glorious child shall be begotten by me there, and from thee he shall be named, even Mongán the Fair (Finn), son of Fiachna the Fair. And I shall go there in thy shape, so that thy wife shall not be defiled by it. And I am Manannán, son of Ler, and thou shalt seize the kingship of Lochlann and of the Saxons and Britons.'

Then the warrior took a venomous hound out of his cloak, and a chain upon it, and said: 'By my word, not a single sheep shall carry its head from here to the fortress of the king of Lochlann, and she will kill three hundred of the hosts of Lochlann, and thou shalt have what will come of it.'

The warrior went to Ireland, and in the shape of Fiachna himself he slept with Fiachna's wife, and in that night she became pregnant. On that day the sheep and three hundred of the nobles of Lochlann fell by the dog, and Fiachna seized the kingship of Lochlann and of the Saxons and Britons.

Now, as to the Cailleach Dubh, Fiachna gave her her due: seven castles with their territory and land, and a hundred of every cattle. And then he went into Ireland and found his wife big-bellied and pregnant, and when her time came, she bore a son.

Now Fiachna the Fair had an attendant, whose name was An Damh, and in that (same) night his wife brought forth a son, and they were christened together, and the son of Fiachna was named Mongán, and the son of the attendant was named Mac an Daimh. And there was another warrior reigning together with Fiachna the Fair, to wit Fiachna the Black, son of Deman who lay heavily on his rule. And to him in the same night a daughter was born, to whom the name Dubh-Lacha

(Black Duck) White-hand was given, and Mongán and Dubh-Lacha were affianced to each other. When Mongán was three nights old, Manannán came for him and took him with him to bring him up in the Land of Promise, and vowed that he would not let him back into Ireland before he were twelve years of age.

Now as to Fiachna the Black, son of Deman, he watched his opportunity, and when he found that Fiachna the Fair, son of Baedan, had with him but a small host and force, he went up to his stronghold, and burnt and destroyed it, and killed Fiachna himself, and seized the kingship of Ulster by force.

And all the men of Ulster desired Mongán to be brought to them when he was six years old, but Manannán did not bring him to Ulster till he had completed sixteen years. And then he came to Ulster, and the men of Ulster made peace between themselves and Fiachna the Black, to wit, one-half of Ulster to Mongán, and Dubh-Lacha to be his wife and consort in retaliation for his father. And it was done so.

One day while Mongán and his wife were playing *fidchell*, they saw a dark black-tufted little cleric at the door-post, who said: 'This inactivity in which thou art, O Mongán, is not an inactivity becoming a king of Ulster, not to go to avenge thy father on Fiachna the Black, son of Deman, though Dubh-Lacha may think it wrong to tell thee so. For he has now but a small host and force with him; and come with me thither, and let us burn the fortress, and let us kill Fiachna.'

'There is no knowing what luck there may be on that saying, O cleric,' said Mongán, 'and we shall go with thee.' And thus it was done, for Fiachna the Black was killed by them, Mongán seized the kingship of Ulster, and the little cleric who had done the treason was Manannán the great and mighty.

And the nobles of Ulster were gathered to Mongán, and he said to them: 'I desire to go to seek boons from the provincial kings of Ireland, that I may get gold and silver and wealth to give away.'

'That is a good plan,' said they. And he went forth into the provinces of Ireland, until he came to Leinster. And the king of Leinster at that time was Brandubh mac Echach. And he gave a hearty welcome to the king of Ulster, and they slept that night in the place, and when Mongán awoke on the morrow, he saw the fifty white red-eared kine, and a white calf by the side of each cow, and as soon as he saw them he was in love with them. And the king of Leinster observed him and said to him: 'Thou art in love with the kine, O king,' saith he.

'By my word,' said Mongán, 'save the kingdom of Ulster, I never saw anything that I would rather have than them.'

'By my word,' said the king of Leinster, 'they are a match for Dubh-Lacha, for she is the one woman that is most beautiful in Ireland, and those kine are the most beautiful cattle in Ireland, and on no condition in the world would I give them except on our making friendship without refusal.'

They did so, and each bound the other. And Mongán went home and took his thrice (sic) fifty white kine with him. And Dubh-Lacha asked: 'What are the cattle that are the most beautiful that I ever saw? And who who got them,' saith she (. . .).

And Mongán told her how he had obtained the kine. And they were not long there when they saw hosts approaching the place, and 'tis he that was there, even the king of Leinster.

'What hast thou come to seek?' said Mongán. 'For, by my word, if what thou seekest be in the province of Ulster, thou shalt have it.'

'It is, then,' said the king of Leinster. 'To seek Dubh- Lacha have I come.'

Silence fell upon Mongán. And he said: 'I have never heard of any one giving away his wife.'

'Though thou hast not heard of it,' said Dubh-Lacha, 'give her, for honour is more lasting than life.'

Anger seized Mongán, and he allowed the king of Leinster to take her with him. Dubh-Lacha called the king of Leinster aside and said to him: 'Dost thou know, O king of Leinster, that the men and one half of Ulster would fall for my sake, except I had already given love to thee? And by my word! I shall not go with thee until thou grant me the sentence of my own lips.'

'What is the sentence?' said the king of Leinster.

'Thy word to fulfil it!' saith she.

The king of Leinster gave his word, with the exception of his being left [till judgement day].

'Then,' said Dubh-Lacha, 'I desire that until the end of one year we be not brought for one night into the same house, and if in the course of a day thou comest into the same house with me, that thou shouldst not sit in the same chair with me, but sit in a chair over against me, for I fear the exceeding great love which I have bestowed upon thee, that thou mayst hate me, and that I may not again be acceptable to my own husband; for if we are a-courting each other during this coming year, our love will not recede.'

And the king of Leinster granted her that condition, and he took her to his house, and there she was for a while. And for that while Mongán was in a wasting sickness continually. And in the night in which Mongán had taken Dubh-Lacha, Mac an Daimh had taken her foster-sister, who was her trusty attendant, and who had gone into Leinster with Dubh-Lacha. So one day Mac an Daimh came into the house where Mongán was, and said: 'Things are in a bad way with thee, O Mongán,' saith he, 'and evil was thy journey into the Land of Promise to the house of Manannán, since thou hast learnt nothing there, except consuming food and practising foolish things, and it is hard on me that my wife has been taken into Leinster, since I have not made "friendship without refusal" with the king of Leinster's attendant, as thou didst with the king of Leinster, thus being unable to follow thy wife.'

'No one deems that worse than I myself,' said Mongán.

And Mongán said to Mac an Daimh, 'Go,' saith he, 'to the cave of the door, in which we left the basket of [. . .], and a sod from Ireland and another from Scotland in it, that I may go with thee on thy back; for the king of Leinster will ask of his wizards news of me, and they will say that I am with one foot in Ireland, and with the other in Scotland, and he will say that as long as I am like that he need not fear me.'

And in that way they set out. And that was the hour and time in which the feast of Moy-Liffey was held in Leinster, and they came to the Plain of Cell Chamain in Leinster, and there beheld the hosts and multitudes and the king of Leinster going past them to the feast, and they recognised him.

'That is sad, O Mac an Daimh,' said Mongán, 'evil is the journey on which we have come.' And they saw the holy cleric going past them, even Tibraide, the priest of Cell Chamain, with his four gospels in his own hand, and the [. . .] upon the back of a cleric by his side, and they reading their offices. And wonder seized Mac an Daimh as to what the cleric said, and he kept asking Mongán: 'What did he say?' Mongán said it was reading, and he asked Mac an Daimh whether he understood a little of it.

'I do not understand,' said Mac an Daimh 'except that the man at his back says "Amen, amen".'

Thereupon Mongán shaped a large river through the midst of the plain in front of Tibraide, and a large bridge across it. And Tibraide marvelled at that and began to bless himself. ''Tis here,' he said, 'my father was born and my grandfather, and never did I see a river here. But as the river has got there, it is well there is a bridge across it.'

They proceeded to the bridge, and when they had reached its middle, it fell under them, and Mongán snatched the gospels out of Tibraide's hand, and sent them [Tibraide and his attendant] down the river. And he asked Mac an Daimh whether he should drown them.

'Certainly, let them be drowned!' said Mac an Dairnh.

'We will not do it,' said Mongán. 'We will let them down the river the length of a mile, till we have done our task in the fortress.'

Mongán took on himself the shape of Tibraide, and gave Mac an Daimh the shape of the cleric, with a large tonsure on his head, and the [. . .] on his back. And they go onward before the king of Leinster, who welcomed Tibraide and gave him a kiss, and "Tis long that I have not seen thee, O Tibraide,' he said, 'and read the gospel to us and proceed before us to the fortress. And let Ceibhin Cochlach, the attendant of my chariot, go with thee. And the queen, the wife of the king of Ulster, is there and would like to confess to thee.' And while Mongán was reading the gospel, Mac an Daimh would say 'Amen, amen.'

The hosts said they had never seen a priest who had but one word except that cleric; for he said nothing but 'amen.'

And Mongán went onward to the front of the fortress in which Dubh-Lacha was. And she recognised him. And Mac an Daimh said: 'Leave the house all of ye, so that the queen may make her confession.'

And her nurse or foster-sister ventured out of boldness to stay there.

Mac an Daimh closed his arms around her and put her out, and said that no one should be with the queen except the woman that had come with her. And he closed the bower after them and put the glazen door to it, and opened the window of glass. And he lifted his own wife into bed with him, but no sooner than Mongán had taken Dubh-Lacha with him. And Mongán sat down by her shoulder and gave her three kisses, and carried her into bed with him, and had his will and pleasure of her. And when that had been done, the hag who guarded the jewels, who was in the corner, began to speak; for they had not noticed her until then. And Mongán sent a swift magical breath at her, so that what she had seen was no longer clear to her.

'That is sad,' said the hag, 'do not rob me of Heaven, O holy cleric! For the thought that I have uttered is wrong, and accept my repentance, for a lying vision has appeared to me, and I dearly love my foster-child.'

'Come hither to me, hag!' said Mongán, 'and confess to me.'

The hag arose, and Mongán shaped a sharp spike in the chair, and the hag fell upon the spike, and found death.

'A blessing on thee, O Mongán,' said the queen, 'it is a good thing for us to have killed the woman, for she would have told what we have done.'

Then they heard a knocking at the door, and 'tis he that was there, even Tibraide, and three times nine men with him. The doorkeepers said: 'We never saw a year in which Tibraides were more plentiful than this year. Ye have a Tibraide within and a Tibraide without.'

''Tis true,' said Mongán.

'Mongán has come in my shape. Come out,' said he, 'and I will reward you, and let yonder clerics be killed, for they are noblemen of Mongán's that have been put into the shape of clerics.'

And the men of the household came out and killed the clerics, and twice nine of them fell. And the king of Leinster came to them and asked them what course they were on. 'Mongán,' said they, 'has come in Tibraide's shape, and Tibraide is in the place.' And the king of Leinster charged them, and Tibraide reached the church of Cell Chamain, and none of the remaining nine escaped without a wound.

And the king of Leinster came to his house, and then Mongán departed. And the king asked: 'Where is Tibraide?' sath he.

'It was not Tibraide that was here,' said the woman, 'but Mongán, since you will hear it.'

'Were you with Mongán, girl?' said he.

'I was,' said she, 'for he has the greatest claim on me.'

'Send for Tibraide,' said the king, 'for [. . .] we have chanced to kill his people.' And Tibraide was brought to them, and Mongán went home and did not come again until the end of a quarter, and during that time he was in a wasting sickness.

And Mac an Daimh came to him and said to him: ''Tis wearisome to me,' said he, 'to be without my wife through a clown like myself, since I have not made "friendship without refusal" with the king of Leinster's attendant.'

'Go thou for me,' said Mongán, 'to get news to Ráith Descirt of Bregia, where Dubh-Lacha of the White Hand is, for I am not myself able to go.'

Thereafter Dubh-Lacha said: 'Let Mongán come to me,' said she, 'for the king of Leinster is on a journey around Leinster, and Ceibhin Cochlach, the attendant of the king's chariot, is with me and keeps telling me to escape, and that he himself would come with me. And Mongán behaves in a weak manner,' said she. And Mac an Daimh went to incite Mongán.

Thereupon Mongán set out to Raith Descirt of Bregia, and he sat down at the shoulder of the girl, and a gilded chess board was brought to them, and they played. And Dubh-Lacha bared her breasts to Mongán, and as he looked upon them, he beheld the great paps, which were soft and white, and the middle small and shining-white. And desire of the girl came upon him. And Dubh-Lacha observed it. Just then the king of Leinster with his hosts was drawing near the fortress, and the fortress was opened before him. And the king of Leinster asked of the girl whether Mongán had been in the house. She said he had been. 'I wish to obtain a request of thee, girl,' said the king of Leinster.

'It shall be granted. Except thy being with me till the year is ended, there is nothing that thou mayst ask which I will not grant thee.'

'If that be so,' said the king, 'tell me when thou longest for Mongán son of Fiachna; for when Mongán has gone, thou wilt long for him.'

At the end of a quarter Mongán returned, and he was longing for her; and all the hosts of the place were there at the time. Then the hosts of the place came out, and Mongán turned back from the fortress and went home. And that quarter he was in a wasting sickness. And the nobles of Ulster assembled into one place and offered Mongán to go with him to make battle for the sake of his wife.

'By my word,' said Mongán, 'the woman that has been taken from me through my own folly, no woman's son of the men of Ulster shall fall for her sake in bringing her out, until, through my own craftiness, I myself bring her with me.'

And in that way the year passed by, and Mongán and Mac an Daimh set out to the king of Leinster's house. There were the nobles of Leinster going into the place, and a great feast was being prepared towards the marriage of Dubh-Lacha. And he [the king] vowed he would marry her. And they came to the green outside.

'O Mongán,' said Mac an Daimh, 'in what shape shall we go?'

And as they were there, they see the hag of the mill, to wit, Cuimne. And she was a hag as tall as a weaver's beams and a large chain-dog with her licking the mill-stones, with a twisted rope around his neck, and Brothar was his name. And they saw a hack mare with an old pack-saddle upon her, carrying corn and flour from the mill.

And when Mongán saw them, he said to Mac an Daimh: 'I have the shape in which we will go,' said he, 'and if I am destined ever to obtain my wife, I shall do so this time.'

'That becomes thee, O noble prince,' [said Mac an Daimh].

'And come, O Mac an Daimh, and call Cuimne of the mill out to me to converse with me.'

'It is three score years,' [said Cuimne], 'since any one has asked me to converse with him.' And she came out, the dog following her, and when Mongán saw them, he laughed and said to her: 'If thou wouldst take my advice, I would put thee into the shape of a young girl, and thou shouldst be as a wife with me or with the king of Leinster.'

'I will do that certainly,' said Cuimne

And with the magic wand he gave a stroke to the dog, which became a sleek white lapdog, the fairest that was in the world, with a silver chain around its neck and a little bell of gold on it, so that it would have fitted into the palm of a man. And he gave a stroke to the hag, who became a young girl, the fairest of form and make of the daughters of the world, to wit, Ibhell of the Shining Cheeks, daughter of the king of Munster. And he himself assumed the shape of Aedh, son of the king of Connaught, and Mac an Daimh he put into the shape of his attendant. And he made a shining-white palfrey with crimson hair, and of the packsaddle he made a gilded saddle with variegated gold and precious stones. And they mounted two other mares in the shape of steeds, and in that way they reached the fortress.

And the door-keepers saw them and told the king of Leinster that it was Aed the Beautiful, son of the king of Connaught, and his attendant, and his wife Ibhell of the Shining Cheek, daughter of the king of Munster, exiled and banished from Connaught, that had come under the protection of the king of Leinster, and he did not wish to come with a greater host or multitude. And the door-keeper made the announcement, and the king came to meet them, and welcomed them. And the king of Leinster called the son of the king of Connaught to his shoulder. 'That is not the custom with us,' said the son of the king of Connaught, 'but that he should sit by the side of the king who is the second best man in the palace, and next to thee I am the second best in the house, and by the side of the king I will be.'

And the drinking-house was put in order. And Mongán put a love-charm into the cheeks of the hag, and from the look which the king of Leinster cast on her he was filled with her love, so that there was not a bone of his of the size of an inch, but was filled with love of the girl. And he called his attendant to him and said to him: 'Go to where the wife of the king of Connaught's son is, and say to her, "the king of Leinster has bestowed great love upon thee, and that a king is better than a king's heir".'

And Mongán understood the whispering, and said to Cuimne: 'There is an attendant coming from the king of Leinster with a message to thee, and I know the secret message which he brings, and if thou wouldst take my advice, thou wouldst not be with a worse man than myself or the king of Leinster.'

'I have no choice of bridegroom, whichever of you will be husband to me."

'If that be so,' said Mongán, 'when he comes to thee, say that by his gifts and precious things thou wilt know him who loves thee, and ask him for the drinking horn which he brings thee.'

And the king of Leinster's attendant came to converse with her, and said: 'Here is a noble horn brought to thee.'

'We should know him who loves us by gifts and precious things.'

And the king of Leinster said to the attendant: 'Give her my horn.'

But the king's household said: 'Do not give thy treasures to the wife of the king of Connaught's son.'

'I will give them,' said the king of Leinster, 'for the woman, and my treasures will come to me.' And Mac an Daimh takes the horn from her and whatever else she got of treasures till the morning.

And Mongán said to Cuimne: 'Ask the king of Leinster for his girdle.' And the girdle was of such a nature that neither sickness nor trouble would seize the side on which it was. And she demanded the girdle, and the king of Leinster gave it her, and Mac an Daimh forthwith took it from her. 'And now say to the king of Leinster's attendant, if the (whole) world were given thee, thou wouldst not leave thy own husband for him.' And the attendant told that to the king of Leinster, who said: 'What is it you notice?'

'Are you in the house . . .?' said they.

'You know this woman by my side, to wit, Dubh-Lacha of the White Hands, daughter of Fiachna Dubh son of Deman. I took her from him on terms of "friendship without refusal," and if thou like, I would exchange with thee.' And great anger and ferocity seized him and he said: 'If I had brought steeds and studs with me, it would be right to ask them of me. However, it is not right to refuse a lord [. . .] though I am loath it should be so, take her to thee.' And as they made the exchange, Mongán gave three kisses to the girl, and said: 'Every one would say that we did not make the exchange from our hearts, if I did not give these kisses.' And they indulged themselves until they were drunk and hilarious.

And Mac an Daimh arose and said: 'It is a great shame that no one puts drink into the hand of the king of Connaught's son.'

And as no one answered him, he took the two best steeds that were in the fortress, and Mongán put swiftness of wind into them. And Mongán placed Dubh-Lacha behind him, and Mac an Daimh his own wife, and they set forth. And when on the morrow the household of the king of Leinster arose, they saw the cloak of the hag, and the grey tall hag on the bed of the king of Leinster. And they saw the dog with a twisted halter round his neck, and they saw the hack mare and the packsaddle [. . . .] And the people laughed and awoke the king of Leinster, who saw the hag by his side and said: 'Art thou the greybacked hag of the mill?'

'I am,' said she.

'Pity that I should have slept with thee, O Cuimne!' [said the King of Leinster].

3. The Death of Fothad Airgdech (Aided Fothaid Airgdig)

Mongán was in Rathmore of Moylinny in his kingship. To him went Forgoll the poet. Through him many a married couple was complaining to Mongán. Every night the poet would recite a story to Mongán. So great was his lore that they were thus from Halloween to May-day. He had gifts and food from Mongán.

One day Mongán asked his poet what was the death of Fothad Airgdech. Forgoll said he was slain at Duffry in Leinster. Mongán said it was false. The poet said he would satirise him with his lampoons, and he would satirise his father and his mother and his grandfather, and he would sing (spells) upon their waters, so that fish should not be caught in their rivermouths. He would sing upon their woods, so that they should not give fruit, upon their plains, so that they should be barren forever of any produce. Mongán promised him his will of precious things as far as (the value of) seven bondmaids, or twice seven bondmaids, or three times seven. At last he offers him one-third, or one-half of his land, or his whole land; at last (anything) save only his own liberty with (that of) his wife Breó thigernd, unless he were redeemed before the end of three days. The poet refused all except as regards the woman. For the sake of his honour Mongán consented. Thereat the woman was

sorrowful. The tear was not taken from her cheek. Mongán told her not
to be sorrowful, help would certainly come to them.

So it came to the third day. The poet began to enforce his bond.
Mongán told him to wait till evening. He and his wife were in their
bower. The woman weeps as her surrender drew near and she saw no
help. Mongán said: 'Be not sorrowful, woman. He who is even now
coming to our help, I hear his feet in the Labrinne.'

They wait a while. Again the woman wept. 'Weep not, woman! He
who is now coming to our help, I hear his feet in the Máin.'

Thus they were waiting between every two watches of the day. She
would weep, he would still say: 'Weep not, woman. He who is now
coming to our help, I hear his feet in the Laune, in Lough Leane, in
the Morning-star River between the Ui Fidgente and the Arada in the
Suir on Moy-Fevin in Munster, in the Echuir, in the Barrow, in the
Liffey, in the Boyne, in the Dee, in the Tuarthesc, in Carlingford
Lough, in the Nid, in the Newry river, in the Larne Water in front of
Rathmore.'

When night came to them, Mongán was on his couch in his palace,
and his wife at his right hand, and she sorrowful. The poet was
summoning them by their sureties and their bonds. While they were
there, a man is announced approaching the rath from the south. His
cloak was in a fold around him, and in his hand a headless spear-shaft
that was not very small. By that shaft he leapt across the three ramparts,
so that he was in the middle of the garth, thence into the middle of the
palace, thence between Mongán and the wall at his pillow. The poet
was in the back of the house behind the king. The question is argued
in the house before the warrior that had come.

'What is the matter here?' said he.

'I and the poet yonder,' said Mongán, 'have made a wager about the
death of Fothad Airgdech. He said it was at Duffry in Leinster. I said
that was false.'

The warrior said the poet was wrong. 'It will be [. . .],' said Forgoll,
'[. . .]' 'That were not good,' said the warrior.

'It shall be proved. We were with thee, with Find,' said the warrior.

'Hush,' said Mongán, 'that is not fair.'

'We were with Find, then,' said he.

'We came from Scotland. We met with Fothad Airgthech here
yonder on the Larn river. There we fought a battle. I made a cast at him,
so that it passed through him and went into the earth beyond him and

left its iron head in the earth. This here is the shaft that was in that spear. The bare stone from which I made that cast will be found, and the iron head will be found in the earth, and the tomb of Fothad Airgdech will be found a little to the east of it. A stone chest is about him there in the earth. There, upon the chest, are his two bracelets of silver, and his two arm-rings, and his neck-torque of silver. And by his tomb there is a stone pillar. And on the end of the pillar that is in the earth there is Ogam. This is what it says: "This is Eochaid Airgdech. Cáilte slew me in an encounter against Find".'

They went with the warrior. Everything was found thus. It was Cáilte Find's foster-son, that had come to them. Mongán however, was Find, though he would not let it be told.

[Note: Fothad Airgdech, also called Oendé, was one of the three Fothads, brothers, who reigned together over Ireland for one year (AD 284).]

4. The Alms of Mongán
(Scel Mongán)

Now once upon a time when Forgoll the poet was with Mongán, the latter at a certain hour of the day went before his stronghold, where he found a bardic scholar [one of Forgal's pupils] learning his lesson. Said Mongán:

> 'All is lasting
> In a cloak of sackcloth;
> In due course thou shalt attain
> The end of thy studies.'

Mongán then took pity on the scholar, who was in the cloak of sackcloth. He had little of any substance. In order to know whether he would be a truthful and good messenger he said to him, promising him [. . . .]

'Go now,' said Mongán, 'until thou reach the fairy knoll of Lethet Oidni, and bring a precious stone which I have there, and for thyself take a pound of white silver, in which are twelve ounces. Thou shalt have help from them. This is thy journey from here, to Cnocc Bane. Thou wilt find welcome in the fairy knoll of Cnocc Bane for my sake.

Thence to Duma Granerit. Thence to the fairy knoll of Lethet Oidni. Take the stone for me, and go to the stream of Lethet Oidni, where thou wilt find a pound of gold, in which are nine ounces. Take that with thee for me.'

The man went on his journey. In the fairy knoll of Cnocc Bane he found a noble-looking couple to meet him. They gave great welcome to a messenger of Mongán's. It was his due. He went further. He found another couple in Duma Granerit, where he had the same welcome. He went to the fairy knoll of Lethet Oidni, where again he found another couple. They gave great welcome to a man of Mongán's. He was most hospitably entertained, as on the other nights. There was a marvellous chamber at the side of the couple's house. Mongán had told him that he should ask for its key. He did so. The key was brought to him. He opens it. He had been told not to take anything out of the house except what he had been sent for. He does so. The key he gave back to the couple; his stone, however, and his pound of silver he took with him. Thereupon he went to the stream of Lethnet Oidni, out of which he took his pound of gold. He went back to Mongán, to whom he gave his stone and gold. He himself takes his silver. These were his wanderings.

5. The Telling of Mongán's Frenzy (Tucait Baile Mongán)

[Mongán's 'Frenzy 'or 'Vision' was the title of a tale which is now lost .]

Findtigernd, Mongán's wife, besought Mongán to tell her the simple truth of his adventures. He asked of her a respite of seven years. It was granted. Then that period arrived. The men of Ireland had a great gathering at Usnech in Meath, the year of the death of Ciarán the son of the Carpenter, and of the slaying of Túathal Maelgarb, and of the taking of the kingship by Diarmait. The hosts were on (the hill of) Usnech. A great hail-storm came upon them there. Such was its greatness that the one shower left twelve chief streams in Ireland for ever. Mongán with seven men arose and went from the cairn aside, and his queen and his shanachie Cairthide, son of Marcán. Then they saw something, a prominent stronghold with a frontage of ancient trees. They go to it. They went into the enclosure. They go into a marvellous house there. A covering of bronze was on the house, a pleasant bower over its windows. Seven conspicuous men were there. Within the house there was a marvellous spread of quilts and covers, and of wonderful jewels. Seven vats of wine there were. Mongán was made welcome in the house. He stayed there. He became intoxicated. It was then and there that Mongán sang the 'Frenzy' to his wife, since he had promised he would tell her something of his adventures. It seemed to them it was not very long they were in that house. They deemed it to be no more but one night. However, they were there a full year. When they awoke, they saw it was Rathmore of Moy-Linny [i.e. Mongán's own palace] in which they were.

6: The Curse upon Mongán's Lineage (from the Yellow Book of Lecan)
Translated by Eleanor Knott

Eochu Rígéigeas, chief poet of Ireland, was invited to make verse for Fiachna, son of Boetán, for Fiachna was king of Ulaid and Eochu was of the Ulaid.

'I should avoid thy presence,' said Eochu, 'more than that of any of the kings of Ireland, for thou hast a young son, Mongán son of Fiachna. He is the most learned youth in Ireland, he will be relating tales and giving instruction, evil people will set him to contradict me, I shall curse him and thou wilt quarrel with me on that account.'

'Nay,' said Fiachna, 'I shall speak to my son that he contradict thee not, it is he will be the most civil towards thee in this household.'

'Well,' said Eochu, 'it shall be done. Let it be thus until the end of a year.'

One day he was relating lore.

'Evil of thee, Mongán, said the boys, 'that thou dost not challenge the lying clown.'

'Good,' said Mongán.

Fiachna went on a royal visitation, accompanied by Eochu. One day on their journey they beheld six large pillar-stones before them, and four young clerics by the stones.

'What do you here, clerics?' said Fiachna.

'We are here seeking knowledge and instruction. God has brought to us, however, the king-poet of Ireland, Eochu, to reveal who planted these stones and how they were arranged.'

'Well,' said Eochu, 'I do not remember all that. I should think the Children of Deda upreared them, to build the City of Cú Roí.'

'Well, Eochu,' said one of them, 'the young clerics say thou art astray.'

'Do not blame him,' said another.

'Perhaps he does not know,' said his companion.

'He does not know,' said another.

'Well,' said Eochu, 'and you, what is your explanation of them?'

'This, then, is our information – these are three stones of a champion-band and three stones of a warrior-band. Conall Cernach placed them, along with Illand, son of Fergus, who slew three here in his first prowess. He was unable to uprear the pillars on account of his youth, and Conall Cernach raised them with him, for it was the custom of the Ulaid, wherever they performed their first act of valour, to raise pillar-stones to the number that they slew – and be off, Eochu, with thy ignorance.'

'Do not be ashamed, Eochu,' said Fiachna, 'the scholars are a match for thee.'

They proceed on their way as before, and they perceived a large lime-washed castle in front of them, and four youths in purple raiment before the door. Eochu approached the enclosure.

'Well,' said Fiachna, 'what do you want?"'

'We want to hear from Eochu what castle this is, and who lived in it.'

'So many build castles,' said Eochu, 'that they do not all find room in the memory.'

'Let be,' said the other, 'for he does not know.'

'What is your information, then?' said Fiachna.

'Not difficult, indeed –

> A while since he was merry,
> drinking mead from a green goblet,
> in the garden on its lawn –

and yet thou hast not remembered its name, Eochu.'

'Good,' said Eochu.

Then they proceeded, and they saw another castle before them, and four youths quarrelling in front of the entrance.

'I am right!'

'Thou art not right!'

'What are you at, boys?' said Fiachna.

'We are contending as to what castle this is, and by whom it was built. God has brought to us, however, a man without any ignorance to reveal it to us.'

'Do not shame him,' said his companion, 'he does not know.'

'What do you know about it?' said Fiachna.

'Not difficult, indeed:

> for the man who dug Ráth Imgat;
> Imgat was the woman who named it,
> daughter of Buise, son of Didracht.

Ráth Imgat, then, is its name, Eochu, and it is not fortunate for thee that thou art ignorant of it.'

Then Eochu was put to shame.

'It is all the same to thee, Eochu,' said Fiachna 'thou shalt not be thought the less of.'

They go home then, and find Mongán and his following within.

Well,' said Eochu, 'thou hast done that, Mongán I know.'

'Thou hast said it,' said Mongán

'It shall not profit thee then,' said Eochu, 'I shall leave a reproach on thee in return for it. The great sport thou hast made for thyself, that thou shalt be without sport in consequence of it. Thou shalt have no issue save horseboys, and thou shalt not leave any great inheritance, neither shall. . . .'(?)

Thus was Mongán, son of Fiachna, deprived of noble issue.

[Coda: from the Annals of Clonmacnois.]

AD 624. Mongán mac Fiaghna, a very well-spoken man, and much given to the wooing of women, was killed by one [Arthur ap] Bicoir, a Welshman, with a stone.

DREAMS
AND VISIONS

The Dream of Oengus

(Aislinge Oenguso)

Translated by Caitlín Matthews

In this tale, the great Oengus mac Og, son of the Dagda, falls into a love-sickness for an unknown woman who visits his bed. It is not so much a dream as a vision that Oengus experiences. From the words of the doctor, Fergne, who, in other sources, is named Fingen, King Conchobar's doctor, we understand that Oengus is suffering the pangs of first love and that he has no prior knowledge to self-diagnose his complaint. We also have to pinch ourselves to realise that the great and powerful dé Danaan faery is himself under a spell stronger than that of any faery magic. The people of the *sí* – a word that means simultaneously 'the faery mounds' and 'the faery people' – pursue their own amours, sometimes with mortal men and women, sometimes, as here, with their own kind.

The instrument that Caer, the shapeshifting daughter of another *sí* mound, plays is the *tiompán* which may have been a psaltery-like instrument of strings laid across a resonating frame, to be plucked or perhaps played with hammers like the Hungarian cimbalon. The sound of wire-strung instruments played in this fashion is particularly enchanting and entrancing.

Our translation of the *Aislinge Oenguso* is from Egerton 1782 in the British Museum, Ed Francis Shaw, *The Dream of Oengus*, Dublin, 1934.

One night when Oengus was sleeping, he saw something that looked like a young woman coming towards him near the head of his bed. She was the most beautiful woman in Ireland. Oengus went to seize her hands in order to take her into his bed, but the one whom he had welcomed to sleep with him made a sudden move away from him and he had no notion who had taken her from him. He remained there until morning and he had no healthful spirit within him. The disappearance of the one who had visited him without a word spoken had rendered him ill. No food went down his throat. He remained there another night when he saw the lovely woman who had fled from him; she had a *tiompán* in her hands, the sweetest he had ever heard, and she played music to him so that he fell asleep. He remained there until the next day when he would take no food.

A full year passed during which she made many such visits to him, and he became enamoured of her, but said nothing to anyone. He fell into a languor and no-one knew what was the matter with him. The doctors of Ireland assembled. They could not agree what was was wrong. Someone went to seek Fergne the doctor of Conn. He came to them. Now Fergne could tell from looking at the face of the sick what illness they had, he could even tell from the way the smoke arose from a house the number of those within who were sick. He could tell that Oengus' sickness was of the mind rather than of the body.

Fergne drew him apart and said to him, 'Perhaps experience has not prepared you but you are in love with one who is absent.'

'You have guessed the cause,' said Oengus. 'And my love is yet unsatisfied.'

None of the other doctors had dared to draw this conclusion.

'You are right!' said Oengus. 'A beautiful young woman has come to me, one whose beauty surpasses all others in Ireland, one who has great distinction. She had a *tiompán* in her hand and she has played to me every night.'

'No matter,' said Fergne, 'she has chosen you to be the recipient of her love. Send messages of this to Boann, your mother, and ask her to come and speak to you.'

This was done. Soon Boann came. 'I am in the process of healing this man,' said Fergne. 'He is ill of a grave malady.' He told Boann the news. 'His mother should look after him while he has this mysterious sickness,' said Fergne, 'Meanwhile, it would be good for you to make a circuit of Ireland to see if you can find a woman who fits the appearance of the one who has appeared to your son.' This search continued for a whole year, but no-one resembling the woman was found. Fergne called on them again.

'We have been unable to find any help for our trouble,' said Boann.

Fergne said, 'Send for the Dagda to come and speak to his son.'

So the Dagda was sent for and came also, 'Why have I been called?'

'To advise your son,' said Boann. 'It would be better if you helped him. He is so low that he is likely to die. He has a languor upon him. He loves someone who is absent from him and we cannot find her without your help.'

'What use will my words be to him?' asked the Dagda, 'I know no more than you yourself.'

'You know of this, certainly,' said Fergne, 'you are the king of all the *sí* in Ireland. Go seek for the help of Bodb, king of the *sí* of Munster, for his knowledge is highly respected throughout Ireland.'

Bodb was found. He gave his welcome, 'Be welcome,' said Bodbh, 'people of the Dagda.'

'It is for this that we have come.'

'Do you have news?' asked Bodb.

'Oengus has seen a young woman while he slept. We do not know where she may be found in the whole of Ireland. He has asked the Dagda to search Ireland for a distinguished woman of this appearance.'

'She will be sought,' said Bodb, 'but give me leave for a year's delay in which I can seek out news of her.'

They returned at the end of that year to the Síd of Femen, the abode of Bodb. 'I have sought the length and breadth of Ireland and I have found the young woman at Bel Dragon Lake, at the Harp of Cliach,' said Bodb.

They returned to the Dagda who bade them welcome. 'Have you news?' he asked.

'We have good news. A young woman of the description you gave us has been found, through the good offices of Bodb. Let Oengus come with us to recognise the young woman and he will be able to see her.'

So Oengus was taken there by chariot towards the Síd of Femen. A great feast was prepared by the king in his honour. He wished him welcome. They spent three days and nights at the feast.

'Tomorrow, we will go out,' said Bodb, 'to see if you recognise the young woman, and for you to see her. But though you may be able to recognise her, I am not able to give her to you, you will be able to do nothing more than see her.'

They left for the lake and saw a hundred and fifty young women. They saw Oengus' beloved among them. The attendant women did not come up to her shoulders. There was a chain of silver between each couple of women. They each had a collar of silver about their necks and a chain of fine gold. Bodb said then, 'Do you recognise the woman below?'

'I know her surely!' said Oengus.

'You are not in the best condition,' remarked Bodb.

'It doesn't matter,' said Oengus, 'I am content to have recognised her even though I will not be able to take her away with me this time. Who is this young woman, Bodb?' asked Oengus.

'Ah, I know that!' said Bodb, 'It is Caer Ibormeith, (Yew-Berry) daughter of Ethal Anbual of the Síd of Uaman in the province of Connacht.'

Oengus and his party departed for their home. Bodb went with him and they spoke to the Dagda and Boann in the Brug of Mac Oc. They told them the news and related how beautiful and distinguished the woman was, superior to those attending her. They told them her name and that of her father and grandfather. 'We regret,' said the Dagda, 'we are not able [to fetch her hither?].'

Bodb said, 'The best thing you can do, Dagda, is to consult Ailill and Medb, because it is within their province that the young woman lives.'

The Dagda went to the province of Connacht with an escort of sixty chariots. He was welcomed by the king and queen. Then they spent an entire week in feasting and serving beer to their guest. 'Why have you come to us?' asked the king.

'There is in your domains,' said the Dagda, 'a young woman beloved of my son, and who is the cause of great regret for him. I ám come to you to ask whether she might be bestowed upon my son.'

'Who is it?' asked Ailill.

'The daughter of Ethal Anbual.'

'We do not have any power over her,' said Ailill and Medb. 'If we did, she would have been given to Oengus.'

'The best you can do, perhaps, is to meet with the king of the síd?' suggested the Dagda.

Ailill's steward went to find Ethal Anbual, her father. 'I am commanded by Ailill and Medb to bid you come that there may be dealings between you.'

'I will not come,' said Ethal Anbual, 'and I will not give my daughter to the son of the Dagda.'

The steward returned with this message to Ailill, 'I cannot persuade him to come; he knows why he has been called.'

'No matter,' said Ailill, 'he will come to us when the heads of his warriors are brought away.'

Then the army of Ailill and the people of the Dagda drove towards the síd and invaded it. They did indeed carry away sixty heads and the king, Ethal Anbual, was led away as a prisoner to Cruachan.

Ailill said then to Ethal Anbual, 'Give your daughter to the son of the Dagda.'

'I am not able to,' said he, 'her power is greater than mine.'

'What greater power does she have then?' asked Ailill.

'Not hard to tell. She can go in the form of a bird for the space of a year; then the next year she will be in human form.'

'In which year is she in the form of a bird?' asked Ailill.

'It is not for me to betray her,' said her father.

'Your head then,' said Ailill, 'if you do not tell us!'

'I will not refuse you much longer,' said Ethal, 'but will tell you, since you have the air of one who has already decided to take her. Next Samhain (eve of November) she will be in the form of a bird at Lake Bel Dragon. You will see a flock of marvellous birds at the same time as she appears: there will be a hundred and fifty swans around her. I am prepared to feast among them.'

'That is no matter to me,' said the Dagda, 'because I know under what form they will be.'

A peace treaty was concluded between Ailill, Ethal and the Dagda, and Ethal was set at liberty. The Dagda took his leave and returned home to tell the news to his son. 'Go, next Samhain, to Lake Bel Dragon ready to call her to you on the lake.' Then Mac Oc went to Lake Bel Dragon and he saw a hundred and fifty white birds on the lake, with silver chains and buckles of gold around their necks. Oengus was in human form at the lake-shore. He called to the young woman, 'Come and speak to me, Caer!'

'Who calls me?' she said.

'It is I, Oengus, who calls you.'

'I will come if you promise me on your honour that you will join me on the lake tomorrow.'

'I hold myself responsible for your protection,' he said.

He went to her and put his arms around her. They slept in the form of two swans and they flew three times round the lake. And there was no loss of honour to him to be in that state. They left in the form of two white birds (swans) and they went to the Brug of Mac Oc. They sang together such a music that all who heard them fell into a sleep for three days and nights. Then the young woman slept with him.

And this is why there came to be a friendship between the Mac Oc,

Ailill and Medb. It is for this reason that Oengus came with three hundred troops to Ailill and Medb in the Cattle Raid of Cooley. And this story is called 'The Dream of Oengus, son of the Dagda', which connects with the 'Cattle Raid of Cooley'. (*Táin Bó Cuailgne.*)

15. The Sick-Bed of Cú Chulainn

(Serglige con Cú Cuhulainn)

Translated by A.H. Leahy

'The Sick-bed of Cú Chulainn,' is a classic account of a visit by mortals to the Otherworld of the sídhe. Like many early Irish sagas, is a compilation based on several versions of the same story. The tale in its earliest form probably told how a mortal hero, having fallen under a fairy spell, was lured by the fairy people to the Otherworld, where he was healed of his malady in order to assist the fairy folk in their tribal dispute. In the present version of the story the two visits of the fairy messengers to the ailing Cú Chulainn, the double account of Loeg's experiences in the fairy realm, as well as other repetitions and inconsistencies are the result of the work of the compiler. Nevertheless, there are some very fine passages of descriptive writing, some excellent poems, and above all a narrative which is full of unexpected twists and turns. Noteworthy also is the fact that here, as in 'The Wooing of Emer' (pp. 345–368), Cú Chulainn's wife plays a significant part. In fact the first time she is mentioned it is by the name Eithne. This confusion is a result of a combination of at least two versions of the story, and we have a break in the middle which shows where the scribe tried to reconcile the two – or rather, gave up trying. We chose to leave the story as it stands rather than attempt to cover the join. A modern retelling of the story, however, appears in *Celtic Love* by Caitlín Matthews.

This still remains a wonderful account of what happens when an immortal woman falls out of love with her immortal husband – in this case the sea-god Manannán mac Lir – and in love with a mortal hero – Cú Chulainnn, who then falls for her but continues to love his wife! In the end it is the druids who are called upon to reconcile matters, though the God himself still has to set the final seal upon everything. This version is edited and translated by A.H. Leahy from the twelfth century *Lebor na h-Uidre,* the Book of the Dun Cow (Dublin, 1929) .

Every year the men of Ulster were accustomed to hold festival together; and the time when they held it was for three days before Samhain, and for three days after that day, and upon Samhain itself. And the time that is spoken of is that when the men of Ulster used to assemble in Mag Muirthemne, and there they used to hold the festival every year; nor was there anything in the world that they would do at that time except sports, and marketings, and splendours, and pomps, and feasting and eating; and it is from that custom of theirs that the Festival of Samhain was descended, that is now held throughout the whole of Ireland.

Now once upon a time the men of Ulster held festival in Mag Muirthenme, and the reason that this festival was held was that every man of them should every Samhain give account of the combats he had made and of his valour. It was their custom to hold that festival in order to give account of these combats, and the manner in which they gave that account was this: each man used to cut off the tip of the tongue of a foe whom he had killed, and carry it with him in a pouch. Moreover, in order to make more great the numbers of their contests, some used to bring with them the tips of the tongues of beasts, and each man publicly declared the fights he had fought, one man of them after the other. And they did this also: they laid their swords over their thighs when they related their combats, and their own swords used to turn against them when the strife that they declared was false; nor was this to be wondered at, for at that time it was customary for demons to scream from the weapons of men, so that for this cause their weapons might be the more able to guard them.

To that festival then came all the men of Ulster except two alone, and these two were Fergus mac Róig, and Conall the Victorious.

'Let the festival be held!' cried the men of Ulster.

'Nay,' said Cú Chulainn, 'it shall not he held until Conall and Fergus come,' and this he said because Fergus was the foster-father of Cú Chulainn, and Conall was his comrade.

Then said Sencha, 'Let us for the present engage in games of chess; and let the druids sing, and let the jugglers perform their feats'; and it was done as he had said.

Now while they were thus employed a flock of birds came down and hovered over a neighbouring lake; never were seen in Ireland more beautiful birds than these. And a longing that these birds should be given to them seized upon the women who were there; and each of them began to boast of the prowess of her husband at bird-catching.

'How I wish,' said Ethne, Conchobar's wife, 'that I could have two of those birds, one of them upon each of my two shoulders.'

'It is what we all long for,' said the women.

'If any should have this gift, I should be the first one to have it,' said Ethne [Emer] Inguba, the wife of Cú Chulainn.

'What are we to do now?' said the women.

'It is easy to answer you,' said Leborcham, the daughter of Oa and Adarc; 'I will go now with a message from you, and will seek for Cú Chulainn.' She then went to Cú Chulainn.

'The women of Ulster would be well pleased,' she said, 'if yonder birds were given to them by thy hand.'

Cú Chulainn reached for his sword to unsheathe it against her. 'Cannot the women of Ulster find any other but us,' he said, 'to give them their bird-hunt to-day?'

'It is not seemly for thee to rage thus against them,' said Leborcham, 'for it is on thy account that the women of Ulster have assumed one of their three blemishes, even the blemish of blindness.' For there were three blemishes that the women of Ulster assumed, that of crookedness of gait, and that of a stammering in their speech, and that of blindness. Each of the women who loved Conall the Victorious had assumed a crookedness of gait; each woman who loved Cuscraid Menn, the Stammerer of Macha, Conchobar's son, stammered in her speech; each woman in like manner who loved Cú Chulainn, had assumed a blindness of her eyes, in order to resemble Cú Chulainn; for he, when his mind was angry within him, was accustomed to draw in one of his eyes so far that a crane could not reach it in his head, and would thrust out the other so that it was as great as a cauldron in which a calf is cooked.

'Yoke for us the chariot, O Loeg!' said Cú Chulainn. At that Loeg yoked the chariot, and Cú Chulainn went into the chariot, and he cast his sword at the birds with a cast like the cast of a boomerang, so that they flapped against the water with their claws and wings. And they seized upon all the birds, and they gave them and distributed them among the women; nor was there any one of the women, except Ethne alone, who had not a pair of those birds.

Then Cú Chulainn returned to his wife.

'Thou art angry,' said he to her.

'I am in no way angry,' answered Ethne, 'for I deem it as being by me that the distribution was made. And thou hast done what was fitting,' she said, 'for there is not one of these women but loves thee; none in whom thou hast no share; but for myself, none has any share in me but thou alone.'

'Be not angry,' said Cú Chulainn, 'if in the future any birds come to Mag Muirthemne or to the Boyne, the two birds that are the most beautiful among those that come shall be thine.'

A little while after this they saw two birds flying over the lake, linked together by a chain of red gold. They sang a gentle song, and a sleep fell upon all the men who were there except Cú Chulainn. Cú Chulainn rose up to pursue the birds.

'If thou wilt listen to me,' said Loeg (and so also said Ethne), 'thou wilt not go against them; behind those birds is some special power. Other birds may be taken by thee at some future day.'

'Is it possible that such claim as this should be made upon me?' said Cú Chulainn. 'Place a stone in my sling, O Loeg!'

Loeg thereon took a stone, and he placed it in the sling, and Cú Chulainn launched the stone at the birds, but the cast missed. 'Alas!' said he. He took another stone, and he launched this also at the birds, but the stone flew past them.

'Wretch that I am,' he cried; 'since the very first day that I assumed arms, I have never missed a cast until this day!' And he threw his spear at them, and the spear went through the shield of the wing of one of the birds, and the birds flew away, and went beneath the lake.

After this Cú Chulainn departed, and he rested his back against a stone pillar, and his soul was angry within him, and sleep fell upon him. Then saw he two women come to him; the one of them had a green mantle upon her, and upon the other was a purple mantle folded in five folds. And the woman in the green mantle approached him, and she laughed a laugh at him, and she gave him a stroke with a horsewhip. And then the other approached him, and she also laughed at him, and she struck him in the same way; and for a long time were they thus, each of them in turn coming to him and striking him, until he was all but dead; and then they departed from him.

Now the men of Ulster perceived the state in which Cú Chulainn was, and they cried out that he should be awakened; but 'Nay,' said Fergus, 'you shall not move him, for he is seeing a vision'; and a little after that Cú Chulainn arose from his sleep.

'What has happened to thee?' said the men of Ulster; but he had no power to bid greeting to them.

'Let me be carried,' he said, 'to the sick-bed that is in Tete Brece; not to Dun Imrith, nor yet to Dun Delgan.'

'Wilt thou not be carried to Dun Delgan, thy stronghold, to seek for Emer?' said Loeg.

'Nay,' said he, 'my word is for Tete Brece'; and thereon they bore him from that place, and he was in Tete Brece until the end of one year, and during all that time he had speech with no-one.

Now upon a certain day before the next Samhain, at the end of a year, when the men of Ulster were in the house where Cú Chulainn was, Fergus being at the side-wall, and Conall the Victorious at his head, and Lugaid Red-Stripes at his pillow, and Ethne Inguba at his feet; – when they were there in this manner, a man came to them, and he seated himself near the entrance of the chamber in which Cú Chulainn lay.

'What has brought thee here?' said Conall the Victorious.

'No hard question to answer,' said the man. 'If the man who lies yonder were in health, he would be a good protection to all of Ulster; in the weakness and the sickness in which he now is, so much the more great is the protection that they have from him. I have no fear of any of you,' he said, 'for it is to give to this man a greeting that I come.'

'Welcome to thee, then, and fear nothing,' said the men of Ulster; and the man rose to his feet, and he sang them the following verses:

> O Cú Chulainn! of thy illness
> Not great will be the length.
> They would heal thee if they were here,
> The daughters of Aed Abrat.

> Thus spoke Liban in Mag Cruach,
> By the side of Labraid the Swift:
> Love holds Fann's heart;
> She longs to be joined to Cú Chulainn.

> Goodly in truth would be the day
> When Cú Chulainn comes to my land.
> If he comes he shall have silver and gold;
> He shall have much wine to drink.

> Could he but love me enough for that,
> Cú Chulainn son of Sualtam!
> I have seen him in slumber,
> Without his arms, in very truth.

'Tis to Mag Muirthemne thou shouldst go,
On the night of Samain, without injury to thyself.
I will send thee Liban,
To heal thy sickness, O Cú Chulainn!

O, Cú Chulainn! of thy illness,
Not great will be the length.
They would heal thee if they were here,
The daughters of Aed Abrat.

'Who art thou, then, thyself?' said the men of Ulster.

'I am Angus, the son of Aed Abrat,' he answered; and the man then left them, nor did any of them know whence it was he had come, nor whither he went.

Then Cú Chulainn sat up, and he spoke to them.

'Fortunate indeed is this!' said the men of Ulster; 'tell us what it is that has happened to thee.'

'Upon Samain night last year,' he said, 'I indeed saw a vision'; and he told them of all he had seen.

'What should now be done, Father Conchobar?' said Cú Chulainn.

'This hast thou to do,' answered Conchobar; 'rise, and go to the pillar where thou wert before.'

Then Cú Chulainn went forth to the pillar, and then saw he the woman in the green mantle come to him. 'This is good, O Cú Chulainn!' said she.

'It is no good thing in my thought,' said Cú Chulainn. 'Wherefore camest thou to me last year?'

'It was indeed to do no injury to thee that we came,' said the woman, 'but to seek for thy friendship. I have come to greet thee,' she said, 'from Fann, the daughter of Aed Abrat; her husband, Manannán mac Lir (Son of the Sea), has abandoned her, and she has thereon set her love on thee. My own name is Liban, and I have brought to thee a message from my husband, Labraid the Swift Sword-Wielder, that he will give thee the woman Fann in exchange for one day's service to him in battle against Senach Siaborthe, and against Eochaid Iuil, and against Eóghan Inber.'

'I am in no fit state,' he said, 'to contend with men to-day.'

'That will last but a little while,' she said; 'thou shalt be whole, and all that thou hast lost of thy strength shall be increased to thee. Labraid shall bestow on thee that gift, for he is the best of all warriors that are in the world.'

'Where is it that Labraid dwells?' asked Cú Chulainn.

'In Mag Mell, the Plain of Delight,' said Liban; 'and now I desire to go to that land,' said she.

'Let Loeg go with thee,' said Cú Chulainn, 'that he may learn of the land from which thou hast come.'

'Let him come, then,' said Liban.

She and Loeg departed after that, and they went forward toward Mag Mell, the place where Fann was. And Liban turned to seek for Loeg, and she placed him beside her shoulder. 'Thou wouldst never go hence, O Loeg!' said Liban, 'wert thou not under a woman's protection.'

'It is not a thing that I have been accustomed to up to this time,' said Loeg, 'to be under a woman's guard.'

'Shame, and everlasting shame,' said Liban, 'that Cú Chulainn is not where thou art.'

'It were well for me,' answered Loeg, 'if it were indeed he who was here.'

They passed on then, and went forward until they came opposite to the shore of an island, and there they saw a skiff of bronze lying upon the lake before them. They entered into the skiff, and they crossed over to the island, and came to the palace door, and there they saw a man, and he came towards them. And thus spoke Liban to the man whom they saw there:

> Where is Labraid, the swift sword-handler,
> The head of victorious troops?
> Victory is in his strong chariot;
> He stains with red the points of his spears.

And the man replied to her thus:

> Labraid, the swift sword-handler –
> He is not slow: he will be strong.
> They are gathering for the battle;
> They are making ready for the slaughter
> That will fill Mag Fidga.

They entered into the palace, and they saw there thrice fifty couches within the palace, and three times fifty women upon the couches; and the women all bade Loeg welcome, and it was in these words that they addressed him:

> Welcome to thee, O Loeg,
> Because of thy quest:
> Loeg, we also
> Hail thee as our guest!

'What wilt thou do now?' said Liban; 'wilt thou go on without a delay, and hold speech with Fann?'

'I will go,' he answered, 'if I may know the place where she is.'

'That is no hard matter to tell,' she answered; 'she is in her chamber apart.'

They went there, and they greeted Fann, and she welcomed Loeg in the same fashion as the others had done.

Fann was the daughter of Aed Abrat; Aed means fire, and he is the fire of the eye: that is, of the eye's pupil: Fann moreover is the name of the tear that runs from the eye; it was on account of the clearness of her beauty that she was so named, for there is nothing else in the world except a tear to which her beauty could be likened.

Now, while they were thus in that place, they heard the rattle of Labraid's chariot as he approached the island, driving across the water. 'The spirit of Labraid is gloomy to-day,' said Liban; 'I will go and greet him.' And she went out, and she bade welcome to Labraid, and she spoke as follows:

> Hail to Labraid, swift sword-handler!
> Heir to an army – small and armed with javelins.
> He hacks the shields – he scatters the spears,
> He cleaves the bodies – he slaughters free men;
> He seeks for bloodshed – bright is he in the conflict:
> To thee, who war against the hosts, Labraid, hail!
>
> Hail to Labraid, the swift sword-handler!
> Heir to an army – small and armed with javelins.

Labraid did not reply to her, and the lady spoke again thus:

> Hail to Labraid, swift sword-handler!
> Ready in giving – generous to all – eager for combat;
> Scarred thy side -fair thy speech -strong thy hand,
> Kindly in ruling – hardy in judgments – powerful in
>   vengeance.
> He fights off the hosts. Hail, Labraid!

Hail to Labraid, swift handler of the battle-sword!

Labraid still made no answer, and she sang another lay thus:

Hail, Labraid, swift sword-handler!
Bravest of warriors – more proud than the sea!
He routs the armies – he joins the combats;
He tests the soldiers – he raises up the weak,
He humbles the strong. Hail, Labraid!

Hail, Labraid, swift sword-handler!

'Thou speakest not rightly, O woman,' said Labraid; and he then addressed her thus:

There is no pride or arrogance in me, oh wife!
And no deluding spell can weaken my judgment.
We are going now into a conflict of doubtful issue, decisive
and severe,
Where red swords strike in powerful hands,
Against the multitudinous and united hosts of Eochaid Iuil.
There is no presumption in me–no pride and no arrogance
in me, oh wife!

'Let now thy mind be appeased,' said the woman Liban to him. 'Loeg, the charioteer of Cú Chulainn, is here; and Cú Chulainn has sent word to thee that he will come to join thy hosts.'

Then Labraid bade welcome to Loeg, and he said to him: 'Welcome, O Loeg! for the sake of the lady with whom thou comest, and for the sake of him from whom thou hast come. Go now to thine own land, O Loeg!' said Labraid, 'and Liban shall accompany thee.'

Then Loeg returned to Emain, and he gave news of what he had seen to Cú Chulainn, and to all others beside; and Cú Chulainn rose up, and he passed his hand over his face, and he greeted Loeg brightly, and his mind was strengthened within him for the news that Loeg had brought him.

(At this point occurs a break in the story, resulting from the fact that the narrative in its present form is made up of at least two earlier accounts. Into the gap are inserted a description of the Bull-Feast at which Lugaid Red-Stripes is elected king over all Ireland; also the exhortation that Cú Chulainn, supposed to be lying on his sick-bed, gives to Lugaid as to the duties of a king. After this insertion, which has no real connection with the *narrative, the story itself proceeds, but from another point, for the thread is taken up at the place where Cú Chulainn has indeed awaked from his trance, but is still on his sick-bed; the message of Angus appears to have been given, but Cú Chulainn does not seem to have met Liban for the second time, and he lies at Emain Macha not at Tete Brece. Ethne has disappeared as an actor from the scene; her place is taken by Emer, Cú Chulainn's wife; and the whole style of the romance is altered for the better. Even if it were not for the want of agreement of the two versions, we could see that we have here two tales founded upon the same legend but by two different hands, the end of the first and the beginning of the second alike missing, and the gap filled in by the story of the election of Lugaid.)*

Now as to Cú Chulainn, it has to be related thus: He called upon Loeg to come to him; and 'Go, O Loeg!' said Cú Chulainn, 'to the place where Emer is; and say to her that fairy women have come upon me, and that they have destroyed my strength; and say also to her that it goes better with me from hour to hour, and bid her to come and see me'; and the young man Loeg then spoke these words in order to hearten the mind of Cú Chulainn:

> Little indeed is its use to a warrior –
> The bed where he lies in sickness.
> His illness is the work of the fairy folk,
> Of the women of Mag Trogach.
> They have beaten thee,
> They have put thee into captivity;
> They have led thee off the track.
> The power of the women has rendered thee impotent.
>
> Awake from the sleep in which thou art fighting
> Against beings who are not soldiers;
> The hour has come for thee to take thy place
> Among heroes who drive their chariots to battle.
> Place thyself upon the seat of thy war chariot.
> Then will come the chance
> To cover thyself with wounds,
> To do great deeds.
>
> When Labraid shows his power,
> When the splendor of his glory shines,

Then must thou arise,
Then wilt thou be great.

Little indeed is its use to a warrior –
The bed where he lies in sickness.
His illness is the work of the fairy folk,
Of the women of Mag Trogach.

And Loeg, after that heartening, departed; and he went to the place
where Emer was; and he told her of the state of Cú Chulainn.

'Ill has it been what thou hast done, O youth!' she said; 'for although
thou art known as one who dost wander in the lands where the fairy folk
dwell, yet no virtue of healing hast thou found there and brought for the
cure of thy lord. Shame upon the men of Ulster!' she said, 'for they have
not sought to do a great deed, and to heal him. Yet, had Conchobar thus
been fettered, had it been Fergus who lost his sleep, had it been Conall
the Victorious to whom wounds had been dealt, Cú Chulainn would
have saved them.' And she then sang a song, and in this fashion she sang
it:

O Loeg mac Riangabra! alas!
Thou hast searched fairyland many times in vain;
Thou tarriest long in bringing thence
The healing of the son of Dechtire.

Woe to the high-souled Ulstermen!
Neither foster-father or foster-brother of Cú Chulainn
Has made a search through the wide world
To find the cure for his brave comrade.
If Fergus, foster-father of Cú Chulainn, were under this
    spell,
And if, to heal him, there was needed the knowledge of a
    druid,
The son of Dechtire would never take repose
Until Fergus had found a druid who could heal him.

If it were the foster-brother of Cú Chulainn, Conall the
    Victorious,
Who was afflicted with wounds,
Cú Chulainn would search through the whole world
Until he found a physician to heal him.

If Loegaire the Triumphant
Had been overborne in rugged combat,
Cú Chulainn would have searched through the green
    meads of all Ireland
To find a cure for the son of Connad mac Iliach.

Alas! sickness seizes upon me, too,
Because of Cú Chulainn, the Hound of Conchobar's smith!
The sickness that I feel at my heart creeps over my whole body!
Would that I might find a physician to heal thee!

Alas! death is at my heart!
For sickness has checked the warrior
Who rode his chariot across the plain,
And now he goes no more
To the assembly of Muirthemne.

Why does he go forth no rnore from Emain?
It is because of the fairy folk that he lingers.
My voice grows weak and dies.

Month, season, year, all have gone by,
And yet sleep has not taken up its accustomed course.
There is no one by him. Not one fair word
Doth ever come to his ears, O Loeg mac Riangabra.

And, after that she had sung that song, Emer went forward to Emain that
she might visit Cú Chulainn; and she seated herself in the chamber
where Cú Chulainn was, and thus she addressed him: 'Shame upon
thee!' she said, 'to lie thus prostrate for a woman's love! Well may this
long sick-bed of thine cause thee to ail!' And it was in this fashion that
she addressed him, and she chanted this lay:

Arise, hero of Ulster!
Awake joyful and sound.
Look upon the king of Ulster, how great he is!
Long enough hast thou slept.

It is ill sleeping too deep;
It is the weakness that follows defeat;
Sleeping too long is like milk to repletion;
It is the lieutenant of death; it has all death's power.

Awake! Sleep is the repose of the sot;
Throw it off with burning energy.
I have spoken much, but it is love that inspires me.
Arise, hero of Ulster!

Arise, hero of Ulster!
Awake joyful and sound.
Look upon the king of Ulster, how great he is!
Long enough hast thou slept.

And Cú Chulainn at her word stood up; and he passed his hand over his face, and he cast all his heaviness and his weariness away from him, and then he arose, and went on his way before him until he came to the enclosure that he sought; and in that enclosure Liban appeared to him. And Liban spoke to him, and she strove to lead him into fairyland; but 'What place is that in which Labraid dwells?' said Cú Chulainn. 'It is easy for me to tell thee!' she said:

Labraid's home is over a pure lake,
Where troops of women congregate.
Easy for thee to go there,
If thou wilt know swift Labraid.

His skilled arm strikes down hundreds;
Wise are they who describe his deeds:
Beautifully purple the colours
Which are on the cheeks of Labraid.

He shakes his head like a wolf in the battle
Before the thin blood-stained swords.
He shatters the arms of his impotent enemies;
He shatters the bucklers of the warriors.

'I will not go thither at a woman's invitation,' said Cú Chulainn.

'Let Loeg go then,' said the woman, 'and let him bring to thee tidings of all that is there.'

'Let him depart, then,' said Cú Chulainn; and Loeg rose up and departed with Liban, and they came to Mag Luada, and to Bile Buada, and over the fair green of Emain, and over the fair green of Fidga, and in that place dwelt Aed Abrat, and with him his daughters.

Then Fann bade welcome to Loeg, and 'How is it,' said she, 'that Cú Chulainn has not come with thee?'

'It pleased him not,' said Loeg, 'to come at a woman's call; more-over, he desired to know whether it was indeed from thee that had come the message, and to have full knowledge of everything.'

'It was indeed from me that the message was sent,' she said; 'and let now Cú Chulainn come swiftly to seek us, for it is for to-day that the strife is set.'

Then Loeg went back to the place where he had left Cú Chulainn, and Liban with him; and 'How appears this quest to thee, O Loeg?' said Cú Chulainn.

And Loeg answered, 'In a happy hour shalt thou go,' said he, 'for the battle is set for to-day'; and it was in this manner that he spake, and described the fairy world thus:

> I went in the twinkling of an eye
> Into a marvellous country where I had been before.
> I reached a cairn of twenty armies,
> And there I found Labraid of the long hair.
>
> I found him sitting on the cairn,
> A great multitude of arms about him.
> On his head his beautiful fair hair
> Was decked with an apple of gold.
>
> Although the time was long since my last visit
> He recognised me by my five-fold purple mantle.
> Said he, 'Wilt thou come with me
> Into the house where dwells Failbe the Fair?'
>
> Two kings are in the house,
> Failbe the Fair and Labraid.
> Three fifties of warriors are about them.
> For all their great number they live in the one house.
>
> On the right are fifty beds,
> And on the beds, as many warriors;
> On the left, fifty beds,
> And a warrior on every bed.
>
> The beds have round columns,
> Beautiful posts, adorned with gold.
> They gleam brightly in the light
> Which comes from a stone, precious and brilliant.

At the door towards the west
On the side towards the setting sun,
There is a troop of grey horses with dappled manes,
And another troop of horses, purple-brown.
At the door towards the east
Are three trees of purple glass.
From their tops a flock of birds sing a sweetly drawn-out song
For the children who live in the royal stronghold.
At the entrance to the enclosure is a tree
From whose branches there comes beautiful and harmonious
    music.
It is a tree of silver, which the sun illumines;
It glistens like gold.

There are thrice fifty trees.
At times their leaves mingle, at times, not.
Each tree feeds three hundred people
With abundant food, without rind.

There is a well in that noble palace of the fairy-mound.
There you will find thrice fifty splendid cloaks,
With a brooch of shining gold
To fasten each of the cloaks.

There is a cauldron of invigorating mead,
For the use of the inmates of the house.
It never grows less; it is a custom
That it should be full forever.
There is a woman in the noble palace.
There is no woman like her in Erin.
When she goes forth you see her fair hair.
She is beautiful and endowed with many gifts.

Her words, when she speaks to anyone,
Have a marvellous charm.
She wounds every man to the heart
With the love she inspires.
The noble lady said,
'Who is the youth whom we do not know?
Come hither if it be thou
That art the servant of the warrior of Muirthemne.'

I yielded to her request with reluctance;
I feared for my honour.
She said to me, 'Will he come,
The only son of the excellent Dechtire?'

It is a pity that thou hast not gone,
O Cú Chulainn! Everyone asks for you.
You yourself should see how it is built,
The grand palace that I have seen.

If I owned the whole of Erin,
With supreme sovereignty over its fair inhabitants,
I would give it up – the temptation would be irresistible!
I would go and live in the country where I have just been.

I went in the twinkling of an eye
Into a country where I had been before.
I reached a cairn of twenty armies,
And there I found Labraid of the long hair.

'The quest then is a good one,' said Cú Chulainn.
    'It is goodly indeed,' said Loeg, 'and it is right that thou shouldst go
to attain it, and all things in that land are good.' And thus further also
spoke Loeg, as he told of the loveliness of the fairy dwelling:

They are beautiful women, victorious,
Never knowing the sorrow of the vanquished,
The daughters of Aed Abrat.
The beauty of Fann deserves glittering renown;
No king or queen is her equal.

I repeat what has been said to me:
She is a mortal daughter of Adam, without sin.
The beauty of Fann in our days,
Is beyond comparison.

I saw the glorious warriors
Armed with trenchant weapons,
With garments of bright colours;
These were not the garments of underlings.
I saw the women, joyous at the feast;
I saw the troop of maidens;

I saw the handsome boys
Walking about the trees on the hill.

In the house I heard the musicians
Playing for Fann.
If I had not made haste to go away
I would have got my hurt from that music.

I saw the hill where the house stands.
Ethne Inguba is a fair woman,
But the woman I speak of now,
Would drive entire armies to madness.

And Cú Chulainn, when he had heard that report, went on with Liban to
that land, and he took his chariot with him. And they came to the island
of Labraid, and there Labraid and all the women that were there bade
them welcome; and Fann gave an especial welcome to Cú Chulainn.

'What is there now set for us to do?' said Cú Chulainn.

'No hard matter to answer,' said Labraid; 'we must go forth and make
a circuit about the army.'

They went out then, and they came to the army, and they let their
eyes wander over it; and the host seemed to them to be innumerable.

'Arise, and go hence for the present,' said Cú Chulainn to Labraid;
and Labraid departed, and Cú Chulainn remained confronting the
army. And there were two ravens there, who spake, and revealed druid
secrets, but the armies who heard them laughed.

'It must surely be the madman from Ireland who is there,' said the
army; 'it is he whom the ravens would make known to us'; and the armies
chased them away so that they found no resting-place in that land.

Now at early morn Eochaid Iuil went out in order to bathe his hands
in the spring, and Cú Chulainn saw his shoulder through the hood of
his tunic, and he hurled his spear at him, and he pierced him. And he
by himself slew thirty-three of them, and then Senach Siaborthe
assailed him, and a great fight was fought between them, and Cú
Chulainn slew him; and after that Labraid approached, and he broke
before him those armies.

Then Labraid entreated Cú Chulainn to stay his hand from the
slaying; and 'I fear now,' said Loeg, 'that the man will turn his wrath
upon us; for he has not found a combat to suffice him. Go now,' said
Loeg, 'and let there be brought three vats of cold water to cool his heat.

The first vat into which he goes will boil over; after he has gone into the second vat, none will be able to bear the heat of it: after he has gone into the third vat, its water will have but a moderate heat.'

And when the women saw Cú Chulainn's return, Fann sang thus:

> Stately the charioteer that steps the road;
> If he be beardless it is because he is young.
> Splendid the course he drives over the plain,
> At eve on Aenach Fidgai.
> There is in each of his two cheeks
> a red dimple like red blood,
> a green dimple, a brown dimple,
> a crimson dimple of light colour.
>
> There are seven lights in his eye,
> It is a fact not to be left unspoken,
> Eyebrows brown, of noblest set,
> Eyelashes of chafer black.
>
> He outstrips all men in every slaughter;
> He traverses the battle to the place of danger
> There is not one with a high hardy blade,
> Not one like Cú Chulainn.
> Cú Chulainn it is that comes hither,
> The young champion from Muirthemne;
> They who have brought him from afar
> Are the daughters of Aed Abrat.
>
> Dripping blood in long red streams,
> To the sides of lofty spears he brings;
> Haughty, proud, high for valour,
> Woe be to him against whom he becomes angered.

Liban, moreover, bade a welcome to Cú Chulainn, and she sang as follows:

> Welcome to Cú Chulainn;
> Relieving king;
> A great prince of Mag Muirthemne;
> Great his noble mind;
> A battle-victorious champion;
> A strong valour-stone;
> Blood-red of anger;

Ready to arrange the champions of valour of Ulster;
Beautiful his complexion;
Dazzler of the eyes to maidens;
He is welcome.

'Tell us now of the deeds thou hast done, O Cú Chulainn!', cried
Liban; and Cú Chulainn replied to her thus:

I threw a cast of my spear
Into the court of Eóghan Inber.
I do not know – path of fame –
Whether it is good I have done, or evil.

A host fair, red-complexioned, on backs of steeds,
They pierced me upon all sides;
The people of Manannán son of Lir,
Invoked by Eóghan Inber.

I heard the groan of Eochaid Luil;
It is in good friendship his lips speak.
If the man has spoken true, it certainly won the battle,
The throw that I threw.

Now, after all these things had passed, Cú Chulainn slept with Fann,
and he abode for a month in her company, and at the end of the month
he came to bid her farewell. 'Tell me,' she said, 'to what place I may go
for our tryst, and I will be there;' and they made tryst at the yew tree by
the strand that is known as Iubar Cinn Trachta (Newry).

Now word was brought to Emer of that tryst, and knives were whetted
by Emer to slay the fairy woman; and she came to the place of the tryst,
and fifty women were with her. And there she found Cú Chulainn and
Loeg, and they were engaged in the chessplay, so that they did not
perceive the women's approach. But Fann marked it, and she cried out
to Loeg: 'Look now, O Loeg!' she said, 'and mark that sight that I see.'

'What sight is that of which thou speakest?' said Loeg, and he looked
and saw it, and thus it was that Fann addressed him:

Loeg! look behind thee!
Close at hand
Wise, well-ranked women
Press on us;
Bright on each bosom

> Shines the gold clasp;
> Knives, with green edges
> Whetted, they hold.
>
> As [towards] the slaughter chariot chiefs race,
> Comes Forgall's daughter; changed is her countenance.

'Have no fear,' said Cú Chulainn, 'thou shalt meet no foe; enter thou my strong car, with its bright seat: I will set thee before me, I will guard thee from harm against women, that swarm from Ulster's four quarters. Though the daughter of Forgall vows war against thee, though her dear foster-sisters she rouses against thee, bold Emer will dare no deed of destruction, though she rageth against thee, for I will protect thee.'

Moreover to Emer he said:

> I avoid thee, O lady, as heroes
> Avoid to meet friends in battle;
> The hard spear thy hand shakes cannot injure,
> Nor the blade of thy thin gleaming knife;
> For the wrath that rages within thee
> Is but weak, nor can cause me fear:
> It were hard if the war my might wages
> Must be quenched by a weak woman's power.

'Speak! and tell me, Cú Chulainn,' said Emer, 'why thou wouldst lay this shame on my head? I stand dishonoured before the women of Ulster, and all women who dwell in Erin, and all folk who love honour beside. Though I came on thee secretly, though I remain oppressed by thy might, and though great is thy pride in the battle, if thou leavest me, naught is thy grin. Why, dear youth, dost thou make such attempt?'

'Speak thou, Emer, and say,' said Cú Chulainn, 'should I not remain with this lady? For she is fair, pure and bright, and well skilled, a fit mate for a monarch, filled with beauty, and can ride the waves of ocean. She is lovely in countenance, lofty in race, and skilled in handicraft, can do fine needlework, has a mind that can guide with firmness.'

'Truly,' answered Emer, 'the woman to whom thou dost cling is in no way better than am I myself! Yet fair seems all that's red; what's new seems glittering; and bright what's set o'erhead; and sour are things well known! Men worship what they lack; and what they have seems weak; in truth thou hast all the wisdom of the time! O youth!' she said, 'once we dwelled in honour together, and we would so dwell again, if only I could find favour in thy sight!' and her grief weighed heavily upon her.

'By my word,' said Cú Chulainn, 'thou dost find favour, and thou shalt find it as long as I am in life.'

'Desert me, then!' cried Fann.

'No,' said Emer, 'it is more fitting that I should be the deserted one.'

'Not so, indeed,' said Fann. 'It is I who must go, and danger rushes upon me from afar.'

And an eagerness for lamentation seized upon Fann, and her soul was great within her, for it was shame to her to be deserted and straightway to return to her home; moreover, the mighty love that she bore to Cú Chulainn was tumultuous in her, and in this fashion she lamented, and lamenting sang this song:

> I it is that will go on the journey;
> I give assent with great affliction;
> Though there is a man of equal fame,
> I would prefer to remain.
>
> I would rather be here,
> To be subject to thee, without grief,
> Than to go, though you may wonder at it,
> To the sunny palace of Aed Abrat.
>
> O Emer! the man is thine,
> And well mayst thou wear him, thou good woman –
> What my arm cannot reach,
> That I am forced to wish well.
>
> Many were the men that were asking for me,
> Both in the court and in the wilderness;
> Never with those did I hold a meeting,
> Because I it was that was righteous.
> Woe! to give love to a person,
> If he does not take notice of it;
> It is better for a person to turn away
> Unless he is loved as he loves.
>
> With fifty women hast thou come hither,
> O Emer of the yellow hair,
> To capture Fann – it was not well –
>   And to kill her in her misery.

> There are thrice fifty, during my days,
> Of women, beautiful and unwedded,
> With me in my court together;
> They would not abandon me.

Now upon this it was discerned by Manannán that Fann the daughter of Aed Abrat was engaged in unequal warfare with the women of Ulster, and that she was like to be left by Cú Chulainn. And thereon Manannán came from the east to seek for Fann, and he was perceived by her, nor was there any other conscious of his presence saving Fann alone. And when she saw Manannán, Fann was seized by great bitterness of mind and by grief, and being thus she made this song:

> Behold the valiant son of Lir,
> From the plains of Eóghan Inber,
> Manannán, lord over the world's fair hills,
> There was a time when he was dear to me.
>
> Even if to-day he were nobly constant,
> My mind loves not jealousy.
> Affection is a subtle thing;
> It makes its way without labour.
>
> One day I was with the son of Lir,
> In the sunny palace of Dun Inber;
> We then thought, without doubt,
> That we should never be separated.
> When Manannán, the great one, espoused me,
> I was a worthy wife for him;
> For his life he could not win from me
> The odd game at chess.
>
> When Manannán the great married me,
> I was a wife worthy of him;
> A wristband of doubly-tested gold
> He gave to me as the price of my blushes.
>
> I had with me at going over the sea
> Fifty maidens of many gifts.
> I gave to them fifty men,
> Without reproach, as their companions.

Four fifties, without deceit,
That was the assembly of one house;
Twice fifty men, happy and perfect,
Twice fifty women, fair and healthy.

I see coming over the sea hither
No erring person sees him
The horseman of the crested wave;
He stays not on his long boats.

At thy coming, no one yet sees,
Anyone but a dweller in the fairy-mound;
Thy good sense is magnified by every gentle host,
Though they be far away from thee.

As for me, I would have cause for anger,
Because the minds of women are silly;
The person whom I loved exceedingly
Has placed me here at a disadvantage.

I bid thee farewell, O beautiful Cú;
We depart from thee with a good heart;
Though we return not, be thy good will with us;
Everything is good, compared with going away.

It is now time for me to take my departure;
There is a person to whom it is not a grief;
It is, however, a great disgrace,
O Loeg, son of Riangabar.

I shall go with my own husband,
Because he will not show me disobedience.
Now that you may not say it is a secret departure,
If you desire it, now behold me.

Then Fann rose behind Manannán as he passed, and Manannán greeted her: 'O woman!' he said, 'which wilt thou do? Wilt thou depart with me, or abide here until Cú Chulainn comes to thee?'

'In truth,' answered Fann, 'either of the two of you would be a fitting husband to adhere to; and neither of you is better than the other; yet, Manannán, it is with thee that I go, nor will I wait for Cú Chulainn, for he has betrayed me; and there is another matter, moreover, that weigheth with me, O noble prince!' said she, 'and that is that thou hast no consort who is of worth equal to thine, but such a one hath Cú Chulainn already.'

And Cú Chulainn saw Fann as she went from him to Manannán, and he cried out to Loeg: 'What does this mean that I see?'

'Tis no hard matter to answer,' said Loeg. 'Fann is going away with Manannán mac Lir, since she hath not pleased thee!'

Then Cú Chulainn bounded three times high into the air, and he made three great leaps towards the south, and thus he came to Tara Luachra, and there he abode for a long time, having no meat and no drink, dwelling upon the mountains, and sleeping upon the high-road that runs through the midst of Luachra.

Then Emer went on to Emain, and there she sought out king Conchobar, and she told him of Cú Chulainn's state, and Conchobar sent out his learned men and his people of skill, and the druids of Ulster, to find Cú Chulainn, and to bind him fast, and bring him with them to Emain. And Cú Chulainn tried to kill the people of skill, but they chanted wizard and fairy spells against him, and they bound fast his feet and his hands until he came a little to his senses. Then he begged for a drink at their hands, and the druids gave him a drink of forgetfulness, so that afterwards he had no more remembrance of Fann nor of anything else that he had then done; and they also gave a drink of forgetfulness to Emer that she might forget her jealousy, for her state was in no way better than the state of Cú Chulainn. And Manannán shook his cloak between Cú Chulainn and Fann, so that they might never meet together again throughout eternity.

BATTLES

16. The Battle of Findchorad

(Cath Findchorad)

Translated by M.E. Dobbs

T his is another of the prelude stories to the *Táin Bó Cuailgne*. It is
found only in one, very defective MS (B IV 1a) in the Royal Irish
Academy. It probably dates from the fifteenth century, but was
discovered bound into a seventeenth century MS. Many of the pages
were damaged and had been bound in the wrong order. The edition
prepared by Maighread Dobbs reconstructs, as far as is possible, the text
as it may once have been, but there are several omissions and the story
ends before the battle is concluded. Other texts which refer to this battle
show that it was intended as a sequel to the saga of *'Cath Ruis na Roig'*,
and that it ended with the Ulstermen as victors. The missing portions of
the story must have included the death of Eochaid mac Luchta.
Nevertheless, despite its fragmentary condition, the story is important
for the vivid descriptions it includes of the great brown and white bulls
which were the chief cause (or excuse) for the famous Cattle-Raid of the
Táin. As they are described, the bulls have a positively god-like aspect,
which recalls the sacred cattle of Indian myth. While there has never
been any sign of a creation myth in Celtic tradition (it seems that the
Celts were more interested in the ever-living present than in finite
beginnings or ends) this story has always seemed to us to have
something of the earth-shaking energy of such a myth. Another
interesting factor is the trios of spirits, Venom, Strife and Poison,
together with Silence, Scream and Wail, who are obviously part of the
array of Otherworld beings who throng Celtic myth and legend.

The possible site of the battle may be Corofin in Co Clare, but this
remains conjectural. However, the original editor points out that the
O'Davoren family lived nearby from the fifteenth to seventeenth
centuries, and that they probably possessed many ancient MSS, of which

this may well have been one. As previously, we have added conjectural words here and there to make for smoother reading.

When the four Fifths of Ireland were at Findchorad around Ailill and Medb and Eochaid mac Luchta, expecting to fight Conchobar and the Ulaid with him, they demanded advice as to how they should give battle. They were telling their druids to find out for them what would be the consequences of the battle and which of them would be defeated. Then the druids went [to] their knowledge and their learning viz.: Crom Déroil, Adna son of Uther, Maoil Cheann Mianach, and Daire [and] Fear Ceartne. They offered sacrifices to Mars, to Osiris, to Jove and to Apollo. These are the sacrifices they offered; the flesh of dogs, pigs and cats. Afterwards they went upon the hides of old hairless [old] bulls and on hurdles of the rowan tree, and their faces [turned] north towards Hell. The gods to whom they sacrificed told them to bring the Brown Bull of Cooley and the White-horned Bull and to start a fight. If the Brown Bull was routed the Ulaid (Ulstermen) would be defeated and, if the White-horn was routed, the Men of Ireland would be beaten.

Then the bulls were brought to the camp. MacRoth the chief herald came into the tent where was Eochaid and said to him: 'The two outstanding bulls of Ireland came to the fortress, the Brown Bull and the White-horn, and after they went to inspect them,' said he.

'What like are these bulls?' said Eochaid.

'Easily answered,' said MacRoth:

> 'to begin with the White-horn:
> that is a white-headed,
> white-footed bull,
> red, blood-red
> as though ruddy with red,
> as though bathed in blood,
> as though mingled with crimson;
> of faultless form
> from his nipple to his hump;
> a triple soft red mane.
> The lad of the herd of Ai,
> [The beast] of vengeance,
> the one who attacks alone;

with weighty tail,
with charger's breast,
with lapdog's bulging eye,
with salmon's snout,
with [furious] loins,
with dull-red horns,
with lustful tricks.
Triumphant birth victorious
pre-eminent and threatening
bellowing and proud,
glowering and fierce of face.
The strong ox of the herd
an arch-fiend . . . .
. . . .
The first plague the sprite
or goblin undertakes.
The chief glory of his territory
or his district
the speckled monster
from the Lands of the Fair,
the white-horn (. . . .)

As to the Brown Bull:
that is a dark-brown bull,
haughty, impetuous, very nimble,
active, terrifying, furious, destructive.
Scourging, victorious (. . .) in many ways.
Thick, plump, smooth-sided,
brave and strong as the other,
deep-chested, maned,
thick-necked, well-necked,
large-eyed, large-nostrilled, snorting.
The head high, deep-lowing,
fierce-eyed, curly,
very active, wrathful, powerful,
warlike, venomous, hostile.
With a forehead of bull's bristles,
with nimble tread,
with bearlike onset,

with snakelike venom,
with bestial heat,
with lionlike fury,
with thievish thrust;
on whom thrice fifty
full-grown boys find room
from neck to (. . .)
from the nipple to his hump.
(. . .)
The greatest ox of Dil,
the guardian bull of the world,
the Brown Bull of Cooley.

Then the king arose and with him an enormous throng of princes [went forth] to look at the bulls. When therefore the bulls saw each other they made great provocations (. . .) roared, heard to the clouds of heaven. They shook their thick hides [across] their foreheads as if they were foreheads of bull-seals. Their eyes reddened as if they were resin-flames. They became bristling and horrific so that the mane of each was as rough as an inlet of the sea. Like an iron crest was the ridge of each bull's back. Each of them dealt a fierce simultaneous stroke head to head as mighty as the impact of Cliodhna's Wave on the rocks, as if they were two rams in a field or two dogs fighting. Afterwards they ceased from the struggle and the conflict.

Then Eochaid went back to the fort and he left his son Lughaid and Maine Mingur (son of Ailill and Meadhb) to keep watch on the bulls as to which would win. Then the bulls felt the chilliness of the night and they encountered, skirmishing with their feet (. . .) against each other's chests (. . .) As huge as a vast mill-pond was the spancelling place of each. They twisted their limbs like boars fighting. They bared their teeth like dogs hunting (. . .) till the Brown Bull thrust his horn under the White-horn's shoulder and his bowels broke out over his left flank and he gave a bellow and fled over the Shannon.

[Then] Fraoch son of Fidach leader of the youths of Erris, and the Gamanraid of Erris Domnand with him viz. the Red Gamain of Rae, the Gamain of the Wood of Cead, the Gamain of Cloadh Cetracha, the Gamain of Trasgrad Triochu et cetera. Eochaid said to them, 'Ye ought,' said he, 'with swift heart attack the Ulaid.'

They came and undertook to give battle to the Ulaid (. . .) Fionn

son of Ros king of Leinster, and his son, and his brother, and Ailill
Gaoide (. . .) Fergus Fairge king of Ui Cennselaig (. . .) and three sons
of Cú (. . .) son of (. . .) Sedna Siothbace son of Nuada Neacht of
Leinster (. . .)

'(. . .) in every district; one hundred in each troop so that my army
numbers two thousand five hundred soldiers. These moreover are my
heroes and champions viz. Fiamain son of Foraoi, and Dearea son of
Cú Roi, and Gabhalglinne son of Dega, Bóclus son of Dega from
whom is named (. . .), (and Colpa was his mother from whom is named
Colpa Ford), (. . .) Cortha Ford and its (. . .)!' said Eochaid. Everyone
lauded the army. While they were there they subsequently saw a trio
coming straight towards them (. . .)

> [They had] red spears in their hands and [red]horses,
>   clothing and arms .
> 'Whence went ye?' said he [and whence have ye come?]'
> 'From the Sidh of Bodhb' said they, 'and to talk with thee
>   have we come!'
> 'What are your names?' said Eochaid.
> 'Easy to say' said one [of the three]. He recited the poem:

> 'Venom and Strife are the names
> [of those who come before you];
> Poison which distributes slaughter
> is in truth the third man.

> The deep colour of blood is on us,
> hairy to the feet, corrupt of head.
> Transgression is lawful for us
> as we are from thy blood.

> Because we are from thy blood
> therefore it is a red stone,
> as it would be from a mine
> of blood or of coal stuff.

> Because we are from thy blood
> therefore it is red gold;
> as they would cross wheels,
> as they would polish rust.

We have for you
news of the great battle.
Not as the ear decrees
shall the clamour be heard.

Since life is cut off
battle is not waged.
His speed is turned,
his course is turned.
His activity, his strength,
his shout, his right is turned.

His death is turned
as all will see.
His dread is turned,
his doom is turned.
His might, his wealth,
his wantonness,
his harshness is turned.

'[Well],' said Eochaid, 'let him be vigorous, let him be furious, and let him approach the Ulaid(. . .)'. The Ulaid simultaneously raised a wail as of bitter accusation:

[Let swords find their] edge
upon shapely well-matched breasts
beauty [destroyed by death,
young] nobles will step
on necks of grown men!'

'The poem the spectres make is beautiful,' said the druid (. . .) While the men of Ireland were there they saw another trio coming towards them. Their three heads were covered with wild-streaming grey hair, they had grey horses, grey spears; they were grey all over, horses and appearance alike. Eochaid asked them, 'whence are ye going?' said he, 'and whom are ye for?'

'We are three demon sisters,' said they, 'and Silence, Scream and Wail are our names and we have come hither from the Sidh of Bodhb,' said they. Then they recited the poem:

'We went from the *sídh* of Bodhb
till there were mysterious incitements,

the multitude of the host
and the destruction of the fort.
. . . .
       [It was]
at our wish and evil incitement
that the host made spear-play.
We are three demon sisters.
Silence is the third woman,
Scream and Wail [the other two]!'

[Then was heard cries of warriors] and the shrill yells of the old men approaching the tremendous conflict. But what is there but the destruction of strong men, the beheading of warriors, the hacking of heroes, the disfiguring of fair features, the whitening of lips; and thereby (. . .) eyes were blinded. After that the hand-to-hand fighting began. Then Fionn son of Ros, king of Leinster, his son MaicNia, Feargal, son of Ros his brother, Boirrach son of Antech and Colla son of Fathemon went into the fray till they met the following five leading soldiers; Little Feithean, Big Feithean, Eo son of Orne, Ogma and Tollchend and they fought together. Fionn and Eo attacked each other and a fierce deadly fight took place which ended in Eo being killed by Fionn. Ogma and Tollchend attacked Cuilleasg of Breg till they and a hundred fighting men who were with each of them fell by Cuilleasg and his men, as is said:

    'By Fionn son of Ros – illustrious course –
    fell Eo son of Orne.
    By Cuilleasg of Breg the smiter
    fell Ogma and Tollcend!'

Big Feithean attacked Borrach and a hard and cruel struggle took place between them till Fethean flung a spear at Borrach which laid him low. Springing up he struck a fierce [hard] blow with his broad-grooved sword at Fethean and beheaded him. Little Fethean attacked Colla son of Fatheman and he slew Fethean, as the verse has it:

    'By Borrach – it was a tragic deed –
    fell Big Fethean.
    Little Fethean was cut down
    by Colla son of Fatheman.'

Then it was that the Leinster army uttered a shout of exultation and boasting about the contest. When Conchobar heard that he sent Aodh the poet to seek Glasne his son; and Mes Deaghad son of Amergen, and Eóghan son of Durthacht and Laegaire the Victorious and the poet said:

> 'Oh Laegaire, victorious hero,
> lion who overthrows the salmon,
> good torch-head,
> good defence in every victory!'

Then these four warriors of the Ulaid came to the battle with mutual strength and sympathy and uttered their war-cry against the Leinstermen. Then Glasne and Mes Deaghad charged at the spot where was the royal crown. They made an attack on Fionn and on his son and on his brother. Then Fionn king of Leinster did indeed fall by them. Feargal son of Ros took the crown. He put it on Male Nía's head. The struggle [never] ceased. Then Rae and Clotholl the Shapely attacked (. . .) Laogaire and four hundred warriors along with them and they all fell by Laogaire. However Eóghan son of Durthacht was (not) reviled for the sake of Ulster for the way he went into battle, for [it was] foot by neck and neck by foot was every path through which he strode in the fight and he slew these four chief soldiers; Connla, Coirpre, Oilill and Imit, as is said:

> 'Rae the shapely, Clotholl the renowned
> (fell) by Laogaire full furious,
> by Eoghan (fell) Connla and Coirpre,
> Oilill and Imit loftily!'

Then three sons of Droighen, Ramh, Aodh and Buan, made an attack on the Redheads, as is in the verse:

> 'Three sons of Droighen,
> Ramh Aodh and Buan,
> with fair clipped heads
> We remember [how they fought].
> There they killed the Red-heads!'

Then Meadhb and Ailill urged the aforesaid Fergus son of Rogh, MacCecht, Fraoch son of Fiodach and the Gamanraid, Fiamain son of Foraoi and Dearea son of CuRoi to go and enter the battle. Then those gentlemen went boldly, audaciously, swiftly to the fight by the advice of Meadhb and Oilill. When Fergus entered the battle lie unsheathed the Calad-bolg (hard blade) and began to hack heroes, to slay [them and] to overthrow champions, to mangle brave soldiers so that he cleared an enormous breach (in his) battle charge. It was trying to stop a tidal wave to rush against [him], for every blow he struck was like the impact of a wave on the shore. Then Fionncadh son of Concobhar and Fionncadh son of Conall Cernach attacked Cano Gall and assaulted him so that a perilous, rough, bitter fight took place between them. Cano Gall threw a spear at Fergus who avoided the spear whirling in mid air. Corbmac Conloinglus gave a rough, powerful, hostile blow at Cano which cut off his head. Then Fergus slew the other two, as is said:

> 'Corpmac Conloingius slew Cano the foreigner
> from over the green sea-stream.
> The other two – it was bitter passion –
> and impetuous is Fergus who caused it!'

Then Corpmac laid his hand on Ferghus and said to him: 'What you have done is wicked, hard-hearted and a desolation of families and (. . .)'

17. The Battle of Mag Mucrama

(Cath Maíge Mucrama)

Translated by Caitlín Matthews

C*ath Maige Mucrama* is a battle fought between two foster-brothers over a faery musician: a dispute that is finally settled by the worst deed that any foster-parent can perform. The war originally breaks out because of Ailill's assault upon the *sídhe* mound of Cnoc Aine, where the king of the *sídhe*, Eogabul, is killed and his daughter, Aine, is raped. Fer Fí, the *tiompán*-player, and brother of Aine, allows himself to be taken and become the cause of a dispute between Ailill's own son Eóghan and his foster-son, Lugaid. The story then follows Lugaid's exile in Alba and the strange account of the mouse-feast, his return to invade Ireland and his eventual overthrow at the hands of his foster-father.

This story would have torn at the loyalties of the Irish listener because fosterage was closer and more sacred than a blood relationship. Foster-siblings and foster-parents had honourable and high respect for each other. The fact that Eóghan and his foster-brother, Lugaid mac Conn, come to blows and then to war is all the more lamentable.

Our translation is from the *Book of Leinster* 288a. ff. as edited by Whitley Stokes. The story has been rendered clearer by the repetition of character's relationships to each other so that the reader can accurately distinguish who is meant between a clump of male pronouns. The curious term, *condailbe* – a form of love for one's people and land that wells up with deep emotion – I have translated as 'tribal affection'.

1. The man in the yew tree

Ailill Olom mac Mug Núadat of the seed of Eber mac Mil of Spain, was king of Munster. His wife was Sadb, daughter of Conn of the Hundred Battles. Her three sons by Ailill were Eóghan, Cian and Cormac, from whom the Eoghanacht, the Cíanacht and Dálcassians are descended. The foster-son of Ailill and Sadb was Lugaid mac Con of the Corco Loígde, who was nursed on the self-same knee and suckled at the same breast as Eóghan mac Ailill.

One Samhain night, Ailill went to round up his horses on Cnoc Aine. A bed was made for him. That night the hill was rendered bare (?of horses) and no-one knew who had done this thing. Twice this happened to Ailill to his great wonderment. He dispatched messengers to the poet, Ferches mac Commán who lived in Mairg in Leinster. The poet was both seer and warrior, and he came to speak to Ailill.

Another Samhain night, they went to the hill. Ailill stood upon the hill, while Ferches hid to one side. While he listened to the grazing of horses, Ailill fell asleep. The horses had come from the *sídhe* followed by Eogabul mac Durgabul, king of the *sídhe*, and Aine, daughter of Eogabul with a bronze *tiompán* in her hand, playing before him.

Ferches sprang up and struck him, but Eogabul jumped up on to the *sídhe* mound. Then Ferches threw his great spear and broke his back. When he reached the *sídhe*, Ailill raped Aine. While he was upon her, the woman sucked his ear so that neither flesh nor sinew ever grew on it again. And this is why he was called Ailill Olom, or Bare-Ear, since that time.

'Badly have you behaved to me,' said Aine, 'in raping me and killing my father. I will violate your person for this and will ensure that none of your belongings will be in your keeping when we part.'

The name of that woman is given to this hill, Cnoc Aine.

Brug Ríg, the Kingly Hostel, was the home of Ailill near the great river, Maigue. A poet said of it,

> The waters of Maigue shall be a stream
> Like a rush-light without luminence
> Because it passes beside the court
> Of Aed in mac Mellán the wise.

Another time, Eóghan mac Ailill and Lugain mac Conn, his foster-brother, visited Art mac Conn, the uncle of Eóghan, when he was making a circuit of Connacht. He was going to fetch horses and bridles from him. As they passed the Maigue, they heard a music coming from a yew-tree above the waterfall. They fell to arguing about the man that was playing a *tiompán* of three strings whom they had taken out of that tree, and took him back to Ailill that he might judge between them.

'What's your name?'

'Fer Fí, son of Eogabul.'

'Why have you come back?' asked Ailill.

'We are arguing over this man,' said the foster-brothers.

'What kind of man is he?'

'A really good *tiompán* player.'

'Let him play his music,' said Ailill.

'Sure enough,' said the man.

First he played them the *golltraigh*, the sorrow-strain, which made them sad with grief and lamentation. He was asked to stop. Then he played the *gentraigh*, the laughter-strain, and they laughed so hard that you could almost see their lungs. Then he played the *suantraigh*, the sleep-strain, so that they fell into a deep sleep until the next day. He made off towards the direction from whence he had come, leaving a good deal of trouble fermenting behind him, just as he'd planned.

Afterwards, they rose.

'Speak your judgement, Ailill!'

'There seems little use!' said Ailill. 'Alright, what did you say when you found the man?'

Lugaid said, 'I said "the music is mine."'

Eóghan said, 'I said "the musician is mine."'

'So be it,' said Ailill, 'the man belongs to Eóghan.'

'That's a bad judgement!' exclaimed Lugaid.

'It is truly given,' said Ailill.

'It's not just!' said Lugaid. 'Your usual justice is absent from your mouth.'

'It's not right for a subject like you to rebuke him!' said Eóghan.

'Well, it will be a subject like me who will sever your head and stamp upon your face,' said Lugaid.

'Oh yes, and how will you do that?' asked Eóghan.

'On the battle-field,' said Lugaid. 'A month from this day, come and meet me me on Cend Abrat.'

And so it was. A month on from that day, they met, each with his army until the battle-lines faced each other. On Lugaid mac Conn's side, was his foster-father Lugaid Lága mac Mug Núadat. Lugaid confered with his jester, Déra of the Dáirine, who had the same appearance and size as Lugaid.

'Good!' said Lugaid. 'Now Eóghan will challenge me to single combat and because of his inflammatory humour, and with him being the son and heir of one king and the grandson of another, he will doubtless overcome me.'

'Those words sit badly on your lips!' said the jester. 'You are ruined! Let me go against him with your crown on my head and me wearing your battle-harness, so that everyone will say that you've been killed there. If I should fall, then go away at once, since everyone will say that it's you who are dead and that the battle is won. But Eóghan will be looking for you in the battle-crush. If he sees the calves of your legs, then you will be wounded.'

So they did this and the jester was killed. But Eóghan knew that it wasn't Lugaid he had killed. He began to search the field for him. 'Lugaid's fallen!' everyone shouted, 'the battle is done!'

And so it was and Lugain was defeated. But then, Eóghan spied amid the battle-press the two calves of Lugaid shining like the snow of one night. Eóghan chased after him, cast at him and struck him in the calf. Which is how the place Brén gairr or 'Prurient Pus' gets its name, from where the pus gushed out.

'Has the blow hit the spot?' asked Eóghan.

Then the battle was truly over. They have sung about it,

> The battle of Cend Abrat overcame
> Mac Conn of the hundred spoils.
> After seven years – hardly impatient –
> he cowardly fought at Mucrama.

2. At the mouse feast

And so that was how Lugaid was unable to stay in Ireland, because of Eoghan. So he retreated to Alba, though nobody knew how far he he gone. Lugaid Lága accompanied him, in a company consisting of three time nine in all. They fled to the king of Alba. Now Lugaid specifically told his followers that they must take care not to be recognised by the king of Alba, because of Art mac Conn, king of Ireland. Lugaid instructed his people to be obedient to each other as if each man was set as king over the other. He also told them not to call him by his name.

The king of Alba welcomed them. But they didn't tell him their names or where they had come from, only saying that they were fellow-Gaels. A pig and an ox were given to them every night for a year in the private house that they had been given.

Now the king could not help wondering about the splendour of their appearance, nor at their accomplished manner of winning in battles and conflict, nor the way at which they excelled everyone in assemblies, games and sports, nor in the playing of *branduch*, *buanbach* and *fidchell*, and he wondered whether one was leader over the others.

One day, when Lugaid was playing at *fidchell* with the king, they saw a man in some foreign clothes coming towards them in the house.

'Where does that man hail from?' asked the king.

'Of the Gael,' he said.

'What art do you practise?' asked the king.

'Poetry,' he said.

'What's the news from the Irishman, then?' asked the king. 'Is the lordship of Art mac Conn good?'

'It is good indeed,' said the man. 'No better lord ever ruled in Ireland as he.'

'Who's the king of Munster now?' asked the king.

'Eóghan mac Ailill,' said the poet, 'since his father is now an old man.'

'And what of Lugaid mac Conn?' asked the king.

'No-one knows what has befallen him since his banishment by Eóghan mac Ailill.'

'What a dreadful thing!' said the king. 'Sorrow upon Ireland to have lost him! But what of Lugaid's people? How are they?'

'In a bad way,' said the poet. 'They suffer in bondage, oppression and slavery to Eóghan.'

And when Lugaid heard this news, he had just taken the king's gold fidchellmen. He placed his finger tips upon two or three of them so that the row in front of him fell over.

The king looked at him, 'A wave of tribal affection comes over you,' he observed.

The poet who had told this news went away and Lugaid went outside.

'Well, my warriors,' said the king. 'I reckon that is Lugaid who's just gone outside. I see it from his demeanour.'

The following day, another man of Lugaid's party was summoned and told the same story. He also behaved in a similar manner.

'It's true then,' said the king. 'This is Lugaid, and from fear of me, they do not tell us their names. Let's try a trick on them to find out. Bring a pig and an ox on the hoof to be given to them, but say that their own people must prepare it. They will cast lots between them. I bet Lugaid will be left out of the lot-casting. Let the steward watch them.'

Nevertheless, Lugaid did participate in the lottery.

'Alright,' said the king to his steward, 'discover for whom the serving is made.'

But there was no-one present, only the steward at the feast.

'Alright then,' said the king, 'kill me some mice.'

Before each of the men, a mouse was served, still in its skin, and they were all told that they would be put to death if they didn't eat the mice. They reddened at the thought of it. Then they became very pale. They had never before been in such a hard place as this.

'How are they doing?' asked the king.

'They are much troubled by the plates heaped before them.'

'Such are the left-overs of Munster, in spite of full dishes,' said the king. 'Tell them that they will be killed if they refuse to eat up.'

'No luck upon the one who issued that command,' said Lugaid, taking the mouse into his mouth while the king watched him.

At that, all the other men put the mice into their mouths. There was one poor fellow who kept retching it up as soon as he felt the mouse's tail upon his lips.

'A sword is against your throat!' said Lugaid, 'The mouse must be eaten right down to the tail!' And he swallowed the tail down.

'I see that you are obeyed,' said the king from the door.

'I give obedience to them also,' said Lugaid.

'I give you welcome,' said the king. 'Why did you conceal yourself from me?'

'Out of fear of you,' said Lugaid.

'If I had known who you were, I would have helped avenge you,' said the king.

'Such help might still assist me today,' said Lugain.

'My assistance is yours,' said the king. 'I am the king of Alba. The daughter of the king of Britain is my mother. The daughter of the king of the Saxons is my wife. Take them with you to avenge your wrong.'

'That contents me,' said Lugaid.

So it was that one man welded these different hosts into a single host. At Port Rig in Alba, there was an assembly of ships, galleys and boats from off the Saxon coast, with the British amd great gathering of curachs with them. They say that there was a one bridge of curachs stretching between Ireland and Alba.

3. The conception of the two sons

Lugaid joined that army together and brought the great and terrible host to Ireland to avenge his wrong. Not one true man did he bring to Ireland. They invaded the land, receiving the submission of many.

They went unopposed until they reached Mag Mucrama in Crích Oc mBethrae, north of Aidne, above Dublin.

Mag Mucrama was named after the magical pigs that had emerged from the cave of Cruachan, which is Ireland's gate to hell. Out of this gate came the three-headed creatures that wasted Ireland until Amairgin father of Conall Cernach fought against them alone before the gaze of Ulster. Also from that cave had come a crocus-coloured flock of birds whose breath had withered up growth in Ireland until the Ulstermen had killed them with their slings. Out of that cave three pigs emerged. Over whatever land they passed, no corn, grass or leaves would grow until seven years had passed. Whenever anyone attempted to count them, they immediately passed into another region. Whoever counted them successfully was invariably wrong in his reckoning.

'There are three of them,' one man would say.

'No, there are seven!' said another.

'There are definitely nine,' said another.

'It's eleven.'

'It's thirteen!'

They were impossible to count, nor could anyone kill them, for whenever you struck at them, they vanished.

Once, Medb of Cruachan and Ailill (her husband) went to Mag Mucrama to count them. So they counted. Medb was in her chariot and one of the pigs leapt into it.

'There's another pig, Medb!' everyone cried.

'No, it's one less,' said Medb, pulling so upon the pig's leg that the skin over its forehead split open and vanished, leaving the skin in her hand with the leg-bone still attached. This is how Mag Mucrama was named.

Lugaid mac Conn was permitted to overcome Ireland until he reached Mag Mucrama, west of Connacht.

'The time has come to give battle to these foreigners,' said Art mac Conn. (Lugaid's brother.)

'Time indeed!' agreed Eóghan mac Ailill.

The day before the battle, Eóghan went to Díl mac Chrecga of the Ossairge, who lived in Druim Díl. He was a blind druid.

'Come with me,' said Eóghan, 'and satirise these men and sing an incantation over them.'

'Well enough,' he said.

'Let me come with you,' said his unmarried daughter, Moncha, for she served as her father's charioteer.

As they reached Mag Clíach, the druid knew from the way Eóghan spoke that he was doomed.

'Well, Eóghan,' said the druid. 'Do you leave any children?'

'Not very many,' said Eóghan.

'Well then, daughter,' said Díl, 'go with Eóghan, for maybe the kings of Munster will be descended from me.'

A bed was made for the couple. The boy that was conceived there was a good one, Fiacha Mullethan mac Eóghan. He was also called Fiacha Fer-da-Líach (man of two sorrows) for his father was killed on the day on which he had been conceived and his mother died on the day he was born. Each of these misfortunes was a sorrow, hence his name.

This was how he came to be called Mullethan of 'Broad Crown.' As the labour pains seized Moncha at Ath Demthend upon the Suir, her father said, 'It's a pity that it's not tomorrow that you went into labour, for then the child would take precedence over Ireland forever.'

'Truly, I will see to it,' she said, 'for unless he comes through my two sides, he shall come no other way.' And she took herself off into the river and lowered herself upon a stone that stood in the middle of the ford. 'This will delay things,' said she. And she remained in that position until the third hour of the next day.

'It's time now,' said her father. At which she collapsed and expired.

The head of the baby had broadened against the stone, which is why he was called Fiacha Mullethan, father of all the Eóghanacht.

Art mac Conn crossed the Shannon westwards, with a great host of Irishmen. The night before the battle, he sheltered with Olc Aiche, the smith of the Connachta. Olc Aiche said to him, 'It's a great host that Lugaid mac Conn has assembled against you. The British and Alban cattle bellow loudly against you. Their minds are not upon retreating because their flight would be far indeed, beyond the Alps some of them come from! You know that there is among your men one who has done badly. From him, Lugaid is owed something, I think. How many children have you left, Art?'

'One son,' said Art.

'Not enough,' said the druid. 'Sleep tonight with my daughter, Achtan. For it was promised that a great honour will come from me.' This was true, for great in honour was Cormac mac Art mac Conn.

And so Art slept with Achtan and Cormac was conceived. Art told her that she would bear a son and that he would be king of Ireland. He also told her about every treasure-hoard he had concealed that might benefit his son. He told her that he would die the next day and left her. And he instructed that she was to bring her son to his Connacht friend for fostering. And so the next day he went into battle.

4. The second Battle of Mag Mucrama

Lugaid had his plans prepared: half of his troops had hidden themselves in the ground, in holes hidden by a hurdle with earth spread over them, and sticking through the hurdles were broken spear points where the best of the Irish men were. The other half were in this battle-order: the leg of an Irish warrior was tied to the leg of an Alban one, so that Irishman might not run away, and there were two Britons placed on each side of a Irishman.

The opposing battle lines were drawn up. The kings were positioned in the forefront of the battle, Lugain mac Conn, with Lugaid Lága and Béinne Brit at the head of on side, and Art mac Conn, with Eóghan mac Ailill and Corbb Cacht mac Ailill at the head of the other.

Lugaid challenged Eóghan to single combat. Eóghan refused, saying that he wouldn't fight him this time since the last time he had behaved badly to Lugaid. But Lugaid said that there would be no jester taking his place this time and that, even if he was killed, he would rather be eaten by the wolves of Ireland rather than be exiled from his land any longer.

The air above them was black with demons waiting to seize their miserable souls into hell. Only two angels were there, but these were over Art, accompanying him everywhere in the host because he was the rightful ruler.

Then each of the battalions rushed towards each other. Their attack was truly dreadful. Terrible sights were seen. Clouds of chalk and lime rose towards the clouds from the clash of shields and targes being struck with swords, and from the double-sided spears and darts being blocked by the warriors. There was a terrible splintering and crash of shields being hit by swords and stones. A sharp hail of weapon-flights rained down. Blood gushed and seeped from the limbs of the fighters and through the sides of the soldiers.

The Lugaids raced through the battle-press like bears falling upon pigs, striking each man down in turn. Each man wore a combed helmet and an iron breastplate, with a great sword in his hand. They fell upon the host, killing hundreds.

In just such a way, Eóghan mac Ailill and Corbb Cacht mac Ailill fought on their side.

Keen and ruthless was the meeting of the Irish and Alban troops. They almost squashed each other's feet as they struck at each other. As they grappled, men would be wounded by the underground troops, wounded in the back of the head and cast down. The Alban troops sprang out of the ground upon the Irish and closed in about them.

Then it was the Art mac Conn and the Irish suffered defeat and were killed. They fled away southwards toward Ath Cliath in Crích Oac mBethrae. Ailill Olom's seven sons have their grave to the north of this ford. But Taurloch Airt, where Lugaid Lága mac Mug Núadat struck off Art's head on the stone of Taurloch, lies far north of it at Art Senbó.

When Béinne Brit was severing the head of Eóghan mac Ailill, Lugaid Lága fell upon him. It is said that a wave of tribal affection came upon him, as Béinne Brit was hacking at his shoulders,

> Low is the blow struck by Béinne,
> high is the blow struck by Béinne;
> that act wrings my spirit to its limit,
> that blow given by Béinne the Brit.

So saying, Eóghan struck Béinne across the neck so that his head fell upon Eóghan's breast. While he was doing this, Lugaid mac Con came upon him, 'That's no way to treat allies, is it, Lugaid?' he said.

'What does it matter to you?' said Lugaid. 'I shall give you the king of Ireland's head instead of this one.'

Then Lugaid went northwards after the retreating Irish until he fell upon Art and cut off his head, which is why Turloch Airt is called that in Crích Oc mBethrae.

After this, Lugaid mac Conn usurped the kingship of Ireland by force and was in Tara for seven years. He took Cormac mac Art into fosterage.

5. The vengeance of Ailill

But Ailill Olom, father of Eóghan, was still alive. And this was his chorus:

> Worn out are my shoes,
> Unfilled by son or grandson.
> This is my chief bequest:
> I swear hate upon Mac Conn.

This was the refrain of Lugaid mac Conn after his jester had been killed:

> I have emitted no laugh
> since the death of Da Déra;
> my grief has reason enough
> from the loss of Dárini's jester.

And this was the chorus of Sadb, daughter of Conn of the Hundred Battles:

> Alas for myself! alas for Clíu!
> since Fer Fí was found within a yew;
> and caused the death of Art mac Conn
> and the seven sons of my Olom.

> Alas for myself! alas for Clíu!
> since Fer Fí was found within a yew;
> unequal combat it brought for Art,
> and a deep-digged grave for Corbb Cacht.

Now it happened, that some sheep ate the woad-crop of Lugaid's queen, and the case was brought to him to judge. 'I pronounce that the sheep should be held forfeit for their deed,' said Lugaid. But the little boy, Cormac, who sat on the couch beside him said, 'No foster-father! The shearing of the sheep's wool would be a fairer judgement for the eating of the woad plants, since the woad will grow as will the sheep's wool.'

'That's a true judgement, alright,' said everyone. 'It's the son of true lord who has uttered it!'

As they said this, one side of the house fell down the hillside, the side in which the bad judgement had been given. So it remains for all time, the Clóenferta or crooked mound of Tara. They have sung of it,

> It seems that Lugaid, salmon of heroes,
> is mystified, gives crooked judgement.
> To one side leans, forever after,
> the lop-side fort to all men's laughter.

And though Lugaid remained another year in the kingship of Tara, no grass pierced the earth, no leaf came on the tree and no head upon the grain. And because of this, the men of Ireland stripped him of the kingship because he was an illegal ruler.

Then Lugaid went westwards into his own lands with his migrant band but Lugaid Lága didn't accompany him. 'I shall come no more to the place where I opposed my brother because of you and where I killed my kindred. I shall submit myself to the son of the king whom I killed.'

Lugaid mac Conn tried three times to persuade Lugain Lága to come with him, then bade him farewell. He went westwards to Ailill to look after his foster-father and came into the court. Sadb, his foster-mother, put her arms about his neck, saying, 'Do not go, my little son! The man you are going to see is bad and unforgiving.'

'You are welcome here,' said Ailill. 'Come let us discuss things and make arrangements for me to become your father in truth and to make you my son, since I have no sons left to support me.'

Then Ailill laid his cheek upon Lugaid's, and grazed his (foster-son's) skin with a poisonous tooth that he had in his head.

'That has struck deeply,' he said, 'soon you will be grieving,' and left him.

Then Lugaid met Sadb, who looked upon him and cried, 'Sorrow!

> 'This is the greeting that kills a king!
> wound of tooth's poison around you rings!
> a drowsing seizes you, changes your shape!
> Alas, the last leave-taking I now make!'

Her words came true. Afterwards, Ferches mac Commán, the poet, came to Ailill who said to him, 'Go, follow Lugaid.' Only three days had elapsed and the skin of Lugaid's cheek had melted away.

Ferches followed him. Lugaid had reached his own territory by that time and laid his back against a hosting stone, when he saw Ferches.

'Do not come near,' said Lugaid. And his men made a shield-wall between them. Then Ferches cast his spear towards him across the host, and it pierced Lugaid's forehead and the pillar-stone which rang out even as Lugaid withered away, lifeless.

Then Ferches retreated before Lugaid's host into the white-water that he might shave the spear-shaft into splinters upon the water. Which is why those waters are called Ess Ferches. Of them, Sadb, daughter of Conn, would say,

> 'Alas for myself! alas for Clíu!
> since Fer Fí was found within a yew;
> this deed heralds my grave before long:
> the cast made by Ferches at Mac Con.'

Then Ailill said,

> 'Thirty years until this day,
> "old, worn-out ancient" has been my lay.
> What's roused me from my long complaint?
> Is Mac Commáin's skilled spear-feint.'

And Ailill held the kingship of Munster for seven years from that day.

This is the battle of Mag Mucrama in which Art son of Conn, the seven sons of Ailill and a mighty number of slaughtered Irishmen fell besides them. It has been said,

> 'The battle of Mag Mucrama
> where many kings fell.
> Lament for Art mac Conn,
> the greatest of them all!'

However others say that Lugaid mac Conn held the kingship of Tara for thirty years. As it is said,

> 'Mac Conn took Banba's land
> each side of the green clear sea.
> For thirty years in honour's hand
> he reigned the king of all Ireland.'

WISDOM
AND LORE

18. Fingen's Nightwatch

(Airne Fingein)

Translated by T.P. Cross and A.C.L. Brown

Essentially this story is a framework for a collection of lore and wisdom drawn from the entire array of Celtic tradition. The formulae, in which Fingen (an obscure king of Munster around 123 CE) is visited by a faery woman with the wonderful name of Wheelsplendour daughter of Fresh-Flowery, and asks her what wonders there are in Ireland on that particular night (or perhaps in the future), enables the author to throw in anything and everything he knows – which is no small amount, as it transpires.

We never learn the precise reason for the nightwatch, though the implication is that Fingen is concerned by the fact that the new high king of Ireland, Conn of the Hundred Battles, is not well disposed towards him – a fact which is borne out by the end of the tale. The faery woman seems to be trying to distract him from gloomy thoughts, and prophesies a number of events that will take place over the next twelve months. In the process of this a number of episodes from other tales are referenced, including several that we have included here. Cross and Brown's own notes are very full, and readers are referred to these for more information. Some of the more notable elements are discussed below.

The Book of Fermoy calls the fairy 'Bacht' and says that she was from Sliabh na m-Ban or Sid Boidb (modern Slieve Naman). Druim Finghin, where the story takes place, is a ridge extending from near Castle-Lyons in the county of Cork to the south side of the Bay of Dungarvan, in the county of Waterford.

According to the *Prose Dindshenchas*, Boand, the wife of Nechtan, son of Labraid, was foolish enough to go widdershins around a secret well on the green of her husband's fairy-mound, which only Nechtan and his three cupbearers, Flesc (Rod), Iam (Hand), and Luam (Pilot), were permitted to visit. As a result of her imprudence the water burst forth, injuring her physically, and then, following her in her flight to the seacoast, formed the river Boyne.

Fintan was said to be the grandson of Noah. Being refused admission to the ark, he came to Ireland with a small company forty days before the flood in order to escape that catastrophe. All but Fintan perished in the waters, or sometimes of a subsequent epidemic. He, however, continued to live for several thousand years, and was thus enabled to preserve a vast amount of legendary material regarding prehistoric conditions in Ireland.

The list of the 'fabrications' – i.e. miraculously created objects are mentioned in *The Book of Lismore* where there are some variants. The text reads (Stokes' translation): 'Three chief fabrics of Ireland were this night found and revealed, to wit, the headpiece of Briuin, son of Smethra: it was the brazier of Oengus, son of Umor, that made it, even a helmet of the pure purple of the land of the Indians with a ball of gold above it!' The *Echtra Nera* mentions the *'barr Briuin'*, or crown of Briuin, and adds: 'That was the third wonderful gift in Erin, and the mantle of Loegaire in Armagh, and the shirt of Dunlaing in Leinster in Kildare!' Another text mentions a *tathlum*, or sling-stone, made by 'Briuin, the son of Bethar, no mean warrior, who on the ocean's eastern border reigned!'

Briain, Iuchorba, and Iuchair are the sons of the goddess Brigit and may be a triple manifestation of one being. They are also known as the Children of Tuirean, and in the story of that name they make a voyage in Manannán's magic boat to procure a whole collection of talismans.

The draught-board of Crimthann Nia Nar, is mentioned again in the poem describing this warrior's ghostly conversation with his lover after his death.

Leand Linflaclach, the maker of the Diadem of Laegaire mac Luchta, is described in more detail in the *Rennes Dindshenchas* . 'Lein Linflaclach mac Bain . . . artificer of Síd Buidb, he it was that dwelt in the loch and wrought the burnished vessels of Flidias' daughter, Fann. Every night after leaving off work he used to hurl his *inneoin* or "anvil" from him eastwards to Inneoin of the Decies, as far as the grave mound; three showers he used to make fly (from this anvil): one of water, one of fire, one of pure crimson gems (the same thing Nemannach too practised when in the north he hammered Conchobar mac Nessa's goblet), and hence Loch Lein is named!' This is very clearly a type of astronomical myth, few of which have survived in Celtic tradition.

Another very interesting reference is to the palisade of Rath Aildinne, which fell down every night after they had been erected. This episode seems to be a prefiguring of the famous story of the building of Vortigern's Tower in the writings of the seventh-century British monk Nennius. Here the child Ambrosius (better known as Merlin) discovers the reason for the failure of the walls to stand, and afterwards gives a long and detailed list of prophecies.

There is also a reference to Fer Fí, the fairy harper whom we meet again in the 'Battle of Mag Mucrama', (pp. 210–242) which relates how after its fairy owners had been dispossessed of Knockany, they revenged themselves by destroying the grass on the hill every Hallowtide. That the fairies control the fertility of the fields is widely accepted in both Irish and Scots tradition.

Much of the rest of the tale deals with land-lore, and many of the sites mentioned can still be visited today. Of particular interest are the five ancient trackways leading to Tara, which probably date back to the beginning of topographical myth in Ireland.

Once upon a time, when Fingen mac Luchtra was in nightwatch on Halloween in Druim Finghin, there came a fairy woman [*bean sídhe*] a-visiting Fingen every Halloween continually, so that she used to tell him whatever there was of marvels and of glories in Erin from one Halloween to another. Rothniamh (Wheelsplendour) the daughter of Umall Urscothach (Fresh-flowery) from the elf-mound of Cliu was (the name of) that woman.

'How many wonders, O woman,' said Fingen,' are there to-night [of] which we do not know in Erin?'

'Fifty wonders,' said the woman.

'Tell them to us,' said Fingen.

'There is a great wonder,' said the woman: 'to wit, a son who is born to-night in Tara to Feidlimed, son of Tuathal Techtmar, king of Erin. And that son will obtain Erin in one lot, and there shall spring from him three fifties of kings of all those who shall take the throne of Erin until (the time of) Oraineach (The Golden-faced-one) of Usnech, and they shall all be kings, though they shall not have the same duration of life.'

Then Fingen sang this quatrain:

> Though this be a long night-watch

> in which there might be the length of seven winter nights,
> The men of Erin would not be sorrowful,
> and would not sleep, during it.

'And what other wonder, O woman?' said Fingen.

'Not hard (to tell),' said the woman. 'To-night there bursts forth a splendid stream over the eastern plain of Erin on the track of the woman-warrior, the wife of the son of Nechtan; that is, from the place where Sidh Nechtain is (located) north-east to the billows (lit. "mane") of the sea. A well,' said she, 'which is deeply hidden with the three cupbearers of Nechtan to wit, Rod and Lazy and Pilot. The Woman-warrior she is who went from them after violating its (the well's) *geasa* (taboos), so that the well made a beautiful river and so that numerous are its many glories: both oak-woods, and plains, and bogs, and fords, and marshes, and rivermouths, and streams. It shall be a bountiful road and it shall be a rod of white-bronze across a plain of refined gold, for its name is the Boyne.'

And Fingen uttered another quatrain:

> Although my aspect be not brilliant,
> and although the night-watch is long,
> Even though it last for me to the end of a winter night,
> it will not bring me into despondence.

'And what other wonder, O woman?' said he.

'Not hard (to tell),' said the woman. 'A tree indeed,' said she, 'which has been hidden in Erin from the time of the Flood, and it sheds three showers of fruit through the mist, so that the plain on which it stands is full of mast thrice yearly; and when the last acorn falls from it, then comes the blossom of the next acorns. And the waves of the flood saved it without destroying it, and the eye of man has not seen it until to-night. The Yew of Ross is the name of that tree,' said she, 'that is to say, (it is) a scion of the tree which is in Paradise. It is to-night, moreover, that it has been revealed to the men of Erin that it may be an eternal glory from beginning to end.'

Then Fingen spoke this quatrain:

> Not sorrowful is the watch
> waiting for the tree which has been hidden since the flood;
> Lasting will be its glory over Bray
> to the tribes over whom it will spread.

'And what other wonder, O woman?' said Fingen.

'Not hard (to tell),' said the woman. 'God, the High King, granted to Fintan mac Bochra that he should be a chief judge of wisdom in this world, and he has been mute from the hour that he heard the wave-roar of the flood against the side of Mt Olivet, he himself being upon the brow of the wave in the south-west part of Erin's. Moreover, he was asleep as long as the flood was upon the world, and he has been in silence from that time onward, and to-night the power of speech has been unlocked for him, to tell the history of Erin; for that history has been in obscurity and in darkness until to-night. For he is the one just man that the flood left in Erin. Therefore to-night a glorious spirit of prophecy has been sent in the shape of a gentle youth and has alighted on his lips from a ray of the sun, until it has extended through the trench of his back (the lower part of the back of his head) so that there are seven good speeches of poetry that are upon his tongue to tell the histories and the synchronisms of Erin.'

Thereupon he said:

> Though it be a long night to me
> from nine o'clock till morning,
> It does not disturb me,
> because of any one of these fair wonderful deeds.

'And what other wonder, O woman?' said Fingen.

'Not hard (to tell),' said the woman. 'There have been completed to-night the three chief [fabrications] of Erin: to wit, the helmet of Brion from the elf-mounds of Cruachu which Breóson of Smeathru, the smith of Aenghus son of Umhor made; that is, the battle-helmet of purple-crystal of the land of India (with) an apple of gold on top of it of the size of a man's head, and a hundred threads of variegated carbuncles and a hundred tresses of very shining red gold and a hundred chains of white bronze adorning it. For a series of years it has been hidden from the Morrigu in the well of the elf-mound of Cruachu. It has, moreover, been hidden until to-night. And the chess-board of Crimthan Nia Nair which he brought from the gathering of Find, on Crimthan's adventure (into fairyland) when he went one day north-eastward of everybody (i.e., of the rest of the world) from the elf-mound of Bodb upon an adventure, so that it has been in Usnech until to-night. And the diadem of Laegaire mac Luchta White-hand, which Leand Linfiaclach son of Bainblodha of the Bann made. The three daughters of Fandle mac Durath, from the elf-mound of Fairfield found it to-night after its being hidden for a long time; to-wit, from the birth of Conchobar Red-eyebrow.'

Then Fingen spoke this quatrain:

> 'Tis a long watch if it were not for you
> a-talking to me so that it was wonderful.
> I was a hero. I was a king.
> At it (?) by the side of the full long stone.

'And what other wonder, O woman?' said Fingen.

'Not hard (to tell),' said the woman. 'The five chief roads of Erin,' said she. 'They were not found until to-night, and neither horses nor chariots have travelled them. They are: the Track of Midhluachar which Midhluachar mac Damairne, the son of the king of Srub Brain, found in reaching Tara for the meeting of the Feast of Tara to-night; and the Track of Cualu which Fear Fí (Man of Poison) mac Eoghabail (Yew Fork) found on reaching Tara to-night before the phantom hosts of fairy; and the Track of Asal which Asal mac Doir Domblais (Bad Tasting) found on reaching Tara before the reavers of Meath; and the Track of Dal which Setna Sithderg (Ever Red) mac Dornbuidhe (Yellow Fist) found before the bandit host of Ormond as he was seeking the Feast of Tara this night to-night; and the Great Track (i.e. the Eskers of Riada to the dark . . . (?) . . .) which Noar mac Aenghusa Umaild found before the heroes of bravery of Irrais Domnand in strife. So that they are the first who have reached Tara tonight, and these five roads did not appear in Erin until to-night.'

And Fingen began a quatrain:

> Although I am in long rest,
> no long sadness seizes me
> No dislike of the black night seizes me
> before the feast of the great host in Tara.

'And what other wonder, O woman?' said Fingen.

'Not hard (to tell),' said the woman. 'Two complete sepulchres of Sliab Mis. There were buried in them two sons of Mil of Spain; to-wit, Eber and Eremon on the occasion of dividing Erin between them; one of them at the end of the mountain to the eastward and the other at the end of the mountain to the westward. And the Sons of Mil said that those two sepulchres would not meet in any manner until the kingship of Erin should reach one grip (i.e. be united under one head). It is they, moreover, who buried them; to-wit, his two druids, Uar and Eithiar their names. To-night those two graves have met so that they were (of) equal length side by side in the midst of the mountain, and in Tara shall be the single grip of Erin till judgment.'

And Fingen sang this quatrain:

> Glory to those of noble clans, with splendour,
> (is) whatever of good you prophesy;
> There has not been heard in Erin till now
> [so many great] glories in one night.

'And what other wonder, O woman?' said Fingen.

'Not hard (to tell),' said she. 'Three wonderful lakes have appeared in Erin to-night before the birth of Conn of the Hundred Battles, to wit: Loch nEchach; a four-branched holly tree which has been placed at the head of it for seven years has turned to stone in so far as it was in the earth, and the portion of it that was in the water has turned to iron, and that portion of it that was above the water has turned to wood. Moreover, Loch Riach,' said the woman 'it is in it that Caoer Abarbaeth (Silly Berry) from the elf-mound of Feadal Ambaid washed the mantle of Mac in Og with a multitude of colours unknown (to the world), so that it is variously coloured and so that it showed a variety of colour upon it every hour, although the men of Erin should be looking at it at one time. Loch Lein, too,' said she; 'there poured a rain upon it to-night of the hail of the Land of Promise so that there have sprung many wonderful treasures from it, to wit: the jewels of Loch Lein. Although they (the lakes) were in Erin, they were not manifested until to-night throughout Erin.'

Thereupon he said:

> Though it be long until thou didst come, O woman,
> there was found with thee something that made it short;
> It is much that thou sayest of wonders
> in Erin before the birth of Conn.

'And what other wonder, O woman?' said Fingen.

'Not hard (to tell),' said she. 'Four men who escaped from the Tuatha dé Danaan in the battle of Moy Tura, so that they were in hiding in Erin a-destroying the corn, the milk, the great fruit, and the mast: one man of them in the plains of Moy Itha, Redg his name;

another man of them in the mountains of Breg, Brea his name; another man in the borders of Cruachau, Tinell his name; and another man in Slieve Finoil, Greand his name. To-night,' said she, 'they have gone into exile from Erin after being driven out by the Morrigu, and by Bodb of the elf-mound of Femen, and by Midir of Bri Leith, and by Mac in Oicc, so that there shall not be robbers from the Fomorians as long as Conn lives.'

And then Fingen sang this quatrain:

> That which has come from the meeting of glory;
> the birth of the descendant of Crimthann Niadh Nair;
> Out of (all) the glorious things which thou prophesiest,
> Erin shall be three times the better from this.

'And what other wonder, O woman?' said Fingen.

'Not hard (to tell),' said she. 'A fabric wonderful, perishable, which is here in thy vicinity,' said she, 'to wit: a palisade of white bronze upon Rath Aildinne; from the day when its making was undertaken, whatever the builders and smiths used to lift of it one day, that fell down in the morning, so that they did not accomplish the fitness of its making nor of its doors and so that they did not complete its beauty nor its smoothness till to-night. And besides,' said she, 'three vixens out of the elf-mound arose, escaping in flight before the rough attack of the Dagda, to wit: Siur, and Eoir (the Nore), and Berba (the Barrow) until they have come together into one place and have met together at one estuary in this night.'

Fingen began a quatrain:

> Thou art blessed in speech, O woman;
> I am blessed in recounting;
> There is no concealing in Erin
> the expectation of Conn of the Hundred Battles.

'And what other wonder, O woman?' said Fingen.

'Not hard (to tell),' said she. 'Three times nine white birds in chains of red gold have come tonight and have sung wonderful music on the walls of Tara, so that there shall not be either grief or distress or sorrow or longing or absence of entertainment in Erin during the time of Conn of the Hundred Battles. And there have come the three sons of Eon mac Ethideoin from the elf-mound of Trum towards him (Conn), and they are the three royal mercenaries who have sat down about him;

to wit, Mael and Bluicne and Blocc. And at the sound of it, Tara and the hosts which are in it and all the chief fortresses of Erin have uttered a cry. And the poet has uttered a royal lay to Conn,' said she, 'when it was at his parturition.'

'Dost thou remember that lay?' said Fingen.

'I remember it indeed very well,' said the woman. '[But] we have addressed you to-night for joy,' said the woman; 'your sorrow will break out again if you hear the lay of the druid.'

'Since I have heard the good,' said Fingen, 'why should I not hear the bad?'

So it is then that the woman began this lay about Conn, and this is the one which the druid uttered at Tara:

> Joyous the cry of the birth of Conn:
> Conn over Erin, Erin under Conn.
> Conn as far as Fál (Ireland);
> It shall be from him that the sovereignty
> of the hosts shall be stretched
> over the ancient plain of Edair till Doomsday;
> There will come cavalcades and chariots,
> roads under them – a noise across the sea.
> His barks and his boats with crooked prows
> will strike the waves across the sea.
> His hosts upon Meath, upon Munster,
> he will be [a restorer?] to the sea's wall.
> In his time men of Leinster shall be bold;
> his help is not backward;
> Upon the breasts of Luachar;
> he will fill with his fury the Old Plain of Sanb
> To Eas Rudah, to Find, to Fanad,
> and as far as Teach Duind, where the dead hold their tryst,
> He shall mix spears in the blood of heroes
> upon the slope of Ulster – a broad track;
> His wrath shall proclaim each tribe
> as far as the wave of the Sea of Wight;
> [bone-] split red spears,
> swords in dark, bitter gore;
> From earth to the blue sky
> fierce flames will fill the air.

He will go upon an adventure into fairie (*eachtra*) from Tara.
The true prince, gentle, prosperous.
He will prophesy to him – noble the series –
three times fifty princes from him;
There will be born a grandson after that,
Cormac grandson of Conn his name;
He will be a rock of justice at every hour
to the [summit] of fierce judgment.
Conn's pride will shake Erin
both wilderness and mountain,
With his prosperity, with his law,
with his race behind him.
Certain (it is) in the eyes of the druids in Tara,
who sing something that is not false.
Perfection of rule as far as the three seas,
all has God granted to him.
Though we be, (I) and thou, O Fingen,
in a long watch here,
Whatever of wonders we talk of,
has been granted beyond everyone to Conn;
There has been granted to him a long blessed time,
triumph over noble clans under his rule,
Kings through battles, hosts . . . (?) . . . sides,
before their cries raise the shout.

'That then,' said the woman, 'is what Ceasard the druid has spoken in Tara on this night to-night when Conn was horn.'
    And Fingen uttered this quatrain:

Whatever thou speakest of wonders,
will, it seems to me, come to me;
It bodes me no good
hearing the lay of the druid.

Then great dejection took hold of Fingen, and he went forth escaping from his own land, so that he did not come at once; i.e. that he might not be in his own patrimony waiting for the might of Conn and his children after him. So Fingen was making a circuit throughout Erin, and Conn assumed the kingship of Erin thereafter.
    (Conn) one day went upon Usnech in Meath so that he beheld all

Erin on every side. He asked his druid: 'Is there in Erin,' said Conn, 'one who does not serve me?'

'There is but one man,' said the druid.

'Who is that man?' said Conn.

'Fingen mac Luchta,' said the druid, 'and since the time that you were born and since you took the kingdom, he has been avoiding your power.'

'In what place is he?' said Conn.

'Between two deserts: Sliab Mis and Luachar,' said the druid.

'I shall not leave that callow bladelet of grass in Erin without law upon him,' said Conn.

'That will not be very easy for thee,' said the druid.

'Why not?' said Conn.

'Not hard (to tell),' said the druid; 'there is a woman of the elf-mound who instructs him,' said the druid.

'But there is,' said Conn,' a covenant made by Bodb Derg (the Red) with me that no encroachment shall be made in my sovereignty by him.'

'What guarantees hast thou?' said the druid.

'There is a guarantee with me,' said Conn, 'to wit: Fear Fí mac Eóghabail; that is, the son of the daughter of Crimthan Niad Nair, and her father is from the elf-mound of Bodb.'

'Pursue him,' said the druid.

And so it was that Fingen went to Conn, and he was for fifty years in his company, so that he won seventeen battles, until in the last battle he perished by the hand of Forannan Foda (the Tall) and the latter by him at Gull and Irguld.

19. Selections from Cormac's Glossary

(Sanas Cormaic)

Translated by Caitlín Matthews

The author of the following is Cormac mac Cuilleanáin, the ninth-century bishop-king of Cashel who brought together a valuable collection of stories and traditions in his *Glossary*, perhaps the West's earliest dictionary of etymological lore. When we say dictionary, this may imply a rigorously researched set of informational meanings drawn from strict etymological derivations: but in Cormac's *Glossary* we find not a bit of this. Cormac, like most Irish scholars, was steeped in euhemerist enthusiasm: if a word from his word-horde sounds like another expression, if the word can be sawn down into nice easy components and made to derive from some other terms, perhaps even from Latin or Greek, then Cormac is your man. This same method of word-derivation is used extensively in the *Dindsenchus*, the origin-stories of places in Ireland, where hills, rivers and plains are given stories that 'explain' their names. Do not be lured into Cormac's web of words: his inspirational etymology is wide of the mark in nearly all cases. But what his writing often shows is the way that poets played with words of similar-sounding syllables in their compositions: Cormac has clearly had a poetic training of sorts before his ecclesiastical one took hold. Despite this, Cormac's *Glossary* is a fascinating hunting-ground for story snippets and dropped trifles from folk and mythic lore.

Cormac wrote in a mixture of Irish and Latin, with more footnotes and scholarly asides than any ogamist could shake a stick at. Here we have attempted to give a readable selection of entries from the *Glossary*, joining in Cormac's fun by putting in our own bracketed commentaries for your clarity. This selection is chosen to help reflect the mythic focus of the present volume and to give you some idea of how the early Irish viewed their own mythic heritage.

ANA: the Irish mother of the gods. Well did she nourish the gods, since she is *ana* or 'the plenteous one'. The Two Paps of Ana, in West Luachair are still called after her. [The Goddess, Ana or Anu is the eponymous ancestress of the Tuatha dé Danann, literally 'the family of Ana'. The Paps of Anu can be found in Kerry.]

BUANANN: foster-mother of the fianna, from *bé n'Anand* or 'woman of Anann', because she and Anu are very like each other. Just as Anu was the mother of the gods, so Buanann was the mother of heroes. Buanann is the good mother because she is buan-ann or 'full of goodness'. Buan is from Latin *bonum*, as we say '*buan* comes out of *ambuan*' or 'goodness comes out of evil'. The *ann* in Buanann means 'mother'. And so Buanann means 'a good mother who teaches warrior-learning to heroes.' [Búanann was indeed a primeval goddess who trained both Cú Chulainn and Fionn in weapon-training. Buan is a title also significantly given to the Mórrígan. Buan is a word meaning 'lasting or enduring'; while a buannach is a recruit or volunteer, in military terms.]

BRIGIT: a female poet, daughter to the Dagda. This is the same Brigit, the female sage and goddess whom the poets venerated. It was because of this that she was called 'the Poet's Goddess'. Her sisters were also called Brigit: Brigit the female doctor and Brigit the female smith, daughters of the Dagda. Under these names did all Irishmen called her the Goddess Brigit. Brigit is from *breo-aigit* or fiery arrow. [Brighid or Brigit, daughter of the Dagda, is here first recorded as having a triple aspect. Poets did indeed regard themselves as her sons. In actuality, she is venerated now more by women as the Goddess of the hearth, who keeps in the fire at night and as the protector of domesticated beasts, especially cattle, and of the whole dairy process of milk, cheese and butter making. Her emblem, the three legged weaving of rushes, still protects homes and barns, so her triple aspect lives on.]

CAILL CRINMON: the hazelnuts of the knowledge trick or the *creth*: 'wise', *mon*: 'feat'. The source of inspirational composition from which the poem emerges. [The source of inspiration was said to derive from the hazels of wisdom that grew over the source of the River Boyne, eaten by the Salmon of Knowledge. To crack the *caill crinmon* is to have made it as a poet, as many ancient texts deplore, 'Ah, if only I had the caill crinmon!']

COIRE BRECCAIN: Corryvrekin, the great whirlpool that whirls between Ireland and Alba (Scotland), where many seas meet – the sea around Ireland at the north-west, the sea surrounding Alba at the north-east, and the Irish sea between Ireland and Alba from the south. Like a pair of compasses, they whirl about, churning the waters between them turn and turn about like a millwheel until they are sucked down into the depths, leaving the opening like a cauldron with its gaping mouth. It could suck the whole of Ireland into its gaping maw. It vomits out great water spouts with thunderous belches as high as the clouds, just like the boiling of a cauldron over the fire.

Breccán, son of Main, son of Niall of the Nine Hostages, had fifty curraghs trading between Ireland and Alba, but one of them was drawn into the cauldron and none of the crew survived, so no news was ever heard about its sinking. No-one knew what had become of them until the blind poet, Lugaid, arrived at Bangor and his people walked along the beach of Inver Béce and found the clean skull of a dog and brought it to Lugaid. They asked him whose it was and he told them to lay it down so that he could touch it with the end of his poet's staff and made a *dichetul do chennaib* upon it, saying, 'This is the skull of Breccán's dog. It is the merest remnant of someone much greater for Breccán himself drowned among his people in this whirlpool.' [The Corryvrekin, in the sea between Rathlinn Island and the Irish coast is a notoriously dangerous whirlpool. See the entry below under *imbas* for more information about the mysterious prophetic skill used by Lugaid.]

DIANCECHT: the name of the wisest healer of Ireland, from *dia na-cecht*: 'a god with powers'. Diancecht is therefore the god of health. As Néde mac Adnai said, referring to its power over him, '*cechtsam dercca aithscenmaim ailcne*', or 'The stone-fragment's rebound has over-powered our sight', after a piece of stone stuck in his eye. It is not too far to connect *cecht sam* with *caech-som*, 'it blinded' (him). [Diancecht, whose real etymology is 'swift power,' was one of the Tuatha dé Danann, the grandfather of Lugh. His extraordinary powers of healing remained in Christian tradition: see p. 289 of *The Encyclopaedia of Celtic Wisdom* for a charm said to take splinters out of things.]

DRAI: *i dorua ái* or 'the magic art', it is through poetry that he breathes his incantations. [The modern form of this word is draoi, drui or druid.

The association of poetry with spell-making is clearly established in Cormac's mind.]

EMAIN: Emain Macha, from *eo-muin* or neck-pin, the brooch across a neck. Emain's shape was so called by Queen Macha when she took the brooch off her cloak to measure the ground with it. While measuring with it, the brooch-pin slipped eastwards a little on the return circuit, which is why the fort is uneven. [Emain Macha or Navan Fort in Co Armagh, the epicentre of the Ulster stories, was founded by the pregnant otherworldly woman, Macha, being made to compete against the horses of the Ultonian king by her husband. She easily beat the horses, but at the finishing line gave birth to twin children. Her circuit encompassed the fortress named after her. The real etymology of the place is derived from *emain* or 'twins,' but many folk traditions retain Cormac's charming fiction.]

FIDCHELL: or *Féth-ciall* or *Fáth-ciall*, for it needs *ciall* or sense and *fáth* or learning to play it. Or from *fuath-cell*, 'shaped like a church', since the fidchell board has four corners and its squares are set at right-angles and have black and white squares upon it, and besides, many different individuals win the game in turns. So it is that the church has four corners, and the world itself has four directions with the four evangelists. Its morals and precepts are likewise straight like those of Scripture, for black and white, good and bad live within the shelter of the church. [Poor Cormac struggles here! The real etymology of fidhchell is fid-ciall or wood-wisdom. It is a board-game played by two opposing individuals, but unlike chess in that one set of pieces are the king-piece and his champions while the opposing pieces are the invaders: the invaders try to prevent the king from reaching the edge of the board, which is seen as the land. This territorial game echoes the effective reign of a good king whose realm should be so well governed that he can travel throughout its regions without being impeded. It is played by a host of characters in Celtic story, the Welsh equivalent being gwyddbwyll, a name also meaning wood-cunning.]

GAILENG: this word was used of Cormac, son of Tadhg, son of Cian on the occasion when he prepared a feast for his father made up of a hundred different kinds of animals, except badgers. Cormac went to the badger's den but it was too boring to wait for them to come out so he could get them. Instead, he invited them out in the name and under the honour and surety of his father Tadhg. But when the badgers emerged, Cormac killed a hundred of them and displayed them at the feast. And Tadhg's heart was sickened by this and by Cormac's actions and he called his son Cormac Gaeleng, or 'Shit-Honour' from treachery or *gaei lang*, or cowardly courage. [Tadhg's disgust is not over the badger genocide perpetrated by his son, but rather by the staining of his family's honour at the slaying of those who had put themselves under its protection. The Cormac here is probably Cormac Gelta Gáeth, a legendary ancestor of the Leinstermen.]

GRETH: the name of Athairne's servant, the one to whom Amairgin son of Eculsach, smith of Búas, said '*Inith greth gruth grínmuine glascrema cue uinn obla grethi gruth?*' This was when Greth came to the house of Ecetsal the smith to ask to borrow something. He saw that the child at the fireside was but a hand high and yet was about seven years old. It was eating a dish of curds, blackberries, sloes, leeks, nuts, onions, and crab apples, and it looked up and asked, 'Does Greth eat curds blackberries, sloes, leeks, nuts, onions, and crab apples and curds?' repeating this over and over. Greth returned to Athairne's house and told his master. Then Athairne came with a billhook to kill the boy. Meanwhile, back at the smithy, Ecetsal came into the house while the iron was in the fire and asked the servant girl who had visited the house. 'Athairne's servant,' she replied, and reported what had happened. 'Listen to me, said Ecetsal, 'Athairne will surely come and kill the boy, so hide him, but leave his tunic where it is.' Athairne entered and aimed a blow at the piece of wood that was inside the tunic. Then the serving girl cried out and he went away. And the honour-price that was set for the boy was that Athairne should become his teacher and instruct him so that the boy should be no less skilful than his teacher. And this was how Amairgin was instructed by Athairne.

[This story tells us how the Ulster poet Amairgin – who is a later poet than the Amairgin of the Milesian Invasion – came to be taught by the satirist Athairne – see p. 369 for Athairne's death. Like the precocious Welsh poet-baby, Taliesin, Amairgin already has distinct poetic skills. He speaks in the iron-tongued, riddling language of the professional poet, his precocity a threat to Athairne who tries to kill him. But because Athairne tried to take his life – albeit that of a block of wood – his intentions to kill are treated with the utmost judicial severity.

Athairne's punishment, under the law, would be to pay the full honour price of a poet; instead of this, he has to raise and educate Amairgin to be as good as himself. Later poetic evidence shows that teacher and pupil became close.]

IMBAS FOROSNA: this reveals every good thing that the poet desires to know or to make clear. It is done like this. The poet masticates the meat of a red pig, or of a dog or cat. Then he puts it upon the threshold stone behind the door and makes an incantation over it, offering it to images of gods. Then he calls his spirits to him to help him and, if what he is looking for is not revealed the next day, he makes incantations over his two palms and calls again upon his spirits that his sleeping should not be disturbed. He places his palms over his eyes and so falls into trance. He is envigilated as that he is not disturbed or interrupted until his searching is completed, which might be a minute or two or three, or as long as he was supposed to be continuing his offering. This is why it is called *imbas*: 'his two palms' *boiss* upon *im* him, one palm over the other upon his cheeks.

Patrick forbade this practice and also that of *teinm laegda*, saying that anyone who practised them should not merit heaven or earth, since it went against their baptismal vows. He did however allow *dichetal do chennaib* to be used in their poetic craft because it didn't involve making offerings to demons; the revelation comes directly from the tips of the poet's fingers.

[This description of the prophetic skills known as the Three Illuminations is one of the only ones we have and it is technically imprecise since Cormac clearly hasn't ever witnessed it. Despite St Patrick's strictures about their performance, the Three Illuminations were considered to be the true mark of a poet. *Imbas forosna* was a very purposeful seeking out of spiritual help by means of a trance-like incubatory sleep, and was used for important decision-making such as king making. *Teinm laegda* was a form of spontaneous, incantatory method for discovering unknown matters: a cracking open of problems by the heat of poetic vision. If we refer to the entry of Coire Breccan above, we see that Lugaid the blind poet uses a form of *dichetal do chennaib*, a kind of psychometric seership, to ascertain the ownership of the dog's skull.]

MORANN: or *mór-fhinn*, the great fair one. This was the name that his mother gave him, saying that whoever refused to say his name would suffer death. His father called him Mac Máin or Son of Great Wealth because his son was a good treasure to him: he said that whoever refused to say this name would be in danger of death. And this is why these two names stuck to him. [Morann mac Maine, son of Cairbre Cinnchait, was a legendary judge or brehon, the owner of several ceremonial chains and collars that closed about his neck if he gave bad judgement. His ordeals and judgements have come to us and can be found on p. 266 of *The Encyclopaedia of Celtic Wisdom*.]

MUG-EIME: this is the name of the first lap-dog in Ireland. Cairpre Musc, son of Conaire, fetched it from the east, from Britain. It was in a time when the Gaels were powerful in Britain, when they divided Alba into regions and knew the homes of their friends. It wasn't only on the eastern sea in Scotland that they built houses and royal forts either. There was Dinn Tradui, the triple-banked fort of Crimthann the Great, son of Fidach, king of Ireland and Alba as far as the Ictian sea (English Channel). There was also Glass, son of Cass, swineherd of Hiruaith (Norway), who kept his pigs; Patrick resurrected him sixty years after he was killed by the warriors of Mac Con. In that region is Dinn map Lethain, among the Cornish Britons. There the tribes continued to grow and expand until they had as many lands to the east as to the west and here they reigned long after the coming of Patrick.

So it was that Cairpre Musc was visiting his family and friends in the east. At this time there were no pet dogs in Ireland, for the Britons had made it a rule that no such specially-bred dog should be given to the Gaels whether they begged them for one, nor could they be freely given out of gratitude or friendship. The British law said that every criminal should be held accountable for his crime.

A friend of Cairpre Musc's possessed such a dog and this is how Cairpre got it. Once, when Cairpre went to his house, he was told to treat everything as his, except the lap-dog. Now Cairpre owned a beautiful knife whose haft was decorated with silver and gold. It was a precious thing. Now Cairpre oiled it, rubbing meat-fat on to the knife and left it lying near the dog. The lap-dog began licking and then gnawing the haft of the knife until it was ruined. The next day, Cairpre complained of this and asked for recompense from his friend. 'Indeed, it is fair that I should pay for damage,' he said. Cairpre replied, 'I will abide by what the law of Britain demands, and nothing less: is it not so that each crime belongs to the animal that perpetrated it?' And so it was that the lap-dog was given to Cairpre and he gave it the name Mug éime or 'Slave of the Haft,' because of the knife it had gnawed. The lap-dog was a bitch and was in pup.

This was the time when Ailill Flann was king of Munster and Cormac mac Conn was king of Tara. They and Cairpre began to argue over the possession of the lap-dog. And this is the way that the dispute was settled: the dog was to stay with each of them for a period of time. After this decision, the bitch gave birth to three puppies and they each had one: from this litter descend all the lap-dogs of Ireland. And long after the original dog had died, it was Connla, son of Tadhg, son of Cian, son of Oilill Olum who found the lap-dog's bare skull and took it as riddle to a poet who had come with his composition to his father's house. The poet was Maen mac Edaine and Maen solved the riddle through *teinm laegda*, saying,

> 'Your pelt was smooth in Eogain's house,
> In Conn's house there was food enough,
> Your fair shaped so admired
> Before your beauty died in Cairpre's dwelling.

Mug-éime! This head is that of Mug-éime, the very first lap-dog ever brought to Ireland.'

[This story relates yet another story about the Three Illuminations, this time an example of *teinm laegda*. We see that the poet Maen deduces information about the skull in a short quatrain and, by so doing, the name of the hound leaps to his lips. This may be compared with the dog-skull in the Coire Breccan entry above. There is something highly familiar about this dispute over a lap-dog. Welsh legend tells of how Cad Goddeu, the Battle of the Trees, was fought over the theft of a white roebuck, a dog and a lapwing by Amaethon, the rightful possessions of Arawn, King of Annwfn, the Welsh Underworld. Cairpre Musc is the legendary ancestor of the Muscraige people of Munster and his rather legalistic taking of the British lap-dog raises more than a glimmer of suspicion that we have a parallel story, although he disputes with other kings of Ireland rather than with any supernatural characters.]

MANANNÁN MAC LIR: a famous merchant from the Isle of Man. He was the best navigator in the west of Europe. By his observation of the skies he could tell when the weather would be good or bad and when the weather would change. Among the Scots and Britons he was called 'of the sea' and son of the sea. The Isle of Mann is named after Manannán. [At last, Cormac gets his etymology correct! But he sadly reduces the great god of the sea and of the otherworldly islands of the blessed west to a mere trader!]

NESCOIT: or 'boils'. This is a Gaelic story. When the Battle of Mag Tuiread was being fought, Goibhniu the smith was forging weapons for the Tuatha dé Danann, while Luchtine the Carpenter was carving shafts for the spears and Creidne the Welder was welding rivets for the same spears. It is said among the Scots that Goibhniu made spears in three motions, after which Luchtine made the shafts with three cuts, so did Creidne make the rivets in three goes. Each of these threes was final one. Goibhniu threw the spearheads from his tongs and they stuck into the door-jamb. Luchtine then threw the shafts to land in the spearheads and then Creidne flung the rivets from his tongs on to the shafts to fasten them.

Now while Goibhniu was doing this, his wife was charged with a crime, which news caused him to be depressed and jealous. When he heard the news, he was holding a pole in his hands. The pole was called Ness, around which the clay furnace was made. Then he spoke a spell over the pole, striking any man who approached with it. Any who escaped the blow was struck with boils very like a burning lump of ore from the forge, which is how boils got their name from Ness – the pole of Goibhniu and scoit, or liquid.

Ness means four things all told: a weasel, Ness as a name, a pole and a name for a furnace, as a smith's wife once noted in an elegy she made for him:

> It was hard to look upon him,
> The flame from his furnace tall to the roof.
> Sweet dronings from his bellows
> Sang to the hole in his furnace.

Ness is also the name for a blow or wound, as it says in the Senchas Mor:

> Measurement begins with grains,
> Every law derives from the Fianna,
> Every worth comes from a treasure,
> From a man's body recompenses are set,

However many his wounds,
The higher they are, the more payment.
than if the wound is under his clothes.

[This story tells us about Goibhniu, the smith god of the Tuatha dé Danann. As we have seen on p. 58 his spear-points tend to have disastrous effects upon those who enter the forge unawares. We have no other context for this story about the crime his wife is charged with: she is not only unnamed in tradition, but her crime is unknown. We may assume adultery, perhaps. Ness is actually the name for the clay moulding block where a smith makes his moulds and pours the molten ore, but we also hear about the wife of Cathbad changing her name from *Assa* or 'peaceful' to *Ni-assa* or Nessa, 'not peaceful'. The text of the Senchas Mor deals with the laws of Ireland and the recompenses due to injury or crime. The spear of Goibhniu, though it may harm, also heals in medical tradition.]

ORC TREITH: a name for a king's son, as the poets state, 'the assembly of a king's son', *Oínach n'uirc tréith*, with food, fine clothes, with down-stuffed quilts, beer and kebabs, branndubh and fidhchell, horses and chariots, greyhounds and other fine things.

Also there is *orcc*, the title of a salmon, as we hear in the story of Lomna the Fool. After his head had been taken from him, he spoke, saying, 'A speckled, whitebellied salmon that has swum with lesser fish under the sea, I will not speak. I am no country pig who indiscriminantly shits oak-mast everywhere. But I say that Cairpre has made a division that is unjust.'

This was how it came about. The fool of Fionn, grandson of Baiscni, was called Lomna the Lousy. One day Fionn went out hunting and Lomna stayed home. There was a woman of the Luigne who slept with Fionn: in nearly every mountain and forest where Fionn and men roamed there was a woman in every region who was available to him. These were female inn-keepers, ready to support the Fianna; for wherever they roamed, no-one would harm them. Fionn came into Tethba with his Fianna and Lomna stayed behind. Lomna went walking and saw Cairpre, one of the Fianna, sleeping with Fionn's woman. Then the woman begged Lomna to say nothing. It felt dreadful to him to betray his master so, when Fionn returned, Lomna cut an ogham inscription upon a four-sided stick, saying,

'A pole of wood within the champion's silver helmet.
The husband of an adulterous whore is made fool of within the
    Fianna.
There's some heather upon naked Ualann of the Luigne.'

And Fionn immediately understood this story and grew disgusted with
the woman. But the woman knew that it was Lomna who had told him
and she sent a messenger to Cairpre to come and kill the fool.

So Cairpre came and cut off his head and carried it off with him.
Fionn returned to camp that evening and saw a body without a head.
'A body without a head,' said Fionn, 'let us discover whose it is.' And he
put his thumb into his mouth and spoke through *teinm laegda*,

'It wasn't done by our folk,
Nor by the Leinstermen,
No modesty has caused this,
No red dog has ravaged him,
No boar has torn him, nor eaten him, nor hidden him,
No secret what has befallen Lomna.'

'This is the body of Lomna,' said Fionn, 'and enemies have carried off
his head.'

Then they unleashed the hounds and let them follow the scent.
Fionn followed the track of the warriors and came upon Cairpre in an
abandoned house, cooking fish upon a stone, and Lomna's head nearby
the fire on a pole. The first serving that he cooked on the stone, Cairpre
divided into twenty seven portions, but he did not put a piece into the
mouth of the head. Now this (lack of hospitality) was *geis* to the fianna,
and Lomna's head spoke, saying, 'A speckled, whitebellied salmon that
has swum with lesser fish under the sea.' Which was the origin of this
saying. With the second serving, Cairpre divided the fish into another
twenty-seven portions and the head said, 'You share an unjust portion
at the second serving. A just judge would divide it differently, even
though I have no belly to digest it. The hatred of the fianna will be upon
Luigne.'

'Oh, throw out that head!' exclaimed Cairpre. 'Since it heaps such
abuse upon us.'

Then the head spoke again: 'At the first assault, the chieftain runs
with his spear. You yourself will be jointed and divided and cut into
collops. Fionn will bring fire and sword upon the Luigne now.'

And after that remark, Fionn came into that place and killed them.

[This story tells of Fionn mac Cumail, who here uses his poetic skills of *teimn laegda* to discover the identity of the unfortunate Lomna. Lomna himself is no mean poet: as with many such magical poetic invocations, these are most obscure and difficult to translate. By discreet means, he informs Fionn about his woman's unfaithfulness, using ogham inscription. He cleverly writes something that would mean nothing much to a casual eye or ear, but which Fionn, with his poetic knowledge, can immediately understand and act upon. Cairpre offends against the fianna's code of hospitality when he divides the salmon and neglects to feed Lomna.]

PRULL: 'greatly'. As was said by the poetess, daughter of Ua Dulsaine to Senchán Torpest, 'My two ears burn me greatly.' To which one of Senchán's students replied, 'That is from the art of the Ua Dulasine poets of Liac in Tursaige.'

This is what happened to Senchán. He arranged to visit the Isle of Mann for a holiday, with fifty poets in his retinue, and other students besides. No other poet before had such a fine set of clothes upon his back, in addition to his fine tugain, his poet's cloak; he wore the best garments of the kind worn by the nobility of the Gael. After they had put to sea and turned their stern against the shore, a staggeringly ugly youth called to them from the land, 'Take me with you,' he cried. Everyone looked at him, not liking what they saw. He was not a bird of their flock, that was clear from his hideous appearance.

Whenever he touched his forehead, streams of pus would squirt out of his ears down his back. Across his skull were two criss-cross streams of it, as if his brains were leaking from his head, and the stench of this would knock you down. The eyes in his head were rounder than blackbird's eggs. His gaze was more frenetically agitated than the turning of a quern. His face was black as death itself. His cheeks bowed out more than a lifting crane and his nose longer than the snout of the smith's anvil. His breath came and went like the labouring bellows when it smelts the ore. The smith's hammer could not strike through the fiery globulous mass that issued from his mouth. He was swifter than the swallow or the hare upon the plain. His pointed teeth were yellower than gold and his gums greener than holly. His two shins were thin, naked and covered with freckles. His two heels were yellow, sharp and black-spotted. His shins were a distaff wide, his thighs a axe-handle's width. His bum was like a full cheese cut in half. His belly capacious as a sack and his neck the length of the stepping crane's. His head was the size of a soldier's pack-bag. His arms were of pitchfork length. His fists the size of a labourer's. If the dirty rag that clothed him had been taken off, it would be very hard for it not to go on a journey all by itself, unless a stone had anchored it, on account of the lice upon him.

The youth shouted loudly to Senchán, 'I would be more use to you than these poets or that stuck-up set of fools you have on board.'

'Set yourself down,' said Senchán, 'but better that you enter the ship from the rudder.'

'I'll try that thing,' said the youth. So he climbed on to the ship's rudder and swifter than a cat after the mouse, or a griffin to its nest or a hawk from a cliff, was the struggle he made until he was in the ship. But it nearly capsized because all the other voyagers moved to one side of the ship, leaving him to occupy the other side all by himself. And Senchán's retinue said, 'A monster has appeared to you, Senchán. And it looks as if it will be the only retinue you have if we ever reach land!' And ever afterwards, he was called Senchán Torpeist, or Senchán of the Monster.

They eventually reached the Isle of Mann and went ashore. While they were on the beach, they saw a weak, decrepit, grey-haired old woman upon the rocks. The old woman said to them,

> 'An old woman and an old priest,
> Both sprout death's broom upon their chins.
> While they do not serve God's Son,
> They do not give forth their first fruits.'

And this was how the old woman on the beach was, cutting sea-weed and gathering shell-fish. About her ankles and wrists were signs of high status but she had no decent clothes on her back. She had the transparency of famine about her. And this was a shame because she was none other than the poetess, daughter of Ua Dulsaine of the Muscraige, from Liac Thuill, in the land of the Ua Fidhgenti, who had gone on her circuit of Ireland and Alba and Mann until her retinue were all dead. And then her brother, a son of the Ua Dulsaine family, one skilled in the songs of the *sídhe*, had been asking for her all over Ireland and not finding her.

And when the old woman had seen the poets, she asked them who they were. And one of the retinue answered proudly, 'The ones you are asking about are good. This is none other than Senchán, Poet of Ireland.'

'Are you willing to lower yourself and answer me yourself, Senchán?' she asked him.

'You shall indeed be answered,' he said.

Then the woman chanted,

> 'I am not accustomed to suffering;
> Like the seaweed, I am soft and blistered.

'Can you quote me the following two lines?' she asked.

But the silence from Senchán and the other poets merely lengthened. Then the ugly youth leapt in front of Senchán and said to her, 'Cailleach, you should not approach Senchán. It is not honourable for you. Ask me instead, for none of these folk here are fit to address you.'

'So then,' said the female poet, 'what are the next two lines?'

'No problem!' said the youth.

> 'From the skin of Mann's rock,
> Much salt has been made.'

The woman said, 'Truly spoken! What is the other half of this quatrain, Senchán?

> What man thinks about me daily,
> For my two ears burn me greatly?'

'Amen!' cried the youth. 'Senchán shall not converse with you yet.'

'Very well,' she said, 'what is the answer according to you?'

'No problem! –

> Who but Mac Ua Dulsaine, the artist,
> From Liac of Tursaige Thuill?'

'Good heavens! Truly you are the lost poetess, daughter of the Ua Dulsaine family, who has been looked for all over Ireland and Scotland,' cried Senchán.

'That is myself,' she said.

Then Senchán rescued her. Some noble clothing suitable to her rank was put upon her and she returned to Ireland with Senchán.

When they reached Ireland they saw the youth who had been with them already upon the shore, but he was utterly changed. Now he was a brilliant, kingly young hero. Long-tailed eyes were in his head, his hair was long and golden. In appearance and dress, he was handsomer than any living man. Then he walked sunwise about Senchán and his retinue, and was seen no more after that time. There is no doubt that this was the spirit of Poetry himself.

[This story deals with who can be considered a true poet. Senchán's poetic retinue think a lot about themselves and Senchán himself as chief poet of Ireland should be able to complete the quotation with which the poetess challenges them. It is the ugly youth, the spirit of Poetry himself, who answers her courteously and correctly. Cormac irritatingly calls the poetess, *lethcerdd* or 'half-poet' throughout, when it is obvious from the context that she is more than a match in poetic skill for her opponents; we have chosen 'poetess' as a more respectful term than the implied dilletantism of 'half-poet'. The reason that Poetry first appears in this horrific guise is because it is one of the hardest of arts at the beginning: only when it is fully developed can its true splendour be known.]

TREFOT: that is Ireland, Mann and Alba, which are called *trefot* because three sods of ore were brought from each land so that they could be druidically made of one kind. As it is told in *Togail Bruigne da Dergae* (the Burning of Da Derga's Hostel), 'the luck of the sovereign earth'. She was is called Fuata, or rather Fotla, is called so because she is queen over three parts of the islands. There are three such queens, Eriu, Fotla and Banba. The *Lebor Gabala Erenn* (the Invasions of Ireland) have much to say on this matter.

[Trefot literally means 'three earths or soils.' This intriguing but infuriating laconic entry refers to a tradition that has not come down to us but which is vitally important for our understanding of Celtic culture. The magical act which binds Ireland, Mann and Alba into one entity may have occured at Trevot in Co Meath, and obviously involves the three sovereign goddesses Eriu, Fotla and Banba to each of whom the poet Amairgin White-Knee made a promise to name Ireland. See pp. 6–15 in *Encyclopaedia of Celtic Wisdom*. The text speaks of three ores being brought. Now this would suggest the forging of some iron object, which perhaps was held as a piece of sacred regalia by the druids of Meath, though we have no evidence of this. The name of the goddess Fotla literally means 'a sod of earth'. The reference to the Burning of Da Derga's Hostel is unclear to us, unless it is an allusion to the confounding of this sacred forging of the three ores in some manner: perhaps in much the same way that, in the Welsh Triads, the disinterment of Bran's head by Arthur oversets Bran's protective and palladian influence in fending off invaders.

The only other magical reference to sods of earth that may be set aside this story occur in the life of Mongán, see p. 174, where he puts a sod of earth from Scotland in one shoe and a sod of Irish earth in the other to confuse the druids who are looking for him.

However, the three-legged symbol of the sunwise triskele is central to Celtic ideology, conveying good fortune. This three-legged symbol is still the emblem of the Isle of Man. Triplicity is commonly found in the groupings of many deities, like the threefold Brighid, see above. We may cross-reference the wider Indo-European tradition and look at India to see a continuing obsession with the *tri-murti* of deities Brahma, Vishnu and Shiva and their consorts Sarasvati, Lakshmi and Parvati/ Durga. Sun-wheel symbols such as the Hindu swastika, which moves sunwise, not like the Nazi reverse swastika which moves widdershins, remain symbols of luck. Hindus still proclaim, 'Svasti, svasti,' or 'Good Fortune,' invoking this life-giving quality of movement and growth.]

SIEGES,
BURNINGS
AND CURSES

20. The Destruction of Dind Rig

(Orgain Denna Ríg)

Translated by Whitley Stokes

There are three copies of this tale of treachery, love, and vengeance. The present version is from the *Book of Leinster*, there is another in the Bodleian library (Rawlinson B. 502) which dates from the twelfth century, and a third in *The Yellow Book of Lecan*. The three copies generally agree, though the one included here is slightly fuller.

The hero of this story is originally called Moén, which means 'dumb', but a chance encounter with a hurley stick causes him to cry out, from which he receives him manhood name of Labraid (Speaking). Craiphtine the harper also appears in the *Táin Bó Froech* and plays the slumber stain, or *goiltraigh*, to deadly effect in both.

Dind Rig (Fortress of Kings) has been identified with the ruins of earthworks on the west bank of the River Barrow near Leighlinbridge, Co Carlow. The final incident may actually be a historical incident, as it appears in the *Annals of Tigernach* as follows: 'Cobthach, the Meagre of Bregia, son of Ugaine the Great, was burnt, with thirty kings around him, at Dind rig of Magh Ailbe, in the palace of Tuaimm Tenbath. Precisely, by Labraid the Dumb, the Exile, son of Ailill of Ane, son of Loeguire Lorc, in revenge for his father.'

Whence is the Destruction of Dind Rig?

Easy (to say). Cobthach the Meagre of Bregia, the son of Ugaine the Great, was king of Bregia, but Loegaire Lorc, son of Ugaine, was king of Erin. He, too, was a son of Ugaine the Great. Cobthach was envious towards Loegaire concerning the kingship of Erin, and wasting and grief assailed him, so that his blood and his flesh wasted away. Wherefore he was surnamed the Meagre of Bregia, and Loegaire's murder was brought about.

So Loegaire was called to Cobthach that he might leave him his blessing before he died. Now when Loegaire went in to his brother the leg of a hen's chick is broken on the floor of the house.

'Unlucky was thine illness,' says Loegaire.

'This is fitting,' says Cobtlhach, 'all has departed, both blood and bone, both life and wealth. Thou hast done me damage, my lad, ill breaking the hen's leg. Bring it hither that I may put a bandage round it.'

'Woe is me,' says Loegaire, 'the man has decay and destruction: he is delivered into neglect.'

'Come tomorrow,' says Cobthach 'that my tomb be raised by thee, and that my pillar-stone be planted, my assembly of mourning be held, and my burial-paean be performed; for I shall die swiftly.'

'Well,' says Loegaire, 'it shall be done.'

'Well, then,' saith Cobthach to his queens and his steward, 'say ye that I am dead, but let none other know it, and let me be put into my chariot – with a razor-knife in my (right) hand. My brother will come to me vehemently, to bewail me, and will throw himself upon me. Mayhap he will get somewhat from me.'

This was true. The chariot is brought out. His brother came to bewail him. He comes and flings himself down upon Cobthach who plunges the knife into Loegaire at the small of his back, so that its point appeared at the top of his heart, and thus Loegaire died, and was buried in Druim Loegairi.

Loegaire left a son, even Ailill of Ane. He assumed the kingship of Leinster. The first parricide did not seem enough to Cobthach so he gave silver to someone who administered a deadly drink to Ailill, and thereof he died.

After that, Cobthach took the realm of Leinster. Now Ailill of Ane had left a son, even Móen Ollam. Now he was dumb until he became a big man. One day then, in the playground, as he was hurling, a hockey-stick chanced over his shin. 'This has befallen me!' says he.

'Móen labraid ("speaks")', say the lads. From that time Labraid was his name.

The men of Erin are summoned by Cobthach to partake of the Feast of Tara. Labraid went, like every one, to partake of it. Now when they were most gloriously consuming the banquet, the eulogists were on the floor, lauding the king and the queens, the princes and the nobles.

'Well then,' says Cobthach, 'know ye who is the most hospitable (man) in Erin?'

'We know,' says Craiphtine (the Harper), 'it is Labraid Loingsech, son of Ailill. I went to him in spring, and he killed his only ox for me.'

Says Ferchertne the Poet: 'Labraid is the most hospitable man we know. I went to him in winter, and he killed his only cow for me, and he possessed nothing but her.'

'Go ye with him then!' says Cobthach, 'since he is more hospitable than I.'

'He will not be the worse of this,' says Craiphtine, 'and thou wilt not be the better.'

'Out of Erin with you then,' says Cobthach, 'so long as thou art alive!'

'Unless we find our place (of refuge) in it,' says the lad.

They are then rejected.

'Whither shall we go?' says the lad.

'Westwards,' answered Ferchertne.

So forth they fare to the king of the Men of Morca, the Men of Morca that dwelt about Luachair Dedad in the west. Scoriath is he that was their king.

'What has brought you?' asked Scoriath.

'Our rejection by the king of Erin.'

'Ye are welcome,' says Scoriath. 'Your going or your staying will be the same (to us) so long as I am alive. Ye shall have good comradeship,' says the king.

Scoriath had a daughter, whose name was Moriath They were guarding her carefully, for no husband fit for her had been found at once. Her mother was keeping her. The mother's two eyes never slept (at the same time), for one of the two was watching her daughter. Howbeit the damsel loved Labraid. There was a plan between her and him. Scoriath held a great feast for the Men of Morca. This is the plan they made – after the drinking, Craiphtine should play the slumber-strain, so that her mother should fall asleep and Labraid should reach the chamber. Now that came to pass. Craiphtine hid not his harp that night, so that the queen fell asleep, and the (loving) couple came together.

Not long afterwards the queen awoke. 'Rise, O Scoriath!' says she. 'Ill is the sleep in which thou art. Thy daughter has a woman's breath. Hearken to her sigh after her lover has gone from her.'

Then Scoriath rose up. 'Find out who has done this,' quoth he, 'that he may be put to the sword at once!'

No one knew who had done it.

'The wizards and the poets shall lose their heads unless they find out who has done it.'

'It will be a disgrace to thee,' says Ferchertne, 'to kill thine own household.'

'Then thou thyself shalt lose thy head unless thou tellest.'

'Tell,' quoth Labraid: ''tis enough that I only should be ruined.'

Then said Ferchertne: 'The lute hid no music from Craiphtine's harp till he cast a death-sleep on the hosts, so that harmony was spread between Moen and marriageable Moriath of Morca. More to her than any price was Labraid.'

'Labraid,' says he, 'forgathered with her after ye had been lulled by Craiphtine's harp.'

In this he betrayed his companions.

'Well then,' says Scoriath, 'until tonight we have not chosen a husband for our daughter, because of our love for her. (But) if we had been choosing one, 'tis he whom we have found here. Let drinking take place within,' says the king, 'and let his wife be put at Labraid's hand. And I will never part from him till he be king of Leinster.'

Then Labraid's wife came to him and sleeps with him.

And thereafter they deliver a hosting of the Munstermen till they reached Dind rig (for) the first destruction. And they were unable to destroy it until the warriors outside made a deceptive plan, namely, that Craiphtine should go on the rampart of the fortress to play the slumber-strain to the host within, so that it might be overturned, and that the host outside should put their faces to the ground and their fingers in their ears that they might not hear the playing.

So that was done there, and the men inside fell asleep and the fortress was captured, and the garrison was slaughtered, and the fortress was sacked.

Now Moriath was on the hosting. She did not deem it honourable to put her fingers into her ears at her own music, so that she lay asleep for three days, no one daring to move her.

Whence said Flann Mac Lónáin:

'As great Moriath slept before the host of Morca –
more than any tale – when Dind rig was sacked –
course without a fight when the hole-headed lute played
    a melody.'

Thereafter Labraid took the realm of Leinster, and he and Cobthach were at peace, and his seat was at Dind rig.

Once upon a time, however, when he had taken it, and Cobthach had the full kingship, he induced this Cobthach to do his will and meet his desire. So a house was built by him to receive Cobthach. Passing strong was the house: it was made of iron, both wall and floor and doors. A full year were the Leinstermen abuilding it, and father would hide it from son, and mother from daughter, husband from wife, and wife from husband, so that no one heard from another what they were going about, and for whom they were gathering their gear and their fittings. To this refers (the proverb): not more numerous are Leinstermen than (their) secrets. Where the house was built was in Dind rig.

Then Cobthach was invited to the ale and the feast, and with him went thirty [. . .] of the kings of Erin. Howbeit Cobthach was unable to enter the house until Labraid's mother and his jester went in. This is what the jester chose (as his reward for doing so): the benediction of the Leinstermen, and the freedom of his children forever. Out of goodness to her son the woman went. On that night Labraid himself was managing household matters.

On the morrow he went to play against the lads in the meadow. His fosterer saw him. He plies a one-stemmed thorn on Labraid's back and head. 'Apparently,' saith he, 'the murder thou hast (to do) is a murder by a boy! Ill for thee my lad, to invite the king of Erin with thirty kings, and not to be in their presence, meeting their desire.'

Then Labraid dons (his mantle) and goes to them into the house. 'Ye have fire, and ale and food (brought) into the house.'

''Tis meet,' says Cobthatch.

Nine men had Labraid on the floor of the house. They drag the chain that was out of the door behind them, and cast it on the pillar-stone, in front of the house; and the thrice fifty forge-bellows they had around it, with four warriors at each bellows, were blown till the house became hot for the host.

'Thy mother is there, O Labraid,' say the warriors.

'Nay, my darling son,' says she. 'Secure thine honour through me, for I shall die at all events.'

So then Cobthach Coel is there destroyed, with seven hundred followers and thirty kings around him, on the eve of great Christmas precisely. Hence is said:

Three hundred years victorious reckoning –

before Christ's birth, a holy conception,
it was not fraternal, it was evil –
(Loegaire) Lorc was slain by Cobthatch Coel.
Cobthach Coel with thirty kings,
Labraid (. . .) slew him.
Loegaire's grandson from the main,
in Dind rig the host was slain.

And 'tis of this that Ferchertne the poet said:

Dind rig, which had been Tuaim Tenbath,
Máin Ollam he was at first,
Labraid Móen afterwards,
but 'Labraid the Exile',
since he went into exile,
when he gained a realm
as far as the Ictian Sea [i.e. English Channel],
and brought the many foreigners
with him (to Ireland),
two thousand and two hundred foreigners
with broad lances in their hands
from which the Laigin (Leinstermen) are so called.

This is the Destruction of Dind rig.

21. The Siege of Howth

(Talland Etair)

Translated by Whitley Stokes

The following story comes from the *Book of Leinster*, with occasional variations from Harlian 5280 f 54b, a fifteenth century copy preserved in the British Museum Library. Much of the action turns upon the character of the Bard and Satirist Athern (Athairne), who was famed for the exorbitant demands he made for tribute. He constantly made as much as he could from the law that said no poet should be refused anything he asked (presumably because of the fear that the poet would satirise anyone who refused, thus very possibly ruining his standing in the community). Much of this story is thus an account of Atherne's outrageous requests and the pains taken by others to fulfil them. The battle itself is caused by the men of Leinster attempting to recover their wives and cattle, which Atherne had demanded. In the course of the fighting, two brothers of the great Ultonian hero Conall Cernach are killed, thus requiring revenge to be taken against those who killed them. The one-handed king Mes-Gegra is perhaps most famous in that the calcified ball made from his brains is later used to kill Conchobar mac Nessa (see p. 458). Howth itself is a site which is mentioned frequently in Irish tradition, in particular as the site of the home of the semi-immortal champion Crimthann Nia Nair. It is identified with a stretch of land which juts into the Irish Sea a few miles north-east of Dublin.

In Ireland there dwelt a hard, merciless man, to wit, Atherne the Urgent of Ulster. A man that asked the one-eyed for his single eye and used to demand the woman in childbed. He was so called from going by Conor's counsel, on a (bardic) circuit. This is the way he went at first, lefthandwise about Ireland till he made the round of Connaught. This is the way he then went, to the king of the midst of Ireland, between the two Fords of Hurdles, namely, to Eochaid son of Luchta, king of the south of Connaught. Eochaid went to deliver Atherne to the men of Munster over the Shannon, southward.

'That thou mayst not shew thanklessness towards us, O Atherne,' saith Eochaid. 'If we have aught of jewels or treasures that are good in thine eyes, take them.'

'There is, forsooth!' saith Atherne, 'the single eye there in thy head, to be given to me into my fist.'

'There shall be no refusal,' saith Eochaid, 'thou shalt have it.'

So then the king put his finger under his eye, and tore it out of his head, and gave it into Atherne's fist.

'Take my hand, O gillie,' saith the king, 'and lead me to the water that I may wash my face.'

Then he poured three waves of the water on his face.

'Has the eye been torn out of my head, O gillie?' saith the king.

'Woe is me!' saith the gillie, 'red (derg), is the lough (derc) with thy blood!'

'This shall be its name forever,' saith the king, '"Redlough", namely "Dergderc".'

For the generosity that the king shewed, to wit, giving his single eye for his honour's sake, as a miracle of generosity God gave him his two eyes.

This is the way Atherne went thereafter, to the king of Munster, even to Tigerna Tétbuillech. Nought then took he for his honour save that the queen should sleep with him that night, or the honour of the men of Munster should be lost for ever. And that night on which the woman was brought to bed, this is the night that she slept with Atherne, for sake of her husband's honour, that his honour might not be taken away.

This is the way Atherne went thereafter, to Leinster, till he abode in Ard Brestine in in the south of Moyfea. And they came to the south of Leinster to meet him and to offer him jewels and treasures, not to come into the country, so that he might not leave invectives. For the treasures of no one whom he assailed would abide unless a gift were given to him. And no folk or tribe by whom he should be slain would get reprisal. So that (any) man would give his wife to him, or his single eye out of his head, or his desire of jewels and treasures. Now this is what he bore in his mind, great invectives to leave on the Leinstermen, so that they should slay him, and that Ulster would thus be for ever avenging him on Leinster. So then he made a demand of (the men of) the south of

Leinster in Brestine (and he said) that he saw not of jewels or treasures aught that he would take from them, but he would leave an *ail bréthre* (verbal insult) on them for ever, so that they should not hold up their faces before the Gael, unless they gave him the jewel that was best on the hill; and (he said) that no one in the hill knew what this jewel was or what place it was in.

That was an outrage and great disgrace to the host. And they all besought the Lord of the Elements to give them help to put away from them the outrage that was inflicted upon them.

Now there was a horseman training his horse on the hill: he used to move towards the meeting: he used to leap from it. And once, while turning the horse over-shanks, the horse flung a great sod from his two hooves. No one in the meeting noticed it till it came into the bosom of the king, to wit, Fergus Fairge. And in the face of the sod, on the clayey side, he saw the brooch wherein were four-score ounces of red gold.

'What is this in my bosom, O Atherne?' saith the king.

Then said Atherne:

> 'A brooch there is in Ard Brestine .
> From a horse's hooves it hath been given
> Over it a great just judgment hath been passed,
> In the mantle of Mane son of Durthacht.'

'That is the brooch whereof I were fain,' says Atherne. 'My father's brother left it, and buried it in the ground after the breaking of a battle-slaughter on the Ulstermen, to wit, the Battle of Brestine.'

So then the brooch was given to him. And he went thereafter to Mes-gegra, the king of Leinster. A brother of his was Mes-róidia. Two sons of two mutes were those. Deaf and dumb were their mother and their father. Mes-gegra made great welcome to Atherne.

'It is well, indeed,' saith Atherne, 'provided thy wife be with me till morning.'

'Wherefore should I give thee my wife,' says the king.

'For thy honour's sake,' saith Atherne, 'or slay me, so that there may be a shame on Leinstermen forever and so that Ulster may never cease to avenge me upon them.'

'If it be for the Ulstermen, thou shalt not find welcome with me, O Atherne. But thou shalt have the woman for my honour's sake. Nevertheless there is not in Ulster a man who could take her unless I gave her to thee for my honour's sake.'

'This is true,' saith Atherne, 'that I will not stop from thee till a man of Ulster bear off thy head and thy wife.'

'That shall not be considered against thee,' saith the king. 'Thou shalt have welcome.'

The woman sleeps with him, even Buan, Mes-gegra's wife. And Atherne keeps on the circuit of Leinster till the end of a year, and he took thrice fifty queens of the wives of princes and nobles of Leinster to carry them with him to his (own) country.

'Well now, my lad,' saith Atherne to his gillie, 'fare thou for me to the Ulstermen that they come to meet me. Meseemeth the Leinstermen will be plotting against me concerning my booty unless I appeal to their honour.'

Then the Leinstermen went to bid farewell to Atherne till they were at the Tolka to the north of Dublin. Then Atherne bids them farewell, and he left (them) no blessing and took none from them.

Sorrowful were the Leinstermen that their wives should be taken from them in captivity to Ulster. So when Atherne came to Ainech Lagen, the Leinstermen went to pursue their booty. Then came the Ulstermen after Atherne: they came to protect him. A battle is fought about him straightway. The Ulstermen are routed, and they went by the sea eastward until they were shut up in Howth. Nine watches were they in Howth without drink, without food, unless they drank the brine of the sea, or unless they devoured the clay. Seven hundred kine, in sooth, had Atherne in the middle of the fort; and there was not a boy or man of Ulster who tasted their milk, but the milking was cast down the cliff, so that of the Ulstermen none might find out Atherne's food to taste it. And the wounded men were brought to him, and he would not let a drop go into their mouths, so that they used to bleed to death alone.

And the chiefs of Ulster used to come to him entreating a drink for Conor, and nought they got from him, so that what supported Conor was what the girl used to bring on her back from Emain Macha at nones, even Leborcham – she it is that used to bring it.

A slave and a slavegirl were in Conor's house, and this is the child that was born to them, even the girl Leborcham. Uncomely, now, was the girl's shape, to wit, her two feet and her two knees behind her, her two hams and her two heels before her. She it is that used to travel through Ireland in one day. Every thing of good or of evil that was done in Ireland she used to relate to Conor in the Red Branch at the end of the day. A loaflet of three score cakes she had before her at the end of the fire, besides her share with the host. She it is that used to bring Conor his share on her back from Emain to Howth.

The fighting used to continue both day and night around the fort. Leinstermen say it was they that built Dún Etair. Cú Chulainn's gap is there without closing. Everyone was inciting him about fencing it.

'Not so,' saith he [Cú Chulainn] 'a heap of spears closes it for me.' Conor used to advise Cú Chulainn not to put forth his prowess until a muster of Ulstermen should come. For Leborcham had gone to muster the Ulstermen that they might come in boats or by land to help them.

Mess-dead, son of Amargen, a foster-son of Cú Chulainn's, a boy of seven years, was put to keep the door of the fort. And nine men every hour of the day were slain by him, and Ulster's hostages were brought forth by the Leinstermen thrice every day, and they were borne-off in like wise, by Mess-dead in combat. Wherefore it is on him that unequal combat was first practised in Ireland.

This then is what they say, when the Ulstermen made land on the east of Howth, then three hundred heroes went to the wicket to stay him. There he gave forth his warcry, as they were cutting off his head. And Cú Chulainn heard it (and said):

'It is the sky that crashes, or the sea that flows, or the earth that quakes, or the warshout of my foster-son at unequal combat being practised against him!' With that Cú Chulainn started out suddenly. The host was cleft in twain behind him. A battle is fought there straightway. Heavy in sooth was the attack that they delivered. Bloody the mutual uplifting: destructive the prowess which the heroes and the champions of valour displayed.

The two lines of battle were joined from terce to none. There the Leinstermen are routed, so that they raised a red wall against the Ulstermen, for it was a prohibition to Ulster to pass over a red wall. *Fe* on this side and *fe* on that was the conflict.

A great multitude of Ulstermen fell there in answering the fight. First there fell Mess-dead son of Amargen, and Brianin Brethach, and Condla, and Beothach, and Conaed son of Morna, and a multitude besides.

Alone fared Conall Cernach in pursuit of the Leinstermen, to avenge his brothers, Mes-dead and Loegaire, who had fallen in the fight. This is the road he went: through Dublin, past Drimnagh, through Hy-Gavla into Forcarthain, by Uachtar Ard, past Naas, to Clane.

Now when the Leinstermen reached their country, each man of them went to his stead. But Mes-gegra (the king) stayed behind the host alone with his charioteer at the Path of Clane.

'I will sleep at present,' saith the charioteer to Mes-gegra, 'and thou shalt sleep then.'

'I deem it well,' saith the king.

Now while Mes-gegra was looking at the water he saw a wonderful nut floating along the river towards him. Larger than a man's head was the nut. And he himself went down, and brought it to him, and cleft it with his skene, [knife] and left half the kernel for the gillie. And he saw tha the gillie was lifted up in his sleep from the ground – and after that the gillie awoke from his sleep.

'How is it with thee, my lad?' saith the king.

'I have seen an evil vision,' saith the gillie.

'Catch the horses, my lad,' saith the king.

The gillie caught the horses.

'Hast thou eaten up the nut?' saith the gillie.

'Yea,' saith the king.

'Didst thou leave the half for me?' saith the gillie.

'I lessened it first,' saith the king.

'The man that ate the little behind my back,' saith the gillie, 'would eat the much.'

The king's hand, with half the kernel therein, was over against him. The gillie attacks him with a sword and cut his hand off from him.

'That is bad, O gillie,' saith the king. 'Open my fist: half the kernel is therein.'

As the gillie saw that, he turned the sword against himself, and it went westwards through his back.

'Woe is me, my lad!' saith the king.

Mes-gegra himself yokes his chariot, and puts his (severed) hand into it before him.

Now when he went out of the ford westwards then came Conall into the ford on the east.

'Is that so, O Mes-gegra?' saith Conall.

'I am here,' saith Mes-gegra.

'What then?' saith Conall.

'What can be wished,' saith Mes-gegra, 'but (this): on him from whom thou claimest debts, make demand with all the might thou mayst have.'

'My brothers are with thee,' saith Conall.

'Not in my girdle are they,' saith Mes-gegra.

'That is a blemish,' saith Conall.

'True valour it is not,' saith Mes-gegra, 'to fight with me who have but one hand.'

'Thus shall it be,' saith Conall, 'my hand shall be tied to my side,' saith Conall.

Triply was Conall Cernach's hand tied to his side. And each smote the other till the river was red from them. Then was Conall's swordplay the mightier.

'Well, then, O Conall,' saith Mes-gegra. 'I wot thou wilt not go till thou takest my head with thee. Take thou my head on thy head and my glory on thy glory.'

Conall severs his head from him in the Path of Clane, and Conall takes the head and put it on the flagstone on the ford's brink. A drop came from the neck of the head and went into the top of the stone and passed through it to the ground. Then he put Mes-gegra's head on the stone, and it went from the top of the stone to the ground, and it fared before him to the river. Conall the Cross-eyed was his name thitherto. For the Ulstermen had three blemishes, to wit, Conall the Cross-eyed and Cú Chulainn the Blind, and Cuscraid the Mute. The women of Ulster divided (themselves) into three. Each loved a man of that triad. The third that loved Cú Chulainn, they used to be blind while conversing with him; the third that loved Conall Cernach used to be cross-eyed while conversing with him; the third that loved Cuscraid the Mute used to be dumb while conversing with him.

Howbeit Conall put his head on his (own) head, and the head went over his shoulder, and he was straight-eyed from that hour.

Then Conall went alone into his chariot, and his charioteer into Mesgegra's chariot. They go forward then into Uachtar Fine till they met with fifty women, namely Mes-gegra's wife Buan, with her maidens, coming southwards from the border.

'With whom art thou, O woman?' saith Conall.

'(I am) the wife of Mes-gegra the king.'

'It hath been enjoined on thee to come with me,' saith Conall.

'Who hath enjoined me?' saith the woman.

'Mes-gegra,' saith Conall.

'Hast thou brought a token with thee?' saith the woman.

'His chariot and his horses here,' saith Conall.

'Many are they on whom he bestows treasures,' saith the woman.

'His head is here then,' saith Conall.

'I am lost to him now!' says the woman.

The head [turned red and then white].

'What is it ails the head?' says Conall.

'I know,' says the woman. 'A dispute arose between him and Atherne. He declared that not one man of Ulster should bear me away. A contest about his word, this it is that ails the head.'

'Come thou to me,' says Conall, 'into the chariot.'

'Stay for me', she says, 'till I bewail my husband.'

Then she lifts up her cry of lamentation, and it was heard even unto Tara and to Aillen, and she cast herself backwards, and she [was] dead.

On the road is her grave, even Coll Buana – [because of] the hazel (*coll*) which grew through her grave.

'Bear it hence, my lad,' says Conall.

'I cannot bear the head with me,' says the gillie.

'Take out its brain therefrom,' says Conall, 'and ply a sword upon it, and bear the brain with thee, and mix lime therewith, and make a ball thereof.'

This is done, and the head is left with the woman. And they fared on till they reached Emain. So the Ulstermen had exultation at the slaying of the king of Leinster.

Hence then is the circuit of Athirne, and the slaying of Mes-gegra by Conall Cernach, and the battle of Howth.

22. The Destruction of Da Derga's Hostel

(Togail Bruidne da Derga)

Translated by Whitley Stokes

'The Destruction of Da Derga's Hostel' is one the few complete narratives of any great extent preserved from ancient Irish literature. The oldest manuscript was copied about the year 1100 CE, but the saga existed in written form as early as the eighth or ninth century. According to the annals, Conaire was high king of Ireland about the beginning of the Christian era. The famous Hostel of Da Derga, which offered such astonishing hospitality, was believed to be situated among the hills overlooking the village of Bray near Dublin, and was built over the Dodder, a little stream that flows through Donnybrook and empties into Dublin Bay. The story, though rambling and disconnected in places, is told with real power and contains some of the finest descriptive passages in early Irish literature, especially the long description of Etain herself on p. 290, which makes her live and breathE before us. Much of the story is, indeed, no more than an excuse for the author to show off his knowledge and descriptive powers, as he takes us through the rooms of the hostel and its many strange and bizarre occupants. In all, it reads much like a *Who's Who* of the warriors and otherworld beings of Ireland at that time, and there are many more rooms which we have omitted here for reasons of space. Thus we find 'The Room of Kitcheners', 'The Room of the Servant Guards', 'The Room of the Swineherds', 'The Room of the Mimes,' and 'The Room of Nar-the-Squinter-with-the-left-eye' – and so on, to the limit of the medieval Irish court.

After giving an account of Conaire's antecedents and birth, the story goes on to tell how the youthful king met his tragic and untimely death. He is represented as the grandson of Etain, whose life history is recorded in 'The Wooing of Etain' (pp. 389–408 in The *Encyclopaedia of Celtic*

Wisdom), though there is some confusion over the fact that there are two Etains, one the granddaughter of the other. Like numerous other characters in early Irish fiction, he is subject to certain *geasa*, or taboos, which he violates only on peril of his life. The fairy folk, in revenge for the injury which Conaire's grandfather had done them in destroying their mound, bring it about that Conaire breaks all his taboos and so falls a victim to the perfidy of his own foster-brothers and of the British pirates who act as their allies.

The mention of the *Tarbh Feis* or Bull Feast is interesting. This curious ritual seems to have been a left over from an older, shamanic tradition in which the druid would sleep on the freshly flayed hide of a bull after eating a broth made from its flesh. It is also a ritualised form of *imbas ferosna*, one of three well-known methods of divination in Celtic tradition.

The following translation is complete except for the omission of a few unimportant repetitious passages. We have added some material from other versions of the text included by Stokes in his full edition. We have also changed the layout of the text in one place – the list of Conaire's *geasa* have been set out as they are in the original, as poetry. The list of names given by the seeress Cailb (p. 304) is omitted in the translation, but we have restored them from the text as they are evidently a kind of magical invocation based on the punning nature of the names. Not all are translatable, but some, such as Caill (wood), Coll (hazel), Dairne (oak-slave) imply that Cailb draws some of her nature from trees; but most are words which suggest that she was ugly and uncouth and generally not the kind of person one would want to have in one's house!

There was a famous and noble king over Erin, named Eochaid Fedlech. Once upon a time he came over the fair-green of Bri Leith, and he saw at the edge of a well a woman with a bright comb of silver adorned with gold, washing in a silver basin wherein were four golden birds and little, bright gems of purple carbuncle in the rims of the basin. A mantle she had, curly and purple, a beautiful cloak, and in the mantle silvery fringes arranged, and a brooch of fairest gold. A kirtle she wore, long, hooded, hardsmooth, of green silk, with red embroidery of gold. Marvellous clasps of gold and silver in the kirtle on her breasts and her shoulders and spaulds on every side. The sun kept shining upon her, so that the glistening of the gold against the sun from the green silk was manifest to the men. On her head were two golden-yellow tresses, in each of which was a plait of four strands, with a bead of gold at the point of each strand. The hue of that hair seemed to the king and his companions like the flower of the iris in summer, or like red gold after the burnishing thereof.

There she was, undoing her hair to wash it, with her arms out through the sleeve-holes of her smock. White as the snow of one night were the two hands, soft and even, and red as foxglove were the two clearbeautiful cheeks. Dark as the back of a stag-beetle the two eyebrows. Like a shower of pearls were the teeth in her head. Blue as a hyacinth were the eyes. Red as rowan-berries the lips. Very high, smooth and softshining the shoulders. Clearwhite and long the fingers. Long were the hands. White as the foam of a wave was the flank, slender, long, tender, smooth, soft as wool. Polished and warm, sleek and white were the two thighs. Round and small, hard and white the two knees. Short and white and rulestraight the two shins. Justly straight and beautiful the two heels. If a measure were put on the feet it would hardly have found them unequal. The bright radiance of the moon was in her noble face; the loftiness of pride in her smooth eyebrows; the light of wooing in each of her regal eyes. A dimple of delight in each of her cheeks, with a variegation in them at one time of purple spots with redness of a calf's blood, and at another with the bright lustre of snow. Soft womanly dignity in her voice; a step steady and slow she had; a queenly gait was hers. Verily, of the world's women 'twas she was the dearest and loveliest and justest that the eyes of men had ever beheld. It seemed to king Eochaid and his followers that she was from the fairymounds. Of her was said: 'Shapely are all till compared with Etain; dear are all till compared with Etain.'

A longing for her straightway seized the king; so he sent forward a man of his people to detain her. The king asked tidings of her and said, while announcing himself: 'Shall I have an hour of dalliance with thee?'

''Tis for that we have come hither under thy safeguard,' said she.

'Whence art thou and whence hast thou come?' asked Eochaid.

'Easy to say,' answered she. 'Etain am I, daughter of Etar, king of Echrad. I have been here for twenty years since I was born in a fairymound. The men of the fairy-mound, both kings and nobles, have been wooing me; but nought was gotten from me, because ever since I was able to speak, I have loved thee and given thee a child's love for the high tales about thee and thy splendour. And though I have never seen thee, I knew thee at once from thy description: it is thou, then, I have found.'

'No "seeking of an ill friend afar" shall be thine,' said Eochaid. 'Thou shalt have welcome, and for thee every other woman shall be left by me, and with thee alone will I live so long as thou hast honour.'

'Pay me my proper bride-price,' she said, 'and afterwards grant my wish.'

'Thou shalt have both,' said Eochaid.

The value of seven bondmaids was given to her, and she became Eochaid's wife.

Then the king, Eochaid Fedlech, died leaving one daughter named, like her mother, Etain, and she was wedded to Cormac, king of Ulster. After the end of a time Cormac, king of Ulster, 'the man of the three gifts,' forsook Eochaid's daughter, because she was barren save for one daughter that she had borne to Cormac after the making of the pottage which her mother – the woman from the fairy mounds – gave her. Then she said to her mother: 'Bad is what thou hast given me: it will be a daughter that I shall bear.'

'That will not be good,' said her mother; 'a king's pursuit will be on her.'

Then Cormac again wedded his wife, even Etain, and this was his desire, that the daughter of the woman who had before been abandoned (i.e., his own daughter) should be killed. So Cormac would not leave the girl to her mother to be nursed. Then his two thralls took her to a pit, but she smiled a laughing smile at them as they were putting her into it. Then their kindly nature came to them. They carried her into the calf shed of the cowherds of Eterscel, great-grandson of Iar king of Tara, and they fostered her till she became a good embroideress; and there was not in Ireland a king's daughter dearer than she.

A fenced house of wickerwork was made by the thralls for her, without any door, but only a window and a skylight. King Eterscel's folk espied that house and supposed that it was food that the cowherds kept there. But one of them went and looked through the skylight, and he saw in the house the dearest, most beautiful maiden! This was told to the king, and straightway he sent his people to wreck the house and carry her off without asking the cowherds. For the king was childless, and it had been prophesied to him by his wizards that a woman of unknown race would bear him a son. Then said the king: 'This is the woman that has been prophesied to me!'

Now while she was there next morning she saw a bird on the skylight coming to her, and he left his birdskin on the floor of the house, and went to her and captured her, and said: 'They are coming to thee from the king to wreck thy house and to bring thee to him perforce. And thou wilt be pregnant by me, and bear a son, and that son must not kill birds. And Conaire, son of Mess Buachalla shall be his name'; for hers was Mess Buachalla, 'the Cowherds' Foster-child.'

And then she was brought to the king, and with her went her fosterers, and she was betrothed to the king, and he gave her the value of seven bondmaids and to her fosterers a like amount. And afterwards they were made chieftains, so that they all became law worthy, whence are the two Fedlimids the stewards. And then she bore a son to the king, called Conaire son of Mess Buachalla, and these were her three urgent prayers to the king – the nursing of her son among three households; that is, the fosterers who had nurtured her, and Mane Honeywords, and herself the third; and she said that such of the men of Erin as should wish to do aught for this boy should give securities to those three households for the boy's protection.

So thus he was reared, and the men of Erin straightway knew this boy on the day he was born. And other boys were fostered with him, to wit, Fer Le and Fer Gair and Fer Rogain, three sons of Donn Desa the champion.

Now Conaire possessed three gifts – the gift of hearing and the gift of eyesight and the gift of judgment; and of those three gifts he taught one to each of his three foster-brothers. And whatever meal was prepared for him, the four of them would go to it. Even though three meals were prepared for him each of them would go to his meal. The same raiment and armour and colour of horses had the four.

Then King Eterscel died. A bull-feast was prepared by the men of Erin in order to determine their future king; that is, a bull was killed by them and thereof one man ate his fill and drank its broth, and a spell of truth was chanted over him in his bed. Whomsoever he would see in his sleep would be king, and the sleeper would perish if he uttered a falsehood.

Four men in chariots were on the Plain of Liffey at their game, Conaire himself and his three foster-brothers. Then his fosterers went to him and summoned him to the bull-feast. The bullfeaster, in his sleep, at the end of the night had beheld a man stark-naked, passing along the road of Tara, with a stone in his sling. 'I will go in the morning after you,' said Conaire.

He left his foster-brothers at their game, and turned his chariot and his charioteer and fared to Dublin. There he saw great white-speckled birds, of unusual size and colour and beauty. He pursued them until his horses were tired. The birds would go a spearcast before him, and would not go any farther. He alighted, took his sling out of the chariot, and went after them until he reached the sea. The birds betook themselves to the waves. He went after them and overcame them. The birds quit their birdskins, and turned upon him with spears and swords. One of them protected him, and addressed him, saying: 'I am Nemglan, king of thy father's birds; and thou hast been forbidden to cast at birds, for here there is no one that should not be dear to thee because of his father or mother.'

'Till to-day,' said Conaire, 'I knew not this.'

'Go to Tara tonight,' said Nemglan; ''tis fittest for thee. A bull-feast is there, and through it thou shalt be king. A man stark-naked, who shall go at the end of the night along one of the roads of Tara, having a stone and a sling – 'tis he that shall be king.'

So Conaire fared forth naked; and on each of the four roads whereby men go to Tara there were three kings awaiting him, and they had raiment for him, since it had been foretold that he would come stark-naked. Then he was seen from the road on which his fosterers were, and they put royal raiment about him, and placed him in a chariot, and he took sureties.

The folk of Tara said to him: 'It seems to us that our bull-feast and our spell of truth are a failure, if it be only a young, beardless lad that we have visioned therein.'

'That is of no moment,' said he. 'For a young, generous king like me to be in the kingship is no disgrace, since the taking of Tara's sureties is mine by right of father and grandsire.'

'Excellent! excellent!' said the host. They set the kingship of Erin upon him. And he said: 'I will take counsel of wise men that I myself may be wise.'

He uttered all this as he had been taught by the bird-man at the sea, who had said this to him: 'Thy reign will be subject to a restriction, but the bird-reign will be noble, and these shall be thy taboos:

'Thou shalt not go righthandwise round Tara
And lefthandwise round Mag Breg.
The evil-beasts of Cerna must not be hunted by thee.
And thou shalt not go out every ninth night beyond Tara.
Thou shalt not sleep in a house

From which firelight is manifest outside after sunset,
And in which light is manifest from without.
And three Reds shall not go before thee to Red's house.
And no rapine shall be wrought in thy reign.
And after sunset a company of one woman
Or one man shall not enter the house in which thou art.
And thou shalt not settle the quarrel of thy two thralls.'

Now there were in Conaire's reign great bounties, to wit, seven ships in every June of every year arriving at Inver Colptha, and oak-mast up to the knees in every autumn, and plenty of fish in the rivers Bush and Boyne in June of each year, and such abundance of good-will that no one slew another in Erin during his reign. And to every one in Erin his fellow's voice seemed as sweet as the strings of lutes. From mid-spring to mid-autumn no wind disturbed a cow's tail. His reign was neither thunderous nor stormy.

Now his foster-brothers murmured at the taking from them of their father's and their grandsire's gifts, namely theft and robbery and slaughter of men and rapine. They thieved the three thefts from the same man – a swine and an ox and a cow, every year, that they might see what punishment therefor the king would inflict upon them, and what damage the theft in his reign would cause to the king. Every year the farmer would come to the king to complain, and the king would say to him, 'Go thou and address Donn Desa's three sons, for 'tis they that have taken the beasts.' Whenever he [the steward] went to speak to them, they would almost kill him and he would not return to the king lest Conaire should add to his hurt.

Since, then, pride and wilfulness possessed them, they took to marauding, surrounded by the sons of the lords of the men of Erin. Thrice fifty men had they as pupils who in the form of were-wolves were destroying in the province of Connacht, until Mane Milscothach's swineherd saw them, and he had never seen that before. He fled in fright. When they heard him they pursued him. The swineherd shouted, and the people of the two Manes came to him, and the thrice fifty men were arrested, along with their auxiliaries, and taken to Tara. They consulted the king concerning the matter, and he said: 'Let each father slay his son, but let my foster-brothers be spared.'

'Let be, let be!' said every one: 'you shall be obeyed.'

'But mind you,' said he; 'there is no lengthening of life in the judgment I have delivered. The men shall not be hanged; but let veterans go with them in banishment that they may wreak their rapine on the men of Scotland and Britain.'

This they did. They put to sea and met the son of the king of Britain, even Ingcel the One-eyed, grandson of Conmac: thrice fifty men and their veterans they met upon the sea.

They made an alliance, and went with Ingcel and wrought rapine with him.

This was the destruction which Ingcel did of his own will. On a certain night his mother and his father and his seven brothers had been bidden to the house of the king of his district. All of them were destroyed by Ingcel in a single night. Then the Irish pirates put out to sea to the land of Erin to inflict equal destruction upon their own people, as payment for that to which Ingcel had been entitled from them.

In Conaire's reign there was perfect peace in Erin, save that in Thomond there was a battle between the two Cairbres. Two foster-brothers of his were they. And until Conaire came it was impossible to make peace between them. 'Twas a taboo of his to go to separate them before they had appealed to him. He went, however, although to do so was one of his taboos, and he made peace between them. He remained five nights with each of the two. That also was a taboo of his.

After settling the quarrel, he was travelling to Tara. The way he took to Tara was past Usnech in Meath; and he saw raiding from east and west, and from south and north, and he saw warbands and hosts, and men stark-naked; and the land of the southern O'Neills was a cloud of fire around him.

'What is this?' asked Conaire. 'Easy to say,' his people answered. 'Easy to know that the king's law has broken down therein, since the country has begun to burn.'

'Whither shall we betake ourselves?' said Conaire.

'To the north-east,' said his people.

So then they went righthandwise round Tara, and lefthandwise round Mag Breg, and the evil beasts of Cerna were hunted by him. But he saw it not till the chase had ended. They that made of the world that smoky mist of magic were the fairy folk, and they did so because Conaire's taboos had been violated. Great fear then fell on Conaire because they had no way to go save upon the Road of Midluachar and the Road of Cualu. So they took their way by the coast of Ireland southward.

Then said Conaire on the Road of Cualu: 'Whither shall we go tonight?'

'By my word, my fosterling Conaire,' said Mac Cecht, son of Snade Teiched, the champion of Conaire son of Eterscel, 'it is more usual that the men of Erin should contend for thee every night than that thou shouldst wander about for a guesthouse.'

'Judgment goes with good times,' said Conaire. 'I had a friend in this country, if only we knew the way to his house.'

'What is his name?' asked Mac Cecht.

'Da Derga ('Two Reds') of Leinster,' answered Conaire. 'He came to me to seek a gift from me, and he did not meet a refusal. I gave him a hundred cows of the drove. I gave him a hundred fatted swine. I gave him a hundred mantles made of close cloth. I gave him a hundred blue-coloured weapons of battle. I gave him ten red, gilded brooches. I gave him ten vats of mead good and brown. I gave him ten thralls. I gave him ten nags. I gave him thrice nine hounds all-white in their silver chains. I gave him a hundred race-horses. There would be no abatement in his case though he should come again, and he on his part make to me a return. It would be strange if he were surly to me tonight when I reach his abode.'

'I am acquainted with his house,' said Mac Cecht; 'the road whereon thou art going is the boundary of his abode. It continues till it enters his house, for through the house passes the road. There are seven doorways into the house, and seven rooms between every two doorways; but there is only one door-way covering, and that covering is turned to every doorway to which the wind blows.'

'With all that thou hast here,' said Conaire, 'thou shalt go with this large company until thou alightest in the midst of the house.'

'If so be,' answered Mac Cecht, 'that thou goest thither, I go on [first] that I may strike fire there ahead of thee.'

When Conaire after this was journeying along the Road of Cualu, he marked before him three horsemen riding towards the house. Three red frocks had they, and three red mantles: three red bucklers they bore, and three red spears were in their hands: three red steeds they bestrode, and three red heads of hair were on them. Red were they all, both body and hair and raiment, both steeds and men.

'Who is it that fares before us?' asked Conaire. 'It was a taboo of mine for those three to go before me – the three Reds to the house of Red.

Who will follow them and tell them to come behind me?'

'I will follow them,' said Le Fri Flaith, Conaire's son.

He went after them, lashing his horse, but he overtook them not. There was the length of a spearcast between them: but they did not gain upon him and he did not gain upon them. He told them not to go before the king. He overtook them not; but one of the three men sang a lay to him over his shoulder: 'Lo, my son, great the news, news from a hostel. Lo, my son!' They went away from him then: he could not detain them.

The boy waited for the company of his father. He told his father what was said to him. Conaire liked it not.

'After them!' said Conaire, 'and offer them three oxen and three bacon-pigs, and so long as they shall be in my household, no one shall be among them from fire to wall.'

So the lad went after them, and offered them that, and overtook them not. But one of the three men sang a lay to him over his shoulder: 'Lo, my son, great the news! A generous king's great ardour whets thee, burns thee. Through ancient men's enchantments a company of nine yields. Lo, my son!'

The boy turned back and repeated the lay to Conaire.

'Go after them,' said Conaire, 'and offer them six oxen and six bacon-pigs, and my leavings, and gifts tomorrow, and so long as they shall be in my household, no one shall be among them from fire to wall.'

The lad then went after them, and overtook them not; but one of the three men answered and said: 'Lo, my son, great the news! Weary are the steeds we ride. We ride the steeds of Donn Tetscorach from the fairy-mounds. Though we are alive we are dead. Great are the signs: destruction of life, sating of ravens, feeding of crows, strife of slaughter, wetting of sword-edge, shields with broken bosses in hours after sundown. Lo, my son!' Then they went from him.

'I see that thou hast not detained the men,' said Conaire.

'Indeed it is not because I failed to try,' said Le Fri Flaith. He recited the last answer that they gave him.

Conaire and his retainers were not pleased thereat; and afterwards evil forebodings of terror were on them. 'All my taboos have seized me tonight,' said Conaire, 'since those Three Reds were the fairy folk.'

The three Reds went forward to the house and took their seats therein, and fastened their red steeds to the door of the house.

That is the Forefaring of the Three Reds in the Hostel of Da Derga.

Then, as Conaire was going to Da Derga's Hostel, a man with black, cropped hair, with one hand and one eye and one foot, overtook them. Rough cropped hair was upon him. Though a sackful of wild apples were flung on his crown, not an apple would fall to the ground, but each of them would stick on a hair. Though his snout were flung on a branch they would remain together. Long and thick as an outer yoke was each of his two shins. Each of his buttocks was the size of a cheese on a withe. A forked pole of iron, black-pointed, was in his hand. A swine, black-bristled, singed, was on his back, squealing continually, and a woman big-mouthed, dark, ugly, hideous, was behind him. Though her snout were flung on a branch, the branch would support it. Her lower lip would reach her knee.

He started forward to meet Conaire, and made him welcome.

'Welcome to thee, O master Conaire! Long hath thy coming hither been known.'

'Who gives the welcome?' asked Conaire.

'Fer Caille here, with his black swine for thee to consume that thou be not fasting tonight, for 'tis thou art the best king that has come into the world!'

'What is thy wife's name?' said Conaire.

'Cichuil,' he answered.

'Any other night,' said Conaire, 'that pleases you, I will come to you, but leave us alone tonight.'

'Nay,' said the churl, 'for we will go to thee in the place wherein thou wilt be tonight, O fair little master Conaire!'

So the churl went towards the house, with his great, big-mouthed wife behind him, and his swine short-bristled, black, singed, squealing continually, on his back. That was one of Conaire's taboos, and that plunder should be taken in Ireland during his reign was another taboo of his.

Now plunder was taken by the sons of Donn Desa, and five hundred there were in the body of their marauders, besides what underlings were with them. This, too, was a taboo of Conaire's. There was a good warrior in the north country, 'Wain Over Withered Sticks', this was his name. Why he was so called was because he used to go over his opponent even as a wain would go over withered sticks. Now plunder was taken by him, and there were five hundred in that body of marauders alone, besides underlings. There was besides a troop of still haughtier heroes, namely, the seven sons of Ailill and Medb of

Connacht, each of whom was called 'Mane'. And each Mane had a nickname, to wit, Mane Fatherlike and Mane Motherlike, and Mane Gentle-pious, Mane Very-pious, Mane Un-slow, and Mane Honeywords, Mane Grasp-them-all, and Mane the Talkative. Rapine was wrought by them. As to Mane Motherlike and Mane Un-slow, there were fourteen score in the body of their marauders. Mane Fatherlike had three hundred and fifty. Mane Honeywords had five hundred. Mane Grasp-them-all had seven hundred. Mane the Talkative had seven hundred. Each of the others had five hundred in the body of his marauders. There was a valiant trio of the men of Cualu of Leinster, namely, the three Red Hounds of Cualu, called Cethach and Clothach and Conall. Now rapine was wrought by them, and twelve score were in the body of their marauders, and they had a troop of madmen. In Conaire's reign a third of the men of Ireland were marauders. He was of sufficient strength and power to drive them out of the land of Erin so as to transfer their marauding to Britain, but after this transfer they returned to their country.

When they had reached the shoulder of the sea, they met Ingcel the One-eyed and Eiccel and Tulchinne, three great-grandsons of Conmac of Britain, on the raging of the sea. A man ungentle, huge, fearful, uncouth was Ingcel. A single eye in his head, as broad as an oxhide, as black as a chafer, with three pupils therein. Thirteen hundred were in the body of his marauders. The marauders of the men of Erin were more numerous than they. The marauders of Erin were about to attack them on the sea. 'Ye should not do this,' said Ingcel; 'do not violate fair play with us, for ye are more in number than we.'

'Nought but a combat on equal terms shall befall thee,' said the reavers of Erin.

'There is somewhat better for you,' said Ingcel; 'let us make peace since ye have been cast out of the land of Erin, and we have been cast out of the land of Scotland and Britain. Let us make an agreement between us. Come ye and wreak your rapine in my country, and I will go with you and wreak my rapine in your country.'

They followed this counsel, and they gave pledges therefor on the one side and the other. These are the sureties that were given to Ingcel by the men of Erin, namely Fer Gair and Gabur (or Fer Le) and Fer Rogain, for the destruction that Ingcel should choose to cause in Ireland and for the destruction that the sons of Donn Desa should choose to cause in Scotland and Britain. A lot was cast upon them to see with which of them they should go first. It fell that they should go with Ingcel to his country. So they made for Britain, and there his father and mother and his seven brothers were slain, as we have said before. Thereafter they made for Scotland, and there they wrought destruction, and then they returned to Erin.

It was just at this time that Conaire son of Eterscel went towards the Hostel of Da Derga along the Road of Cualu. 'Tis then that the reavers came till they were on the sea off the coast of Breg over against Howth. Then said the reavers: 'Strike the sails, and make one band of you on the sea that ye may not be sighted from land; and let some lightfoot be found from among you to go on shore to see if we could save our honour with Ingcel; that is, a destruction in exchange for the destruction he has given us.'

'Who will go on shore to act as spy? Let some one go,' said Ingcel, 'who should have there three gifts, namely, gift of hearing, gift of far sight, and gift of judgment.'

'I,' said Mane Honeywords, 'have the gift of hearing.'

'And I,' said Mane Un-slow, 'have the gift of far sight and of judgment.'

'Tis well for you to go thus,' said the reavers: 'good is that plan.'

Then nine men went till they were on the Hill of Howth, to discover what they might hear and see.

'Be still a while!' said Mane Honeywords.

'What is that?' asked Mane Un-slow.

'The sound of a cavalcade under a king I hear.'

'By the gift of far sight, I see,' said his comrade.

'What seest thou there?'

'I see there,' said he, 'cavalcades splendid, lofty, beautiful, warlike, somewhat slender, wary, active, keen, whetted, vehement, a good course that shakes a great covering of land. They fare to many heights, with wondrous waters and estuaries.'

'What are the waters and heights and estuaries that they traverse?'

'Easy to say: Indeoin, Cult, Cuilten, Mafat, Ammat, Iarmafat, Finne, Goiste, Guistine, grey spears over chariots, ivory-hilted swords on thighs, silvery shields above their elbows. Half-wheels and half horses. Garments of every colour about them. Thereafter I see before them special horses, thrice fifty dark-grey steeds. Small-headed are they, red-nosed, pointed, broad-hoofed, big-nosed, red-chested, fat, easily-stopped, easily-yoked, battle-nimble, keen, whetted, vehement, with their thrice fifty bridles of red enamel upon them.'

'I swear by what my tribe swears,' said the man of the long sight, 'these are the steeds of some good lord. This is my judgment thereof: it is Conaire son of Eterscel, with multitudes of the men of Erin around him, who is travelling the road.'

Back then they went that they might tell the reavers. 'This,' they said, 'is what we have heard and seen.'

Of this host, then, there was a multitude, both on this side and on that, namely, thrice fifty boats, with five thousand in them, and ten hundred in every thousand. Then they hoisted the sails on the boats, and steered them thence to shore, till they landed on the Strand of Fuirbthe. Just at the time when the boats reached land, then was Mac Cecht striking fire in Da Derga's Hostel. At the sound of the spark the thrice fifty boats were hurled out, so that they were on the shoulders of the sea.

'Be silent a while!' said Ingcel. 'Liken thou that, O Fer Rogain?'

'I know not,' answered Fer Rogain, 'unless it be Luchdonn the satirist in Emain Macha, who makes this hand-smiting when his food is taken from him perforce: or the scream of Luchdonn in Tara Luachra: or Mac Cecht's striking a spark, when he kindles a fire before a king of Erin where he sleeps. Every spark and every shower which his fire would let fall on the floor would broil a hundred calves and two half-pigs.'

'May God not bring Conaire there tonight!' said Donn Desa's sons, Conaire's foster-brothers. 'Sad that he is under the hurt of foes!'

'It seems to me,' said Ingcel, 'it should be no sadder for me than the destruction I gave you. It is a feast for me that Conaire should chance to come there.'

Their fleet was steered to land. The noise that the thrice fifty vessels made in running ashore shook Da Derga's Hostel so that no spear nor shield remained on its rack therein, but the weapons uttered a cry and fell all on the floor of the house.

'Liken thou that, O Conaire,' said every one; 'what is this noise?'

'I know nothing like it unless it be the earth that has broken, or the Leviathan that surrounds the globe and strikes with its tail to overturn the world, or the ships of the sons of Donn Desa that have reached the shore. Alas, that it should not be they who are here! Beloved foster-brothers of our own were they! Dear were the champions. We should not have feared them tonight.' Then came Conaire out upon the green of the Hostel.

When Mac Cecht heard the tumultuous noise, it seemed to him that warriors had attacked his people. Thereat he leapt into his armour to help them. Vast as the thunder-feat of three hundred did they deem his act in leaping to his weapons. Thereof there was no profit.

Now in the bow of the ship wherein were Donn Desa's sons was the champion, greatly-accoutred, wrathful, the lion-hard and awful, Ingcel the One eyed, great-grandson of Conmac. Wide as an oxhide was the single eye protruding from his forehead, with seven pupils therein, which were black as a chafer. Each of his knees as big as a stripper's cauldron; each of his two fists was the size of a reaping-basket; his buttocks as big as a cheese on a withe; each of his shins as long as an outer yoke.

So after that, the thrice fifty boats, and those five thousands – with ten hundred in every thousand – landed on the Strand of Fuirbthe.

Then Conaire with his people entered the Hostel, and each took his seat within, both taboo and non-taboo. And the three Reds took their seats, and Fer Caille with his swine took his seat. Thereafter Da Derga came to them, with thrice fifty warriors, each of them having a long head of hair to the hollow of his poll, and a short cloak to their buttocks. Speckled-green drawers they wore, and in their hands were thrice fifty great clubs of thorn with bands of iron.

'Welcome, O master Conaire,' said he. 'Though the bulk of the men of Erin were to come with thee, they themselves would have a welcome.'

When they were there they saw a lone woman coming to the door of the Hostel, after sunset, and seeking to be let in. As long as a weaver's beam was each of her two shins, and they were as dark as the back of a stag-beetle. A greyish, woolly mantle she wore. Her lower hair reached as far as her knee. Her lips were on one side of her head. She came and put one of her shoulders against the doorpost of the house, casting the evil eye on the king and the youths who surrounded him in the Hostel. He himself addressed her from within.

'Well, O woman,' said Conaire, 'if thou art a soothsayer, what fortune seest thou for us?'

'Truly I see for thee,' she answered, 'that neither fell nor flesh of thine shall escape from the place into which thou hast come, save what birds will bear away in their claws.'

'It was not thy omen we foreboded, O woman,' said he: 'it is not thou that always augurs for us. What is thy name, O woman?'

'Cailb,' she answered.

'That is not much of a name,' said Conaire.

'Lo, many are my names besides.'

'What are they?' asked Conaire.

'Easy to say,' quoth she. 'Samon, Sinand, [Seisclend, Sodb, Soéglend, Samlocht, Caill, Coll, Dichóem, Dichiúil, Dithim, Dichuimne, Dichruidne, Dairne, Dáirine, Déruaine, Egem, Agam, Ethamne, Gnim, Cluiche, Cethardam, Níth, Némain, Nóennen, Badb, Blosc, Bloár, Huae. And Aife la Sruth, Mache, Méde, Mod.']

On one foot, and holding up one hand, and breathing one breath she sang all that to them from the door of the house.

'I swear by the gods whom I adore,' said Conaire, 'that I will call thee by none of these names whether I shall be here a long or a short time. What dost thou desire?'

'That which thou, too, desirest,' she answered.

''Tis a taboo of mine,' said Conaire, 'to admit the company of one woman after sunset.'

'Though it be a taboo,' she replied, 'I will not go until my guesting come at once this very night.'

'Tell her,' said Conaire, 'that an ox and a bacon-pig shall be taken out to her, and my leavings, provided that she stays tonight in some other place.'

'If in sooth,' she said, 'it has befallen that the king has not room in his house for the meal and bed of a lone woman, they will be got from some one else possessing generosity – if the hospitality of the prince in the Hostel has departed.'

'Savage is the answer!' said Conaire. 'Let her in, though it is a taboo of mine.'

Great loathing they felt after that from the woman's converse and ill foreboding; but they knew not the cause thereof.

The reavers afterwards landed, and went on till they were at Cinn Slebe, on the way to Da Derga's Hostel. Ever open was the Bruden (Hostel). . . .

Great was the fire which was kindled by Conaire every night; that is, a *torc caille* (Boar of the Wood). Seven outlets it had. When a log was taken out of its side every flame that used to come forth at each outlet was as big as the blaze of a burning oratory. There were seventeen of Conaire's chariots at every door of the house, and by the robbers from the vessels who were looking on, that great light was clearly seen through the wheels of the chariots.

'Canst thou say, O Fer Rogain,' said Ingcel, 'what that great light yonder resembles?'

'I cannot liken it to anything,' answered Fer Rogain, 'unless it be the fire of a king. May God not bring that man here tonight! 'Tis a pity to destroy him!'

'What then deemest thou,' said Ingcel, 'of that man's reign in the land of Erin?'

'Good is his reign,' replied Fer Rogain. 'Since he assumed the kingship, no cloud has veiled the sun for the space of a day from the middle of spring to the middle of autumn. And not a dewdrop has fallen from grass till midday, and wind would not touch a cow's tail until noon. And in his reign, from year's end to year's end, no wolf has attacked anything save one bullcalf of each byre; and to maintain this rule there are seven wolves in hostageship at the sidewall in his house, and behind this a further security, that is, Maclocc, and 'tis he that pleads for them at Conaire's house. In Conaire's reign are the three crowns on Erin, namely, a crown of corn ears, and a crown of flowers, and a crown of oak mast. In his reign, too, each man deems the other's voice as melodious as the strings of lutes, because of the excellence of the law and the peace and the good-will prevailing throughout Erin. May God not bring that man there tonight! 'Tis sad to destroy him. 'Tis "a branch through its blossom." 'Tis "a swine that falls before mast." 'Tis "an infant in age." Sad is the shortness of his life!'

'It was my good luck,' said Ingcel, 'that he should be there and there should be one destruction for another. His destruction is not more grievous to me than my father and my mother and my seven brothers, and the king of my country, whom I gave up to you before coming on the exchange of the rapine.'

'"Tis true, 'tis true!' said the evildoers who were along with the British marauders.

The robbers made a start from the Strand of Fuirbthe, and brought a stone for each man to make a cairn; for this way the distinction which at first the Fians made between a 'Destruction' and a 'Rout'. A pillar-stone they used to plant when there would be a Rout. A cairn, however, they used to make when there would be a Destruction. At this time, then, they made a cairn, for it was a Destruction. Far from the house was this, that they might not be heard or seen therefrom.

For two causes they built their cairn: first, since this was a custom in marauding; and, secondly, that they might find out their losses at the

Hostel. Every one that would come safe from it would take his stone from the cairn: thus the stones of those that were slain would he left, and thence they would know their losses. And this is what men skilled in story recount, that for every stone in Carn Lecca there was one of the reavers killed at the Hostel. From that Carn Lecca in O'Kelly's country is named.

A 'boar of a fire' was kindled by the sons of Donn Desa to give warning to Conaire. So that was the first warning-beacon that was made in Erin, and from it to this day every warning beacon is kindled. This is what others recount: that it was on the eve of Samhain the destruction of the Hostel was wrought, and that from that beacon the beacon of Samhain followed, and stones are placed in the Samhain-fire.

Then the reavers held a council at the place where they had put the cairn.

'Well, then,' said Ingcel to the guides, 'what is nearest to us here?'

'Easy to say: the Hostel of Da Derga, chief-hospitaller of Erin.'

'Good men indeed,' said Ingcel, 'were likely to seek their fellows at that Hostel tonight.'

This, then, was the counsel of the reavers, to send one of them to see how things were there.

'Who will go there to espy the house?' asked every one.

'Who should go,' said Ingcel, 'but I, for 'tis I that am entitled to dues.'

Ingcel went to reconnoitre the Hostel with one of the seven pupils of the single eye which stood out of his forehead, to fit his eye into the house in order to destroy the king and the warriors who were around him therein. And Ingcel saw them through the wheels of the chariots. Then Ingcel was perceived from the house. He hurried from it after being perceived. He went till he reached the reavers in the place wherein they were. Each circle of them was set around another to hear the tidings, the chiefs of the reavers being in the very centre of the circles. There were Fer Ger and Fer Gel and Fer Rogel and Fer Rogain and Lomna the Buffoon, and Ingcel the One-eyed-six in the centre of the circles. And Fer Rogain questioned Ingcel.

'How is it, O Ingcel?' asks Fer Rogain.

'However it be,' answered Ingcel, 'royal is the behaviour, hostful is the tumult: kingly is the noise thereof. Whether a king be there or not, I will take the house for what I have a right to. Thence my return for your depredations comes.'

'We have left it in thy hand, O Ingcel!' said Conaire's foster-brothers. 'But we should not wreak the destruction till we know who may be present in the Hostel.'

'Question: hast thou examined the house well, O Ingcel?' asked Fer Rogain.

'My eye cast a rapid glance around it, and I will accept it for my dues as it stands.'

'Thou mayest well accept it, O Ingcel,' said Fer Rogain: 'the foster-father of us all is there, Erin's overking, Conaire son of Eterscel. Question: what sawest thou in the champion's high seat of the house, facing the king, on the opposite side?'

The Room of Cormac Conlonges

'I saw there,' said Ingcel, 'a man of noble countenance, large, with a clear and sparkling eye, an even set of teeth, a face narrow below, broad above; fair, flaxen, golden hair upon him, and a proper fillet around it; a brooch of silver in his mantle, and in his hand a gold-hilted sword. A shield with five golden circles upon it; a five-barbed javelin in his hand. A visage just, fair, ruddy he has; he is also beardless. Modest-minded is that man!'

'And after that, whom sawest thou there?' said Fer Rogain

The Room of Cormac's Nine Comrades

'There,' said Ingcel, 'I saw three men to the west of Cormac, and three to the east of him, and three in front of the same man. Thou wouldst deem that the nine of them had one mother and one father. They are of the same age, equally goodly, equally beautiful, all alike. Greenish mantles they all wore. Thin rods of gold in their mantles. Curved shields of bronze they bear. Ribbed javelins above them. An ivory hilted sword in the hand of each. An unique feat they have, to wit, each of them takes his sword's point between his two fingers, and they twirl the swords round their fingers, and the swords afterwards extend themselves by themselves. Liken thou that, O Fer Rogain,' said Ingcel.

'Easy,' said Fer Rogain, 'for me to liken them. It is Conchobar's son Cormac Conlonges, the best hero behind a shield in the land of Erin.

Of modest mind is that boy! Evil is what he dreads tonight. He is a champion of valour for feats of arms: he is an hospitaller for house-holding. These are the nine who surround him, the three Dungusses, and the three Doelgusses, and the three Dangusses, the nine comrades of Cormac Conlonges son of Conchobar. They have never slain men on account of their misery, and they never spared them on account of their prosperity. Good is the hero who is among them, even Cormac Conlonges. I swear what my tribe swears, nine times ten will fall by Cormac in his first onset, and nine times ten will fall by his people, besides a man for each of their weapons, and a man for each of themselves. And Cormac will share prowess with any man before the Hostel, and he will boast of victory over a king or crown-prince or noble of the reavers; and he himself will chance to escape, though all his people be wounded. (. . .)'

The Room of the Picts

'And whom sawest thou next?' said Fer Rogain.

'I saw another room there, with a huge trio in it: three brown, big men: three round heads of hair on them, even, equally long at nape and forehead. Three short black cowls about them reaching to their elbows: long hoods were on the cowls. Three black, huge swords they had, and three black shields they bore, with three dark broad-green javelins above them. Thick as the spit of a cauldron was the shaft of each. Liken thou that, O Fer Rogain!'

'Hard it is for me to find their like. I know not at all that trio, unless it be the trio of Pictland, who went into exile from their country, and are now in Conaire's household. These are their names: Dublonges son of Trebuat, and Trebuat son of O'Lonsce, and Curnach son of O'Faich. The three who are best in Pictland at taking arms are that trio. Nine times ten will fall at their hands in their first encounter, and a man will fall for each of their weapons, besides one for each of themselves. And they will share prowess with every trio in the Hostel. They will boast a victory over a king or a chief of the robbers; and they will afterwards escape though wounded. Woe to him who shall wreak the Destruction, though it be only on account of those three! (. . .) And whom sawest thou there afterwards?'

The Room of the Pipers

'There,' said Ingcel, 'I beheld a room with nine men in it. Hair fair and yellow was on them: they all are equally handsome. Mantles speckled with colour they wore, and above them were nine bagpipes, four-tuned, ornamented. Enough light in the palace were the ornaments on those four-tuned pipes. Liken thou them, O Fer Rogain.'

'Easy for me to liken them,' said Fer Rogain. 'Those are the nine pipers that came to Conaire out of the fairy-mound of Breg, because of the noble tales about him. These are their names: Bind, Robind, Riarbind, Sibe, Dibe, Deichrind, Umall, Cumal, Ciallglind. They are the best pipers in the world. Nine times nine will fall before them, and a man for each of their weapons, and a man for each of themselves. And each of them will boast a victory over a king or a chief of the robbers. And they will escape from the destruction; for a conflict with them will be a conflict with a shadow. They will slay, but they will not be slain, for they are out of a fairy-mound. Woe to him who shall wreak the Destruction, though it be only because of those nine! (. . .) And after that, whom sawest thou there?' said Fer Rogain.

The Room of Conaire's Steward

'There,' said Ingcel, 'I saw a room with one man in it. Rough cropped hair upon him. Though a sack of crab-apples should be flung on his head, not one of them would fall on the floor, but every apple would stick on his hair. His fleecy mantle was over him in the house. Every quarrel therein about seat or bed comes to his decision. Should a needle drop in the house, its fall would be heard when he speaks. Above him is a huge black tree, like a millshaft, with its paddles and its cap and its spike. Liken thou him, O Fer Rogain!'

'Easy for me is this. Tuidle of Ulster is he, the steward of Conaire's household. 'Tis needful to hearken to the decision of that man, the man that rules seat and bed and food for each. 'Tis his household staff that is above him. That man will fight with you. I swear what my tribe swears, the dead at the destruction slain by him will be more numerous than the living. Thrice his number will fall by him, and he himself will fall there. Woe to him who shall wreak the Destruction! (. . .) What sawest thou there after that?' said Fer Rogain.

The Room of Mac Cecht, Conaire's Champion

'There I beheld another room with a trio in it, three half-furious nobles: the biggest of them in the middle, very noisy, rock-bodied, angry, smiting, dealing strong blows, who beats nine hundred in battle-conflict. A wooden shield, dark, covered with iron, he bears, with a hard rim, a shield whereon would fit the proper litter of four troops of ten weaklings. A boss thereon, the depth of a cauldron, fit to cook four oxen, a hollow maw, a great boiling, with four swine in its mid-maw. At his two smooth sides are two five-thwarted boats fit for three parties of ten in each of his two strong fleets. A spear he has, blue-red, hand-fitting, on its strong shaft. It stretches along the wall on the roof and rests on the ground. An iron point upon it, dark-red, dripping. Four amply-measured feet between the two points of its edge. Thirty amply-measured feet in his deadly-striking sword from dark point to iron hilt. It sends forth fiery sparks which illumine the Mid-court House from roof to ground. 'Tis an overpowering sight that I saw. A swoon from horror almost befell me while staring at those three. There is nothing stranger.

'Two bald men were there by the man with hair. Two lakes by a mountain, two hides by a tree. Two boats near them full of thorns of a white thorntree on a circular board. And there seemed to me some-thing like a slender stream of water on which the sun is shining, and its trickle down from it, and a hide arranged behind it, and a palace-housepost shaped like a great lance above it. A good weight of a plough-yoke is the shaft that is therein. Liken thou that, O Fer Rogain?'

'Easy to liken him!' answered Fer Rogain. 'That is Mac Cecht son of Snaide Teichid; the battle-soldier of Conaire son of Eterscel. Good is the hero Mac Cecht! Supine he was in his room, in his sleep, when thou beheldest him. The two bald men which thou sawest by the man with hair, these are his two knees by his head. The two lakes by the mountain which thou sawest, these are his two eyes by his nose. The two hides by a tree which thou sawest, these are his two ears by his head. The two five-thwarted boats on a circular board, which thou sawest, these are his two sandals on his shield. The slender stream of water which thou sawest, whereon the sun shines, and its trickle down from it, this is the flickering of his sword. The hide which thou sawest arranged behind him, that is his sword's scabbard. The palace-housepost which thou sawest, that is his lance; and he brandishes this spear till its two ends meet, and he hurls a wilful cast of it when he pleases. Good is the hero Mac Cecht!

'Six hundred will fall by him in his first encounter, and a man for each of his weapons, besides a man for himself. And he will share prowess with every one in the Hostel, and he will boast of triumph over a king or chief of the robbers in front of the Hostel. He will chance to escape though wounded. And when he shall come upon you out of the house, as numerous as hailstones, and grass on a green, and stars of heaven will be your cloven heads and skulls, and the clots of your brains, your bones and the heaps of your bowels, crushed by him and scattered throughout the ridges.'

Then with trembling and terror of Mac Cecht the robbers fled over three ridges. (. . .)'

'And whom sawest thou next, O Ingcel?' said Fer Rogain.

The Room of Conaire's three sons, Oball and Oblin and Corpre

'There I beheld a room with a trio in it, to wit, three tender striplings, wearing three silken mantles. In their mantles were three golden brooches. Three golden-yellow manes were on them. When they undergo headcleansing their golden-yellow mane reaches the edge of their haunches. When they raise their eye it raises the hair so that it is not lower than the tips of their ears, (and it is) as curly as a ram's head. A cloth of gold and a palace-flambeau above each of them. Every one who is in the house spares them, voice and deed and word. Liken thou that, O Fer Rogain,' says Ingcel.

Fer Rogain wept, so that his mantle in front of him became moist. And no voice was gotten out of his head till a third of the night (had passed).

'O little ones,' says Fer Rogain, 'I have good reason for what I do! Those are three sons of the king of Erin: Oball and Obline and Corpre Findmor.'

'It grieves us if the tale be true,' say the sons of Donn Desa.

'Good is the trio in that room. Manners of ripe maidens have they, and hearts of brothers, and valours of bears, and furies of lions. Whosoever is in their company and in their couch, and parts from them, he sleeps not and eats not at ease till the end of nine days, from lack of their companionship. Good are the youths for their age! Thrice ten will fall by each of them in their first encounter, and a man for each weapon, and three men for themselves. And one of the three will fall there. Because of that trio, woe to him that shall wreak the Destruction!'

'Ye cannot,' says Ingcel: 'clouds of weakness are coming to you, etc. And whom sawest thou afterwards?'

The Room of the Fomorians

'I beheld there a room with a trio in it, to wit, a trio horrible, unheard of, a triad of champions. (. . .) 'Liken thou that, O Fer Rogain,' said Ingcel.

''Tis hard for me to liken that trio. Neither of the men of Erin nor of the men of the world do I know it, unless it be the trio that Mac Cecht brought out of the land of the Fomorians by dint of combats. Not one of the Fomorians was found to fight him, so he brought away those three, and they are in Conaire's house as sureties that, while Conaire is reigning, the Fomorians destroy neither corn nor milk in Erin beyond their fair tribute. Well may their aspect be loathly! Three rows of teeth in their heads from one ear to the other. An ox with a bacon-pig, this is the ration of each of them, and that ration which they put into their mouths is visible till it comes down past their navels. Bodies of bone without a joint in them all those three have. I swear what my tribe swears, more will be killed by them at the destruction than those they leave alive. Six hundred warriors will fall by them in their first conflict, and a man for each of their weapons, and one for each of the three themselves. And they will boast a triumph over a king or chief of the robbers. It will not be more than with a bite or a blow or a kick that each of those men will kill, for no arms are allowed them in the house since they are in "hostageship at the wall" lest they do a misdeed therein. I swear what my tribe swears, if they had armour on them, they would slay us all but a third. Woe to him that shall wreak the Destruction, because it is not a combat against sluggards. And whom sawest thou there after that?' said Fer Rogain.

The Room of Munremur mac Gerrcind and Birderg son of Rua and Mal son of Telband

'I beheld a room there, with a trio in it,' said Ingcel. 'Three brown, big men, with three brown heads of short hair. Thick ankles they had. As thick as a man's waist was each of their limbs. Three brown and curled masses of hair upon them, with a thick head; three cloaks, red and speckled, they wore; three black shields with clasps of gold, and three five-barbed javelins; and each had in hand an ivory-hilted sword. This is the feat they perform with their swords: they throw them high up, and they throw the scabbards after them, and the swords, before reaching the ground, place themselves in the scabbards. Then they throw the scabbards first, and the swords after them, and the scabbards meet the swords and place themselves round them before they reach the ground. Liken thou that, O Fer Rogain!'

'Easy for me to liken them! Mal son of Telband, and Munremur mac Gerrcind, and Birderg son of Ruan. Three crown princes, three champions of valour, three heroes the best behind weapons in Erin! A hundred heroes will fall by them in their first conflict, and they will share prowess with every man in the Hostel, and they will boast of the victory over a king or chief of the robbers, and afterwards they will chance to escape. The Destruction should not be wrought even because of those three. And after that whom sawest thou?' said Fer Rogain.

The Room of Conall Cernach

'There I beheld in a decorated room the fairest man of Erin's heroes. He wore a tufted purple cloak. White as snow was one of his cheeks, the other was red and speckled like foxglove. Blue as hyacinth was one of his eyes, dark as a stag-beetle's back was the other. The bushy head of fair golden hair upon him was as large as a reaping-basket, and it touches the edge of his haunches. It is as curly as a ram's head. If a sackful of red-shelled nuts were spilt on the crown of his head, not one of them would fall on the floor, but remain on the hooks and plaits and swordlets of that hair. A gold-hilted, sword in his hand: a blood-red shield which has been speckled with rivets of white bronze between plates of gold. A long, heavy, three-ridged spear: as thick as an outer yoke is the shaft that is in it. Liken thou that, O Fer Rogain.'

'Easy for me to liken him, for the men of Erin know that scion. That is Conall Cernach, son of Amorgen. He has chanced to be along with Conaire at this time. 'Tis he whom Conaire loves beyond every one, because of his resemblance to him in goodness of form and shape. Goodly is the hero that is there, Conall Cernach! To that bloodred shield on his fist, which has been speckled with rivets of white bronze, the Ulaid have given a famous name, to wit, the Bricriu of Conall Cernach.

'(Another name for it is Conall Cernach's Lámthapad, because of the quickness and readiness with which that shield of Conall Cernach is seized and wielded.)

'I swear what my tribe swears, plenteous will be the rain of red blood over it to-night before the Hostel! That ridged spear above him, many will there be unto whom to-night, before the Hostel, it will deal drinks of death. Seven doorways there are out of the house, and Conall Cernach will contrive to be at each of them, and from no doorway will he be absent. Three hundred will fall by Conall in his first conflict, besides a man for each (of his) weapons and one for himself. He will share prowess with every one in the Hostel, and when he shall happen to sally upon you from the house, as numerous as hailstones and grass on green and stars of heaven will be your half-heads and cloven skulls, and your bones under the point of his sword. He will succeed in escaping though wounded. Woe to him that shall wreak the Destruction, were it but for this man only!'

'Ye cannot,' says Ingcel. 'Clouds of weakness are coming to you etc. After that whom sawest thou?'

The Room of Conaire Himself

'There I beheld a room, more beautifully decorated than the other rooms of the house. A silvery curtain around it, and there were ornaments in the room. I beheld a trio in it. The outer two of them were, both of them, fair, with their hair and eyelashes; and they are as bright as snow. A very lovely blush on the cheek of each of the twain. A tender lad in the midst between them. The ardour and energy of a king has he, and the counsel of a sage. The mantle I saw around him is even as the mist of Mayday. Diverse are the hue and semblance each moment shewn upon it. Lovelier is each hue than the other. In front of him in the mantle I beheld a wheel of gold which reached from his chin to his navel. The colour of his hair was like the sheen of smelted gold. Of all the world's forms that I ever beheld, this is the most beautiful. I saw his golden-hilted sword down beside him. A forearm's length of the sword was outside the scabbard. That part was so bright that a man down in the front of the house could see a fleshworm by the shadow of the sword! Sweeter is the melodious sounding of the sword than the melodious sound of the golden pipes that accompany music in the palace.

'Now the young warrior was asleep, with his feet in the lap of one of the two men and his head in the lap of the other.'

'Liken thou him, O Fer Rogain,' said Ingcel.

'Easy for me to liken him,' said Fer Rogain. 'No "conflict without a king" this. He is the most splendid and noble and beautiful and mighty king that has come into the whole world. He is the mildest and gentlest and most perfect king that has come to it, that is, Conaire son of Eterscel. 'Tis he that is high king of all Erin. There is no defect in that man, whether in form or shape or vesture: whether in size or fitness or proportion, whether in eye or hair or brightness, whether in wisdom or skill or eloquence, whether in weapon or dress or appearance, whether in splendour or abundance or dignity, whether in knowledge or valour or kindred.

'Great is the tenderness of the sleepy, loveable man till he has chanced on a deed of valour; but if his fury and his courage be awakened when the champions of Erin and Alba are with him in the house, the Destruction will not be wrought so long as he is therein. Six hundred will fall by Conaire before he shall attain his arms, and seven hundred will fall by him in his first conflict after attaining his arms. I swear what my tribe swears, unless drink be taken from him, though there be no one else in the house but he alone, he would hold the Hostel until help would reach it which men would prepare for him from the Wave of Clidna and the Wave of Assaroe while ye are at the Hostel.

'Nine doors there are to the house, and at each door a hundred warriors will fall by his hand. And when every one in the house has ceased to ply his weapon, 'tis then he will resort to a deed of arms. And if he chance to come upon you out of the house, as numerous as hailstones and grass on a green will be your halves of heads and your cloven skulls and your bones under the edge of his sword.

' 'Tis my opinion that he will not chance to get out of the house. Dear to him are the two that are with him in the room, his two fosterers, Dris and Snithe. Thrice fifty warriors win fall before each of them in front of the Hostel, and not farther than a foot from him, on this side and that, will they fall,' said Fer Rogain.

'Woe to him who shall wreak the Destruction, were it only because of that pair and the prince that is between them, the high-king of Erin, Conaire son of Eterscel! Sad were the quenching of that reign!' said Lomna the Buffoon son of Donn Desa. (. . .)

'And after that, whom sawest thou there?' said Fer Rogain.

The Room of Tulchinne the Juggler

'There,' said Ingcel, 'I beheld a great champion, in front of the same room, on the floor of the house. The shame of baldness is on him. White as mountain cotton-grass is each hair that grows through his head. Earrings of gold around his ears. A mantle speckled, coloured, he wore. Nine swords in his hand, and nine silvern shields, and nine apples of gold. He throws each of them upwards, and none of them falls on the ground, and there is only one of them on his palm; each of them rising and falling past another is like the movement to and fro of bees on a day of beauty. When he was swiftest, I beheld him at the feat, and as I looked, the company uttered a cry about him and his implements were all on the house-floor. Then the prince who is in the house said to the juggler: "We have been together since thou wast a little boy, and till tonight thy juggling never failed thee."

' "Alas, alas, fair master Conaire, good cause have I. A keen, angry eye looked at me: a man with the third of a pupil which sees the going of the nine bands. Not much to him is that keen, wrathful sight! Battles are fought with it," said he. "It should be known till doomsday that there is evil in front of the Hostel." '

'And after that whom sawest thou?' said Fer Rogain.

The Room of the Harpers

'To the east of them I beheld another ennead. Nine branchy, curly manes upon them. Nine grey, floating mantles about them, nine pins of gold in their mantles. Nine rings of crystal round their arms. A thumbring of gold round each man's thumb: an ear-tie of gold round each man's ear: a torque of silver round each man's throat. Nine bags with golden faces above them on the wall. Nine rods of white silver in their bands. Liken thou (them).'

'I know those,' quoth Fer Rogain. 'They are the king's nine harpers, with their nine harps above them: Side and Dide, Dulothe and Deichrinne, Caumul and Cellgen, and Olene and Olchói. A man will perish by each of them.'

The Room of the Conjurers

'I saw another trio on the dais. Three bedgowns girt about them. Four-cornered shields in their hands, with bosses, of gold upon them. Apples of silver they had, and small inlaid spears.'

'I know them,' says Fer Rogain, 'Cless and Clissine and Clessamun, the king's three conjurers. Three of the same age are they: three brothers, three sons of Naffer Rockless. A man will perish by each of them.'

The Room of the three Lampooners

'I beheld another trio hard by the room of the King himself. Three blue mantles around them, and three bedgowns with red insertion over them. Their arms had been hung above them on the wall.'

'I know those,' quoth he. 'Dris, Draigen, and Aitlit' Thorn and Bramble and Furze, the king's three lampooners, three sons of Sciath foilt. A man will perish by each of their weapons.'

The Room of Sencha and Dubtach and Goibniu Son of Lurgnech

'I beheld the room that is next,' said Ingcel. 'Three chief champions, in their first greyness, are therein. As thick as a man's waist is each of their limbs. They have three black swords, each as long as a weaver's beam. These swords would split a hair on water. A great lance in the hand of the midmost man, with fifty rivets through it. The shaft therein is a good

load for the yoke of a plough team. The midmost man brandishes that
lance so that its edge studs hardly stay therein, and he strikes the shaft
thrice against his palm. There is a great boiler in front of them, as big
as a calf's cauldron, wherein is a black and horrible liquid, and he
plunges the lance into that black fluid. If its quenching be delayed, it
flames on its shaft and then thou wouldst suppose that there is a fiery
dragon in the top of the house. Liken thou that, O Fer Rogain!'

'Easy to say. Three heroes who are best at grasping weapons in Erin,
namely, Sencha the beautiful son of Ailill, and Dubtach Chafertongue
of Ulster, and Goibniu son of Lurgnech. And the spear Luin of Celtchar
mac Uthecair, which was found in the battle of Mag Tured, this is in
the hand of Dubtach Chafertongue of Ulster. That feat is usual for it
when it is ripe to pour forth a foeman's blood. A cauldron full of poison
is needed to quench it when a deed of manslaying is expected. Unless
this come to the lance, it flames on its haft and will go through its bearer
or the master of the palace wherein it is. It will kill a man at every blow,
when it is at its work, from one hour to another, even though it may not
reach him. It will kill nine men at every cast, and one of the nine will
be a king or crownprince or chieftain of the robbers.

'I swear what my tribe swears, there will be a multitude unto whom
tonight the Luin of Celtchar will deal drinks of death in front of the
Hostel. I swear what my tribe swears, that in their first encounter three
hundred will fall by those three heroes, and they will share prowess with
every three in the Hostel tonight. And they will boast of victory over a
king or chief of the robbers, and the three will chance to escape. And
after that, whom sawest thou there?' said Fer Rogain.

The Room of the Three Manx Giants

'There I beheld a room with a trio in it,' said Ingcel. 'Three men mighty,
manly, overbearing, which see no one abiding at their three hideous,
crooked aspects. A fearful view because of the terror of them. A dress of
rough hair covers them; their savage eyes look out through a thatch of
cows' hair, without garments, enwrapping them down to the heels.
With three manes, equine, awful, majestic, down to their sides. Fierce
heroes who wield against foemen hard-smiting swords. A blow they give
with three iron flails having seven chains triple-twisted, three-edged,
with seven iron knobs at the end of every chain: each of them as heavy

as an ingot of ten smeltings. Three big brown men. Dark equine back-manes on them, which reach their two heels. Two good thirds of an oxhide in the girdle round each one's waist, and each quadrangular clasp that closes it as thick as a man's thigh. The raiment that is round them is the hairy coat that grows on them. Tresses of their back-manes were outspread, and a long staff of iron, as long and thick as an outer yoke, was in each man's hand, and an iron chain out of the end of every club, and at the end of every chain an iron pestle as long and thick as a middle yoke. They stand in their sadness in the house, and enough is the horror of their aspect. There is no one in the house that would not be avoiding them. Liken thou that, O Fer Rogain?'

Fer Rogain was silent. 'Hard for me to liken them. I know none such of the world's men unless they be that trio of giants to whom Cú Chulainn gave quarter at the beleaguerment of the Men of Falga (the Isle of Man), and when they were getting quarter they killed fifty warriors . . . But Cú Chulainn would not let them be slain, because of their wondrousness. These are the names of the three: Srubdaire son of Dordbruige, and Conchenn of Cenn Maige, and Fiad Sceme son of Scipe. Conaire bought them from Cú Chulainn; so they are along with him. Three hundred will fall by them in their first encounter, and they will surpass in prowess every three in the Hostel; and if they come forth upon you, the fragments of you will be fit to go through the sieve of a cornkiln, from the way in which they will destroy you with the flails of iron. Woe to him that shall wreak the Destruction, though it were only on account of those three! And after that, whom sawest thou there?' said Fer Rogain.

The Room of Da Derga

'There I beheld another room,' said Ingcel, 'with one man therein and in front of him two servants with two manes upon them, one of the two dark, the other fair. Red hair on the warrior, and red eyebrows. Two ruddy cheeks he had, and an eye very blue and beautiful. He wore a green cloak and a shirt with a white hood and a red insertion. In his hand was a sword with a hilt of ivory, and he supplied attendants of every room in the house with ale and food, and he quick-footed in serving the whole host. Liken thou that, O Fer Rogain!'

'I know those men. The chief one is Da Derga. 'Tis by him that the

Hostel was built, and since it was built its doors have never been shut save on the side to which the wind comes – the opening is closed against it – and since he began house-keeping his cauldron was never taken from the fire, but it has been boiling food for the men of Erin. The pair before him, those two youths, are his fosterlings, two sons of the king of Leinster, namely Muredach and Cairbre. Three tens will fall by that trio in front of their house and they will boast of victory over a king or a chief of the robbers. After this they will chance to escape from it. (. . .) And after that whom sawest thou there?' said Fer Rogain.

The Room of the Three Champions from the Fairy-Mounds

'There I beheld a room with a trio in it,' said Ingcel. 'Three red mantles they wore, and three red shirts, and three red heads of hair were on them. Red were they all even together with their teeth. Three red shields above them. Three red spears in their hands. Three red horses in their bridles in front of the Hostel. Liken thou that, O Fer Rogain!'

'Easily done. Three champions who wrought falsehood in the fairy-mounds. This is the punishment inflicted upon them by the king of the fairy-mounds, to be destroyed thrice by the king of Tara. Conaire son of Eterscel is the last king by whom they are destroyed. Those men will escape from you. To fulfil their own destruction, they have come. But they will not be slain, nor will they slay anyone.' (. . .)

'Rise up, then, ye champions,' said Ingcel, 'and get you on to the Hostel!'

With that the marauders marched to the Hostel, and made a murmur about it.

'Silence a while!' said Conaire. 'What is that?

'Champions at the house,' said Conall Cernach of Ulster.

'There are warriors for them here,' answered Conaire.

'They will be needed tonight,' Conall Cernach rejoined.

Then went Lomna the Buffoon before the host of robbers into the Hostel. The door-keepers struck off his head. Then the head was thrice flung into the Hostel, and thrice cast out of it.

Then Conaire himself sallied out of the Hostel together with some of his people, and they fought with the host of robbers, and six hundred fell by Conaire before he could get to his arms. Then the Hostel was thrice set on fire, and thrice put out by the other side: and it was found that the Destruction would never have been wrought had not the use of his weapons been taken from Conaire. Thereafter Conaire went to seek his arms, and he donned his battledress, and fell to plying his weapons on the marauders, together with the band that he had. Then, after getting his arms, six hundred fell by him in his first encounter.

After this the reavers were routed. 'I have told you,' said Fer Rogain son of Donn Desa, 'that if the champions of the men of Erin and Alba attack Conaire at the house, the Destruction will not be wrought unless Conaire's fury and valour be quelled.'

'Short will his time be,' said the wizards along with the robbers. This was the quelling they brought: a great thirst that seized him.

Thereafter Conaire entered the house, and asked for a drink. 'A drink to me, O master Mac Cecht,' says Conaire.

Says Mac Cecht: 'This is not the office that I have fulfilled for thee, to give thee a drink. There are waiters and cupbearers who bring drink to thee. The command I have hitherto had from thee is to protect thee when the champions of the men of Erin and Alba may be attacking thee around the Hostel. Thou wilt go safe from them, and no spear shall enter thy body. Ask a drink of thy waiters and thy cupbearers.'

Then Conaire asked a drink of his waiters and his cupbearers who were in the house.

'In the first place there is none,' they said; 'all the liquids that had been in the house have been spilt on the fires.' The cupbearers found no drink for him in the River Dodder, and the Dodder had flowed through the house.

Then Conaire again asked for a drink. 'A drink to me, O fosterer, O Mac Cecht! 'Tis equal to me what death I shall die, for anyhow I shall perish.'

Then Mac Cecht gave a choice to the champions of valour of the men of Erin who were in the house, whether they cared to protect the king or to seek a drink for him. Conall Cernach answered this in the house – and cruel he deemed the choice offered, and afterwards he had always a feud with Mac Cecht – 'Leave the defence of the king to us,' says Conall, 'and go thou to seek the drink, for of thee it is demanded.'

So then Mac Cecht fared forth to seek the drink, and he took Conaire's son, Le Fri Flaith, under his armpit, and Conaire's golden cup, in which an ox with a bacon-pig would be boiled; and he bore his shield and his two spears and his sword, and he carried the cauldron-spit, a spit of iron.

He burst forth upon the marauders, and in front of the Hostel he dealt nine blows with the iron spit, and at every blow nine robbers fell. Then he made a sloping feat of the shield and an edgefeat of the sword about his head, and he delivered a hostile attack upon them. Six hundred fell in his first encounter, and after cutting down hundreds he went through the band outside.

The doings of the folk of the Hostel, this is what is here examined, presently. (. . .)

Howbeit then, but it is long to relate, 'tis weariness of mind, 'tis confusion of the senses, 'tis tediousness to hearers, 'tis superfluity of narration to go over the same things twice. But the folk of the Hostel came forth in order, and fought their combats with the robbers, and fell by them, as Fer Rogain and Lomna the Buffoon had said to Ingcel, to wit, that the folk of every room would sally forth still and deliver their combat, and after that escape. So that none were left in the Hostel in Conaire's company save Conall and Sencha and Dubtach.

Now from the vehement ardour and the greatness of the contest which Conaire had fought, his great drouth of thirst attacked him, and he perished of a consuming fever, for he got not his drink. So when the king died those three sallied out of the Hostel, and delivered a cunning deed of reaving on the marauders, and fared forth from the Hostel, wounded, broken and maimed.

As for Mac Cecht, however, he went his way till he reached the Well of Casair [the source of the River Dodder], which was near him in the district of Cualu; but of water he found not therein the full of his cup, that is, Conaire's golden cup which he had brought in his hand. Before morning he had gone round the chief rivers of Erin; to wit, Bush, Boyne, Bann, Barrow, Neim, Luae, Laigdae, Shannon, Suir, Sligo, Samair, Find, Ruirthech, Slaney, and in them he found not the full of his cup of water.

Then before morning he had travelled to the chief lakes of Erin; to wit, Loch Derg, Loch Luimnig, Loch Foyle, Loch Mask, Loch Corrib, Loch Laig, Loch Cuan, Loch Neagh, Morloch, and of water he found not therein the full of his cup.

He went his way till he reached Uaran Garad on Mag Ai. It could not hide itself from him: so he brought thereout the full of his cup, and the boy fell under his covering. After this he went on and reached Da Derga's Hostel before morning.

When Mac Cecht went across the third ridge towards the house, there were two men striking off Conaire's head. Then Mac Cecht struck off the head of one of the two men who had beheaded Conaire. The other man then was fleeing with the king's head. A pillar-stone chanced to be under Mac Cecht's feet on the floor of the Hostel. He hurled it at the man who had Conaire's head and drove it through his spine, so that his back broke. After this Mac Cecht beheaded him. Mac Cecht then spilt the cup of water into Conaire's gullet and neck. Then said Conaire's head, after the water had been put into its neck and gullet:

> A good man Mac Cecht! An excellent man Mac Cecht!
> A good warrior without, good within;
> He gives a drink he saves a king, he doth a noble deed;
> Well he ended the champions I found;
> He sent a flagstone on the warriors;
> Well he hewed by the door of the Hostel . . .
> So that it is at one hip that he is cut.
> Good should I be to far-renowned Mac Cecht
> If I were alive. A good man!

After this Mac Cecht followed the routed foe. (. . .)

Now when Mac Cecht was lying wounded on the battlefield, at the end of the third day, he saw a woman passing by. 'Come hither, O woman!' said Mac Cecht.

'I dare not go thus,' said the woman, 'for horror and fear of thee.'

'There was a time, O woman, when people had horror and fear of me; but now thou shouldst fear nothing. I accept thee on the truth of my honour and my safeguard.' Then the woman went to him.

'I know not,' said he, 'whether it is a fly, or a gnat, or an ant that nips me in the wound.'

It really was a hairy wolf that was there, as far as its two shoulders in the wound! The woman seized it by the tail, dragged it out of the wound, and it took the full of its jaws out of him.

'Truly,' said the woman, 'this is "an ant of ancient land".'

Said Mac Cecht, 'I swear what my people swears, I deemed it no bigger than a fly, or a gnat, or an ant.'

And Mac Cecht took the wolf by the throat, and struck it a blow on the forehead, and killed it with a single blow.

Then Le Fri Flaith son of Conaire died under Mac Cecht's armpit, for the warrior's heat and sweat had dissolved him.

Thereafter Mac Cecht, having cleansed the slaughter, at the end of the third day, set forth, and he dragged Conaire with him on his back, and buried him at Tara, as some say. Then Mac Cecht departed into Connacht, to his own country, that he might work his cure in Mag Brengair. Wherefore the name clave to the plain from Mac Cecht's misery, that is, Mag Brengair.

Now Conall Cernach escaped from the Hostel, and thrice fifty spears had gone through the arm which upheld his shield. He fared forth till he reached his father's house, with half his shield in his hand, and his sword, and the fragments of his two spears. Then he found his father before the enclosure surrounding his stronghold in Tailltiu.

'Swift are the Wolves that have hunted thee, my son,' said his father.

'This is what we have had of conflict against warriors, thou old hero,' Conall Cernach replied.

'Hast thou then news of Da Derga's Hostel?' asked Amergin. 'Is thy lord alive?'

'He is not alive,' said Conall.

'I swear by the gods by whom the great tribes of Ulster swear, it is cowardly for the man who went thereout alive, having left his lord with his foes in death,' said the father of Conall Cernach.

'My wounds are not white, thou old hero,' said Conall. He showed him his shield-arm, whereon were thrice fifty wounds which had been inflicted upon it. The shield that guarded it is what saved it. But the right arm had been played upon, as far as two thirds thereof, since the shield had not been guarding it. That arm was mangled and maimed and wounded and pierced, save that the sinews kept it to the body without separation.

'That arm fought tonight, my son,' says Amergin.

'True is that, thou old hero,' says Conall Cernach. 'Many there are unto whom it gave drinks of death tonight in front of the Hostel.'

Now as to the marauders, every one of them that escaped from the Hostel went to the cairn which they had built on the night before last, and they brought thereout a stone for each man not mortally wounded. So this is what they lost by death at the Hostel, a man for every stone that is now in Carn Lacca.

23. The Debility of the Ulstermen

(Ces Noínden Ulað)

Translated by Eleanor Hull

Like 'The Sickbed of Cú Chulainn' (pp. 195–218) and 'The Dream of Oengus,' (pp. 189–194) this story is one of several which deal with blighted love between mortals and Otherworldly beings. Crunnchu ignores the conditions set for a faery-human marriage and so brings disaster both upon Ulster and himself. The story seems to have been composed largely to explain the fact that when Queen Medb, with her allies, sought to invade Ulster, all the warriors except Cú Chulainn were unable to fight. It also accounts for the origin of the name Emain Macha by one of those fanciful etymologies common in the 'Dinnshenchas'. Macha is almost certainly the goddess of that name, as the way in which she announces herself to the assembly implies. The detail of her turning right, sunwise, for luck, when she enters Crunnchu's house is to bring good luck. Queen Medb, before beginning her campaign in the *Táin Bó Cuailgne*, orders her charioteer to make a sunwise turn to avoid evil. The king, though not named, lives in the times before the Red Branch warriors and their honourable code. Macha's curse still resounds in the troubled history of Ireland today. This appears to be the only story in which the unfortunate Crunnchu appears. Agnoman is one of the legendary ancestors of the Nemedians (see 'The Invasions of Ireland' pp. 14–16) The version printed here appears at the beginning of certain texts of the *Tain Bó Cuailgne*.

There lived on the heights and in the solitudes of the hills a rich cowlord of the Ulstermen, Crunnchu mac Agnoman by name. In his solitude great wealth accumulated to him. He had four sons around him. His wife, the mother of his children, died. For a long time he lived without a wife. As he was one day alone on the couch in his house, he saw coming into the mansion a young stately woman, distinguished in her appearance, clothing, and demeanour. Macha was the woman's name, the scholars say. She sat herself down on a chair near the hearth, and stirred the fire. She passed the whole day there, without exchanging a word with any one. She fetched a kneading-trough and a sieve and began to prepare food. As the day drew to an end she took a vessel and milked the cow, still without speaking.

When she returned to the house, she turned right about, [i.e. sunwise] went into his kitchen and gave directions to his servants; then she took a seat next to Crunnchu. Each one went to his couch; she remained to the last and put out the fire, turned right about again and laid herself down beside him, laying her hand on his side. For a long time they dwelt together. Through his union with her, he increased yet more in wealth. His handsome appearance was delightful to her.

Now the Ulstermen frequently held great assemblies and meetings. All, as many as could go, both of men and women, went to the gathering. 'I, too,' said Crunnchu, 'will go like every one else to the assembly.'

'Go not,' said his wife, 'lest thou run into danger by speaking of us; for our union will continue only if thou dost not speak of me in the assembly.'

'I will not utter a word,' said Crunnchu.

The Ulstermen gathered to the festival, Crunnchu also going with the rest. It was a brilliant festival, not alone in regard to the people, but as to horses and costumes also. There took place races and combats, tournaments, games, and processions.

At the ninth hour the royal chariot was brought upon the ground, and the king's horses carried the day in the contests. Then bards appeared to praise the king and the queen, the poets and the druids, his household, the people and the whole assembly. The people cried: 'Never before have two such horses been seen at the festival as these two horses of the king: in all Ireland there is not a swifter pair!'

'My wife runs quicker than these two horses,' said Crunnchu.

'Seize the man,' said the king, 'and hold him until his wife can be brought to the race-contest!'

He was made fast, and messengers were despatched from the king to the woman. She bade the messengers welcome, and asked them what had brought them there. 'We have come for you that you may release your husband, kept prisoner by the king's command, because he boasted that you were swifter of foot than the king's horses.'

'My husband has spoken unwisely,' said she; 'it was not fitting that he should say so. As for me, I am ill, and about to be delivered of a child.'

'Alas for that,' said the messengers, 'for thy husband will be put to death if thou dost not come.'

'Then I must needs go,' she said.

Forthwith she went to the assembly. Every one crowded round to see her. 'It is not becoming,' said she, 'that I should be gazed at in this condition. Wherefore am I brought hither?'

'To run in contest with the two horses of the king,' shouted the multitude.

'Alas!' she cried, 'for I am close upon my hour.'

'Unsheath your swords and hew yonder man to death,' said the king.

'Help me,' she cried to the bystanders, 'for a mother hath borne each one of you. Give me, O King, but a short delay, until I am delivered.'

'It shall not be so,' replied the king.

'Then shame upon you who have shown so little respect for me,' she cried. 'Because you take no pity upon me, a heavier infamy will fall upon you.'

'What is thy name?' asked the king.

'My name,' said she, 'and the name of that which I shall bear, will for ever cleave to the place of this assembly. I am Macha, daughter of Sainreth mac Imbaith (Strange son of Ocean). Bring up the horses beside me!'

It was done, and she outran the horses and arrived first at the end of the course. Then she gave vent to a cry in her pain, but God helped her, and she bore twins, a son and a daughter, before the horses reached the goal. Therefore is the place called Emain Macha, 'the Twins of Macha'.

All who heard that cry were suddenly seized with weakness, so that they had no more strength than the woman in her pain. And she said, 'From this hour the ignominy that you have inflicted upon me will rebound to the shame of each one of you. When a time of oppression falls upon you, each one of you who dwells in this province will be overcome with weakness, as the weakness of a woman in child-birth, and this will remain upon you for five days and four nights; to the ninth generation it shall be so.'

Thus it was. It continued from the days of Crunnchu to the days of Fergus mac Donnell, or till the time of Fore, son of Dallan, son of Mainech, son of Lugaid. Three classes there were upon whom the debility had no power, namely, the children and the women of Ulster, and Cú Chulainn, because he was not descended from Ulster; none, also, of those who were outside the province were afflicted by it.

This is the cause of the *Noínden Ulad*, or the Debility of the Ulstermen.

LOVE AND LONGING

24. The Story of Baile of the Clear Voice

(Scel Baili Binnberlaig)

Translated by Kuno Meyer

In this brief eleventh-century tale a Romeo and Juliet story plays itself out. The theme of the intertwining trees, which is common to folksong the world over, is here given a particularly Irish twist when the two trees are made into writing tablets. The practice of 'kenning', wordplay, formed an important part of the aspiring *fili* (poet), who had to master this skill in the sixth year of his or her apprenticeship (see Introduction). This version of the story is translated from MS Harl 5280 f48a, in the British Museum.

Baile the Sweet-spoken, son of Buan. Three grandsons had Caba son of Cing, son of Ross, son of Rugraide: Monach and Bitan and Fercorb, de quibus Dal m-Buain, and Dal Cuirb and Monaig Arad. Buan's only son was Baile. He was the special love of Aillinn, daughter of Lugaid, soil of Fergus of the Sea; or of the daughter of Eóghan, son of Dathi; and he was the special amour of every one who saw him or heard of him, both men and women, on account of the tales about him. And they (he and Aillinn) agreed to meet in a love-tryst, at Ross na Rig, at the house of Maelduib, on the brink of the Boyne in Breg.

The man (Baile) came from the north to meet her, from Emain Macha, across Sliab Fuaid, over Murthemne to Traig Baili. They un-yoked their chariots and put their horses on the turf to graze. And there was glee and merry-making.

As they were there, they saw the horrible apparition of a man coming towards them from the south. Fitful was his course and his approach. He sped over the earth like the darting of a hawk from a cliff, or the wind from the green sea. His left was towards the land.

'To him!' said Baile, 'and ask him whither he goes or whence he comes, or what is the cause of his haste.'

'To Tuaig-Inber I am going and back northward now from Mount Leinster, and I have no news but that the daughter of Lugaid, son of Fergus, has given love to Baile, son of Buan, and was coming to meet him when the warriors of Leinster overtook her and killed her, as druids and good seers foretold of them, that they would not meet in life, and that they would meet after their deaths, never to part. This is my news.'

And he went from them after that, and they were not able to detain him.

When Baile heard that, he falls dead without life; and his tomb is raised and his rath, his stone is put up and his funeral games are held by the men of Ulster. And a yew grew up through his grave, and on its top the form and shape of Baile's head was visible. Hence [it] is called Tráig Baili.

Then the same man [who had told the lie to Baile] went southward to the place where was the maiden Aillinn, and went into the bower.

'Whence cometh he whom we know not?'said the maiden.

'From the north of Erin, from Tuaig-Inber, and past this place to Mount Leinster.'

'Hast thou news?' said the maiden.

'I have no news worth lamenting here, but by the side of Traig Baili I saw the men of Ulster at funeral games, digging a rath and placing a stone and writing the name of Baile, son of Buan, the royal heir of Ulster, who was coming to meet a sweetheart and lady-love to whom he had given love; for it is not their fate to meet in life, nor that one of them should see the other alive.'

He darted out when he had completed his evil tale. Aillinn fell dead without life, and her grave is dug, etc.

And an apple-tree grew through her grave and was a large tree at the end of the seventh year, and the shape of Aillin's head on its top. At the end of seven years princes and seers and prophets cut down the yew which was over Baile and make a poet's tablet of it; and the visions and feasts and loves and wooings of Ulster are written in it. In the same manner the wooings of Leinster are written in the tablet (made of the tree that grew on Aillinn's grave).

Then came Hallowe'en and its feast was made by Cormac son of Art. Poets and men of every art came to that feast, as was the custom, and they brought their tablets with them. And Art saw them [the tablets] and when he saw them he asked for them. And the two tablets were brought to him, and they were in his hands face to face. The one tablet of them sprang upon the other, and they twined together as the woodbine round a branch, nor was it possible to sever them. And they were (kept) like any other jewel in the treasury at Tara, until Dunlang, son of Enna, burnt [them] when he slew the maidens. Hence said the poet said:

> The apple tree of noble Aillinn,
> The yew of Bailé – small inheritance –
> Although they are introduced into poems,
> They are not understood by unlearned people.

And [Ailbhé] the daughter of Cormac, the grandson of Conn, said:

> What I liken Aluime to,
> Is to the yew of Ráith Bailé
> What I liken the other to,
> Is to the apple tree of Aillinn.

Flann Mac Lonan said:

> Let Cormac decide with proper sense,
> So that he be envied by the hosts;
> Let him remember – the illustrious saint –
> The tree of the strand of Bailè Mac Buain.

> There grew up a tree under which companies could sport,
> With the form of his face set out on its clustering top;
> When he was betrayed, truth was betrayed,
> It is in that same way they betray Cormac.

Cormac said:

> Here was entombed the son of White Buan.

25. Trystan and Essyllt

(Ystori Trystan)

Translated by Tom Peete Cross

The story below may well be the oldest extant episode from the saga of Trystan (Tristan) and Essyllt (Isolt) which from these early beginnings metamorphosed into the romantic story of medieval Arthurian literature. There is some evidence to suggest that the characters of Trystan, Essyllt and March (Mark) originated in a Northern region of the country, possibly even in the kingdom of the elusive Picts. Certainly documents mentioning a Drustan map Tallorch who appears to have flourished during the fifth or sixth centuries, seem to point to a far older origin than the more usual medieval sources would indicate.

The episode which follows here appears in four manuscripts, of which only one is complete (MSS 6 and 43 in the Cardiff Library). It dates from the fifteenth century but was certainly based on a much earlier text, as the language of the poems indicates. It tells an old story, not dissimilar from that of Diarmuid and Grainne, in which the hero Trystan runs off to the woods with the wife of his king. Kae (Cei, or Kay in later versions), who happens to be in love with Essyllt's serving maid, sees what has taken place and tells Arthur, who intervenes to save bloodshed and because he is Trystan's uncle. He sends Gwalchmai (better known as Gawain) to persuade Trystan to come out of hiding in the woods and there follows a long exchange of poetic verses, which are in a notably older style than the prose sections of the text. Gwalchmai finally persuades Trystan to speak with Arthur, and after a further exchange agrees to abide by his uncle's judgement. The denouement is suprising and dramatic, with Essyllt proving she has a sharp mind as well as great beauty.

In the interim Trystan ap Tallwch and Essyllt the wife of March y Meirchion, fled into the forest of Clyddon (Kelyddon), Golwg Hafddydd

(Summer Day Aspect), her handmaiden, and Bach Bychan (Little Small), his page, carrying pasties and wine with them. A couch of leaves was made for them.

And then March y Meirchion went to complain to Arthur against Trystan, and to entreat him to avenge upon Trystan the insult offered him, because he was nearer of kindred to him (Arthur) than Trystan was, for March y Meirchion was first cousin to Arthur and Trystan was but the nephew-son of a first cousin to Arthur.

'I will go, I and my family,' said Arthur, 'to seek either satisfaction or bloodshed.'

And then they surrounded the wood of Kelyddon.

One of the peculiarities of Trystan was that whoever drew blood upon him died, and whoever Trystan drew blood upon died also.

When Essyllt heard the talking around the wood, she trembled against the two hands of Trystan. And then Trystan asked her why she trembled, and she said it was because of fear for him. Then Trystan sang this *englyn* [poetic verse form]:

> Fair Essyllt, be not fearful;
> while I am protecting thee,
> three hundred knights
> will not succeed in carrying thee off,
> nor three hundred armed men.

And then Trystan rose up and hastily took his sword in his hand, and approached the first battalion as quickly as he could until he met March y Meirchion. And then March y Meirchion said, 'I will kill myself in order to kill him.'

And then the other men all said, 'Shame upon us if we interfere with him.' Thereupon Trystan went through the three battalions uninjured.

Kae Hír (Cai the Long) was in love with Golwg Hafddydd. Thus he did: he (went to) the place where Essyllt was and spoke, singing this *englyn*:

> Blessed Essyllt, loving sea-gull,
> Speaking in conversation,
> (I say that) Trystan has escaped.

ESSYLLT: Blessed Kae, if it is true what thou sayest,
> in conversation with me,
> thou wilt obtain a golden mistress.

> KAE: A golden mistress I desire not
> because of what I have said (. . . .)
> Golwg Hafddydd I seek.

> ESSYLLT: If it is true the tale
> thou hast just told me with thy mouth,
> Golwg Hafddydd will be thine.

And then March y Meirchion went a second time to Arthur and lamented to him because he obtained neither satisfaction nor blood for his wife. And Arthur said, 'I know no counsel to give thee except to send instrumental musicians to sound toward him from afar, and after that to send vocal musicians with *englynion* (epigrams) of praise.' So they did. Thereupon Trystan called to him the artists and gave them handfuls of gold and silver.

After that someone was sent to him concerning Gwalchmai. And Gwalchmai sang this *englyn*:

> Heavy is the immense wave
> when the sea is at the centre (of its course);
> who art thou, impetuous warrior?

> TRYSTAN: Heavy are the wave and the thunder (together),
> though their separation be unwieldy;
> in the day of battle I am Trystan.

> GWALCHMAI: Trystan of irreprovable qualities,
> I find no fault with thy discourse;
> Gwalchmai was thy companion.

> TRYSTAN: I should perform for Gwalchmai, on the day
> he should have on hand the bloody work,
> what brother would not do for brother.

> GWALCHMAI: Trystan, noble chieftain,
> Heavy (the blows) thy effort has struck.
> I am Gwalchmai, nephew of Arthur.

> TRYSTAN: Quicker than an instant, O Gwalchmai,
> if thou shouldst have on hand the work of combat,
> I would make gore up to the two knees.

GWALCHMAI: Trystan of perfect qualities,
            if Archgrwn did not refuse (service),
            I would do the best I could.

TRYSTAN: I ask in order to pacify,
            I ask not out of asperity;
            what is the number which is before (me)?

GWALCHMAI: Trystan of noble qualities,
            they do not know thee;
            it is the family of Arthur which is ambushing thee.

TRYSTAN: Because of Arthur I do not threaten;
            nine hundred battalions I shall provoke;
            unless I am slain, I shall slay.

GWALCHMAI: Trystan, friend of women,
            before entering upon the bloody work,
            the best thing is peace.

TRYSTAN: If I have my sword on my hip,
            and my right hand to defend me,
            am I worse off than they?

GWALCHMAI: Trystan of shining qualities,
            who breakest the lance-shaft with thy effort,
            do not reject Arthur as a kinsman.

TRYSTAN: Gwalchmai of pre-eminent qualities,
            the shower has over-drenched a hundred hosts;
            as he may love me, I shall love him.

GWALCHMAI: Trystan, whose habit is to be foremost,
            The shower has over-drenched a hundred oaks;
            Come and converse with thy kinsman.

TRYSTAN: Gwalchmai of crossgrained qualities,
            the shower over-drenches a hundred furrows;
            I will go wherever thou mayest wish.

Then Trystan went with Gwalchmai to Arthur, and Gwalchmai sang this *englyn*:

> Arthur of courteous habits,
> the shower has overdrenched a hundred trees;
> here is Trystan, be joyful.

Then Arthur sang this *englyn*:

> Gwalchmai of faultless manners,
> who wast not wont to conceal thyself
> on the day of battle;
> I welcome to Trystan my nephew.

Notwithstanding that, Trystan said nothing; and Arthur sang the second *englyn*:

> Blessed Trystan, army chieftain,
> Love thy kindred as well as thyself,
> and me as head of the tribe.

And notwithstanding that, Trystan said nothing; and Arthur sang the third *englyn*:

> Trystan, chief of battles,
> Take as much as the best,
> and love me sincerely.

In spite of that, Trystan said nothing; and Arthur sang the fourth *englyn*:

> Trystan of exceedingly prudent manners,
> love thy kindred, it will not bring thee loss;
> coldness grows not between one kinsman and another.

Then answered Trystan and sang this *englyn* to Arthur, his uncle:

> Arthur, I will consider of what thou sayest,
> and thee first will I adorn with praise;
> whatever thou mayest wish, I will do.

And then peace was made by Arthur between Trystan and March y Meirchion, and Arthur conversed with the two of them in turn, and neither of them was willing to be without Essyllt.

Then Arthur adjudged her to one while the leaves should be on the wood, and to the other during the time that the leaves should not be on the wood, the husband to have the choice. And the latter chose the time when the leaves should not be on the wood, because the night is longest during that season. And Arthur announced that to Essyllt, and she said, 'Blessed be the judgement and he who gave it!' And Essyllt sang this *englyn*:

> Three trees are good in nature:
> the holly, the ivy, and the yew,
> which keep their leaves throughout their lives:
>
> I am Trystan's as long as he lives!

And in this way March y Meirchion lost his wife forever. And so ends the story.

26. The Noble Youth

(Y Melwas)

Translated by John Matthews

The first edition of this poem, edited from MS Llanstephan 122,426, in The Myvyrian Archaeology of Wales (1870) was mistakenly given the title 'A Dialogue between Arthur and his second wife Gwenhwyfar who was taken away by Melwas of, Lord of Alban'. In fact, the poem, which probably dates from the thirteenth century, is a dialogue between Gwenhwyfar (Guinevere) and Melwas himself, who does indeed, in a number of early versions of the Arthurian literature of Wales, carry off Arthur's queen. The poem, together with a second, independent version (Wynnstay I, 91, now in the Library of Wales) was subsequently edited and translated by Mary Williams in a 1938 article entitled 'An early Ritual Poem in Welsh' *(Speculum* Vol 13. pp. 38–51). In this, Miss Williams endeavoured to prove that the poems formed the basis of a ritual dialogue in which Gwenhwyfar represented a goddess and Melwas her neophyte, requesting initiation. A careful examination of the two poems suggests another possibility: that this is a kind of riddling, boasting exchange between Gwenhwyfar and Melwas, of a kind frequently found in Celtic mythlore (see Cú Chulainn's dialogue with Emer for instance, pp. 349–359). This could have been a prelude to Melwas' flight with Gwenhwyfar. The 'old man' with his chin propped up on his sword, may be Arthur himself, who is sometimes portrayed as older than Guinevere. There is little doubt that the story of the stealing of Arthur's queen does represent a very ancient theme, probably dating back to the Greek myth of Persephone, and forming part of the oldest superstructure of Arthurian literature. Melwas himself, who is elsewhere referred to as the 'King of the Summer Country' (i.e. the County of Somerset or the Otherworld) has long been recognised as a type of Underworld King, whose rape of the queen parallels that of Hades (see *King Arthur and the Goddess of the Land* by Caitlín Matthews). The version offered here is still tentative, and based on a conflation of both poems. I am indebted to Mary Williams' notes and her reproduction of both texts in the original Welsh. The title of the poem, which in fact heads the Wynnstay MS, derives from the description Melwas gives himself: 'Y Melwas', the Noble Youth.

GWENHWYFAR: Who is that man at the lower table,
In the midst of the feast,
Seated below the salt?

MELWAS: Melwas from Ynys Witryn
[Glass Isle = Glastonbury]
Of the many, gilded caskets –
I have drunk none of your wine.

GWENHWYFAR: I do not pour wine
For anyone who fails to stay –
The coward in the affray.
Cai could drink far more than you.

MELWAS: I could ford a river in spate,
Though it were fathoms deep –
Even in a coat of mail –
I could easily stand up to Cai.

GWENHWYFAR: Be quiet, boy! Enough of your idle words!
Unles you are stronger than you look
You could never stand up to Cai –
Not you and seven more!

MELWAS: Gwenhwyfar of the Deer's Glance
Don't despise me. I may be young
But I could stand up to Cai alone.

GWENHWYFAR: You, boy – not even with a squad!
With your pink complexion,
You are hardly Cai's size!

MELWAS: Men in their cups seem weak,
But let's leave that aside.
I am Melwas, none other!

GWENHWYFAR: Since you have begun
Continue with your speech –
A boy knows who likes him!

MELWAS: Gwenhwyfar of the rejecting glance,
Tell me if you know
Where you saw me before.

GWENHWYFAR: In an honourable court
Drinking wine with the Cymru
In the land of Dyfneint.   [Devon]

MELWAS: I hate this old man's smile
His chin propped on his sword
He who has desire but cannot rise!

GWENHWYFAR: Still more do I hate
Proud men with loud voices
Who won't be silent or draw a sword!

MELWAS: Black is my steed and powerful
Water he fears not,
Before no man turns aside.

GWENHWYFAR: Green is my steed, the colour of leaves.
He is utterly despised
Who fails to fulfil his promise.

MELWAS: Gwenhwyfar of the silver glance.
Don't reject me. Though I am young
I could stand against a hundred.

GWENHWYFAR: Silly boy in your black and yellow!
After looking long and hard
I believe I have seen you before.

MELWAS: Gwenhwyfar of facetious speech,
Vain words come naturally to you –
There indeed you saw me.

WOOINGS

27. The Wooing of Emer

(Tochmarc Emer)

Translated by Kuno Meyer

According to the most ancient tradition, the great Ultonian hero Cú Chulainn had no wife; but a number of *tochmarca*, 'wooings,' exist in which he pursues deep and magical relationships with various women, two of which at least lead to marriage. 'The Wooing of Emer', who is the great love of Cú Chulainn's life, exists in several versions, the oldest of which was composed as early as the eighth century. The present version, from the Stowe MS 992, is later, but less fragmentary. Dr Meyer described it as 'wandering and incoherent', and blamed the endless additions made by the author – or perhaps compiler would be a better word – of the story; but in fact there is a gradual unfolding of Cú Chulainn's adventures, which are in the end neatly tied in to the promises he makes to Emer. All those who have commented upon the story have drawn attention to the strange and baffling nature of the dialogue between Cú Chulainn and Emer. However, most of this yields to a careful reading – the seeming obscurity of the language being of the kind called *kenning*, (riddling or elusive metaphor) referring to a thing by comparing it to something else. The love talk between the two is actually both touching and funny. Cú Chulainn's boasts and Emer's tart responses read like a true account of a dialogue between two remarkable people.

The long disquisition by Cú Chulainn to his charioteer Loeg in which he explains the meaning of the dialogue to pass the time on their journey home, has been restored to the text here between pp. 353 and 359. It is usually omitted on the grounds that it holds up the action, but we felt that it deserved to be included as an example of the way that poets could, when they wished, decipher the mystery of their own texts, and also because of the amount of lore that is preserved there. Those who wish to pass over this and read the story though without interruption, should turn from pp. 353 to 359.

Another fascinating episode is that which refers to Cú Chulainn's education in the arts of war by the Scottish Amazonian warrior Scathach, who teaches him the extraordinary tricks of the warrior, listed (sadly without glosses) in the text. The episode where Cú Chulainn avoids marriage to Dervogill by first wounding her then sucking out the wound and thus, by the laws of the time, becoming related to her, is a splendid example of the use of law to defeat fate.

PartI
Cuchulainn's Wooing

There lived once upon a time a great and famous king in Emain Macha, whose name was Conchobar, son of Fachtna Fathach. In his reign there was much store of good things enjoyed by the men of Ulster. Peace there was, and quiet, and pleasant greeting; there were fruits and fatness and harvest of the sea; there was power and law and good lordship during his time among the men of Erin. In the king's house at Emain was great state and rank and plenty. Of this form was that house, the Red Branch of Conchobar, namely, after the likeness of the Tech Midchuarta of Tara. Nine compartments were in it from the fire to the wall. Thirty feet was the height of each bronze partition in the house. Carvings of red yew therein. A wooden floor beneath, and a roofing of tiles above. The compartment of Conchobar was in the front of the house, with a ceiling of silver with pillars of bronze. Their headpieces glittered with gold and were set with carbuncles, so that day and night were equally light therein. There was a gong of silver above the king, hung from the roof-tree of the royal house. Whenever Conchobar struck the gong with his royal rod, all the men of Ulster were silent. The twelve cubicles of the twelve chariot-chiefs were round about the king's compartment. All the valiant warriors of the men of Ulster found space in that king's house at the time of drinking, and yet no man of them would crowd the other. Splendid, lavish, and beautiful were the valiant warriors of the men of Ulster in that house. In it were held great and numerous gatherings of every kind, and wonderful pastimes. Games and music and singing there, heroes performing their feats, poets singing, harpers and players on the *tiompán* striking up their sounds.

Now, once the men of Ulster were in Emain Macha with Conchobar, drinking from the beer vat known as the 'Iron-Chasm'. A hundred fillings of beverage went into it every evening. Such was the drinking of the 'Iron-Chasm', which at one sitting would satisfy all the men of Ulster. The chariot-chiefs of Ulster were performing on ropes stretched across from door to door in the house at Emain Macha. Fifteen feet and nine score was the size of that house. The chariot-chiefs were performing three feats, the spear-feat, the apple-feat, and the sword-edge feat. The chariot-chiefs who performed those feats were these: Conall the Victorious, son of Amergin; Fergus, son of Roig, the Over-bold; Loegaire the Triumphant, son of Connad; Celtchar, son of Uithechar; Dubtach, son of Lugaid; Cú Chulainn, son of Sualtam; Scel, son of Barnene (from whom the Pass of Barnene is named), the warder of Emain Macha. From him is the saying 'a story of Scel's', for he was a mighty story-teller. Cú Chulainn surpassed them all at those feats for quickness and deftness.

The women of Ulster loved Cú Chulainn greatly for his dexterity in the feats, for the nimbleness of his leap, for the excellence of his wisdom, for the sweetness of his speech, for the beauty of his face, for the loveliness of his look. For in his kingly eyes were seven pupils, four of them in his one eye, and three of them in the other. He had seven fingers on either hand, and seven toes on either of his two feet. Many were his gifts. First, his gift of prudence until his warrior's flame appeared, the gift of feats, the gift of *buanfach* (a game like draughts), the gift of chessplaying, the gift of calculating, the gift of sooth-saying, the gift of discernment, the gift of beauty.

But Cú Chulainn had three defects: that he was too young, for his beard had not grown, and all the more would unknown youths deride him, that he was too daring, and that he was too beautiful. The men of Ulster took counsel about Cú Chulainn, for their women and maidens loved him greatly. For Cú Chulainn had no wife at that time. This was their counsel, that they should seek out a maiden whom Cú Chulainn might choose to woo. For they were sure that a man who had a wife to attend to him would be less likely to spoil their daughters and accept the love of their women. And, besides, they were troubled and afraid that Cú Chulainn would perish early, so that for that reason they wished to give him a wife that he might leave an heir; knowing that his rebirth would be of himself.

Then Conchobar sent out nine men into each province of Erin to seek a wife for Cú Chulainn, to see if in any stronghold, or in any chief place in Erin they could find the daughter of a king, or of a chief, or of a hospitaller, whom it might please Cú Chulainn to woo.

All the messengers returned that day a year later, and had not found a maiden whom Cú Chulainn chose to woo. Thereupon Cú Chulainn himself went to woo a maiden that he knew in Luglochta Loga ('the Gardens of Lug'), namely Emer, the daughter of Forgall the Wily. Cú Chulainn himself, and his charioteer Loeg son of Riangabar, went in his chariot. That was the one chariot which the host of the horses of the chariots of Ulster could not follow, on account of the swiftness and speed of the chariot, and of the chariot-chief who sat in it. Then Cú Chulainn found the maiden on her playing-field, with her foster-sisters around her, daughters of the land-owners that lived around the stronghold of Forgall. They were learning needlework and fine handiwork from Emer. Of all the maidens of Erin, she was the one maiden whom he deigned to address and to woo. For she had the six gifts: the gift of beauty, the gift of voice, the gift of sweet speech, the gift of needlework, the gifts of wisdom and chastity. Cú Chulainn had said that no maiden should go with him but she who was his equal in age and form and race, in skill and deftness, who was the best handiworker of the maidens of Erin, for that none but such as she was a fitting wife for him. Now, as Emer was the one maiden who fulfilled all these conditions, Cú Chulainn went to woo her above all.

It was in his festal array that Cú Chulainn went forth that day to address Emer, and to show his beauty to her. As the maidens were sitting on the bench of gathering at the stronghold, they heard coming towards them the clatter of horses' hoofs, with the creaking of the chariot, the cracking of straps, the grating of wheels, the rush of the hero, and the clanking of weapons.

'Let one of you see,' said Emer, 'what it is that is coming toward us.'

'Truly, I see,' said Fial, daughter of Forgall, 'two steeds alike in size, beauty, fierceness, and speed, bounding side by side. Spirited they are and powerful, pricking their ears: their manes long and curling, and with curling tails. At the right side of the pole of the chariot is a grey horse, broad in the haunches, fierce, swift, wild; thundering he comes along, taking small bounds, with head erect and chest expanded. Beneath his four hard hoofs the firm and solid turf seems aflame. A flock of swift birds follows, but, as he takes his course along the road, a flash of breath darts from him, a blast of ruddy flaming sparks is poured from his curbed jaws.

'The other horse is jet-black, his head firmly knit, his feet broad-hoofed and slender. Long and curly are his mane and tail. Down his broad forehead hang heavy curls of hair. Spirited and fiery, he fiercely gallops along, stamping firmly on the ground. Beautifully he sweeps along as having outstripped the horses of the land; he bounds over the smooth dry sward, following the levels of the mid-glen, where no obstacle obstructs his pace.

'I see a chariot of fine wood with wicker work, moving on wheels of white bronze. A pole of white silver, with a mounting of white bronze. Its frame very high of creaking copper, rounded and firm. A strong curved yoke of gold; two firm-plaited yellow reins; the shafts hard and straight as sword-blades.

'Within the chariot a dark sad man, comeliest of the men of Erin. Around him a beautiful crimson five-folded tunic, fastened at its opening on his white breast with a brooch of inlaid gold, against which it heaves, beating in full strokes. A shirt with a white hood, interwoven red with flaming gold. Seven red dragon-gems on the ground of either of his eyes. Two blue-white, bloodred cheeks that breathe forth sparks and flashes of fire. A ray of love burns in his look. Methinks, a shower of pearls has fallen into his mouth. As black as the side of a charred beam each of his eye-brows. On his two thighs rests a golden-hilted sword, and fastened to the copper frame of the chariot is a blood-red spear with a sharp mettlesome blade, on a shaft of wood well-fitted to the hand. Over his shoulders a crimson shield with a rim of silver, chased with figures of golden animals. He leaps the hero's salmon-leap into the air, and does many like swift feats. This is the description of the chariot-chief of the single chariot.

'Before him in that chariot there is a charioteer, a very slender, tall, much-freckled man. On his head is very curly bright-red hair, held by a fillet of bronze upon his brow which prevents the hair from falling over his face. On both sides of his head patins of gold confine the hair. A shoulder mantle about him with sleeves opening at the two elbows, and in his hand a goad of red gold with which he guides the horses.'

Meanwhile Cú Chulainn had come to the place where the maidens were. He wished a blessing to them. Emer lifted up her lovely face and recognised Cú Chulainn, and she said, 'May God make smooth the path before you!'

'And you,' he said, 'may you be safe from every harm!'

'Whence comest thou?' she asked.

'From Intide Emna,' he replied.

'Where did you sleep?' said she.

'We slept,' he said, 'in the house of the man who tends the cattle of the plain of Tethra.'

'What was your food there?' she asked.

'The ruin of a chariot was cooked for us there,' he replied.

'Which way didst thou come?'

'Between the Two Mountains of the Wood,' said he.

'Which way didst thou take after that?'

'That is not hard to tell,' he said. 'From the Cover of the Sea, over the Great Secret of the Tuatha dé Danann, and the Foam of the two steeds of Emain Macha; over the Mórrígu's Garden, and the Great Sow's Back; over the Glen of the Great Dam, between the god and his prophet; over the Marrow of the Woman Fedelm, between the boar and his dam; over the Washingplace of the horses of Dea; between the King of Ana and his servant, to Monnehuile of the Four Corners of the World; over Great Crime and the Remnants of the Great Feast; between the Vat and the Little Vat, to the Gardens of Lug, to the daughters of Tethra's nephew, Forgall, the king of the Fomorians. And what O maiden, is the account of thee?' said Cú Chulainn.

'Truly, that is not hard to tell,' said the maiden. 'Tara of the women, whitest of maidens, the paragon of chastity, a prohibition that is not taken, a watcher that yet sees no one. A modest woman is a dragon, which none comes near. The daughter of a king is a flame of hospitality, a road that cannot be entered. I have champions that follow me to guard me from whoever would carry me off against their will, without their and Forgall's knowledge of my act.'

'Who are the champions that follow thee, O maiden?' said Cú Chulainn.

'Truly, it is not hard to tell,' said Emer. 'Two called Lui, two Luaths; Luath and Lath Goible, son of Tethra; Triath and Trescath, Brion and Bolor; Bas, son of Omnach; eight called Connla; and Conn, son of Forgall. Every man of them has the strength of a hundred and the feats of nine. Hard it were, too, to tell the many powers of Forgall himself. He is stronger than any labourer, more learned than any druid, more acute than any poet. It will be more than all your games to fight against Forgall himself. For many powers of his have been recounted of manly deeds.'

'Why dost thou not reckon me, O maiden, with those strong men?' said Cú Chulainn.

'If thy deeds have been recounted, why should I not reckon thee among them?'

'Truly, I swear, O maiden,' said Cú Chulainn, 'that I shall make my deeds to be recounted among the glories of the strength of heroes.'

'What then is thy strength?' said Emer.

'That is quickly told,' said he; 'when my strength in fight is weakest, I fight off twenty. A third part of my strength is sufficient for thirty. Alone, I make combat against forty. Under my protection a hundred are secure. From dread of me, warriors avoid fords and battlefields. Hosts and multitudes and many armed men flee before the terror of my face.'

'Those are goodly fights for a tender boy,' said the maiden, 'but thou hast not yet reached the strength of chariot-chiefs.'

'Truly, O maiden,' said he, 'well have I been brought up by my dear foster-father Conchobar. Not as a churl strives to bring up his children, between flag[stone] and kneading-trough, between fire and wall, nor on the floor of a single larder have I been brought up by Conchobar; but among chariot-chiefs and champions, among jesters and druids, among poets and learned men, among the nobles and landlords of Ulster have I been reared, so that I have all their manners and gifts.'

'Who then were they who brought thee up in all those deeds of which thou dost boast?' said Emer.

'That, truly, is easily told. Fair-speeched Sencha has taught me, so that I am strong, wise, swift, deft. I am prudent in judgment, my memory is good. Before wise men, I make answer to many; I give heed to their arguments. I direct the judgments of all the men of Ulster, and, through the training of Sencha, my decisions are unalterable.

'Blai, the lord of lands, on account of his racial kinship, took me to himself, so that I got my due with him. I invite the men of Conchobar's province with their king. I entertain them for the space of a week, I settle their gifts and their spoils, I aid them in their honour and their fines.

'Fergus has so fostered me, that I slay mighty warriors through the strength of valour. I am fierce in might and in prowess, so that I am able to guard the borders of the land against foreign foes. I am a shelter for every poor man, I am a rampart of fight for every wealthy man; I give comfort to him who is wretched, I deal out mischief to him who is strong: all this through the fosterage of Fergus.

'Amergin the poet, to his knee I came. Therefore I am able to praise a king for the possession of any excellency; therefore I can stand up to any man in valour, in prowess, in wisdom, in splendour, in cleverness, in justice, in boldness. I am a match for any chariot-chief. I yield thanks to none, save Conchobar the Battle-Victorious.

'Finnchoem has reared me, so that Conall the Victorious is my foster-brother. For the sake of Dechtire, [his mother] Cathbad of the gentle face has taught me, so that I am an adept in the arts of the gods of druidism, and learned in the excellencies of knowledge.

'All the men of Ulster have taken part in my bringing up, alike charioteers and chariot-chiefs, kings and chief poets, so that I am the darling of the host and multitude, so that I fight for the honour of them all alike. Honourably was I called into being by Lug son of Conn mac Ethlenn, when Dechtire went to the house of the Mighty One of the Brug. And thou, O maiden,' said Cú Chulainn, 'how hast thou been reared in the Gardens of Lug?'

'It is not hard to relate that to thee, truly,' answered the maiden. 'I was brought up,' said she, 'in ancient virtues, in lawful behaviour, in the keeping of chastity, in rank equal to a queen, in stateliness of form, so that to me is attributed every noble grace of demeanour among the hosts of Erin's women.'

'Good indeed are those virtues,' said Cú Chulainn. 'Why, then, should it not be fitting for us both to become one? For I have not hitherto found a maiden capable of holding converse with me at a meeting in this wise.'

'One more question,' said the maiden. 'Hast thou a wife already?'

'Not so,' said Cú Chulainn.

Said the maiden, 'I may not marry before my sister is married, for she is older than I; namely, Fial, daughter of Forgall, whom thou seest with me here. She is excellent in handiwork.'

'It is not she, truly, with whom I have fallen in love,' said Cú Chulainn. 'Nor have I ever accepted a woman who has known a man before me, and I have been told that yon girl was once Cairbre Niafer's.'

While they were thus conversing, Cú Chulainn saw the breasts of the maiden over the bosom of her smock. And he said: 'Fair is this plain, the plain of the noble yoke.'

Then the maiden spake these words: 'No one comes to this plain who does not slay as many as a hundred on every ford from the Ford of Scenn Menn at Ollbine to Banchuing Arcait, where swift Brea breaks the brow of Fedelm.'

'Fair is this plain, the plain of the noble yoke,' said Cú Chulainn.

'No one comes to this plain,' said she, 'who has not achieved the feat of leaping over three walls and slaying three times nine men at one blow, one of each of my brothers being in each group of nine, and yet preserve the brother in the midst of each nine of them alive; and then, accompanied by them and my foster-sister, bring out of Forgall's stronghold my weight in gold.'

'Fair is this plain, the plain of the noble yoke,' said Cú Chulainn.

'None comes to this plain,' said she, 'who does not go without sleep from summer's end to the beginning of spring, from the beginning of spring to May-day, and again from May-day to the beginning of winter.'

'Even as thou hast commanded, so shall all by me be done,' said Cú Chulainn.

'And by me thy offer is accepted, it is taken, it is granted,' said Emer. 'Yet one question more. What is thy account of thyself?' said she.

'I am the nephew of the man that disappears in another in the wood of Badb,' said he. [A pun on the name Conchobar – a stream bearing his name unites with the Dofolt in the woods of Ros.]

'And thy name?' she said.

'I am the hero of the plague that befalls dogs,' said he.

After those notable words, Cú Chulainn went from thence, and they did not hold any further converse on that day.

While Cú Chulainn was driving across Breg, Loeg, his charioteer, asked him: 'Now,' said he, 'the words that thou and the maiden Emer spoke, what didst thou mean by them?'

'Dost thou not know,' answered Cú Chulainn, 'that I am wooing Emer? And it is for this reason that we disguised our words, lest the girls should understand that I am wooing her. For, if Forgall knew it, we should not meet with his consent.' Cú Chulainn then repeated the conversation from the beginning to his charioteer, explaining it to him, to beguile the length of their way.

'By Intide Emna which I said when she asked me "whence hast thou come?" I meant from Emain Macha. It is called Emain Macha from this. Macha, the daughter of Sainreth Mac in Botha, wife of Crundchu son of Agnoman, ran a race against two steeds of the king, after she had been forced to it by a strong injunction. She beat them, and bare a boy and a girl at one birth. And from those twins (*emuin*) is called, and from that Macha is named the plain of Macha. Or again, it is from this that Emain Macha is, as it is in the following tale. Three kings were reigning together over Erinn. They were from Ulster. Dithorba son of Diman from Uisnech of Meath; Aed the Red, son of Badurn, son of Aircet the Bald, in the land of Aed; Cimbaeth, son of Findairgret, from Finnabair of Mag Inis. It is he who brought up Ugaine the Great, son of Eochu the Victorious. Then the men made an agreement, that each of them was to reign seven years. Three times seven sureties were pledged between them, seven druids to revile them for ever; or seven poets to lampoon and satirise, and upbraid them; or seven chiefs to wound them and burn them; unless each man gave up his reign at the end of seven years, having preserved true government, the produce of each year, without decay of any kind, and without the death of a woman from concubinage. Each of them reigned three times in his turn, during sixty-six years. Aed the Red was the first of them to die, or rather he was drowned in Ess Ruaid, and his body was taken into the *síd* there, whence Sid Aeda and Ess Ruaid. He left no children, except one daughter, whose name was Macha the Red-haired. She demanded the kingship in its due time. Cimbaeth and Dithorba said they would not give kingship to a woman. A battle was fought between them. Macha routed them. She was sovereign for seven years. Meanwhile Dithorba had fallen. He left five noble sons behind, Baeth and Brass and Betach Uallach and Borbchass. These now demanded the kingship. Macha said she would not give it to them, "for not by favour did I obtain it," said she, "but by force in the battlefield." A battle was fought between them. Macha routed the sons of Dithorba, who left a slaughter of heads before her, and went into exile in the wilds of Connaught. Macha then took Cimbaeth to her as her husband and leader of her troops. When now Macha and Cimbaeth were united, Macha went to seek the sons of Dithorba in the shape of a leper. She smeared herself with rye-dough and . . . She found them in Buirend Connacht, cooking a wild boar. The men asked tidings of her, and she gave them. And they let her have food by the fire. Said one of them "Lovely is the eye of the girl, let us lie with her." He took her with him into the wood. She bound that man by dint of her strength, and left him in the wood. She came back to the fire. "Where is the man who went with thee?" they asked. "He is ashamed to come to you," she replied, "after having lain with a leper." "There is no shame," said they, "for we shall all do the same." Each man took her into the wood. She bound every one of them, one after the other and brought them all in one chain to Ulster. The men of Ulster wanted to kill them. "No," said she, "for that would be the ruin of my true government. But they shall be thralls, and shall dig a rath round me, and that shall be the eternal seat of Ulster for ever." Then she marked out the dun for them with her brooch, a golden pin on her neck – a brooch on the neck of Macha (*eo imma muin Macha*). Hence is Emain Macha in truth.

'The man, I said, in whose house we slept, he is the fisherman of Conchobor. Roncu is his name. It is he that catches the fish on his line under the sea; for the fish are the cattle of the sea, and the sea is the plain of Tethra, a king of the kings of the Fomori.

'The cooking-hearth, I said. A foal was cooked for us on it. A foal is the ruin of a chariot to the end of three weeks' [*Nómad*, a period of nine nights] . . . and there is a *gess* on a chariot to the end of three weeks for any man to enter it after having last eaten horseflesh. For it is the horse that sustains the chariot.

'Between the Two Mountains of the Wood, I said. These are the two mountains between which we came, Sliab Fuait to the west of us, and Sliab Cuillinn to the east of us. We were in Oircel, the wood which is between them, on the road I meant between the two.

'The road, I said, from the Covering of the Sea, that is from the Plain of Murthemne. The sea was on it for thirty years after the deluge, whence is Teme Mara, the shelter, or covering of the sea. Or again, it is from this that it is called the Plain of Murthemne, [for] a magic sea was on it with [islands] in it, so that one could sit on it, so that a man with his armour might sit down on the ground of (. . .) until the Dagda came with his club of anger, and sang the following words at it, so that it ebbed away at once:

> Silent thy hollow head,
> Silent thy dirty body,
> Silent thy muddy brow.

'Over the Great Secret of the men of Dea, that is a wonderful secret and a wonderful whisper. It is called the Marsh of Dolluid to-day. Dolluid, son of Carpre Niafer, was wounded by Matu. Before that, however, its name was Great Secret of the Men of Dea, because it was there that the gathering of the battle of Moytura was first planned by the Tuatha dé Danann, for the purpose of throwing off the tribute which the Fomori exacted from them, that is two-thirds of corn and milk and offspring.

'Over the Foam of the Two Steeds of Emain. There was a famous youth reigning over the Gaels. He had two horses reared for him in *Síd* Eremon of the Tuatha dé. Nemed, son of Nama, was the name of that king. Then those two horses were let loose from the *síd*, and a splendid stream burst after them from the *síd*, and there was great foam on that stream, and the foam spread over the land for a great length of time, and was thus to the end of a year, so that hence that water was called Uanub, foam on the water, and it is Uanub to-day.

'The Garden of the Mórrígan, I said. That is Ochtur Netmon. The Dagda gave that land to the Mórrígan, and she lived there. After a year she killed Ibor Boiclid, son of Garb, in her garden. The [plants] which her garden grew were [barren] in that year, for the son of Garb was her relation.

'The Back of the Great Sow, I said, that is, Druirnin n-Ebreg. For the shape of a sow appeared to the sons of Milid on every hill and on every height in Erinn, when they crossed over and wanted to land in it by force, after a spell had been cast on it by the Tuatha dé Danann.

'The Glen of the Great Dam, I said, that is Glenn m-Breogain. Glenn m-Breogain and Moy Bray were named after Breoga, son of Breogán Sendacht, son of Milid. It was called Glen of the Great Dam because Dam of Dile, son of Smirgoll, son of Tethra, who was king over Erinn, lived there. This Dam died in [congress with] a woman [from the *síd*] of Moy Bray to the west of the mouth (. . .)

'The road, I said, between the God and his Seer. That is, between Mac Oc of the *síd* of the Brug and his seer, Bresal. Bresal was a seer to the west of the Brug. Between them was the one woman, the wife of the smith. That is the way I went. Mairne, then, is between the hill of the *síd* of the Brug in which Oengus is, and the *síd* of Bresal, the druid.

'Over the Marrow of the Woman Fedelm, I said. That is, the Boyne. It is called Boyne from Boand, the wife of Nechtan, son of Labraid. She went to guard the hidden well at the bottom of the dun with the three cupbearers of Nechtan, Flex and Lesc and Luain. Nobody came without blemish from that well, unless the three cupbearers went with him. The queen went out of pride and overbearing to the well, and said nothing would ruin her shape, nor put a blemish on her. She passed left-hand-wise round the well to deride its power. Then three waves broke over her, and smashed her two thighs and her right hand and one of her eyes. She ran out of the *síd* to escape from this injury, until she came to the sea. Wherever she ran, the well ran after her. Segais was its name in the *síd*, the river Segsa from the *síd* to the Pool of Mochua the Arm of the Wife of Nuadu and the Thigh of the Wife of Nuadu after that; the Boyne in Meath; Manchuing Arcait it is called from the Finda

to the Troma, the Marrow of the Woman Fedelm, from the Troma to
the sea.

'The Boar (*triath*) I said and his Dam, that is Cleitech and Fessi. For
triath is the name for a boar, the leader of herds; but it is also a name
for a king, the leader of the great host. Cleitech then is [a bull] of battle.
Fessi, again, is a name for a great sow of a farmer's house. A boar and
his dam, and between a boar and his sow then we went.

'The King of Ana, I said, and his Servant (*gnia*), that is, Cerna,
through which we passed. *Síd* Cirine was its name of old. Cerna is its
name since the (. . .) Enna Aignech, slew Cerna, the king of Ana on
that hill, and he slew his steward in the east of that place. Gnia was his
name, from which is Rath Gniad in Cerna ever. On Gese, the king of
the sons of Emne, did Enna do it, for there was great friendship
between Gese and Cerna.

'The Washing of the Horses of Dea, I said, that is: Ange. The
Washing of the Horses of Dea was its name originally, because in it the
Men of Dea washed their horses when they came from the battle of
Moytura. It was called Ange after the king whose horses the Tuatha dé
Danann washed in it.

'The four-cornered Mannchuile, I said, that is, Muin Chille. It is
there where Mann the farmer was. There was a great mortality of cattle
in Erinn in the reign of Bresal Brece, son of Fiachu Fobrecc of Leinster.
Then Mann made large deep chambers underground in the place
which is called Uachtar Mannchuile to-day. And [spells] were made to
keep off the plague. Afterwards he gave an entertainment to the king
with twenty-four couples to the end of seven years. Mannchuile, then,
are the corners of Mann, that is, Ochtar Muinchille.

'Great Crime again, I said, that is, Ailbine. There was a famous king
here in Erinn: Ruad, son of Rigdond, of Munster. He had an appointment of meeting with foreigners. He went to the meeting with the
foreigners round the south of Alba with three ships. Thirty were in each
ship. The fleet was arrested from below in the midst of the sea.
Throwing jewels and precious things into the sea did not get them off.
Lots were cast among them for who should go into the sea and find out
what it was that held them fast. The lot fell upon the king himself. Then
the king Ruad, son of Rigdond leapt into the sea. The sea at once closed
over him. He lighted upon a large plain on which nine beautiful
women met him. They confessed to him that it had been they that had
arrested the ships, in order that he should come to them. And they gave

him nine vessels of gold to sleep with them for nine nights, one night with each of them. He did so. Meanwhile his men were not able to proceed quickly through the power of the women. Said one woman of then it was her time of conceiving, and she would bear a son, and he should come to them to fetch his son on his return from the east. Then he joined his men, and they went on their voyage. They stayed with their friends to the end of seven years, and then went back a different way and did not go near the same spot. And they landed in the bay of Ailbine. There the women came up to them. The men heard their music in their brazen ship. While they were stowing their fleet, the women came ashore and put the boy out of their ship on the land where the men were. The harbour was stony and rocky. Then the boy [ate] one of the stones, so that he died of it. The women saw it and cried all together: Ollbine, Ollbine! "great crime". Hence it is called Ailbine.

'The Remnants of the Great Feast, I said, that is Taillne. It is there that LugScimaig gave the great feast to Lug son of Ethle, to comfort him after the battle of Moytura, for that was his wedding feast of kingship. For the Tuatha dé made this Lug king after Nuadu had been killed. As to the place in which their remnants were put, he made a large hill of them. The name was Knoll of the Great Feast, or Remnants of the Great Feast, that is Taillne to-day.

'Of the daughters of Tethra's nephew, Forgall the Wily, is the nephew of Tethra, king of the Fomori, that is the son of his sister, for *nia* and a sister's son is the same, and a champion is also called *nia*.

'As to the account of myself I gave her. There are two in the land of Ross, Conchobor is the name of one of them, and Dofolt (without hair, bald) the name of the other. Now the Conchobor falls into the Dofolt; it mixes with it, so that they are one river.

'I am the nephew (*nia*) of that man, of Conchobor. That is I am the son of Dechtire, Conchobor's sister, or I am a champion of Conchobor's.

'In the Wood of Badb, that is, of the Mórrígu, for that is her wood, the land of Ross, and she is the Battle-Crow and is called the Wife of Neit, that is: the Goddess of Battle, for Neit is the same as God of Battle.

'The name I said I had: "I am the hero (*núada*) of the plague [of wild fierceness] that befalls dogs I am *núada*. I am a strong warrior of that plague, I am wild and fierce in battles and fights."

'When I said: "Fair is this plain, the plain of the noble yoke," it was not the plain of Bray that I praised then, but the shape of the maiden. For I beheld the yoke of her two breasts through the opening of her smock, and it is of that said "plain of the noble yoke," of the breasts of the maiden.

'When she said: "No one comes to this plain, who does not kill as many as *argat*" – *argat* in the language of the poets means "a hundred". That is the interpretation, and this is what it means; that it is not easy to carry off the maiden, unless I slay a hundred men at each ford from Ailbine to the Boyne, together with Scennmenn the Wily, the sister of her father, who will change herself into every shape there, to destroy my chariot and to bring about my death,' said Cú Chulainn.

'*Geni grainde*, she said, [meaning that] she would not come with me, unless I jumped the hero's salmon-leap across the three ramparts to reach her. For three brothers of her will be guarding her, Ibur and Scibur and Catt, and a company of nine each of them, and I must deal a blow on each nine, from which eight will die, but no stroke will reach any of her brothers among them; and I must carry her and her foster-sister with their load of gold and silver out of the dun of Forgall.

'Bend Suain, son of Rose Melc, which she said, this is the same thing: that I shall fight without harm to myself from Samhain – that is: the end of summer. For two divisions were formerly on the year; the summer from Beltaine (the first of May) and winter from Samhain to Beltaine. Or *samfuin*, from which *suain* (sounds), for it is then that gentle voices sound, that is to say: sám-son "gentle sound". To Oimolc, the beginning of spring, different (*ime*) is its wet (*folc*), that is, the wet of spring, and the wet of winter. Or, *oi-melc*. *Oi* in the language of poetry, is a name for sheep, whence *oibá* (sheep's death) is named, *coinbá* (dogs death), *echbá* (horse's death), *duineba* (men's death), as *bath* is a name for 'death.' *Oi-melc* then, is the time in which the sheep come out and are milked, whence *oisc* (an ewe), may be *oi-sesc*, a barren sheep. To *Beldin*, that is Beltine, a favouring fire. For the druids used to make two fires with great incantations, and to drive the cattle between them against the plagues, every year. Or to *Beldin* that is: Bel the name of an idol. At that time the young of every neat were placed in the possession of Bel. Beldine, then Beltine. To *Brón Trogain*, Lammas-day, the beginning of autumn – for it is then the earth is afflicted, that is: the earth under fruit. *Trogan* is a name for earth.'

Cú Chulainn went driving on his way, and slept that night in Emain Macha.

Then the daughters of the land-owners told their parents of the youth who had come in his splendid chariot, and of the conversation held between him and Emer; that they did not know what they had said to one another; and that he had turned from them across the plain of Breg northward. The land-owners related all this to Forgall the Wily, and told him that the girl had spoken to Cú Chulainn.

'It is true,' said Forgall the Wily. 'The madman from Emain Macha has been here to converse with Emer and the girl has fallen in love with him: that is why they talked one to another. But it shall avail them nothing. I shall hinder them,' he said.

Thereupon Forgall the Wily went to Emain Macha disguised in the garb of a foreigner, as if it were an embassy from the King of the Gauls that had come to confer with Conchobar, with an offering to him of golden treasures, and wine of Gaul, and all sorts of good things besides. In number they were three. Great welcome was made to him. When on the third day he had sent away his men, Cú Chulainn and Conall and other chariot-chiefs of Ulster were praised before him. He said that it was true, that the chariot-chiefs performed marvellously, but that were Cú Chulainn to go to Donall the Soldierly in Alba (Scotland), his skill would be more wonderful still; and that if he went to Scathach to learn soldierly feats, he would excel the warriors of all Europe. But the reason for which he proposed this to Cú Chulainn was that he might never return again. For he thought that if Cú Chulainn became Scathach's friend, he would come to his death thereby, through the wildness and fierceness of that warrior. Cú Chulainn consented to go, and Forgall bound himself to give Cú Chulainn whatever he desired, if he should go within a certain time. Forgall went home, and the warriors arose in the morning and set themselves to do as they had vowed.

So they started; Cú Chulainn and Loegaire the Triumphant, and Conchobar; and Conall the Victorious, some say, went with them. But Cú Chulainn first went across Mag Breg to visit the maiden. He talked to Emer before going into the ship, and the maiden told him that it had been Forgall who in Emain Macha had desired him to go and learn soldierly feats, in order that they two might not meet. And she bade him be on his guard wherever he went, lest Forgall should destroy him. Either of them promised the other to keep their chastity until they should meet again, unless either of them died meanwhile. They bade each other farewell, and he turned towards Alba.

Part II
Cú Chulainn's Education in Arms

When they reached Donall in Alba, they were taught by him to blow a leathern bellows under the flagstone of the small hole. On it they would perform till their soles were black or livid. They were taught another thing on a spear, on which they would jump and perform on its point; this was called 'the champion's coiling round the points of spears,' or 'dropping on its head.' Then the daughter of Donall, Dornolla, Big-Fist by name, fell in love with Cú Chulainn. Her form was very gruesome, her knees were large, her heels turned before her, her feet behind her; big dark-grey eyes in her head, her face as black as a bowl of jet. A very large forehead she had, her rough bright-red hair in threads wound round her head. Cú Chulainn refused her. Then she swore to be revenged on him for this.

Donall said that Cú Chulainn would not have perfect knowledge of their learning until he went to Scathach, who lived to the east of Alba. So the four went across Alba, Cú Chulainn, Conchobar King of Ulster, Conall the Victorious, and Loegaire the Triumphant. Then before their eyes appeared unto them in a vision Emain Macha, past which Conchobar and Conall and Loegaire were not able to go. The daughter of Donall had raised that vision in order to sever Cú Chulainn from his companions to his ruin. Other versions say that it was Forgall the Wily who raised this vision before them to induce them to turn back, so that by returning Cú Chulainn should fail to fulfil what he had promised him in Emain Macha, and thereby he would be shamed; or that, were he peradventure in spite of it to go eastward to learn soldierly feats, both known and unknown, of Scathach, he would be still more likely to be killed, being alone. Then, of his own free will, Cú Chulainn departed from them along an unknown road, for the powers of the girl Dornolla were great, and she wrought evil against him, and severed him from his companions.

Now, when Cú Chulainn went across Alba, he was sad and gloomy and weary for the loss of his comrades; neither knew he whither he should go to seek Scathach. For he had promised his comrades that he would not return again to Emain Macha, unless he either reached Scathach or met his death. Now, seeing that he was lost, he lingered; and while he was there, he beheld a terrible great beast like a lion coming towards him, which kept watching him, but did not do him any harm. Whichever way he went, the beast went before him, turning its side towards him. Then he took a leap and was on its back. He did not guide it, but went wherever the beast liked. In that wise they journeyed four days, until they came to the uttermost bounds of men, and to an island where lads were rowing on a small loch. The lads laughed at the unwonted sight of the hurtful beast doing service to a man. Cú Chulainn then leaped off, and the beast parted from him, and he bade it farewell.

He passed on, and came to a large house in a deep glen, wherein was a maiden fair of form. The maiden addressed him, and bade him welcome. 'Welcome art thou, O Cú Chulainn!' said she. He asked her how she knew him. She answered that they both had been dear foster-children with Wulfkin the Saxon, 'when I was there, and thou learning sweet speech from him,' said she. She then gave him meat and drink and he turned away from her. Then he met a brave youth who gave him the same welcome. They conversed together, and Cú Chulainn inquired of him the way to the stronghold of Scathach. The youth taught him the way across the Plain of Ill-luck that lay before him. On the hither half of the plain the feet of men would stick fast; on the farther half the grass would rise and hold them fast on the points of its blades. The youth gave him a wheel, and told him to follow its track across one-half of the plain. He gave him also an apple, and told him to follow the way along which the apple ran, and that in such wise he would reach the end of the plain. Thus Cú Chulainn went across the plain; afterwards proceeding farther on. The youth had told him that there was a large glen before him, and a single narrow path through it, which was full of monsters that had been sent by Forgall to destroy him, and that his road to the house of Scathach lay across terrible mountain fastnesses. Then each of them wished a blessing to the other, Cú Chulainn and the youth Eochaid Bairche. It was he who taught him how he should win honour in the house of Scathach. The same youth also foretold to him what he would suffer of hardships and straits in the Cattle-Raid of Cooley, and what evil and exploits and contests he would achieve against the men of Erin.

Then Cú Chulainn, following the young man's instructions, went on that road across the Plain of Ill-luck and through the Perilous Glen. This was the road that Cú Chulainn took to the camp where the scholars of Scathach were. He asked where she was.

'In yonder island,' said they.

'Which way must I take to reach her?'

'By the Bridge of the Cliff, which no man can cross until he has achieved valour.'

For thus was that bridge: it had two low ends and the mid-space high, and whenever anybody leaped on one end of it, the other end would lift itself up and throw him on his back. Some versions relate that a crowd of the warriors of Erin were in that stronghold learning feats from Scathach; namely, Ferdiad son of Daman, and Naisi son of Usnech, and Loch Mor son of Egomas, and Fiamain son of Fora, and an innumerable host besides. But in this version it is not told that they were there at that time.

Cú Chulainn tried three times to cross the bridge and could not do it. The men jeered at him. Then in a frenzy he jumped upon the head of the bridge, and made 'the hero's salmon-leap', so that he landed on the middle of it; and the other head of the bridge had not fully raised itself up when he reached it; he threw himself from it, and was on the ground of the island. He went up to the stronghold, and struck the door with the shaft of his spear, so that it went through it. Scathach was told. 'Truly,' said she, 'this must be someone who has achieved valour elsewhere.' And she sent her daughter Uathach to know who the youth might be. Then Uathach came and conversed with Cú Chulainn. On the third day she advised him, if it were to achieve valour that he had come, that he should go through the hero's salmon-leap to reach Scathach, in the place where she was teaching her two sons, Cuar and Cett, in the great yew tree; that he should set his sword between her breasts until she yielded him his three wishes: namely, to teach him without neglect; that without the payment of wedding-gifts he might wed Uathach; and that she should foretell his future, for she was a prophetess.

Cú Chulainn then went to the place where Sathach was. He placed his two feet on the two edges of the basket of the feats, and bared his sword, and put its point to her heart, saying, 'Death hangs over thee!'

'Name thy three demands!' said she; 'thy three demands, as thou canst utter them in one breath.'

'They must be fulfilled,' said Cú Chulainn. And he pledged her. Uathach then was given to Cú Chulainn, and Scathach taught him skill of arms.

During the time that he was with Scathach, and was the husband of

Uathach her daughter, a certain famous man who lived in Munster, by name Lugaid son of Nos son of Alamac, the renowned king and foster-brother of Cú Chulainn, went eastwards with twelve chariot-chiefs of the high kings of Munster, to woo twelve daughters of Cairbre Niafer, but they had all been betrothed before. When Emer's father, Forgall the Wily, heard this, he went to Tara, and told Lugaid that the best maiden in Erin, both as to form and chastity and handiwork, was in his house unmarried. Lugaid said it pleased him well. Then Forgall betrothed the maiden to Lugaid; and to the twelve under-kings that were together with Lugaid, he betrothed twelve daughters of twelve landed proprietors in Breg.

The king accompanied Forgall to his stronghold for the wedding. When now Emer was brought to Lugaid, to sit by his side, she took between both her hands his two cheeks, and laid it on the truth of his honour and his life, confessing that it was Cú Chulainn she loved, that Forgall was against it, and that any one who should take her as his wife would suffer loss of honour. Then, for fear of Cú Chulainn, Lugaid did not dare to take Emer, and so he returned home again.

Scathach was at that time carrying on war against other tribes, over whom the Princess Aife ruled, The two hosts assembled to fight, but Cú Chulainn had been put in bonds by Scathach, and a sleeping-potion given him beforehand to prevent him going into the battle, lest anything should befall him there. She did this as a precaution. But after an hour Cú Chulainn suddenly started out of his sleep. This sleeping-potion, that would have held anybody else for twenty-four hours in sleep, held him for only one hour. He went forth with the two sons of Scathach against the three sons of Ilsuanach, namely, Cuar, Cett, and Cruife, three warriors of Aife's. Alone he encountered them all three, and they fell by him. On the next morning again the battle was set, and the two hosts marched forward until the two lines met, face to face. Then the three sons of Ess Enchenn advanced, namely, Cire, Bire, and Blaiene, three other of Aife's warriors, and began to combat against the two sons of Scathach. They went on the path of feats. Thereupon Scathach uttered a sigh, for she knew not what would come of it; first, because there was no third man with her two sons against those three, and next, because she was afraid of Aife, who was the hardest woman-warrior in the world. Cú Chulainn, however, went up to her two sons, and sprang upon the path, and met all three, and they fell by him.

Aife then challenged Scathach to combat, and Cú Chulainn went forth to meet Aife. Before going he asked what it was Aife loved most. Scathach said: 'What most she loves are her two horses, her chariot, and her charioteer.' Cú Chulainn and Aife went on the path of feats, and began combat there. Aife shattered Cú Chulainn's weapon, and his sword was broken off at the hilt. Then Cú Chulainn cried: 'Ah me, the charioteer of Aife, her two horses, and her chariot have fallen down the glen, and all have perished!' At that Aife looked up.

Then Cú Chulainn sprang towards her, seized her under her two breasts, took her on his back like a shoulder-load, and bore her away to his own host. Then he threw her from him to the ground, and over her held his naked sword.

'Life for life, O Cú Chulainn!' said Aife.

'My three demands to me!' said he.

'Thou shalt have them as thou breathest them,' she said.

'These are my three demands,' he said, 'that thou give hostages to Scathach, nor ever afterwards oppose her, that thou remain with me this night before thy stronghold, and that thou bear me a son.'

'I promise all this to thee,' said she. And thus it was done. Cú Chulainn went with Aife and remained with her that night. Then Aife said she was with child, and that she would bear a boy. 'On this day seven years I will send him to Erin,' she said, 'and leave thou a name for him.'

Cú Chulainn left a golden finger-ring for him, and told her that the boy was to go and seek him in Erin, so soon as the ring should fit on his finger. And he said that Connla was the name to be given him, and charged her that he should not make himself known to any one man; also, that he should not turn out of the way of any man; nor refuse combat to any. Thereupon Cú Chulainn returned again to his own people.

As he went along the same road, he met an old woman on the road, blind of her left eye. She asked him to beware, and to avoid the road before her. He said there was no other footing for him, save on the cliff of the sea that was beneath him. She besought him to leave the road to her. Then he left the road, only clinging to it with his toes. As she passed over him she hit his great toe to throw him off the path, down the cliff. He had foreseen it, and leaped the hero's salmon-leap up again, and struck off the woman's head. She was Ess Enchenn, the mother of the last three warriors that had fallen by him, and it was in order to destroy him that she had come to meet him.

After that the hosts returned with Scathach to her own land, and hostages were given to her by Aife. And Cú Chulainn stayed there for the day of his recovery.

At last, when the full lore of soldierly arts with Scathach had been mastered by Cú Chulainn – as well as the apple-feat, the thunder-feat, the blade-feat, the supine-feat, and the spear-feat, the rope-feat, the bodyfeat, the cat's-feat, the salmon-feat of a chariot-chief, the throw of the stall, the whirl of a brave chariotchief, the *gae bulga* (bag spear), the wheel-feat, the breath-feat, the hero's whoop, the blow, the counter-blow, running up a lance and righting the body on its point, the scythe-chariot, and the hero's twisting round spear points – then came to him a message to return to his own land, and he took his leave.

Then Scathach told him what would befall him in the future, and sang to him in the seer's large shining ken, and spoke these words:

> Welcome, oh victorious, warlike Cú Chulainn;
> At the Raid of the Cattle of Breg,
> Thou wilt be a chariot-chief in single combat.
> Great peril awaits thee,
> Alone against a vast herd.
> The warriors of Cruachan, thou wilt scatter them.
> Thy name shall reach the men of Scotland.
> Thirty years I reckon the strength of thy valour;
> Further than this I do not add.

Then Cú Chulainn went on board his ship, to set out for Erin. These were the voyagers in the ship: Lugaid and Luan, the two sons of Loch; Ferbaeth, Larin, Ferdiad, and Durst son of Serb. They came to the house of Ruad, king of the Isles, on Samain night. Conall the Victorious, and Loegaire the Triumphant, were there before them levying tribute; for at that time a tribute was paid to Ulster from the Isles of the Foreigners (the Western Isles).

Then Cú Chulainn heard sounds of wailing before him in the stronghold of the king. 'What is that lamentation?' asked Cú Chulainn.

'It is because Dervorgil, the daughter of Ruad, is given as tribute to the Fomorians,' said they.

'Where is the maiden?' he said.

They answered, 'She is on the shore below.'

Cú Chulainn went down to the strand, and drew near to the maiden. He asked her the meaning of her plight, and she told him fully.

Said he, 'Whence do the men come?'

'From that distant land yonder. Remain not here,' she said, 'in sight of the robbers.'

But he remained there awaiting them, and he killed the three Fomorians in single combat. The last man wounded him in the wrist, and the maiden gave him a strip from her garment to bind round his wound. Then he departed without making himself known to her. The maiden came to the stronghold, and told her father the whole story; and afterwards came Cú Chulainn to the stronghold, like every other guest. Conall and Loegaire bade him welcome, and there were many in the stronghold who boasted of having slain the Fomorians, but the maiden believed them not. Then the king had a bath prepared, and afterwards each one was brought to her separately. Cú Chulainn came, like all the rest, and the maiden recognised him.

'I will give the maiden to thee,' said Ruad, 'and I myself will pay her wedding-dowry.'

'Not so,' said Cú Chulainn. 'But if it please her, let her follow me this day year to Erin; there she will find me.'

Then Cú Chulainn came to Emain Macha and related all his adventures. When he had cast his fatigue from him, he set out to seek Emer at the rath of Forgall. For a whole year he remained near it, but could not approach her for the number of the watch.

At the end of the year he came and said to his charioteer, 'It is to-day, O Loeg, that we have our tryst with the daughter of Ruad, but we know not the exact place, for we were not wise. Let us go to the coast.'

When they came to the shore of Loch Cuan (Strangford Lough), they beheld two birds on the sea. Cú Chulainn put a stone in his sling, and aimed at the birds. The men ran up to them, after having hit one of the birds. When they came up to them, lo! they saw two women, the most beautiful in the world. They were Dervorgil, the daughter of Ruad, and her handmaid. 'Evil is the deed that thou hast done, O Cú Chulainn,' said she; 'it was to meet thee we came, and now thou hast hurt us.'

Cú Chulainn sucked the stone out of her, with its clot of blood round it.

'I cannot wed thee now,' said Cú Chulainn, 'for I have drunk thy blood. But I will give thee to my companion here, Lugaid of the Red Stripes.'

And so it was done.

Then Cú Chulainn desired to go to the rath of Forgall. And that day the scythe-chariot was prepared for him. It was called the scythe-chariot (*carpat serrda*) on account of the iron scythes that stood out from it, or perhaps because it was first invented by the Serians. When he arrived at the rath of Forgall, he jumped the hero's salmon-leap across the three ramparts, so that he was on the ground of the stronghold. And he dealt three blows in the liss, so that eight men fell from each blow, and one escaped in each group of nine, namely, Scibur, Ibur, and Cat, three brothers of Emer. Forgall made a leap on to the rampart of the rath without, fleeing from Cú Chulainn, and he fell lifeless. Then Cú Chulainn carried off Emer, and her foster-sister, with their two weights of gold and silver, leaping back again across the third rampart, and so went forth.

From every direction cries were raised around them. Scenn Menn rushed against them. Cú Chulainn killed her at the ford, hence called the Ford of Scenn Menn. Thence they escaped to Glondath, and there Cú Chulainn killed a hundred of them. 'Great is the deed (*glond*) that thou hast done,' said Emer; 'to have killed a hundred armed able-bodied men.'

'Glond-ath (Ford of Deeds) shall be its name for ever,' said Cú Chulainn. He reached Crufoit (Blood-turf), which until then had been called Rae-ban (White Field). He dealt great angry blows on the hosts in that place, so that streams of blood broke over it on every side. 'By thy work, the hill is covered with a blood-stained turf to-day, O Cú Chulainn,' cried the maiden. Hence it is called Cru-foit (Turf of Blood).

The pursuers overtook them at Ath n-Imfuait on the Boyne. Emer left the chariot, and Cú Chulainn pursued them along the banks, the clods flying from the hoofs of the horses across the ford northward. Then he turned, and pursued them northward, so that the clods flew over the ford southward from the hoofs of the horses. Hence is it called the Ford of the Two Clods, from the flying of the sods hither and thither. Now at each ford from Ath Scenn Menn at Ollbine to the Boyne of Breg, Cú Chulainn killed a hundred, and so he fulfilled all the deeds that he had vowed to the maiden, and he came safely out of all, and reached Emain Macha towards the fall of night.

Emer was brought into the House of the Red Branch to Conchobar and to the men of Ulster, and they bade her welcome. Cú Chulainn then took to himself his wife, and thenceforward they were not separated until they died.

28. The Wooing of Luaine and the Death of Athirne

(Tochmarc Luaine agus Aidedh Aithairne Andso)

Translated by Whitley Stokes

*T*ochmarc Luaine agus Aidedh Aithairne Andso is a sequel to the death of Deirdriu, as told in The Exile of the Sons of Uisliu (see pp. 444–453). Then, as now, great stories had a way of continuing into fresh episodes; the greatest most sorrowful love tale of how the unwilling Deirdriu, promised in marriage to an ageing King Conchobor, met her death was no exception. A double for the dead Deirdriu is sought to assuage the king's grief, but after the betrothal of the king to the girl, Luaine, Manannán mac Athgno, the dear friend of Deirdriu and her husband, Naoisi, both betrayed to their deaths by Conchobor's possessive greed, alters the course of events by laying waste to Ulster and allowing Conchobor to become distracted from his wooing. This text gives a clear account of the many Manannáns in Irish tradition, differentiating this son of Athgno from the mythological deity of the sea and the otherworld, Manannán mac Lír.

Together with his two sons, Athirne, a poetic satirist of scorching tongue, lays suit to Luaine, the chosen bride of Conchobor. They lay a *glám dicinn* upon her, a form of excoriating satire. The formula for this curse was that the poet stand like a crane, upon one leg, with one eye closed and one arm stretched out pointing to the object of his satire. The effect of a *glám dicinn* might result in anything from blisters on the face to death, with the added drawback of social exclusion, since no-one wanted to be associated with someone from whom all luck had fled. This may sound extremely unlikely today, but we should recall the Australian

Aboriginal ability to sing someone to death from long distances, and the efficacy of African witch doctors to curse their victims to death. In a society where the power of the word was wholly oral, not written, where the sophisticated mesh of civilisation relied upon memory, custom and the honour due to poets as the conservers of these traditions, the poet's word was magical in effect.

Cathbad, the king's own father and most powerful druid, warns his son about Athirne's murderous intentions and the men of Ulster, backed by Conchobor, determine to kill Athirne, quite contrary to the supposedly inviolate poetic immunity that protected the *aes dána* – the people of the gift. It is the chief poet of Ulster, Amairgen, Athirne's own foster-child and pupil who sings his eulogy.

This text is from the *Yellow Book of Lecan*, col 880, edited and translated by Whitley Stokes in *Révue Celtique* XXIV 1903.

After Derdriu's death, Conchobar mac Nessa was in grief and sorrow and exceeding great dejection; and nought of music, or brightness, or beauty, or delight in the world appeased his spirit, but he was ever and always sad and mournful. The magnates of Ulster were telling him to search the provinces of Erin if perchance he might find therein the daughter of a king or lord, who would drive away from him his grief for Derdriu. To that he assented.

His two messengers were brought to him, namely Lebarcham, daughter of Ae and Adarc, and Lebarcham Rannach, daughter of Uangaimain. Hideous indeed and horrible were the forms of those messengers [. . . .]

Then the two messengers searched Erin, both forts and goodly towns, and in them they found no unmarried woman who could heal Conchobar's grief. Now Lebarcham, daughter of Ae and Adarc, chanced on the dwelling of Domanchenn son of Dega in the province of Ulster itself, and there she beheld a maiden loveable, curly-headed, pure-coloured, who surpassed the world's women in her time, namely, Luaine, daughter of Domarchenn. Lebarcham asked whose daughter she was. (The daughter of Domanchenn son of Dega), they answer. Lebarcham said that it was Conchobar who had sent her to seek Luaine for him, for she was the one girl in Ireland who had upon her the ways of Derdriu, both in shape and sense and handiness. 'That is well,' says her father; and thus he accepts in consideration of a proper bride-price to her.

The messenger came to the place where Conchobar was biding, and tells him the tidings of the girl; so then she said: 'There I beheld a maiden gentle-beautiful, ripe for marriage, yellow-haired [. . . .]

So love for the girl filled his mind and he could not bear not to go himself and see her clearly. Now when he beheld the maiden there was no bone in him the size of an inch that was not filled with long-lasting love for the girl. She was afterwards betrothed to him, and the maiden's bride-price was bound upon him, and he turned back again to Emain.

At that time came Manannán son of Athgno, king of Mann and the Foreigners' Isles, with a vast sea-fleet, to raid and ravage Ulster and take vengeance on it for the sons of Uisnech; for this Manannán had been a friend of theirs, and 'tis he that fostered the children of Naisi and Derdriu to wit, Gaiar the son and Aib-grene the daughter.

There were four Manannáns and not at the same time were they.

Manannán son of Allot, a splendid wizard of the Tuatha dé Danann and in the time of the Tuatha dé Danann was he. Orbsen, now, (is) his proper name. 'Tis that Manannán who dwelt in Arran, and from him Emain Ablach is called, and 'tis he that was killed in the battle of Cuillenn by Uillenn of the Red Eyebrows, son of Caither, son of Nuada Silverhand, contending for the kingship of Connaught. And when his grave was dug, 'tis there Loch n-Oirbsen broke forth under the earth, so that from him, the first Manannán Loch n-Oirbsen is named.

Manannán son of Cerp, king of the Isles and Mann. He was in the time of Conaire son of Etirscel and 'tis he that wooed Tuag daughter of Conall Collamair, Conaire's foster-son, and from her Tuag Inber is named.

Manannán 'son of the sea', to wit, a famous merchant who traded between Erin and Alba and the Isle of Mann. He was also a wizard, and 'tis he was the best pilot who was frequenting Ireland. 'Tis he too that would find out by heavenly science (i.e.) by inspecting the air, the time there would be fair weather or storm, and Manannán was named *dea en* (?), *el ideo*, etc.

Manannán son of Athgno was the fourth Manannán. 'Tis he that came with the great fleet to avenge the sons of Uisnech, and 'tis he that had supported them in Alba. Sixteen years were the sons of Uisnech in Alba, and they conquered from Slamannan to the north of Alba; and 'tis they that expelled the three sons of Gnathal son of Morgann, namely Iatach and Triatach and Mani Rough-hand, from that territory. For their father held sway over that land, and it was the sons of Uisnech that killed him. So the trio came in exile to Conchobar, and 'tis they that killed the three sons of Uisnech as deputies of Eóghan son of Durthacht.

So Manannán fell to plundering Ulster greatly. The Ulstermen gathered to give battle to Manannán. They said that Conchobar's ordeal of battle against the sons of Náisi was not good. A movement of peace was made between them (the Ulstermen) and Manannán and Bobarán the poet, the fosterer of Gaiar son of Náisi was sent at the time of the peace and the answer. Then said Bobarán:

> Gaiar son of famous Náisi
> fosterling of great-pure Manannán,
> therefore he came hither,
> to raid this country [. . . .]

And peace was then made between (Conchobar and) Manannán and friendship with Conchobar; and the *eric* for his father was given to Gaiar by desire of the lords of Ulster, and the two others, Annli and Ardan, were left against Conchobar's honour. A cantred of Liathmaine was given for land to Gaiar, to wit, the land of Dubthach Chafertongue, for he was (then) warring against Ulster along with Fergus. Thus they parted in peace, and thenceforward they were friends.

The doings of Luaine, however, this is now enquired into here.

Then Athirne the Importunate and his two sons, Cuindgedach and Apartach, heard of the plighting of the maiden to Conchobar, they went to solicit her, to beg for boons from her. So when they beheld the damsel, the three of them gave love to her, and desire for her filled them so that they preferred not to be alive unless they should forgather with her. They took by turns to beseeching the damsel, and they declared that they would cease to live, and that for each man of them they would make for her a *glám dicinn*, unless she would have commerce with them.

Said the damsel: 'Unmeet it is for you to say this, and I to be a wife with Conchobar.'

'We cannot remain alive,' say they, 'unless we go in unto thee.'

The damsel refused to lie with them. So then they make three satires on her, which left three blotches on her cheeks, to wit, Shame and Blemish and Disgrace, black and red and white.

Thereafter the damsel died of shame and bashfulness.

So then Athirne fled with his sons to Benn Athirni above the Boyne, for he feared that for the deed he had done vengeance would be inflicted upon him by Conchobar and the Ulstermen.

Now touching Conchobar. Long it seemed to him to be sleeping without a wife. So he came, and beside him the magnates of Ulster, to wit, Conall Cernach and Cú Chulainn and Celtchair and Blai Brugaid, and Eóghan son of Durthacht, and Cathbad and Sencha, to the fort of Domanchenn son of Dega – of the Tuatha dé was his kin, and there was his land. So there they found the damsel dead, and the people of the fort bewailing her. Great silence fell on Conchobar concerning that matter, and the grief upon him was second (only) to his grief for Derdriu.

Conchobar was saying, 'What vengeance would he just therein?'

The magnates of Ulster answered that this would be the fitting punishment for it, to kill Athirne with his sons and his household: 'And many a time,' say they, 'Ulster has found reproach of battle by means of him.'

Thereafter came the damsel's mother, even Be-guba and was wailing sadly and sorrowfully in the presence of Conchobar and the magnates of Ulster.

'O king,' she said, 'it is not the death of one person only which will result from yonder deed, for I and her father will die of grief for her. That yon death would carry us off was fated and promised according to the wizard's prophecy, when he was saying: "Women-troops grieve at the destruction of men by Athirne's words, etc."'

Then said Cathbad: 'Beasts of prey,' quoth he, 'will be sent against you by Athirne, namely, Satire and Disgrace and Shame, Curse and Fire and Bitter word. 'Tis he that hath the six sons of Dishonour, to wit, Niggardliness and Refusal and Denial, Hardness and Rigour and Rapacity. Those will be hurled against you,' quoth he, 'so that they will be in battles against you.'

Then too was Domanchenn egging on and censuring the men of Ulster.

'A question,' says Conchobar: 'how will ye act, O men of Ulster?'

It was Cú Chulainn who counselled the destruction of Athirne the severe. It was Conall the combative, the righteous, who looked on. It was Celtchair the wounding that conspired. It was Munremar the famous that planned. It was Cumscraid the custodian (?) that decided. It was the heroic, haughty, severe, two-edged youths of Ulster that determined that counsel, to go and destroy the abode of Athirne.

Then said [Domanchenn to Luaine's mother]:

'Sad indeed is that, O Be-guba, sad is the lot that has slain thee:

'tis heavy grief one has from it, to see thee over Luaine's grave' [. . .]

A mighty lamentation was then made about the damsel, and her death-chant and her funeral game[s] were performed, and her grave-stone was planted. Sad and sorrowful indeed were her father and her mother, and sad it was to be in presence of the wail that they were making.

Then said

CONCHOBAR: On the plain is this grave of Luaine, daughter of
            red Domanchenn
            never came to yellow Banba a woman that was
            harder to entreat.

CELTCHAIR: Will you tell us how that is, O champion, O
            Conchobar,
            Luaine and Derdriu of the companies, whose was
            the fairer converse?

CONCHOBAR: I will tell thee how that is, O Celtchar, son of
            Uthechar:
            Better was Luaine, who never uttered falsehood,
            there was no rivalry between them.
            Sad is any prophecy that carries her off, that from it
            she should go to death,
            That from it her barrow should be dug, that from it
            her grave should be conspicuous.
            Be-guba and Dega's son, and Luaine – 'tis death
            that will cut me off –
            On the same day they went on the journey, so that
            they have only one grave.
            Athirne of the four children, evil for him the deed
            lie has done:
            They all will fall, man, sons, wives, in vengeance
            for this grave.

Conchobar was then mightily bewailing the damsel and after that he took to egging-on the Ulstermen against Athirne.

Then the Ulstermen followed Athirne to Berm Athirni, and walled him in with his sons and all his household, and killed Mor and Midseng his two daughters, and burnt his fortress upon him.

The doing of that deed seemed evil to the poets of Ulster, wherefore

Amargen said then:

Great grief, great pity, the destruction of Athirne the greatly famous
     [. . .]
Athirne's tomb here, let it not be dug by you, O poets [. . .]
Woe (to him) that wrought the man's destruction, woe to him that
     caused his slaughter!
He had a hard javelin – lasting its brightness – which Crideribel the
     satirist used to make.
He had a spear which would slay a king [. . .]
I will make his death-chant here, and I will make his lamentation,
and I will plant his grave here, and build his fair barrow.

ADVENTURES

29. The Adventure of Eachdach's Sons

(Echtra mac nEchach Muigmedóin)

Translated by Whitley Stokes

In this story Niall of the Nine Hostages encounters the Goddess of Sovereignty, who in this instance represents the land of Ireland itself. According to the annals, Niall was high-king of Ireland from 379 to 405 CE, and as the eponymous ancestor of the O'Neills, is reputed to have been one of the most powerful kings of ancient Ireland. The tale which follows is full of magic and the plot itself may well be familiar to the reader in the form given to it by the Wife of Bath in Chaucer's *Canterbury Tales*. The story in its present form is found in both the *Yellow Book of Lecan* and the *Book of Ballymote* and as such dates no further back than the eleventh century, but it very clearly reflects beliefs from a much older time, when kingship among the Celts was won from the hands of the goddess herself.

There was a wondrous and noble king over Erin, namely, Eochaid Mugmedon. Five sons he had: Brian, Ailill, Fiachra, Fergus and Niall. The mother of Brian, Fiachra, Fergus and Ailill was Mongfinn, daughter of Fidach. The mother of Niall was Cairenn the curly-black, daughter of Sachell Balb, king of the Saxons. Niall was hated by Queen Mongfinn, for Eochaid had begotten him on Cairenn instead of on her. Great then was the hardship which Cairenn suffered from the queen: so great was the hardship that she was compelled to draw the water of Tara, apart, and every handmaid in turn in sight of her; and even when she was with child with Niall, she was forced to do all that in order that the babe might die in her womb.

The time of her lying-in arrived, and yet she ceased not from the service. Then on the green of Tara, beside the pail, she brought forth a man-child, and she durst not take up the boy from the ground, but she left him there exposed to the birds. And not one of the men of Erin dared carry him away, for dread of Mongfinn; since great was her magical power, and all were in fear of her. Then Torna the poet came across the green, and beheld the babe left alone, with the birds attacking it. So Torna took the boy into his bosom, and to him was revealed all that would be thereafter. And he said:

> Welcome, little guest;
> he will be Niall of the Nine Hostages.
> In his time he will redden a multitude.
> Plains will be greatened, hostages will be overthrown,
> battles will be fought.
> Longside of Tara, host-leader of Mag Femin,
> custodian of Maen-mag.
> Revered one of Almain,
> veteran of Liffey, white-knee of Codal.
> Seven-and-twenty years he will rule Erin,
> and Erin will be inherited from him for ever.

Good indeed was Niall's beginning and his success, manly, rough-haired, till he died in the afternoon on a Saturday by the sea of Wight, slain by Eochaid son of Enna Cennselach.

Torna took the boy with him, and fostered him; and after that neither Torna nor his fosterling came to Tara until the boy was fit to be king. Then Torna and Niall came to Tara. 'Twas then that Cairenn, Niall's mother, as she was bringing water to Tara, chanced to meet them. Said Niall to her:

'Let this work alone.'

'I dare not,' she answered, 'because of the queen.'

'My mother,' said he, 'shall not be serving, and I the son of the king of Erin.'

Then he took her with him to Tara, and clad her in purple raiment.

Anger seized Mongfinn, for that seemed evil to her. But this was the will of the men of Erin, that Niall should be king after his father. Wherefore Mongfinn said to Eochaid: 'Pass judgment among thy sons, as to which of them shall receive thy heritage.'

'I will not pass judgment,' he answered; 'but Sithchenn the wizard will do so.'

Then they sent to Sithchenn the smith, who dwelt in Tara, for he was a wise man and a wondrous prophet.

The smith set fire to his forge in which the four sons were placed. Niall came out carrying the anvil and its block.

'Niall vanquishes,' said the wizard, 'and he will be a solid anvil forever.' Brian came next, bringing the sledgehammers. 'Brian to be your fighters,' said the wizard.

Then came Fiachra, bringing a pail of beer and the bellows.

'Your beauty and your science with Fiachra,' said the wizard.

Then came Ailill with the chest in which were the weapons.

'Ailill to avenge you,' said the wizard.

Last came Fergus with the bundle of withered wood and a bar of yew therein.

'Fergus the withered!' said the wizard.

That was true, for the seed of Fergus was no good, excepting one, Cairech Dergain of Cloonburren. And hence is the saying 'a stick of yew in a bundle of firewood.'

To bear witness of that the shanachie sang:

> Eochaid's five sons: Niall the great anvil,
> Brian the sledge-hammer for true striking,
> Ailill the chest of spears against a tribe,
> Fiachra the blast, Fergus the withered.

> Fiachra has the drink of ale,
> Ailill has the warlike spears,
> Brian has the entrance to battle,
> But Niall has the prize.

Now this was grievous to Mongfinn, and she said to her sons, 'Do you four sons quarrel, so that Niall may come to separate you, and then kill him.'

Then they quarrelled.

'I wish to separate them,' said Niall.

'Nay,' said Torna, 'let the sons of Mongfinn be peaceful.'

Hence is the proverb.

Then Mongfinn said that she would not abide by Sithchenn's judgment. So she sent her sons to the same Sithchenn to ask for arms. They went to the smith, and he made arms for them; the weapon that was finest he put into Niall's hand, and the rest of the arms he gave to the other sons. 'Now go to hunt and try your arms,' said the smith. So the sons went and hunted, and it happened that they went far astray.

When they ceased from straying they kindled a fire, broiled some of their quarry, and ate it until they were satisfied. Then they were thirsty and in great drouth from the cooked food. 'Let one of us go and seek for water,' they said. 'I will go,' said Fergus. The lad went seeking water, till he chanced on a well and saw an old woman guarding it.

Thus was the hag: every joint and limb of her, from the top of her head to the earth, was as black as coal. Like the tail of a wild horse was the grey bristly mane that came through the upper part of her headcrown. The green branch of an oak in bearing would be severed by the sickle of green teeth that lay in her head and reached to her ears. Dark smoky eyes she had: a nose crooked and hollow. She had a middle fibrous, spotted with pustules, diseased, and shins distorted and awry. Her ankles were thick, her shoulder blades were broad, her knees were big, and her nails were green. Loathsome in sooth was the hag's appearance.

'That is so,' said the youth.

'"Tis so indeed,' said she.

'Art thou guarding the well?' asked the youth.

'Yea truly,' she answered.

'Dost thou permit me to take away some of the water?' said the youth.

'I will permit,' she answered, 'provided there come from thee one kiss on my cheek.'

'By no means!' said he.

'Then no water shalt thou get from me,' said she.

'I give my word,' he answered, 'that I would rather perish of thirst than give thee a kiss.'

The lad then went back to the place where his brothers were biding, and told them that he had not found water. So Ailill went to look for water, and chanced on the same well. He too refused to kiss the hag, returned without water, and did not confess that he had found the well. Then Brian, the eldest of the sons, went to seek water, chanced on the same well, refused to kiss the old woman, and returned waterless. Fiachra then went, found the well and the hag, and asked her for water.

'I will grant it,' said she; 'but give me a kiss.'

'I would give few kisses for it.'

'Thou shalt visit Tara,' said she.

That fell true, for two of his race took the kingship of Erin, namely Dathi and Ailill Wether, and no one of the race of the other sons, Brian, Ailill, Fergus, took it. So Fiachra returned without water.

So then Niall went seeking water and happened on the same well.

'Give me water, O woman,' said Niall.

'I will give it,' she answered, 'but first give me a kiss.'

'Besides giving thee a kiss, I will lie with thee!' Then he threw himself down upon her and gave her a kiss. But then, when he looked at her, there was not in the world a damsel whose figure or appearance was more loveable than hers! Like the snow in trenches was every bit of her from head to sole. Plump and queenly forearms she had: fingers long and slender: calves straight and beautifully coloured. Two blunt shoes of white bronze between her little, soft-white feet and the ground. A costly full-purple mantle she wore, with a brooch of bright silver in the clothing of the mantle. Shining pearly teeth she had, an eye large and queenly, and lips red as rowanberries.

'That is many-shaped, O lady!' said the youth.

'True,' said she.

'Who art thou?' said the youth.

'I am the Sovereignty of Erin,' she answered; and then she said: 'O king of Tara, I am the Sovereignty: I will tell thee its great goodness (. . .) Go now to thy brothers,' she said, 'and take water with thee, and the kingship and the domination will for ever abide with thee and thy children, save only with twain of the seed of Fiachra, namely, Dathi and Ailill Wether, and one king out of Munster, namely Brian Boru ('of the Tribute') and all these will be kings without opposition. And as thou hast seen me loathsome, bestial, horrible at first and beautiful at last, so is the sovereignty; for seldom it is gained without battles and conflicts; but at last to anyone it is beautiful and goodly. Howbeit, give not the water to thy brothers until they have granted thee seniority over them, and that thou mayst raise thy weapon a hand's-breadth above their weapons.'

'So shall it be done,' said the youth.

Then he bade her farewell, and took water to his brothers; but did not give it to them until they had granted to him every boon that he asked of them, as the damsel had taught him. He also bound them by oaths never to oppose himself or his children.

Then they went to Tara. There they raised their weapons, and Niall raised his the breadth of a hero's hand above them. They sat down in their seats with Niall among them in the midst. Then the king asked tidings of them. Niall made answer and related the adventure, and how they went seeking water, and how they chanced on the well and came to the woman, and what she had prophesied to them.

'What is the cause,' said Mongfinn, 'that it is not the senior, Brian, that tells these tales?'

They answered, 'We granted our seniority and our kingship to Niall for the first time in exchange for the water.'

'You have granted it permanently,' said Sithchenn, 'for henceforward he and his children will always have the domination and kingship of Erin.'

Now that was true, for from Niall onward no one, except with opposition, took the kingship of Erin save one of his children or descendants, until the Strong-Striker of Usnech, Maelsechlann son of Domnall. For it was taken by six and twenty of the O'Neills of the North or of the South, that is, ten kings of the kindred of Conall and sixteen of the kindred of Eóghan; as said the poet:

> I know the number that took
> Erin after Niall of the lofty valour,
> From Loegaire's reign, if it be a fault,
> To the Strong-Striker of Usnech.
> Loegaire and his sons, I will not conceal,
> Diarmaid and mighty Tuathal,
> Nine of sound Aed Slane,
> And seven of the clans of Colman.
>
> Sixteen kings of lofty Eóghan,
> Ten of cruel-savage Conall:
> Niall got with speedy course
> The kingship always for his race.

30. The Adventures of Connla

(Echtra Connla)

Translated by Caitlín Matthews

*E*chtra *Connla* has been identified as one of the earliest surviving Irish stories, originally part of the lost story *Cin Dromma Snechta*, dating from about the seventh or eighth century CE. Connla and his younger brother Art, are the sons of Conn Cétchathach (Conn of the Hundred Battles), a shadowy king whom the annals situate historically in the second century CE. Connla's grandfather is Tuathal Techtmar, he who was responsible for the levying of the tribute known as the Boroma upon the Leinstermen.

The unnamed faery woman who visits Connla speaks of coming from the *síd*: a word that simultaneously means 'faery hill' and 'peace'. She invites Connla to come with to the Otherworld where his youthful beauty shall endure forever: incongruously, a twelfth century scribe has put the Christian term, 'till judgment day' into the faery woman's mouth and makes her prophesy the coming of Christian missionaries who will overcome druidism. Conn's druid, Córan, then enters into a magical singing battle against the *ban mberair,* 'the spells of women'. These spells were the subject of much clerical anguish, and even appear as one of the dangers against which divine protection must be invoked in St Patrick's Breastplate, where the petitioner invokes God's help against the spells of smiths, druids and women! (See my essay 'The Spells of Women' in *The Celtic Seer's Source Book* ed. J. Matthews.) The woman contrasts the lot of mortals and immortals, inviting him to enter the otherworldly race of Tethra, a Fomorian king who became identified as a God of the Otherworld: in Amairgin's praises of Ireland (see p. 11 of *Encyclopaedia of Celtic Wisdom*) the fish of the sea are called 'the cattle of Tethra.'

Our translation has drawn upon Hans P.K. Oskamp's intelligent reading of the seven extant textual editions, but is based largely upon MS 23 N 10 from the Royal Irish Academy.

One day, Connla the Ruddy, son of Conn of the Hundred Battles, stood with his father upon the hill of Uisnech when he saw a woman in a dress of unknown material.

Connla asked her, 'Woman, where have you come from?'

And the woman replied, 'My home is in the Lands of the Living where there is no death, no sin and no criminality. We enjoy ever-lasting banquets without having to prepare them. We have peace without dispute. We live in a great fairy hill and that is why we are called the people of peace.'

'Who are you speaking to?' Conn asked his son, because Connla was the only one able to see the woman.

It was the woman who answered him, 'He is speaking to a lovely young woman of noble lineage who looks forward to neither death nor aging. I love Connla the Ruddy, and I invite him to the Honey Plain of Boadach, that undying king, that sorrowless king whose land no sadness has touched since he took sovereignty.

'Connla the Ruddy, with your radiant, red, studded neckband, come with me! The yellow hair that falls across your celebrated face is the princeliest feature of your royal shape. If you follow me, your fair form will not lose its youth or beauty until the day of judgment.'

Then, since everyone heard what the invisible woman had said, Conn asked his druid, Córan, 'Tell me, Córan, you who are so clever, so full of lore. This overwhelming request is more than I can take, something beyond my experience. It's a dilemma I've never had to face in all the days of my reign. This invisible shape wages an unequal, supernatural challenge by trying to take my handsome son away from me through its unnatural customs. He is being stolen away from royal protection by the spells of women.'

Then the druid sang against the woman in such a way that no-one could hear her voice, nor could Connla see the woman any more.

Before the druid's loud singing caused the woman to go away, she threw an apple towards Connla. For the space of a month, Connla went without drink or food; no food pleased him as much as the apple. But however much of it he ate, it did not diminish the apple but rather it remained whole.

After that Connla was seized by a great longing for the woman he had seen. One day at the end of the month, Connla was beside his father on the plain of Arcommin. Connla saw the same woman coming towards him, saying, 'It is a royal seat which Connla looks to inherit, but one ruling over a race of mortals bound for death. The life-bearing immortals invite you. It is you who are the champion of the people of Tethra. They look upon you every day as you attend the gatherings of your closest friends in your own land.'

When Conn heard the woman's voice, he commanded his people, 'Call the druid to me! I see that her tongue has been set free today.'

Then the woman addressed him, 'Conn of the Hundred Battles, don't admire druidism too much because it's of little benefit. A man of integrity with his companions will cross the far strand to bring the truth. He will soon establish the right among you. He will overcome the authority of druids, all their devilish spells and their dark sorceries.'

And it seemed strange to Conn that Connla would only talk when the woman was near.

Conn asked him, 'Do you fully understand what this woman is asking, Connla?'

And Connla replied, 'This isn't easy for me, because I love my people. But I am gripped by a great longing for the woman.'

The woman said, 'You are swimming against a wave of longing to leave them and come in my glass ship so that we can come to the *síd* of Boadach. There is another country you could do worse than visit. There the sun sets. Though it is far from here, we will reach it before dark. There lies the country that refreshes the hearts of all who visit it. No other people live there but women and maidens.'

Then Connla gave a great leap into the glass ship, and everyone saw him going away from them until the distance robbed them of his progress. They rowed out into the deep sea and were never seen again.

Then Conn looked at Art, Conn's brother, saying, 'Art is lonely today.'

And this is why Art is called Art Oenfher or Art the Solitary (son).

FEASTS AND VISITATIONS

31. Bricriu's Feast

(Fled Bricriu)

Translated by George Henderson

'**B**ricriu's Feast' is one of the longest narratives of the Ulster cycle. It exists in several versions, the oldest of which is based on an original composed probably as early as the eighth century. Though at times repetitious and contradictory, the tale remains one of the best and most lively in early Irish literature. It consists of a series of episodes describing various tests of valour which the three bravest warriors of Ulster – Cú Chulainn, Conall, and Loegaire – undergo in order to determine who is most worthy to receive the choicest portion of a feast prepared by Bricriu of the Poison Tongue. This character also appears in the *Táin Bó Flidais* (pp. 83–86) where he is a poet with an ascerbic rather than trouble-making tongue. In 'Bricriu's Feast' and another romance 'Mac Datho's Pig', he adopts the role of inciter to battle among the heroes. Elsewhere Bricriu is described as the brother of the one-eyed giant Goll mac Carbada, which suggests that he was of supernatural origin.

The antiquity of the motif around which the narrative centres is vouched for by a Greek writer who relates that at ancient Celtic feasts the choicest titbit, or 'Champion's portion,' was assigned to the bravest warrior present, whose pre-eminence was sometimes established by a fight on the spot. Cú Roi is a semi-supernatural being who probably belonged originally, not to the Ulster cycle, but to the legendary history of the south of Ireland. Perhaps the most famous episode is the so-called 'Beheading Game' which actually appears twice, probably as a result of the scribe compiling two versions. Later it appears as a theme in several Arthurian romances, including the fourteenth century poem *Sir Gawain and the Green Knight*, which has been shown to have close parallels with Bricriu's Feast. The version printed here includes most of the text – which is very long – omitting certain repetitive portions, but restoring some not always included, such as the fascinating 'Women's War of Words', in which the wives of the heroes extol their own virtues as well as that of their menfolk, and the visit to Terror son of Great Fear. The descriptions of Cú Chulainn, of the chariots and their horses, of various monsters, and of course of the famous *bachlach*, are all set pieces of descriptive writing. The story comes from the eleventh century *Lebor na hUidre*, the *Book of the Dun Cow*.

Bricriu Poison-tongue held a great feast for Conchobar mac Nessa and for all the Ulstermen. The preparation of the feast took a whole year. For the entertainment of the guests a spacious house was built by him. He erected it at Dun Rudraige after the likeness of the Red Branch in Emain Macha. Yet it surpassed the buildings of that period entirely for material, for artistic design, and for beauty of architecture – its pillars and frontings splendid and costly, its carving and lintel-work famed for magnificence. The house was made in this fashion: on the plan of Tara's Mead-Hall, having nine compartments from fire to wall, each fronting of bronze thirty feet high, overlaid with gold. In the fore part of the palace a royal couch was erected for Conchobar high above those of the whole house. It was set with carbuncles and other precious stones which shone with a lustre of gold and silver, radiant with every hue, making night like day. Around it were placed the twelve couches of the twelve tribes of Ulster. The nature of the workmanship was on a par with the material of the edifice. It took a wagon team to carry each beam, and the strength of seven Ulstermen to fix each pole, while thirty of the chief artificers of Erin were employed on its erection and arrangement.

Then a balcony was made by Bricriu on a level with the couch of Conchobar and as high as those of the heroes of valour. The decorations of its fittings were magnificent. Windows of glass were placed on each side of it, and one of these was above Bricriu's couch, so that he could view the hall from his seat, as he knew the Ulstermen would not allow him within.

When Bricriu had finished building the hall and the balcony, supplying it with both quilts and blankets, beds and pillows, providing meat and drink, so that nothing was lacking, neither furnishings nor food, he straightway went to Emain Macha to meet Conchobar and the nobles of Ulster.

It fell upon a day when there was a gathering of the Ulstermen in Emain. He was at once made welcome, and was seated by the shoulder of Conchobar. Bricriu addressed himself to him as well as to the body of Ulstermen. 'Come with me,' said Bricriu, 'to partake of a banquet with me.'

'Gladly,' rejoined Conchobar, 'if that please the men of Ulster.'

Fergus mac Roig and the nobles of Ulster made answer, 'No; for if we go our dead will outnumber our living, when Bricriu has incensed us against each other.'

'If ye come not, worse shall ye fare,' said Bricriu.

'What then,' asked Conchobar, 'if the Ulstermen go not with thee?'

'I will stir up strife,' said Bricriu, 'between the kings, the leaders, the heroes of valour, and the yeomen, till they slay one another, man for man, if they come not to me to share my feast.'

'That shall we not do to please thee,' said Conchobar.

'I will stir up enmity between father and son so that it will come to mutual slaughter. If I do not succeed in doing so, I will make a quarrel between mother and daughter. If that does not succeed, I will set each of the Ulster women at variance, so that they come to deadly blows till their breasts become loathsome and putrid.'

'Sure it is better to come,' said Fergus.

'Do ye straightway take counsel with the chief Ulstermen,' said Sencha son of Ailill.

'Unless we take counsel against this Bricriu, mischief will be the consequence,' said Conchobar.

Thereupon all the Ulster nobles assembled in council. In discussing the matter Sencha counselled them thus: 'Take hostages from Bricriu, since ye have to go with him, and set eight swordsmen about him so as to compel him to retire from the house as soon as he has laid out the feast.'

Furbaide Ferbenn son of Conchobar brought Bricriu their reply and explained the whole matter.

'It is happily arranged,' said Bricriu.

The men of Ulster straightway set out from Emain Macha, host, battalion, and company, under king, chieftain, and leader. Excellent and admirable the march of the brave and valiant heroes to the palace.

The hostages of the nobles had gone security on his behalf, and Bricriu accordingly considered how he should manage to set the Ulstermen at variance. His deliberation and self-scrutiny being ended, he betook himself to the presence of Loegaire Buadach (the Triumphant), son of Connad mac Iliach. 'Hail now, Loegaire the Triumphant, thou mighty mallet of Breg, thou hot hammer of Meath, flame-red thunderbolt, thou victorious warrior of Ulster, what hinders the championship of Ulster being thine always?'

'If so I choose, it shall be mine,' said Loegaire.

'Be thine the sovereignty of the nobles of Erin,' said Bricriu, 'if only thou act as I advise.'

'I will indeed,' said Loegaire.

'Sooth, if the Champion's Portion of my house be thine, the championship of Emain is thine forever. The Champion's Portion of my house is worth contesting, for it is not the portion of a fool's house,' said Bricriu. 'Belonging to it is a cauldron full of generous wine, with room enough for three of the valiant heroes of Ulster; furthermore a seven-year-old boar; nought has entered its mouth since it was little save fresh milk and fine meal in springtime, curds and sweet milk in summer, the kernel of nuts and wheat in autumn, beef and broth in winter; a cow-lord full seven-year-old; since it was a little calf neither heather nor twig-tops have passed its lips, nought but sweet milk and herbs, meadow-hay and corn. Add to this five-score cakes of wheat cooked in honey. Five-and-twenty bushels, that is what was supplied for these five-score cakes – four cakes from each bushel. Such is the Champion's Portion of my house. And since thou art the best hero among the men of Ulster, it is but just to give it to thee, and so I wish it. By the end of the day, when the feast is spread out, let thy charioteer get up, and it is to him the Champion's Portion will be given.'

'Among them shall be dead men if it is not done so,' said Loegaire.

Bricriu laughed at that, for it pleased him well.

When he had done inciting Loegaire the Triumphant to enmity, Bricriu went to Conall Cernach (the Victorious). 'Hail to thee, Conall the Victorious! Thou art the hero of victories and of combats; great are the victories thou hast already scored over the heroes of Ulster. By the time the Ulstermen go into foreign bounds thou art three days and three nights in advance over many a ford; thou protectest their rear when returning so that an assailant may not spring past thee nor through thee nor over thee; what then should hinder the Champion's Portion of Emain being thine always?' Though great his treachery with regard to Loegaire, he showed twice as much with Conall the Victorious.

When he had satisfied himself with inciting Conall the Victorious to quarrel, he went to Cú Chulainn. 'Hail to thee, Cú Chulainn! Thou

victor of Breg, thou bright banner of the Liffey, darling of Emain,
beloved of wives and of maidens, for thee today Cú Chulainn is no
nickname, for thou art the champion of the Ulstermen. Thou wardest
off their great feuds and forays; thou seekest justice for each man of
them; thou attainest alone to what all the Ulstermen fail in; all the men
of Ulster acknowledge thy bravery, thy valour, and thy achievements
surpassing theirs. What meaneth therefore thy leaving of the Champion's
Portion for some one else of the men of Ulster, since no one of the men
of Erin is capable of contesting it against thee?'

'By the gods of my tribe,' said Cú Chulainn, 'his head shall he lose
who comes to contest it with me.'

Thereafter Bricriu severed himself from them and followed the host
as if no contention had been made among the heroes.

Whereupon they entered Bricriu's stronghold, and each one
occupied his couch therein, king, prince, noble, yeoman, and young
hero. The half of the hall was set apart for Conchobar and his retinue
of valiant Ulster heroes; the other half was reserved for the ladies of
Ulster attending on Mugan daughter of Eochaid Fedlech, wife of
Conchobar. Those who attended on Conchobar were the chief Ulster
warriors with the body of youths and entertainers.

While the feast was being prepared for them, the musicians and
players performed. The moment Bricriu spread the feast with its
savouries he was ordered by the hostages to leave the hall. They
straightway got up with their drawn swords in their hands to expel him.
Whereupon Bricriu and his wife went out to the balcony. As he arrived
at the threshold of the stronghold he called out, 'That Champion's
Portion, such as it is, is not the portion of a fool's house; do ye give it to
the Ulster hero ye prefer for valour!' And then he left them.

Then the waiters got up to serve the food. The charioteer of Loegaire
the Triumphant, that is, Sedlang mac Riangabra, rose up and said to
the distributors: 'Give to Loegaire the Triumphant the Champion's
Portion which is by you, for he alone is entitled to it before the other
young heroes of Ulster.'

Then Id mac Riangabra, charioteer to Conall the Victorious, got up
and spoke to like effect. And Loeg mac Riangabra spoke as follows:
'Bring it to Cú Chulainn; it is no disgrace for all the Ulstermen to give
it to him; it is he that is most valiant among you.'

'That's not true,' said Conall the Victorious and Loegaire the
Triumphant.

They got up upon the floor and donned their shields and seized their swords. They hewed at one another until half the hall was an atmosphere of fire with the clash of sword and spear-edge, the other half one white sheet from the enamel of the shields. Great alarm got hold upon the stronghold; the valiant heroes shook; Conchobar himself and Fergus mac Roig were furious on seeing the injury and injustice of two men attacking one, namely Conall the Victorious and Loegaire the Triumphant attacking Cú Chulainn. There was no one among the Ulstermen who dared separate them until Sencha spoke to Conchobar.

'Part the men,' said he.

Thereupon Conchobar and Fergus intervened; the combatants immediately let drop their hands to their sides.

'Execute my wish,' said Sencha.

'Your will shall be obeyed,' they responded.

'My wish, then,' said Sencha, 'is to-night to divide the Champion's Portion there among all the host, and after that to decide with reference to it according to the will of Ailill mac Matach, for it is accounted unlucky among the Ulstermen to close this assembly unless the matter be adjudged in Cruachan.'

The feasting was then resumed; they made a circle about the fire and got drunken and merry.

Bricriu, however, and his queen were in their balcony. From his couch the condition of the palace was visible to him, and how things were going on. He exercised his mind as to how he should contrive to get the women to quarrel as he had the men. When Bricriu had done searching his mind, it just chanced as he could have wished that Fedelm Fresh-Heart came from the stronghold with fifty women in her train, in jovial mood. Bricriu observed her coming past him.

'Hail to thee to-night, wife of Loegaire the Triumphant! Fedelm Fresh-Heart is no nickname for thee with respect to thy excellence of form and wisdom and of lineage. Conchobar, king of a province of Erin, is thy father, Loegaire the Triumphant thy husband; I should deem it but small honour to thee that any of the Ulster women should take precedence of thee in entering the banqueting-hall; only at thy heel should all the Ulster women tread. If thou comest first into the hall to-night, the sovereignty of the queenship shalt thou enjoy over all the ladies of Ulster forever.'

Fedelm at that takes a leap over three ridges from the hall.

Thereafter came Lendabair, daughter of Eóghan mac Durthacht,

wife of Conall the Victorious. Bricriu addressed her, saying, 'Hail to
thee, Lendabair! For thee that is no nickname; thou art the darling and
pet of all mankind on account of thy splendour and of thy lustre. As far
as thy husband hath surpassed all the heroes of mankind in valour and
in comeliness, so far hast thou distinguished thyself above the women
of Ulster.'

Though great the deceit he applied in the case of Fedelm, he
applied twice as much in the case of Lendabair.

Then Emer came out with half a hundred women in her train.
'Greeting and hail to thee, Emer, daughter of Forgall Monach, wife of
the best man in Erin! Emer of the Fair Hair is no nickname for thee;
Erin's kings and princes contend for thee in jealous rivalry. As the sun
surpasseth the stars of heaven, so far dost thou outshine the women of
the whole world in form and shape and lineage, in youth and beauty
and elegance, in good name and wisdom and address.'

Though great his deceit in the case of the other ladies, in that of
Emer he used thrice as much.

The three companies [of women] thereupon went out until they met
at a spot three ridges from the hall. None of them knew that Bricriu had
incited them one against the other. To the hall they straightway return.
Even and easy and graceful their carriage on the first ridge; scarcely did
one of them raise one foot before the other. But on the ridge following,
their steps were shorter and quicker. On the ridge next to the house it
was with difficulty each kept up with the other; so they raised their robes
to the rounds of their hips to complete the attempt to go first into the
hall. For what Bricriu had said to each of them with regard to the other
was that whosoever entered first should be queen of the whole
province. The amount of confusion then occasioned by the
competition was as it were the noise of fifty chariots approaching. The
whole stronghold shook and the warriors sprang to their arms and tried
to kill one another within.

'Stay,' cried Sencha; 'they are not enemies who have come; it is
Bricriu who has set to quarrelling the women who have gone out. By
the gods of my tribe, unless the door be closed against them, our dead
will outnumber our living.'

Thereupon the door-keepers closed the doors. Emer, the daughter of
Forgall Monach, wife of Cú Chulainn, by reason of her speed, outran
the others and put her back against the door, and straightway called
upon the door-keepers before the other ladies came, so that the men

within got up, each of them to open the door for his own wife that she might be the first to come in.

'Bad outlook to-night,' said Conchobar. He struck the silver sceptre that was in his hand against the bronze pillar of the couch, and the company sat down.

'Stay,' said Sencha; 'it is not a warfare of arms that shall be held here; it will be a warfare of words.' Each woman went out under the protection of her husband, and then followed 'The Ulster Women's War of Words.'

Fedelm of the Fresh-Heart, wife of Loigaire the Triumphant, made speech:

> Born of a mother in freedom,
> one in rank and in race mine elders;
> Sprung from loins that are royal,
> in the beauty of peerless breeding;
> Lovely in form I am reckoned,
> and noted for figure and comely.
>
> Fostered in warrior virtues,
> In the sphere of goodly demeanour:
> Loigaire's hand – all-noble,
> What triumphs it scoreth for Ulster!
> Ulster's marches from foemen,
> Ever equal in strength, ever hostile –
> All by himself were they holden:
> From wounds a defence and protection,
> Loigaire, more famous than heroes,
> In number of victories greater,
> Why should not Fedelm the lovely
> Step first in the mead-hall so festive,
> Shapelier than all other women,
> Triumphant and jealous of conquest?

Thereupon spake Lendabair, daughter of Eóghan mac Derthacht, wife of Conall Cernach, son of Amorgen:

> Mine is a mien too of beauty,
> Of reason, with grace of deportment,
> Finely and fairly stepping
> In front of the women of Ulster,

See me step to the mead-hall,
My spouse and my darling the Conall.
Big is his shield and triumphant,
Majestic his gait and commanding,
Up to the spears of the conflict,
In front of them all as he strideth:
Back to me comes he proudly,
With heads in his hands as his trophies;
Swords he getteth together
For the clashing in conflict of Ulster;
Guardian of every ford-way,
He destroyeth them too at his pleasure;
Fords he defendeth from foemen,
The wrongful attack he avengeth,
Holdeth himself as a hero
Upon whom shall be raised a tombstone:
Son of Amorgen noble,
His is the courage that speaketh;
Many the arts of the Conall
And therefore he leadeth the heroes.
Lendabair, great is her glory,
In every one's eye is her splendour;
Why not the first when she enters
The hall of a king so queenly?

Emer, daughter of Forgall the tricky, wife of Cú Chulainn, made
speech:

I am the standard of women,
in figure, in grace and in wisdom;
None mine equal in beauty,
for I am a picture of graces.
Mien full noble and goodly,
mine eye like a jewel that flasheth;
Figure, or grace, or beauty,
or wisdom, or bounty, or chasteness,
joy of sense, or of loving,
unto mine has never been likened.
Sighing for me is Ultonia –
a nut of the heart I am clearly.

(Now were I welcoming wanton,
no husband were yours tomorrow.)
My spouse is the hound of Culann,
and not a hound that is feeble;
Blood from his spear is spurting,
with life-blood his sword is dripping;
Finely his body is fashioned,
but his skin is gaping with gashes,
Wounds on his thigh there are many,
but nobly his eye looks westward;
Bright is the dome he supporteth
and ever red are his eyen,
Red are the frames of his chariot,
and red are also the cushions;
Fighting from ears of horses
and over the breaths of men-folk,
Springing in air like a salmon
when he springeth the spring of the heroes,
Rarest of feats he performeth,
the leap that is birdlike he leapeth,
Bounding o'er pools of water,
he performeth the feat *cless nonbair*; [the feat of nine]
Battles of bloody battalions,
the world's proud armies he heweth,
Beating down kings in their fury,
mowing the hosts of the foemen.
Others to *cron* [a kind of base metal] I liken,
shamming the travail of women,
Ulster's precious heroes
compared with my spouse Cú Chulainn.
He unto blood may be likened,
to blood that is clear and noble,
They to the scum and the garbage,
as *cron* their value I reckon;
Shackled and shaped like cattle,
as kine and oxen and horses,
Ulster's precious women
beside the wife of Cú Chulainn.

Thus did the men in the hall behave on hearing the laudatory addresses of the women – Loegaire and Conall each sprang into his hero's light, and broke a stave of the palace at a like level with themselves, so that in this way their wives came in. Cú Chulainn upheaved the palace just over against his bed, till the stars of heaven were to be seen from underneath the wattle. By that opening came his own wife with half a hundred of her attendants in her train, as also a hundred in waiting upon the other twain. Other ladies could not be compared with Emer, while no one at all was to be likened to Emer's husband. Thereupon Cú Chulainn let the palace down until seven feet of the wattle entered the ground; the whole stronghold shook, and Bricriu's balcony was laid flat to the earth in such a way that Bricriu and his queen toppled down until they fell into the ditch in the middle of the courtyard among the dogs.

'Woe is me,' cried Bricriu, as he hastily got up, 'enemies have come into the palace.' He took a turn round and saw how it was lop-sided and inclined entirely to one side. He wrung his hands, then betook himself within, so bespattered that none of the Ulstermen could recognise him.

Then from the floor of the house Bricriu made speech: 'Alas! that I have prepared you a feast, O Ulstermen. My house is more to me than all my other possessions. Upon you, therefore, it is taboo to drink, to eat, or to sleep until you leave my house as you found it upon your arrival.'

Thereupon the valiant Ulstermen went out of the house and tried to tug it, but they did not raise it so much that even the wind could pass between it and the earth. That matter was a difficulty for the Ulstermen. 'I have no suggestion for you,' said Sencha, 'except that you entreat of him who, left it lop-sided to set it upright.'

Whereupon the men of Ulster told Cú Chulainn to restore the house to its upright position, and Bricriu made a speech: 'O King of the heroes of Erin, if thou set it not straight and erect, none in the world can do so.' All the Ulstermen then entreated Cú Chulainn to solve the difficulty. That the banqueters might not be lacking for food or for ale, Cú Chulainn got up and tried to lift the house at a tug and failed. A distortion thereupon got hold of him, whilst a drop of blood was at the root of each single hair, and he drew his hair into his head, so that, looked on from above, his dark-yellow curls seemed as if they had been shorn with scissors, and taking upon himself the motion of a millstone he strained himself until a warrior's foot could find room between each pair of ribs.

His natural resources and fiery vigour returned to him, and he then heaved the house aloft and set it so that it reached its former level. Thereafter the consumption of the feast was pleasant to them, with the kings and the chieftains on the one side round about Conchobar the illustrious, the noble high-king of Ulster.

Again it was their hap to quarrel about the Champion's Portion. Conchobar with the nobles of Ulster interposed with the view of judging between the heroes. 'Go to Cú Roi mac Dairi, the man who will undertake to intervene,' said Conchobar.

'I accept that,' said Cú Chulainn.

'I agree,' said Loegaire.

'Let us go, then,' said Conall the Victorious.

'Let horses be brought and thy chariot yoked, O Conall,' said Cú Chulainn.

'Woe is me!' cried Conall.

'Every one,' said Cú Chulainn, 'knows the clumsiness of thy horses and the unsteadiness of thy going and thy turnout; thy chariot's movement is most heavy; each of the two wheels raises turf every way thy big chariot careers, so that for the space of a year there is a well marked track easily recognised by the warriors of Ulster.'

'Dost thou hear that, Loegaire?' said Conall.

'Woe is me!' said Loegaire. 'But I am not to blame or reproach. I am nimble at crossing fords, and more, to breast the storm of spears, outstripping the warriors of Ulster. Put not on me the pretence of kings and champions against single chariots in strait and difficult places, in woods and on confines, until the champion of a single chariot tries not to career before me.'

Thereupon Loegaire had his chariot yoked and he leaped into it. He drove over the Plain-of-the-Two-Forks, of the Gap-of-the-Watch, over the Ford of Carpat Fergus, over the Ford of the Morrigu, to the Rowan Meadow of the Two Oxen in the Fews of Armagh, by the Meeting of the Four Ways past Dundalk, across Mag Slicech, westwards to the slope of Breg.

A dim, dark, heavy mist overtook him, confusing him in such a way that it was impossible for him to fare farther. 'Let us stay here,' said Loegaire to his charioteer, 'until the mist clears up.' Loegaire alighted from his chariot, and his gillie put the horses into the meadow that was near at hand.

While there, the gillie saw a huge giant approaching him. Not beautiful his appearance: broad of shoulder and fat of mouth, with sack eyes and a bristly face; ugly, wrinkled, with bushy eyebrows; hideous and horrible and strong; stubborn and violent and haughty; fat and puffing; with big sinews and strong forearms; bold, audacious, and uncouth. A shorn black patch of hair on him, a dun covering about him, a tunic over it to the ball of his rump; on his feet old tattered brogues, on his back a ponderous club like the wheel-shaft of a mill.

'Whose horses are these, gillie?' he asked, as he gazed furiously at him.

'The horses of Loegaire the Triumphant.'

'Yes! a fine fellow is he!' And as he thus spoke he brought down his club on the gillie and gave him a blow from top to toe.

The gillie gave a cry, whereupon Loegaire came up.

'What is this you are doing to the lad?' asked Loegaire.

'It is by way of penalty for damage to the meadow,' said the giant.

'I will come myself, then,' said Loegaire; and they struggled together until Loegaire fled to Emain leaving his horses and gillie and arms.

Not long thereafter Conall the Victorious took the same way and arrived at the plain where the druidical mist overtook Loegaire. The like hideous black, dark cloud overtook Conall the Victorious, so that he was unable to see either heaven or earth. Conall thereupon leapt out and the gillie unharnessed the horses in the same meadow. Not long thereafter he saw the same giant coming towards him. He asked him whose servant he was.

'I am the servant of Conall the Victorious,' he said.

'A good man he!' said the giant, and he raised his hands and gave the gillie a blow from top to toe. The fellow yelled. Then came Conall. He and the giant came to close quarters. Stronger were the wrestling turns of the giant, and Conall fled, as Loegaire had done, having left behind his charioteer and his horses, and came to Emain.

Cú Chulainn then went by the same way till he came to the same place. The like dark mist overtook him as fell upon the two preceding. Cú Chulainn sprang down, and Loeg brought the horses into the meadow. He had not long to wait until he saw the same man coming towards him. The giant asked him whose servant he was.

'Servant to Cú Chulainn.'

'A good man he!' said the giant, plying him with the club.

Loeg yelled. Then Cú Chulainn arrived. He and the giant came to close quarters and either rained blows upon the other. The giant was worsted. He forfeited horses and charioteer, and Cú Chulainn brought along with him his fellows' horses, charioteers, and accoutrements, till he reached Emain in triumph.

'Thine is the Champion's Portion,' said Bricriu to Cú Chulainn, and to the others, 'well I know from your deeds that you are in no way on a par with Cú Chulainn.'

'Not true, Bricriu,' said they, 'for we know it is one of his friends from the fairy world that came to him to play us mischief and coerce us with regard to the championship. We shall not forego our claim on that account.'

The men of Ulster, with Conchobar and Fergus, failed to effect a settlement. And the conclusion the nobles in Conchobar's following arrived at was, to accompany the heroes and have the difficulty adjudged at the abode of Ailill mac Matach and of Medb of Cruachan Ai with reference to the Champion's Portion and the mutual rivalry of the women. Fine and lovely and majestic the march of the Ulstermen to Cruachan. Cú Chulainn, however, remained behind the host entertaining the Ulster ladies, performing nine feats with apples and nine with knives, in such wise that one did not interfere with the other.

Loeg mac Riangabra then went to speak to him in the feat-stead and said: 'You sorry simpleton, your valour and bravery have passed away, the Champion's Portion has gone from you; the Ulstermen have reached Cruachan long since.'

'Indeed we had not at all perceived it, my Loeg. Yoke us the chariot, then,' said Cú Chulainn. Loeg accordingly yoked it and off they started. By that time the Ulstermen had reached Mag Breg, Cú Chulainn, having been incited by his charioteer, travelled with such speed from Dun Rudraige, the Grey of Macha and the Black Sainglenn racing with his chariot across the whole province of Conchobar, across Sliab Fuait and across Mag Breg, that the third chariot arrived first in Cruachan.

In virtue then of the swiftness and impetuous speed with which all the valiant Ulstermen reached Cruachan under the lead of Conchobar and the body of chiefs, a great shaking seized Cruachan, till the war-arms fell from the walls to the ground, seizing likewise the entire host of the stronghold, till the men in the royal keep were like rushes in a stream. Medb thereupon spoke: 'Since the day I took up home in Cruachan I have never heard thunder, there being no clouds.' Thereupon Finnabair, daughter of Ailill and Medb, went to the balcony over the high porch of the stronghold. 'Mother dear,' said she, 'I see a chariot coming along the plain.'

'Describe it,' said Medb, 'its form, appearance, and style; the colour of the horses; how the hero looks, and how the chariot courses.'

'Truely I see,' quoth Findabair, 'the two horses that are in the chariot. Two fiery dappled greys, alike in colour, shape and excellence, alike in speed and swiftness, prancing side by side. Ears pricked, head erect, of high mettle and strangely bounding pace. Nostril fine, mane flowing, forehead broad, full dappled; full slim of girth and broad of chest, manes and tails curled, they career along. A chariot of fine wood with wicker-work, having two black revolving wheels. Its *fertsi* hard and straight as a sword, its body of wicker-work new and freshly polished, its curved yoke silver-mounted. Two rich yellow looped reins. In the chariot a fair man with long curling hair; his tresses tri-coloured: brown at the skin, blood-red at the middle, as a diadem of yellow gold the hair at the tips. Three haloes encircle his upturned head, each merging into the other. About him a soft crimson tunic, having five stripes of glittering gold. A shield spotted and indented, with a bright edge of bronze. A barbed five-pronged javelin flames at his wrist. An awning of the rare plumage of birds over his chariot's frame.'

'We recognise that man,' quoth Medb, 'from his description.'

> Compeer of kings, an old disposer of conquest,
> A fury of war, a fire of judgment,
> A flame of vengeance; in mien a hero,
> In face a champion, in heart a dragon
> The long knife of proud victories which will hew us to pieces;
> The all-noble, red-handed Loigaire;
> His the vigour that cuts the leek with the swordedge –
> The back-stroke of the wave to the land.

'By the god of my people,' quoth Medb, 'I swear if it be with fury of hostile feeling Loigaire the Triumphant comes to us, that like as leeks are cut to the ground by a sharp knife, such will be the nicety of the slaughter he will inflict on us, whatever our number at Cruachan Ai, unless his glowing fury, wrath and high dudgeon are guarded against and assuaged in accordance with his very wish.'

'Mother dear,' quoth the daughter, 'I see anon another chariot coming along the plain, not a whit inferior to the first.'

'Describe it,' said Medb.

'Sooth I see,' she quoth, 'in the chariot, on the one hand, a roan spirited steed, swift, fiery and bounding, with broad hoof and expanded chest, taking strong vigorous strides across fords and estuaries, over obstacles and winding roads, scouring plains and vales, raging with triumph. Judge it from the likenesses of soaring birds, among which my very quick eye gets lost from their most smooth careering in emulous course. On the other a bay horse, with broad forehead, heavy locks and wavy tresses; of light and long dashing pace; of great strength; full swiftly he courses the bounds of the plain, between stone enclosures and fastnesses. He finds no obstacle in the land of oaks, careering on the way. A chariot of fine wood with wicker-work, on two bright wheels of bronze; its pole bright with silver mounting; its frame very high and creaking, having a curved, firmly mounted yoke with two rich yellow looped reins. In the chariot a fair man with wavy hanging hair. His countenance white and red, his jerkin clean and white, his mantle of blue and crimson red. His shield brown with yellow bosses, its edge veined with bronze. In his hand flames a fiery, furious spear. And an awning of the rare plumage of birds over the wicker frame of his chariot.'

'We recognise the man from his description,' quoth Medb.

> A lion that groaneth, a flame of Lug,
> that diamonds can pierce;
> A wolf among cattle; battle on battle,
> Exploit on exploit, head upon head he heaps;
> As a trout on red sandstone is cut
> Would the son of Findchoimi cut us;
> should he rage against us, no peace!

'By my people's god, as a speckled fish is cut upon a shining red stone with flails of iron, such I swear will be the minuteness of the slaughter Conall the Victorious will execute on us should he rage against us.'

'I see another chariot coming along the plain.'

'Give us its description,' quoth Medb.

'I see, in sooth,' the daughter quoth, 'two steeds, alike for size and beauty, fierceness and speed, bounding together, with ears pricked, head erect, spirited and powerful (. . .) with fine nostril, long tresses and broad foreheads – full dappled, with girth full slim and chest expanded, mane and tail curled, dashing along. Yoked in the chariot, the one, a grey steed, with broad thighs, eager, swift and fleet – wildly impetuous, with long mane and broad haunches, thundering and trampling – mane curled, head on high, breast broadly expanded. From out the hard course he fiercely casts up clods of earth from his four hard hoofs – a flock of swift birds in pursuit. As he gallops on the way a flash of hot breath darts from him; from his curbed jaws gleams a blast of flame-red fire.

'The other horse, dark-grey, head firmly knit, compact, fleet, broad-hoofed and slender. Firm swift, and of high mettle, with curl and plait and tress – broad of back and sure of foot, lusty, spirited and fiery, he fiercely bounds and fiercely strides the ground. Mane and tail long and flying, heavy locks adown his forehead broad. Grandly he careers the country after winning the horse-race. Soon he bounds the straths, casts off languor, traverses the plains of the Mid Glen, finding no obstacle in the land of oak, coursing the way. A chariot of fine wood with wicker-work, having two yellowish iron wheels and a bright silver pole with bright bronze mounting. A frame very high and creaking, with metal fastenings. A curved yoke richly gilt – two rich yellow looped reins. The *fertsi* hard and straight as sword-blades.

'In the chariot a dark, melancholy man, comeliest of the men of Erin. Around him a soft crimson pleasing tunic fastened across the breast, where it stands open, with a salmon-brooch of inlaid gold, against which his bosom heaves, beating in full strokes. A long-sleeved linen kirtle with a white hood, embroidered red with flaming gold. Set in each of his eyes eight red dragon gem-stones. His two cheeks blue-white and bloodred. He emits sparks of fire and burning breath, with a ray of love in his look. A shower of pearls, it seems, has fallen into his mouth. Each of his two eyebrows as black as the side of a black spit. On his two thighs rests a golden-hilted sword and fastened to the copper frame of the chariot is a blood-red spear with a sharp mettlesome blade on a shaft of wood well fitted to his hand. Over both his shoulders a crimson shield with a rim of silver, chased with figures of animals in gold. He leaps the hero's salmon-leap into the air and does many like swift feats besides. Such is the chief of a chariot-royal. Before him in that chariot is a charioteer, a very slender, tall, much-freckled man. On his head very curled bright-red hair, with a fillet of bronze upon his brow which prevents the hair from falling over his face. On both sides of his head patins of gold confine the hair. A shoulder-mantle about him with sleeves opening at the two elbows, and in his hand a goad of red gold with which he guides the horses.'

'Truly, it is a drop before a shower; we recognise the man from his description,' said Medb.

> An ocean fury, a whale that rages,
> A fragment of flame and fire;
> A bear majestic, a grandly moving billow,
> A beast in maddening anger.
> In the crash of glorious battle
> Through the hostile foe he leaps,
> His shout the fury of doom;
> A terrible bear, he is death to the herd of cattle:
> Feat upon feat, head upon head he piles:
> Praise ye the hearty one, he who is completely victor.
> As fresh malt is ground in the mill
> Shall we be ground by Cú Chulainn.

'By the god of my people,' said Medb, 'I swear if it be in fury Cú Chulainn comes to us, like as a mill of ten spokes grinds very hard malt, so he alone will grind us into mould and gravel, should the whole province attend on us in Cruachan, unless his fury and violence are subdued.'

'How do they come this time?' said Medb.

> Wrist to wrist and palm to palm,
> Tunic to tunic they advance,
> Shield to shield and frame to frame.
> A shoulder-to-shoulder band,
> Wood to wood and car to car,
> This they all are, fond mother.
> As thunder when crashing on the roof,
> With speed the chargers dash,
> As heavy seas which storms are shaking,
> The earth in turn they pound;
> Anon it vibrates as they strike,
> Their strength and weight are like and like.
> Their name is noble,
> No ill fame!

Then Medb made speech:

> 'Women to meet them, and many, half naked,
> Full-breasted and bare and beautiful, numerous;
> Bring vats of cold water where wanting, beds ready for rest,
> Fine food bring forth, and not scanty, but excellent,
> Strong ale and sound and well malted, warriors' keep;

At the gates of the stronghold be set open, open the enclosure.
The batallion that is rushing on won't kill us, I hope.'

Thereupon Medb went out by the high door of the palace into the court, thrice fifty maidens in her train, with three vats of cold water for the three valiant heroes in front of the hosts, in order to alleviate their heat. Choice was straightway given them so as to ascertain whether a house apiece should be allotted them or one house among the three.

'To each a house apart,' said Cú Chulainn.

Thereafter such as they preferred of the thrice fifty girls were brought into the house, fitted up with beds of surprising magnificence. Finnabair in preference to any other was brought by Cú Chulainn into the apartment where he himself was. On the arrival of the Ulstermen, Ailill and Medb with their whole household went and bade them welcome.

'We are pleased,' said Sencha son of Ailill, responding.

Thereupon the Ulstermen came into the stronghold, and the palace is left to them as recounted: seven circles and seven compartments from fire to partition, with bronze frontings and carvings of red yew. Three stripes of bronze in the arching of the house, which was of oak, with a covering of shingles. It had twelve windows with glass in the openings. The couch of Ailill and Medb in the centre of the house, with silver frontings and stripes of bronze round it, with a silver wand by the partition facing Ailill, that would reach the mid hips of the house so as to cheek the inmates unceasingly.

The Ulster heroes went round from one door of the palace to the other, and the musicians played while the guests were being prepared for. Such was the spaciousness of the house that it had room for the hosts of valiant heroes of the whole province in the retinue of Conchobar. Moreover, Conchobar and Fergus mac Roig were in Ailill's apartment with nine valiant Uister heroes besides. Great feasts were then prepared for them and they were there until the end of three days and three nights.

Thereafter Ailill inquired of Conchobar with his Ulster retinue what was the purpose of his visit. Sencha related the matter on account of which they had come: the three heroes' rivalry as to the Champion's Portion, and the ladies' rivalry as to precedence at feasts. 'They could not stand being judged anywhere else than here by thee.'

At that Ailill was silent and was not in a happy mood. 'Indeed,' said he, 'it is not to me this decision should be given as to the Champion's Portion, unless it be done from hatred.'

'There is really no better judge,' said Sencha.

'Well,' said Ailill, 'I require time to consider. For that then three days and three nights suffice for me,' said Ailill.

'That would not forfeit friendship,' answered Sencha.

The Ulstermen straightway bade farewell; being satisfied, they left their blessing with Ailill and Medb and their curse with Bricriu, for it was he who had incited them to strife. They then departed from the territory of Medb, having left Loegaire and Conall and Cú Chulainn to be judged by Ailill. The like supper as before was given to each of the heroes every night.

One night as their portion was assigned to them, three cats from the cave of Cruachan were let loose to attack them, that is, three beasts of magic. Conall and Loegaire made for the rafters, leaving their food with the beasts. In that wise they slept until the morrow. Cú Chulainn fled not from the beast which was attacking him. When it stretched its neck out for eating, Cú Chulainn gave a blow with his sword on the beast's head, but the blade glided off as it were from stone. Then the cat set itself down. Under the circumstances Cú Chulainn neither ate nor slept, but he kept his place. As soon as it was early morning the cats were gone. In such condition were the three heroes seen on the morrow.

'Does not that trial suffice for adjudging you?' asked Ailill.

'By no means,' said Conall and Loegaire, 'it is not against beasts we are striving but against men.'

Ailill, having gone to his chamber, set his back against the wall. He was disquieted in mind, for he took the difficulty that faced him to be fraught with danger. He neither ate nor slept till the end of three days and three nights. 'Coward!' Medb then called him; 'if you do not decide, I will.'

'Difficult for me to judge them,' Ailill said; 'it is a misfortune for one to have to do it.'

'There is no difficulty,' said Medb, 'for Loegaire and Conall Cernach are as different as bronze and white bronze; and Conall Cernach and Cú Chulainn are as different as white bronze and red gold.'

It was then, after she had pondered her advice, that Loegaire the Triumphant was summoned to Medb. 'Welcome, O Loegaire the Triumphant,' said she; 'it is meet to give thee the Champion's Portion. We assign to thee the sovereignty of the heroes of Erin from this time forth, and the Champion's Portion, and a cup of bronze with a bird chased in silver on its bottom. In preference to every one else, take it with thee as a token of award. No one else is to see it until, at the day's end, thou hast come to the Red Branch of Conchobar. On the Champion's Portion being exhibited among you, then shalt thou bring forth thy cup in the presence of all the Ulster nobles. Moreover, the Champion's Portion is therein. None of the valiant Ulster heroes will dispute it further with thee. For the thing thou art to take away with thee shall be a token of genuineness in the estimation of all the Ulstermen.'

Thereupon the cup with its full of luscious wine was given to Loegaire the Triumphant. On the floor of the palace he swallowed the contents at a draught. 'Now you have the feast of a champion,' said Medb; 'I wish you may enjoy it a hundred years at the head of all Ulster.'

Loegaire thereupon bade farewell. Then Conall Cernach was likewise summoned to the royal presence. 'Welcome,' said Medb, 'O Conall Cernach; proper it is to give thee the Champion's Portion, with a cup of white bronze besides, having a bird on the bottom of it chased in gold.' Thereafter the cup was given to Conall with its full of luscious wine.

Conall bade farewell. A herald was then sent to fetch Cú Chulainn. 'Come to speak with the king and queen,' said the messenger. Cú Chulainn at the time was busy playing chess with Loeg mac Riangabra, his own charioteer. 'No mocking!' he said; 'you might try your lies on some other fool.' He hurled one of the chessmen, and it pierced the center of the herald's brain. He got his death blow therefrom, and fell between Ailill and Medb.

'Woe is me,' said Medb; 'sorely doth Cú Chulainn work on us his fury when his fit of rage is upon him.' Whereupon Medb got up and came to Cú Chulainn and put her two arms round his neck.

'Try a lie upon another,' said Cú Chulainn.

'Glorious son of the Ulstermen and flame of the heroes of Erin, it is no lie that is to our liking where thou art concerned. Were all Erin's heroes to come, to thee by preference would we grant the quest, for, in regard to fame, bravery, and valour, distinction, youth, and glory, the men of Erin acknowledge thy superiority.'

Cú Chulainn got up. He accompanied Medb into the palace, and Ailill bade him a warm welcome. A cup of gold was given him full of luscious wine, and having on the bottom of it birds chased in precious stone. With it, in preference to every one else there was given him a lump, as big as his two eyes, of dragonstone. 'Now you have the feast of a champion,' said Medb. 'I wish you may enjoy it a hundred years at the head of all the Ulster heroes.'

'Moreover, it is our verdict,' said Ailill and Medb, 'inasmuch as thou art not to be compared with the Ulster warriors, neither is thy wife to be compared with their women. Nor is it too much, we think, that she should always precede all the Ulster ladies when entering the Mead Hall.'

At that Cú Chulainn drank at one draught the full of the cup, and then bade farewell to the king, queen, and whole household.

Thereafter he followed his charioteer.

'My plan,' said Medb to Ailill, 'is to keep those three heroes with us again to-night, and to test them further.'

'Do as thou deemest right,' said Ailill.

The men were then detained and brought to Cruachan and their horses unyoked. Their choice of food was given them for their horses. Conall and Loegaire told them to give oats two years old to theirs. But Cú Chulainn chose barley grains for his. They slept there that night. The women were apportioned among them. Finnabair, with a train of fifty damsels, was brought to the place of Cú Chulainn. Sadb the Eloquent, another daughter of Ailill and Medb, with fifty maids in attendance was ushered into the presence of Conall Cernach. Concend, daughter of Cet mac Matach, with fifty damsels along with her, was brought into the presence of Loegaire the Triumphant. Moreover, Medb herself was accustomed to visit the couch of Cú Chulainn. They slept there that night.

On the morrow they arose early in the morning and went to the house where the youths were performing the wheel-feat. Then Loegaire siezed the wheel until it reached half up the sidewall. Upon that the youths laughed and cheered him. It was in reality a jeer, but it seemed to Loegaire a shout of applause. Conall then took the wheel. It was on the ground. He tossed it as high as the ridge-pole of the hall. The youths raised a shout at that.

It seemed to Conall that it was a shout of applause and victory. To the youths it was a shout of scorn. Then Cú Chulainn took the wheel. It was in mid-air he caught it. He hurled it aloft till it cast the ridge-pole from off the hall; the wheel went a man's cubit into the ground in the outside enclosure. The youths raised a shout of applause and triumph in Cú Chulainn's case. It seemed to Cú Chulainn, however, it was a laugh of scorn and ridicule they then gave vent to.

Cú Chulainn then sought out the womenfolk and took thrice fifty needles from them. These he tossed up one after the other. Each needle went into the eye of another, till in that wise they were joined together. He returned to the women, and gave each her own needle into her own hand. The young warriors praised Cú Chulainn. Whereupon they bade farewell to the king, the queen, and household as well.

'Go to the abode of my foster-father and to that of my step-mother,' quoth Medb, 'that is, Ercol and Garmna – and there put up as guests to-night.'

They kept on their way, and after running a race at the Cruachan Gathering, thrice did Cú Chulainn win the victory of the games. They then went to the abode of Garmna and of Ercol, who bade them welcome.

'For what are ye come?' asked Ercol.

'To be adjudged by thee,' they quoth.

'Go to the abode of Samera; he will adjudge ye.'

They went accordingly and guides were sent with them. They were welcomed by Samera, whose daughter Buan fell in love with Cú Chulainn. They told Samera it was in order to be judged they had come to him. Samera despatched them in order to the Amazons of the Glen.

Loigaire went first, but left his accoutrements and clothing with them [the Amazons]. Conall also went, and left his spears with them, but took his chief weapon, to wit, his sword, away with him. On the third night Cú Chulainn went. The Amazons shrieked at him. He and they fought each other till his spear was splintered, his shield broken, his raiment torn off. The Amazons were beating and overpowering him.

'O Cú Chulainn,' said Loig, 'you sorry coward, you squinting savage! gone are your valour and your bravery when it is sprites that beat you.'

Then Cú Chulainn was enraged at the sprites. He turned back upon the Horrors, and cut and gashed them till the glen was filled with their blood. He brought off his company's brave banner with him and turned back in triumph to the seat of Samera, the place where his companions were.

Samera bade him welcome; 'twas then he made speech:

> Not right to share the champion's fare of the cooking pit,
> Fatted kine, well-fed swine, honey and bread;

Through ladies' cunning take not his share
From Culann's Hound, of name and fame.
Cleaver of shields, raven of prey,
That bravery wields, eager for fray-boar of battle.
As wood takes fire, strikes his ire Emain's foes;
Of victory-loving women belov'd – plague of death.
A judge in deeming, not in seeming, eye flashing far
Hostile ports where ships resort his tributes know;
His chariot rides the mountain-side,
Pride of his clan, he leads the van, an eagle of war.
Why to Loigaire, lion of fences, liken him?
Why unto Conall, rider of fame?
Why should not Emer, of mantle shining –
it is our pleasure through grace divining
Of Ultonian ladies high-born and all –
enter first the merry Mead-Hall.
Cú Chulainn's share, well I wot,
It is not just [elsewhere] to allot.

'My verdict to ye then: the Champion's Portion to Cú Chulainn, and to his wife the precedence of the ladies of Ultonia – Cú Chulainn's valour to rank above that of every one else, Conchobar's excepted.'

After that they went [back] to the abode of Ercol, who bade them welcome. They slept there that night. Ercol challenged them to combat with himself and with his horse. Whereupon Loigaire and his horse went against them. The gelding of Ercol killed the horse of Loigaire, who was himself overcome by Ercol, before whom he fled. He took his way to Emain across Assaroe, and brought tidings with him of his comrades having been killed by Ercol. Conall likewise fled, his horse having been killed by Ercol's; the way he went was across Snam Rathaind (Rathand's Pool) on the route to Emain. Moreover, Conall's gillie, Rathand, was drowned in the river there, and after him Snam Rathaind takes its name since.

The Grey of Macha, however, killed the horse of Ercol, and Cú Chulainn took Ercol himself bound behind his chariot along with him to Emain. Buan, daughter of Samera, went on the track of the three chariots. She recognised the track of Cú Chulainn's framed chariot, inasmuch as it was no narrow track it used to take, but undermining walls, either enlarging or else leaping over breaches. The girl at last

leapt a fearful leap, following him behind in his chariot's track till she
struck her forehead on a rock, whereof she died. From this is named
Buan's Grave.

When Conall and Cú Chulainn reached Emain, they found the
Ultonians holding a keen for them, inasmuch as they felt certain they
were killed. Such the report Loigaire brought. They then related their
adventures and told their news to Conchobar and to the Ultonian
nobles generally. But the chiefs of chariots and the men of valour as a
body were reproaching Loigaire for the lying story he told concerning
his fellows.

Then Cathbad [the Driuid] made speech to this effect:

> A tale inglorious!
> Base Outlaw, black and false,
> For shame! thy face from sight!
> Ultonia's Champion's Portion
> Unhappily didst thou dispute,
> Nor won it by right,
> Thy lying upset
> Cú Chulainn with Ercol has coped,
> Victor in battle-fight;
> Tied at the tail of his car,
> Hercules-strong he held;
> Nor do men conceal his feats,
> His great havoc they tell.
> A champion glorious, battle-victorious,
> When rageth the fray,
> Slaughter-head of the hosts,
> A lord that careers in might,
> Zealous of valour and stout;
> With him to dispute
> The Champion's Portion,
> Unworthy a hero's repute.

The heroes ceased their discussions and their babblings and fell to
eating and enjoying themselves. It was Sualtam mac Roig, father of Cú
Chulainn himself, who that night attended upon the Ulstermen.
Moreover, Conchobar's ladder-vat was filled for them. Their portion
having been brought into their presence, the waiters began to serve, but
at the outset they withheld the Champion's Portion from distribution.

'Why not give the Champion's Portion,' said Dubtach Chafertongue, 'to some one of the heroes; those three have not returned from the King of Cruachan, bringing no sure token with them, whereby the Champion's Portion may be assigned to one of them.'

Thereupon Loegaire the Triumphant got up and lifted on high the bronze cup having the silver bird chased on the bottom. 'The Champion's Portion is mine,' said he, 'and none may contest it with me.'

'It is not,' said Conall Cernach. 'Not alike are the tokens we brought off with us. Yours is a cup of bronze, whereas mine is a cup of white bronze. From the difference between them the Champion's Portion clearly belongs to me.'

'It belongs to neither of you,' said Cú Chulainn as he got up and spoke. 'You have brought no token that procures you the Champion's Portion. Yet the king and the queen whom you visited were loath in the thick of distress to intensify the strife. But no less than your desserts have you received at their hands. The Champion's Portion remains with me, seeing I have brought a token distinguished, above the rest.'

He then lifted on high a cup of red gold having a bird chased on the bottom of it in precious dragonstone, the size of his two eyes. All the Ulster nobles in the train of Conchobar mac Nessa saw it. 'Therefore it is I,' he said, 'who deserve the Champion's Portion, provided I have fair play.'

'To thee we all award it,' said Conchobar and Fergus and the Ulster nobles as well. 'By the verdict of Ailill and Medb the Champion's Portion is yours.'

'I swear by my people's god,' said Loegaire the Triumphant and Conall the Victorious, 'that the cup you have brought is purchased. Of the jewels and the treasures in your possession you have given to Ailill and Medb for it in order that a defeat might not be on record against you, and that the Champion's Portion might be given to no one else by preference. By my people's god, that judgment shall not stand; the Champion's Portion shall not be yours.'

They then sprang up one after the other, their swords drawn. Straightway Conchobar and Fergus intervened, whereupon they let down their hands and sheathed their swords.

'Hold!' said Sencha. 'Do as I bid.'

'We will,' they said.

'Go forth to the ford of Yellow, son of Fair. He will adjudge ye.' Accordingly the three heroes went to the abode of Yellow (Budi). They told their wants and the rivalries which brought them.

'Was not judgment given you in Cruachan by Ailill and by Medb?' said Yellow.

'In sooth there was,' quoth Cú Chulainn, 'but those fellows don't stand by it.'

'Stand by it,' quoth the other men, 'we will not; what has been given us is no decision at all.'

'It is not easy for another to adjudge ye then,' quoth Yellow, 'seeing ye did not abide by Medb and Ailill's arrangement. I know,' he continued, 'one who will venture it: Terror, son of Great Fear (Uath mac Imomain), at yonder loch. Off then in quest of him; he will adjudge ye.'

A big powerful fellow was Terror, son of Great Fear. He used to shift his form into what shape he pleased, was wont to do tricks of magic and such like arts. He in sooth was the wizard from whom Muni, the Wizard's Pass, is named. He used to be called 'wizard' from the extent to which he changed his diverse shapes.

To Terror at his loch they accordingly went. Yellow had given them a guide. To Terror they told the cause for which they had sought him out. He said he should venture on adjudgment provided only they would adhere to it.

'We will adhere to it,' they quoth; whereupon he solemnly pledges them. 'I have a covenant to make with you,' he quoth, 'and whoever of you fulfils it with me, he is the man who wins the Champion's Portion!'

'What is the covenant?' they said.

'I have an axe, and the man into whose hands it shall be put is to cut off my head to-day, I to cut off his to-morrow.'

Thereupon Conall and Loigaire said they would not agree to that arrangement for it would be impossible for them to live after having been beheaded, although he might. Therefore they declined that. Cú Chulainn, however, said he would agree to the covenant (bargain) were the Champion's Portion given to him. Conall and Loigaire said they would allow him that if he agreed to a wager with Terror. Cú Chulainn solemnly pledged them not to contest the Champion's Portion if he made covenant with Terror. And they then pledged him to ratify it. Terror, having put spells on the edge of the axe, lays his head upon the stone for Cú Chulainn. Cú Chulainn with his own axe gives the giant a blow and cuts off his head. [Terror] then went off from them into the loch, his axe and his head on his breast.

On the morrow he comes back on his quest. Cú Chulainn stretches himself out for him on the stone. The axe with its edge reversed he draws down thrice on Cú Chulainn's neck.

'Get up,' quoth Terror, 'the sovereignty of the heroes of Erin to Cú Chulainn, and the Champion's Portion without contest.'

The three heroes then hied them to Emain. But Loigaire and Conall disputed the verdict given in favour of Cú Chulainn and the original contest as to the Champion's Portion continued. The Ulstermen advised them to go to Cú Roi for judgment. To that too they agreed.

On the morning of the morrow the three heroes – Cú Chulainn, Conall and Loegaire – set off to Cú Roi's stronghold (Cathair Con Roi). They unyoked their chariots at the gate of the hold, then entered the court. Whereupon Blathnat, Minn's daughter, wife of Cú Roi mac Dairi, bade them a warm welcome. That night on their arrival Cú Roi was not at home, but knowing they would come, he counselled his wife regarding the heroes until he should return from his Eastern expedition into Scythia. From the age of seven years, when he took up arms, until his death, Cú Roi had not reddened his sword in Erin, nor ever had the food of Erin passed his lips. Nor could Erin retain him for his haughtiness, renown, and rank, overbearing fury, strength, and gallantry. His wife acted according to his wish in the matter of bathing and washing, providing them with refreshing drinks and beds most excellent. And they liked it well.

When bedtime was come, she told them that each was to take his night watching the fort until Cú Roi should return. 'And, moreover, thus said Cú Roi, that you take your turn watching according to seniority.' In whatsoever quarter of the globe Cú Roi should happen to be, every night he chanted a spell over his stronghold, so that the fort revolved as swiftly as a mill-stone. The entrance was never to be found after sunset.

The first night, Loegaire the Triumphant took the watch, inasmuch as he was the eldest of the three. As he kept watch into the later part of the night, he saw a giant approaching him as far as his eyes could see from the sea westwards. Exceedingly huge and ugly and horrible Loegaire thought him, for, in height, it seemed to him, he reached into the sky, and the reflection of the sea was visible between his legs. Thus did he come, his hands full of stripped oaks, each of which would form a burden for a wagonteam of six, at whose root not a stroke had been repeated after a single sword-stroke. One of the stakes he cast at

Loegaire, who let it pass him. Twice or thrice he repeated it, but the stroke reached neither the skin nor the shield of Loegaire. Then Loegaire hurled a spear at him but it did not hit him.

The giant stretched his hand towards Loegaire. Such was its length that it reached across the three ridges that were between them as they were throwing at each other, and thus in his grasp the giant seized him. Though Loegaire was big and imposing, he fitted like a year-old child into the clutch of his opponent, who then ground him between his two palms as a chessman is turned in a groove. In that state, half-dead, the giant tossed him out over the fort, so that he fell into the mire of the ditch at the gate. The fort had no opening there, and the other men and inmates of the hold thought Loegaire had leapt outside over the fort, as a challenge for the other men to do likewise.

There they were until the day's end. When the night-watch began, Conall went out as sentry, for he was older than Cú Chulainn. Everything occurred as it did to Loegaire the first night.

The third night Cú Chulainn went on watch. That night the three Greys of Sescind Uarbeil, the three Ox-feeders of Breg, and the three sons of Big-fist the Siren met by appointment to plunder the stronghold. This too was the night of which it was foretold that the Spirit of the Lake by the fort would devour the whole population of the hold, man and beast.

Cú Chulainn, while watching through the night, had many uneasy forebodings. When midnight came he heard a terrific noise drawing near to him.

'Holloa, holloa,' Cú Chulainn shouted, 'who is there? If friends they be, let them not stir; if foes, let them flee.' Then they raised a terrific shout at him. Whereupon Cú Chulainn sprang upon them, so that the nine of them fell dead to the earth. He heaped their heads in disorder into the seat of watching and resumed his post. Another nine shouted at him. In like manner he killed three nines, making one cairn of them, heads and accoutrements.

While he was there far on into the night, tired and sad and weary, he heard the rising of the lake on high as if it were the booming of a very heavy sea. However deep his dejection, he could not resist going to see what caused the great noise he heard. He then perceived the upheaving monster, and it seemed to him to be thirty cubits in curvature above the loch. It raised itself on high into the air and sprang towards the fort, opening its mouth so that one of the halls could go into its gullet.

Then Cú Chulainn called to mind his swooping feat, sprang on high, and was as swift as a winnowing riddle right round the monster. He entwined his two arms about its neck, stretched his hand into its gullet, tore out the monster's heart, and cast it from him on the ground. Then the beast fell from the air and rested on the earth, after having sustained a blow on the shoulder. Cú Chulainn then plied it with his sword, hacked it to bits, and took the head with him into the sentry-seat along with the other heap of skulls.

While there, depressed and miserable in the morning dawn, he saw the giant approaching him westwards from the sea. 'Bad night,' says he.

'It will be worse for thee, thou oaf,' said Cú Chulainn. Then the giant cast one of the branches at Cú Chulainn, who let it pass him. He repeated it twice or thrice, but it reached neither the skin nor the shield of Cú Chulainn. Cú Chulainn then hurled his spear at the giant, but it did not reach him. Whereupon the giant stretched out his hand towards Cú Chulainn to grip him as he had the others. Cú Chulainn leapt the hero's salmon-leap and called to mind his swooping feat with his sword drawn over the giant's head. As swift as a hare he was, and in mid-air circling round the giant, until he made a water-wheel of him

'Life for life, O Cú Chulainn,' he said.

'Give me my three wishes,' said Cú Chulainn.

'Thou shalt have them as they come at a breath,' he said.

'The sovereignty of Erin's heroes be henceforth mine, the Champion's Portion without dispute, the precedence to my wife over the Ulster ladies forever.'

'It shall be thine,' he said at once. Then he who had been talking with Cú Chulainn vanished, he knew not whither.

Then Cú Chulainn mused to himself as to the leap as his fellows had leapt over the fort, for their leap was big and broad and high. Moreover, it seemed to him that it was by leaping that the valiant heroes had gone over it. He tried it twice and failed.

'Alas!' said Cú Chulainn, 'my exertions for the Champion's Portion have exhausted me, and now I lose it through not being able to take the leap the others took.'

As thus he mused, he assayed the following feats: he would spring backwards in mid air a shot's distance from the fort, and then he would rebound from there until his forehead struck the fort. Then he would spring on high until all that was within the fort was visible to him, and again he would sink up to his knees in the earth owing to the pressure

of his vehemence and violence. At another time he would not take the
dew from off the tip of the grass by reason of his buoyancy of mood,
vehemence of nature, and heroic valour. What with the fit and fury that
raged upon him he stepped over the fort outside and alighted at the
door of the hall. His two footprints are in the flag on the floor of the hold
at the spot where the royal entrance was. Thereafter he entered the
house and heaved a sigh.

Then Minn's daughter, Blathnat, wife of Cú Roi, spoke: 'Truly not
the sigh of one dishonoured, but a victor's sigh of triumph.'

The daughter of the king of the Isle of the Men of Falga (i.e.,
Blathnat) knew full well of Cú Chulainn's evil plight that night. They
were not long there when they beheld Cú Roi coming towards them,
carrying into the house the standard of the three nines slain by Cú
Chulainn, along with their heads and that of the monster. He put the
heads from off his breast on to the floor of the stead, and spoke: 'The
gillie whose one night's trophies are these is a fit lad to watch the king's
stronghold forever. The Champion's Portion, over which you have
fallen out with the gallant youths of Erin, truly belongs to Cú
Chulainn. The bravest of them, were he here, could not match him in
number of trophies.'

Cú Roi's verdict upon them was:

> The Champion's Portion to be Cú Chulainn's,
> With the sovereignty of valour over all the Gael,
> And to his wife the precedence
> on entering the Mead Hall before all the ladies of Ulster.

And the value of seven bond-maidens in gold and silver Cú Roi gave to
Cú Chulainn in reward for his one night's performance.

The three heroes of Ulster straightway bade Cú Roi farewell and kept
on until they were seated in Emain Macha before the day closed. When
the waiters came to deal and divide, they took the Champion's Portion
with its share of ale out of the distribution that they might have it apart.

'Indeed, sure are we,' said Dubtach Chafertongue, 'you think not
tonight of contending for the Champion's Portion. Perhaps the man
you sought out has undertaken to pass judgment.'

Whereupon said the other folk to Cú Chulainn, 'The Champion's
Portion was not assigned to one of you in preference to the other. As to
Cú Roi's judgment upon these three, not a whit did he concede to Cú
Chulainn upon their arriving at Emain.' Cú Chulainn then declared

that he by no means coveted the winning of it; for the loss thence resulting to the winner would be on a par with the profit got from it. The championship was therefore not fully assigned until the advent of the Champion's Covenant in Emain, which follows.

One day as the Ulstermen were in Emain Macha, fatigued after the gathering and the games, Conchobar and Fergus mac Roig, with the Ulster nobles as well, proceeded from the playing field outside and seated themselves in the Red Branch of Conchobar. Neither Cú Chulainn nor Conall the Victorious nor Loegaire the Triumphant were there that night. But the hosts of Ulster's heroes were there. As they were seated, it being eventide, and the day drawing towards the close, they saw a big uncouth fellow of exceeding ugliness drawing nigh them into the hall. To them it seemed as if none of the Ulstermen would reach half his height. Horrible and ugly was the carle's disguise. Next to his skin he wore an old hide with a dark dun mantle around him, and over him a great spreading club-tree branch the size of a winter-shed under which thirty bullocks could find shelter. Ravenous yellow eyes he had, protruding from his head, each of the twain the size of an ox-vat. Each finger was as thick as a person's wrist. In his left hand he carried a stock, a burden for twenty yoke of oxen. In his right hand was an axe weighing thrice fifty glowing molten masses of metal. Its handle would require a yoke of six to move it. Its sharpness such that it would lop off hairs, the wind blowing them against its edge.

In that guise he went and stood by the fork-beam beside the fire.

'Is the hall lacking in room for you,' said Dubtach Chafertongue to the uncouth clodhopper (*bachlach*), 'that ye find no other place than by the fork-beam, unless ye wish to be an illumination to the house? – only sooner will a blaze be to the house than brightness to the household.'

'Whatever property may be mine, you will agree that no matter how big I am the household will be lighted, while the hall will not be burned. That, however, is not my sole function; I have others as well. But neither in Erin nor in Alba nor in Europe nor in Africa nor in Asia, including Greece, Scythia, the Isles of Gades, the Pillars of Hercules, and Bregon's Tower have I accomplished the quest on which I have come, nor a man to do me fair play regarding it. Since ye Ulstermen have excelled all the peoples of those lands in strength, prowess and valour; in rank, magnanimity, and dignity; in truth, generosity, and worth, get one among you to grant the boon I ask.'

'In truth it is not just that the honour of a province be carried off,' said Fergus mac Roig, 'because of one man who fails in keeping his word of honour. Death certainly is not a whit nearer to him than to you.'

'It is not I that shun it.'

'Make thy quest known to us, then,' said Fergus.

'Only if fair play is offered me will I tell it.'

'It is right to give fair play,' said Sencha son of Ailill, 'for it is not seemly for a great people to break a mutual covenant over any unknown individual. It seems to us, furthermore, that if you at last find a person such as you seek, you will find him here.'

'Conchobar I put aside,' said he, 'for the sake of his sovereignty, and Fergus mac Roig also on account of his like privilege. These two excepted, come whosoever of you that may dare, that I may cut off his head tonight, he mine tomorrow night.'

'Sure then there is no warrior here,' said Dubtach, 'after these two.'

'By my troth there will be at this moment,' cried Munremur mac Gerrcind as he sprung on to the floor of the hall. The strength of Munremur was as the strength of a hundred warriors, each arm having the might of a hundred 'centaurs'.

'Bend down, *bachlach*,' said Munremur, 'that I may cut off thy head tonight, thou to cut off mine tomorrow.'

'Were that the object of my quest I could get it anywhere,' said the *bachlach*; 'let us act according to our covenant – I to cut off your head tonight, you to avenge it tomorrow night.'

'By my people's gods,' said Dubtach Chafertongue, 'death is thus for thee no pleasant prospect, should the man killed tonight attack thee on the morrow. It is given to thee alone if thou hast the power, being killed night after night, and to avenge it the next day.'

'Truly I will carry out what you all as a body agree upon by way of counsel, strange as it may seem to you,' said the *bachlach*. He then pledged the other to keep his troth in this contention as to fulfilling his tryst on the morrow.

With that Munremur took the axe from the *bachlach*'s hand. Seven feet apart were its two angles. Then the bachlach put his neck across the block. Munremur dealt a blow across it with the axe until it stood in the block beneath, cutting off the head so that it lay by the base of the fork-beam, the house being filled with the blood.

Straightway the *bachlach* rose, recovered himself, clasped his head, block, and axe to his breast, and made his exit from the hall with the blood streaming from his neck. It filled the Red Branch on every side. Great was the people's horror, wondering at the marvel that had appeared to them. 'By my people's gods,' said Dubtach Chafertongue, 'if the *bachlach*, having been killed tonight, come back tomorrow, he will not leave a man alive in Ulster.'

The following night he returned, and Munremur shirked him. Then the *bachlach* began to urge his pact with Munremur. 'Truly it is not right for Munremur not to fulfill his covenant with me.'

That night, however, Loegaire the Triumphant was present.

'Who of the warriors that contest Ulster's Champion's Portion will carry out a covenant with me tonight? Where is Loegaire the Triumphant?' said he.

'Here,' said Loegaire. He pledged him, too, yet Loegaire did not keep his agreement. The *bachlach* returned on the morrow and similarly pledged Conall Cernach, who came not as he had sworn.

The fourth night the *bachlach* returned, and fierce and furious was he. All the ladies of Ulster came that night to see the strange marvel that had come to the Red Branch. That night Cú Chulainn was there also. Then the *bachlach* began to upbraid them. 'Ye men of Ulster, your valour and your prowess are gone. Your warriors greatly covet the Champion's Portion, yet are unable to contest it. Where is the mad fellow called Cú Chulainn? I would like to know whether his word is better than the others.'

'No covenant do I desire with you,' said Cú Chulainn.

'Likely is that, thou wretched fly; greatly dost thou fear to die.' Whereupon Cú Chulainn sprang towards him and dealt him a blow with the axe, hurling his head to the top rafter of the Red Branch until the whole hall shook. Cú Chulainn then again caught up the head and gave it a blow with the axe and smashed it. Thereafter the *bachlach* rose up.

On the morrow the Ulstermen were watching Cú Chulainn to see whether he would shirk the *bachlach* as the other heroes had done. As Cú Chulainn was awaiting the *bachlach*, they saw that great dejection seized him. It would have been fitting had they sung his dirge. They felt sure that his life would last only until the *bachlach* came. Then said Cú Chulainn with shame to Conchobar, 'Thou shalt not go until my pledge to the *bachlach* is fulfilled; for death awaits me, and I would rather have death with honour.'

They were there as the day was closing and they saw the *bachlach* approaching.

'Where is Cú Chulainn?' said he.

'Here I am,' he replied.

'Thou art dull of speech tonight, unhappy one; greatly you fear to die. Yet, though great your fear, death you have not shirked.'

Thereafter Cú Chulainn stretched his neck across the block, which was of such size that his neck reached but half way. 'Stretch out thy neck, thou wretch,' cried the *bachlach*.

'Thou art keeping me in torment,' said Cú Chulainn; 'dispatch me quickly. Last night, by my troth, I tormented thee not. Verily I swear that if thou torment me I will make myself as long as a crane above you.'

'I cannot slay thee,' said the *bachlach*, 'what with the shortness of your neck and your side and the size of the block.'

Then Cú Chulainn stretched out his neck so that a warrior's foot would have fitted between any two of his ribs; his neck he stretched until his head reached the other side of the block. The *bachlach* raised his axe until it reached the roof-tree of the house. The creaking of the old hide that was about him and the crashing of the axe – both his arms being raised aloft with all his might were as the loud noise of a wood tempest tossed in a night of storm. Down it came then on his neck – its blunt side below, all the nobles of Ulster gazing upon them.

'O Cú Chulainn, arise! Of the warriors of Ulster and Erin, no matter their mettle, none is found to compare with thee in valour, bravery, and truthfulness. The sovereignty of the heroes of Erin to thee from this hour forth and the Champion's Portion undisputed, and to thy wife the precedence always of the ladies of Ulster in the Mead-Hall. And whosoever shall lay wager against thee from now, as my tribe swears I swear, all his life he will be in danger.'

Then the *bachlach* vanished. It was Cú Roi mac Dairi who in that guise had come to fulfill the promise he had given to Cú Chulainn.

32. The Excuse of Guile's Daughter

(Ceasacht Inghine Guile)

Translated by Caitlín Matthews

This story relates the unplanned visit of King Fedlimid of Munster to a satirist called Guile, who is unprepared for such a large party. It is an outrageous account of how to refuse a guest and would have been enjoyed all the more since hospitality among the Gaels was a sacred duty. The story has a surprising ending, and we understand that the excuse has been merely a delaying tactic while the household is made ready for Fedlimid. Parts of this story remind one inevitably of the French cartoon strip, 'Asterix the Gaul,' by Uderzo and Goscinny, with its humorously well-named characters and incidents. Fedlimid swears by 'St Patrick's Stone,' rather than by 'Toutatis' but he does have a set of poets who sound remarkably like 'Cacophonix'. When the apparently shy Guile Beag, who has never been outside in her life, sees three poets suffering dreadful diarrhoea, with their backsides wedged in a ditch, she equates their positions to that of calves being born. Her long, long excuse to avoid giving hospitality to Fedlimid is one of the best ones we've ever heard. We think she does pretty well for a girl as appallingly shy as this!

Our translation is taken from a comparison of MSs from Royal Irish Academy 24 P 12, National Library of Ireland G 448, and Trinity College Dublin H.6.8, in the edition by Caoimhín Breatnach.

There was a noble and eminent king who took the kingship and overlordship of the two level and mild provinces of Munster. He was Fedlimid mac Criomthan, a king who had reached the seven ranks of nobility, in addition to being a cleric who had won the seven ecclesiastical ordinations, as well being a poet who had achieved the seven grades of poetry. Among the Gaels he had no equal in knowledge, devotion and high learning, unless it be Cuimín Foda mac Fiachra or Coluim Chille mac Fedlimid.

Fedlimid took a great circuit of Munster with his retinue until he came to the lands of the Eóghanacht of Locha Léin. It snowed so prodigiously upon the company, with such a weight of snow, that their horses were unable to carry them. It was early spring, to tell the truth. Fedlimid said, 'My companions, do you know whose house is nearest this night? For this would be a good time to look up a distant friend.' They replied, 'The only one we know about is that of your own friend, Guile of Atha Lóich.'

'By the stone of Patrick in Cashel,' said Fedlimid, 'although there is love between us, the nature of his hospitality is uncertain. Time was when that acquaintance would make certain requests of me. Three visits he made to me at Cashel and was given payments of goods without having to ask. When we studied together in Armagh, learning the scriptures, he bade me visit his house if I were ever to find myself in the vicinity of Locha Léin. What better this night for me to go and redeem that promise?'

Then Fedlimid made his way to Guile's house where the noise and cacophony of the great company resounded throughout the place. Three of Guile's poets were outside on the green at that moment. Their names were Piosdal (Stirrer), Samthacht (Lanky) and Seimdille (Slimy). Faints and trances overcame them upon seeing the host, and it was in the grip of these fainting spells that they came before Guile, who asked them what had caused them to assume this condition.

They said to him, 'If you had seen with your own eyes what we have seen, it wouldn't be fainting but death itself that would overcome you. Neither the wall nor the heath surrounding the house here were plain to us because of the quantity of the hosts and multitudes.'

When Guile and his people heard this, their spirits were considerably depressed, and the only person capable of speech in that company was Guile's young daughter, called Guile Beag. When that elder, who was reclining upon his side, raised his elbow from the cushion and looked about the house and saw that it was only his daughter who was capable of utterance, he said to the young girl, 'Would you like to earn my blessing, daughter?'

'If so I'm able!' she said.

'Alright then,' said Guile, 'go out and give welcome to the king of Munster and the notables in his retinue while the house and outbuildings are being tidied and the floor swept. Speak fair words in an honest way to him for a bit. For he is worthy our welcome here since we have benefited from his gold and valuables without our asking for it.'

'You have my word,' said the girl, 'that if any other person but yourself had asked me that, I would have raised blisters upon his cheeks. I was not raised for this, but was rather reared between the quern and the kneading trough, between the kneading trough and the floor, between the floor and the door. I have never gone out of doors from this house, and had I ever seen two or three people together I would have died of shame, shyness and modesty. But there are three things that a foster-father should not bear: distress because of a woman, disappointment over being offered valuables, and the denial of his direct commands. Never have I done any of these things, and though it is hard because of my shame and because I want to merit your blessing, but I will indeed go to Fedlimid.' And the poem was exchanged thus between them:

GUILE: Make discovery, bold Guile,
             whose are those great, fine mounts
             that neigh out over the walls
             on the green before my good house?

GUILE BEAG: Don't ever ask me, dear Guile!
             I'm more retiring than heaven;
             if anyone so much as laughs at me,
             I'll die of mortification!

GUILE: Put on your best silk dress!
             Your gold-bordered checked cloak!
             Take up your engraved staff!
             Come out and discover!

When the poem was done, the daughter put on her best silk clothes and went out on to the green, looking to all points of the compass with her keen, all-seeing eyes, to east, west, south and north. Then it was that the girl saw the great hosts upon the green and she walked determinedly towards them, walking about the host in a great circuit. She met with three poets with their backsides towards the ditch, groaning heartily. She asked them, 'Were you all conceived at the same time?'

'What's that to you?' they said.

'Well, it's just that all the calves are born at the same season,' she said.

'Wait until their faces emerge before you put ropes around them,' they joked.

'No, that's not right,' she said, 'the mothers usually lick them three times before that.'

And the poets conceived a fear of her and left her.

After she had got clear of these three in this way, she approached Fedlimid and welcomed him like this, 'God give you long life, noble Fedlimid!' she said.

'God give you health, girl!' said Fedlimid. 'Timely is the manner of your greeting.'

'It is fitting indeed, noble Fedlimid,' she said, 'for we know that you cannot have had any such acquaintance nor acknowledgement nor accomplishment in this region when you intended to come to Guile's house tonight. Had you done so, it would have given us warning; as it is, he has neither meat nor drink prepared for you. But it is clear to us that it is the downfall of lordship, the failure of accomplishment, and a painful ignorance on your part that you seek hospitality at the house of Guile the satirist this night. We would need notice of a month or three or even a year to prepare for you, noble Fedlimid.'

'What's your meaning?' asked Fedlimid.

'O, Fedlimid!' she said, 'my meaning is that hunger dwells with us. Do you not see that house yonder?'

'I do,' said Fedlimid.

'Well then, the crooked stepping stones lead to the door of that house, at the narrow mouth of its entrance, there's a hurdle offering no cover nor protection lying against it. On the dirty, wispy, slimy floor there's a thin, roaming, wet-legged cat and a short, grumpy dog, and a naked, withered hag, perpetually farting her foulness throughout the house. There's a black, mucky-smoked fire; and some bent narrow beds; and a bare, runny-eyed female cook; and a great sorrow is upon the folk of the house. No-one ever left the house feeling satisfied or happy.'

'By Patrick's stone in Cashel!' said Fedlimid, 'if we had known things were as bad as that, we'd never have visited you!'

'Do you believe me, noble Fedlimid?' she said. 'I'm not saying that you shouldn't have come, only that you should have given us more warning when it would have been a better time to visit. There's a wuthering in the wind but the high passes are pleasant; here, the service is slow, and the hound's chest is thin while the raven's chest is full. We have had to decide between our cows and our stomachs, and we have been without the separation of chaff from grain, and we have no sweet music, nor anything left in our barns, and the women's noses run like milk though their breasts are dry and empty. Our dairy cows give only thin blue milk for they have been sucked dry by their calves, and our men do not even have the power of women in childbirth, and there are swift, grey, parsimonious mice licking the hard, hollowed-out threshing floors, noble Fedlimid,' she said and recited this quatrain:

> What brings Felimid to visit me,
> for your perception is good;
> it's bad to visit a place
> where food's not available.

'By St Patrick's stone in Cashel,' swore Fedlimid, 'if we'd any idea of this, we would not have come here.'

'What's this, noble Fedlimid?' she asked. 'Have you not heard the three herons of Guile's house?'

'I've not heard them,' said Fedlimid, 'What are they called?'

'"Shun the Wall" is the first heron's name, "Avoid the Rampart" is the second heron, and "Don't Come, Don't Come" is the third heron. Have you never heard of the three janitors of Guile's house?'

'I never did,' said Fedlimid. 'What are their names?'

'Scraping, Squeaking and Dragging they are called,' she said. 'Did you hear about the three dogs of Guile's house?'

'No, never,' said Fedlimid, 'What are they called?'

'Giant, Howler and Worrier are their names,' she said. 'And it doesn't matter whether it's a few or a great number who comes to the place, but no-one escapes without being bitten and chewed so that they can barely make it up the mountain yonder, and they suffer infection for a month or three or even a year as a result of them. Did you never hear of the three workmen of Guile's house?'

'I never did,' said Fedlimid. 'What are their names?'

'Lying, Circuitous and Do Nothing. Did you hear about the three musicians of Guile's house?'

'No, I didn't,' said Fedlimid. 'What are they called?'

'Deafening, Blustering and Bawling are their names. And their wives are called Bad, Worse and Worse Than That. Did you ever hear about the three servers of Guile's house?'

'No, never,' said Fedlimid. 'What are their names?'

'Ebb, Luckless and Disastrous. Did you hear about the male cooks of Guile's house?'

'No, I haven't,' said Fedlimid. 'What are they called?'

'Plunder, Theft and Criminal,' she said. 'Did you hear about the twelve hags of Guile's house?'

'I didn't,' said Fedlimid. 'What are they called?'

'Caw, Wrinkle and Peer, Trouble and Provocation, Gloomy, Refusal and Guilty, Tearful and Grumbling, Pilferer and Lip-licker, and they sweep the floor each morning with their sharp, bristly grey beards.'

'Well, girl!' said Fedlimid. 'Is there any of your folk who is worse than these?'

'Oh yes indeed!' she said. 'There's my own foster-father himself, the man who brought me up and cared for me. He's Guile's chief steward.'

'And what's this man's name?' asked Fedlimid.

'Frail, son of Feeble, a mean, hard-bargaining man of the Tuatha dé Danaan, and he was baptised by Denial, the priest who poured three waves over at that ceremony: a wave of niggardliness, a wave of pinnickityness and a wave of meagerliness, and, noble Fedlimid,' she said, 'you come to a troubled house this night. You see, there is only thawed dung on our fields, and our mills hunger for grain and our old supplies are used up and our new supplies have not yet come, and the place to which you have come tonight is like the high field, having only grass enough for one cow, grazing for one beast alone and one goose, and if my older sister was here to back me up, her excuse would be believed, I tell you. If I was older, then I would have some knowledge of cows and spancels, but I've no ability to describe the state of this house tonight. I have no skill at addressing noble folk until now and no-one taught me how to talk to a great host of people like this. Good God, Fedlimid! Whatever gave you the idea that you'd get food from poor, sad Guile tonight?'

'By the Stone of St Patrick in Cashel!' said Fedlimid. 'If it had been your older sister who came out we would have awarded her the land from Luachair to the west, but since it is yourself, we'll assign from Mangartaich of the red heather to Léim Lárach across the sea.'

Then Fedlimid came forward and Guile Beag followed him, saying, 'Come back tonight, Fedlimid!' she said, 'even though this is a bad place for you.' And she said this poem:

> Pity the guest who stays with me,
> whether it be one man or three.
> Nothing remains of our estate
> But the lickings of a plate.
>
> Sad the victory of the host
> in sweet Guile's great big house;
> nothing but empty houses here
> and the thin rind of famine's leer.
>
> The great assembly gathered far,
> complaining from each separate airt;
> pity the one who's journeyed long,
> O noble, generous Crimthann's son!

At that poem, the king grew angry and commanded his servant to bring his horse, which he mounted without the girl noticing. The girl chased after him, grabbing the bridle of the horse. 'Every good thing come to you, noble Fedlimid,' she said. 'Don't be cross! It's not fitting for a king to lose his temper!'

'No, it isn't, girl,' said Fedlimid. 'But this is no time for discussion. The day draws to its close now, and, what with the storm and filthy weather, we've no notion which way to go tonight.'

'It's no wasteland the land about here,' said the girl. 'It is yourself who has the rulership and ordering of it, noble Fedlimid,' said the girl. 'I myself will tell you about this place so that your suspicions about the food will be quietened. There were four guests came here this spring, and there was scarcely any food available to them,' she said. 'Only the eighth share of a lean, mouldy haunch of calf, and a half share of thin, mangy calf's rib, which made the wild dogs throw up because of the smell coming off of it; there was about as much of a skinny groin of a wandering, muddy, mean, miserable pig, and a third portion of dry bannock made of the burnt bits of gleaned oats grubbed up in the far north-west of the fallow field where the sun never shines. And all that was available to them was about as much pale-blue butter that might butter a butterfly's wing, which had been rolled upon the backs of thieving slaves and then strained through the crooked spout of a small jug. That was the drink we offered them after that great feast. It was served in a wooden bowl that was narrow at the base and shallow to the rim, made from the end of a stick of alder firewood; it was empty in the middle and dry above, and it was pledged in a distant land overseas, and the son or brother of Guile had to be left as a surety until I was able to make the downpayment on the food that we'd promised.'

'Girl!' said Fedlimid, 'it's time for us to be off.'

'Much better if you didn't do that,' said the girl. 'Come in with me tonight and we'll give you the nearly-thatched houses and the half-full cups and the half-empty plates and the tree tops for gnawing upon and the bone-fragments for you to split between you and a wet covering to the bottoms of your ears.'

'Upon my word!' said Fedlimid's people, 'what a truly dreadful idea of hospitality. Staying here is much worse than going, let's leave speedily!'

'We will not leave!' said Fedlimid. 'What she offers us is quite suitable. For what are the half-thatched houses save those that are thatched on the outside and unthatched within, and what are the half-empty plates she speaks of but those that have food on the upper part and none on the bottom, and what are the tops of trees but the nuts, and what are the bone-fragments but the teeth we use to crack them open, and what is the wet covering, but a washing? We will go with her,' said Fedlimid, accompanying her into the spacious houses with their white quilts spread smoothly for them. There their hair was smoothed and dressed, and the freshest foods and the most aged drinks of every kind were given to them.

There were twenty four saints accompanying Fedlimid, among whom were Mael Ruagháin, Maol Tuile, Maol Anghaid, Mo-ling, Eochaidh, Cionaodh, Labhrán, Uiathne, Durbhadh, Cuilfhion, Aoinghus mac Aíbléin, Diarmuid of Innis Clothrann, another Aonghus, with Fearadhach, Duibhtíre and Flann mac Ciacheallach, Flann mac Dubh Conna, Flannán, Maol Díothraibh and Fedlimid himself.

By all accounts, they enjoyed that feast for the length of six weeks and it was no worse at the end than it had been on the first night for them. Then Fedlimid's groom came and said, 'Since this is not the appointed place where the court of Munster should stay, we think that we've been here long enough.'

'Curse your words, boy!' said Fedlimid. 'But since you have reminded us of our duty, we will go now. But it is not from lack of food or drink that we are leaving here, despite our long stay.'

Fedlimid took his leave of Guile and set off, wishing him good luck in his excuses. With Guile at his side, Fedlimid emerged from the oratory and Guile Beag came to ask something of Fedlimid.

'It just so happens that I have nothing in my hands now,' said Fedlimid, 'But the next time we meet together, you will receive something from me.'

Fedlimid went round the oratory one way and Guile Beag came round the other side, meeting him, 'To every word it's own truth,' she said. 'You promised something to me when we next met.'

'I will give you my horse and my clothing,' said Fedlimid.

And so the proverb came about, 'The respite of Guile around the oratory.'

Then Fedlimid said farewell to Guile and recited this poem:

> Long life to you, Guile my dear!
> Long life to your wife and daughter!
> Your son will enjoy the benefit
> for the joy of time together.
>
> Our full host, our drinking companions,
> As if Locha Léin had been old mead,
> As if Leamhain had been bragget,
> That was the way of our drinking.
>
> Though the food of your house was meagre,
> according to the words of your girl,
> in such measure were we fed
> that Mount Brandon must have fed us.
>
> I am Fedlimid the generous,
> Crimthann's son, hero's ruin;
> we leave your house, Guile,
> with every good gift and blessing.

And that is the excuse given by Guile's daughter.

EXILES

33. The Exile of Conall Corc

(Longes Chonaill Corc)

Translated by Caitlín Matthews

*L*onges Chonaill Corc is all that we have remaining of a once longer story about Conall Corc, the eponymous king who gives his name to Co Cork. He was the founder of the Eoghanacht dynasty that reigned in Munster, with their headquarters at Cashel in Co Cork. The story has many thematic similarities with that of Amlodius or Amleth, the original Hamlet, as told by Saxo Grammaticus. They, like Corc, were inconvenient individuals who were sent overseas to be quietly disposed of while abroad. We learn how Corc not only survives his murderous relative's attempt to be rid of him, but how he founds his dynasty with the choice of a wife from Pictish Scotland.

The double theme of enslavement and freedom runs through this story and it is important to realise here a notable historical feature which contextualises this prime story of Munster. The island of Ireland was traditional split into two halves, Leth Con and Leth Mug. Conn's half designated the area north of Eiscir Riada, a line drawn between Galway and Dublin, claimed by Conn Cétchatach; while Mug's half were the lands south of this line, southern Ireland, claimed by Eógan Mór or Mug Nuadat. Now Conn means both 'head' and 'chief' but Mug means 'slave,' and Mug's half of the island traditionally had a lower status than the northern half of Ireland.

It is prophesied that Corc's reign will be aided by the freeing of slaves and hostages, and this he does to his later advantage. Under Irish law, every person had an honour price, or *éric*: the price that must be paid to a dead person's family by the perpetrator in the event of his slaying. We see how the poet Gruibne sets Corc's *éric* at the equivalant of King Feredach's weight in silver, but that later, Feredach gives Corc three men's weight in silver when he leaves Alba: from being a man accounted so worthless that his relatives exile him in order to be killed (thus avoiding payment of his *éric* or death price), and his arrival as a landless man of no particular connections, Corc does well to return to Ireland and establish himself on the plain of Femen at Cashel as over-king of all Munster.

The theme of slavery and freedom is also well established in Corc's canny ploy of secretly sleeping with King Feredach's daughter. Refusing to implicate Corc, the daughter risks burning on the pyre before the righteous men of Alba, but she faces it out and gives Corc the upper hand in his dealings with her father. Corc argues so skilfully that she and her son are saved and duly acknowledged. Instead of them becoming outcasts and slaves, Corc liberates and elevates them

The taking of hostages was a necessary part of kingship in ancient Ireland: it meant, in effect, having a hostage for a neighbouring tribe's good behaviour. Fosterage was another more subtle means of keeping the peace: a fosterchild became part of the foster-family and linked often disputing tribal factions in bonds of sacred kinship. King Crimthann thus proves himself to be an archetypally 'bad king' in his murderous intentions towards his nephew and foster-son. By contrast, Corc proves himself to be noble and magnanimous.

Pigs play an important part in the establishment of Corc's sovereignty. Pigs and pig-keeping were the business of slaves, work forbidden to kings. But it is when Gruibne goes to look for straying pigs that he finds Corc nearly dead after a blizzard that Corc's destiny is sealed, and when the Munster swineherd sees his kingship vision that Corc is recognised as the over-king. The swineherd himself is awarded with a high-status ritual office in perpetuity. Pigs in Irish and Welsh myth traditionally arise from the underworld and denote the under-class. They feature strongly in the First and Third Branch of the Mabinogion, in the story of Pwyll and his son Pryderi, as heralds of sovereignty, and, in the Fourth Branch, as the cause of sovereignty's disruption.

'The Exile of Corc' below has lost its beginning and we append a bracketed section ahead of it which summarises what went before, including the birth of Corc, from the most detailed extant MS in the *Book of Leinster* as transcribed by Vernam Hull.

Birth of Corc

[Conall Corc Mac Lugaid's mother was the female satirist, Bolce Ben-bretnach of Briton. One day she put a *geis* upon the king that she should sleep with him and this was how Conall Corc was conceived. Fedelm Láir Derg or Red Mare, the daughter of Móethaire of the Corco Ochae tribe, was the Conall Corc's fostermother. She was a witch, and, on the night that Corc was born, she was spending the night in King Lugaid's house and so Bolce put her son under Fedelm's protection, and it was she who raised him. Now the night after his birth, a meeting of her band of witches was due and, because they would destroy any boys who came into the house, Fedelm prudently hid her foster-son under the hearth beneath the ground. The witches began assembling. As one entered, she perceived that there was some child in the room and said, 'I do not vent my malice save on that which is beneath the cauldron.' And a flame from the heart shot out and burned the child's ear, as result of which Corc mac Lugaid was red (lit. *corc*). The following day, in the house of Fedelm, a seer examined Corc's hand and proclaimed to him, 'You must free captives wherever you see them and whenever you have the power to do so. If you do this, your race will be renowned and your name will be associated with it. Your fame rests upon acting like this.'

After that, when he was older, he was given in fosterage to Crimthan mac Fidaig, his uncle, brother to King Lugaid and King of all Ireland. Corc was sent to Leinster to collect a tribute of sixty cows and while on this mission, he freed various captives, among them an Alban (Scottish) poet called Gruibne who later returned home. Now King Crimthan grew jealous of Corc over the fact that the king's wife had made eyes at his nephew. When Corc spurned her, she accused him of rape. So it was that Crimthan banished Corc to Alba and caused a secret ogam to be written on his shield that would result in his death.]

The exile of Corc

[Corc arrived at] . . . Dublin and saw the ships crossing the sea. He embarked for the eastward searoute and at length saw the mountains of Alba. He was released into that land by his captors. He made his way to a mountain on the west of Alba where so much snow fell that it reached his belt. He was without food or drink for five days and he finally threw himself down, expecting death in that glen. But the learned Gruibne, poet of Feredach King of Alba, came with a party of twelve men to seek his straying pigs. He saw the edge of a mantle sticking out from the snow and said, 'Look! A dead man!' But when he touched the body he found it was still warm. 'Frost has nearly done for him,' he said. 'Quickly kindle a fire about him to thaw out his limbs.'

When the fire had caused his body to steam, Corc stirred.
'Be easy, warrior,' said Gruibne. 'You have nothing to fear.'
Then, looking closely into his face, Gruibne exclaimed,

'Welcome to you, fair Conall Corc!
You who subdued every territory in the west beyond the far seas.
It would seem that this brine of the air has drugged you into
    long sleeping.
A dumb troop on silent feet has bravely besieged you and
    bawled its deep blasts
for thrice three hours so that you yourself were rendered dumb.

It is fortunate indeed that you came upon me and that
you did not wrap yourself in the mantle of another territory.
It was malignantly planned that you should be betrayed,
that swordpoints should pin the cloak of your flesh,
O Corc, son of Lugaid mac Aililla,
praised be your father's name, he was an honourable man!

O great Corc, around whom these very logs flame their flags,
Sweet Cashel itself mantles you so that you will reign over
    Femen with fine feasting.

Your good reign will deter bad weather.
In Munster of the hosts, you will receive hostages
so that you will be known as the Lion of Loch Léin.
Your name will spread over Ireland's great plain
and the family of Oengus will cover the surface of every land.
And shaven heads will come over the ocean carrying crooked
    staves.'

Now it happened that the poet who had recited this poetry was one of two
captives whom Corc had protected from the Leinstermen. He threw both
arms around Gruibne who said, "It is fitting indeed for us to welcome you.
But, tell me, who thought to benefit you by inscribing your shield with this
ogam. It was hardly good luck that he intended to befall you!'
    'What does it say?' Corc asked him.
    'This is what the writing says, "If the bearer of this shield arrives by day
at the court of Feredach, then we instruct that his head must be removed
before evening. If he arrives at night, then his head must be struck off
before morning." But that's not what will happen.'

Gruibne took Corc to his own house, borne on a hurdle by eight men. A month later, the poet went to speak with Feredach and left Corc outside. He told the king the whole story about how he had gone to look for his pigs and had been going to kill the man that he found, but that, when he read the ogam inscription, he was loathe to do so for, he said, 'The ogam on the shield read, "A son of Munster's kings is sent to you. If he arrives during the day, then your daughter is to be given to him before evening. If he arrives at night, she is to sleep with him before morning."'

'What appalling news!' said Feredach. 'Surely most people would be grieved if you brought him away alive.'

Then Gruibne set an honour price upon Corc to the value of King Feredach's weight in silver and Corc was invited in. Feredach welcome him honourably but did not give his daughter to Corc because the King was damned if he would give his daughter to a foreign mercenary. But this did not help him because the couple slept together secretly and she grew pregnant. They brought her out and she bore a son, though she did not tell anyone it was Corc's. It was judged that she should be burned, and the men of Alba gathered for the burning. It was a custom among them that any maiden who slept around before her betrothal should be burnt. Which is why those hills are called Mag Breg, or the Plain of Burning. It was decided by the men of Alba that the girl should be spared until the year's ending to see whether her son began to show any of the features, shapes, or voice of any of the tribe.

They came again to burn her, but she said, 'I will not bring the boy out to you.'

'You shall indeed, and in the presence of Feredach,' they said.

Before she was due to be burned, she brought the boy before Feredach and Corc.

'Now then, woman. Is this boy one of Corc's?'

'He is.'

Corc then said to her, 'I'll not take him from you, for he remains a bastard unless his grandfather acknowledges him.'

'I do acknowledge him,' said Feredach, 'The boy is yours.'

'Now he will be recognised,' said Corc.

Feredach then said to her, 'Get out, woman! and may no luck follow you!'

'No! she shall not go!' said Corc. 'There is no way that she is guilty.'

'She certainly is,' riposted Feredach.

'But she is not guilty,' said Corc. 'Each son belongs to his mother. Her guilt falls upon her son, upon her womb-burden.'

'Then let the boy be cast out,' said Feredach.

'He will not be cast out!' said Corc. 'He has not yet reached manhood. The son will pay for his mother's misdeed.'

'You have saved them both,' said Feredach.

'That is fortunate,' said Corc.

'Well, Corc,' said Feredach. 'Go sleep with your wife. You are the husband I would have chosen for her if I had had the deciding of it. I will pay her bride-price to the men of Alba.'

And so it was. Corc stayed in the east until she had borne him three sons.

The return of Corc

Feredach said, 'Well, Corc, take your sons and your wife to your own land, for it is not right that they should be away from their own country. Take with you the weight of three men in silver, as well as thirty warriors to accompany you.'

And so it was done. Corc arrived from the east with his thirty-strong warrior band, and made for Mag Femen. But such a strong blizzard fell upon them that they missed their path at Cnoc Graffand. (Now Corc's father was stricken with a sickness.) Corc and his company came northwards into the northern reaches of mag Femen.

That day, the swineherd of Aed, king of Muscraige, was guarding his pigs and later that night he went to King Aed and told him, 'I witnessed a wonder today on the northern ridges. I saw a yew-bush upon a stone, and a little oratory before it with a flag-stone near it. There were angels ascending and descending from that flagstone.'

Aed's druid said, 'Truly, that place will be the residence of the king of Munster for all time. Whoever is the first to kindle a fire beneath that yew, from him the line of the Munster kings shall descend.'

'Then let's go and light it,' said Aed.

'Wait until morning,' advised the druid.

Corc came to that same wondrous place after his wanderings and kindled there a fire for his wife and sons, so that when Aed came the next day, he found Corc with his family about him. Aed immediately recognised him and made him welcome, and gave Corc one of his sons to be held in honourable hostageship.

Now it happened that, after the death of Corc's father, Lugaid, there had been a dispute about the succession of the Munster kingship. But, a week after Corc's coming, he was established as the undisputed over-king of all Munster, with his residence at Cashel.

The hostage-surety offered to Corc by the Muscraige was the very first ever to be offered. After that, they were given freedom and one of their people became a queen at Cashel. As for the swineherd who had seen the foundation of Cashel, he and his descendents were forever afterwards free of tribute and taxes from the steward or king of Cashel. It became his task to raise the cry of kingship at the accession of a king of Cashel, receiving as a reward for his services the royal robe of the king. And this is how Corc's Cashel came into being, and why the descendants and seed of Corc mac Lugaid reigned at Cashel forever afterwards from that time.

34. The Exile of the Sons of Uisliu

(Longes mac nUislenn)

Translated by Vernam Hull

This story gives the history of Deirdriu from her conception and ill-starred love for Naoisi to their exile in Scotland and eventual return under the ageing Conchobor's treacherous protection. It remains one of the greatest love stories of Ireland. This early version omits much of the middle development of the story but is an earlier, leaner account of the lovers' exile and betrayal. The translation, by Vernam Hull, is taken from three MS sources, including *Lebor Laignech* of the twelfth century, *Leabhar Buidhe Leacain* of the fourteenth century and Egerton 1782 in the British Museum.

Why was the exile of the Sons of Uisliu? It is not hard [to relate].

The Ulstermen were drinking in the house of Feidlimid mac Daill, the storyteller of Conchobor. Now the wife of Feidlimid was attending upon the host, standing up and she being pregnant. Drinking horns and portions [of food] circled around, and they uttered a drunken shout. When they were about to go to bed, the woman came to her bed. While she was going across the middle of the house, the infant in her womb screamed so that it was heard throughout the whole enclosure. At that scream each man within arose from the other so that they were shoulder to shoulder in the house. Then Sencha mac Ailella issued a prohibition:

'Do not stir,' he said. 'Let the woman be brought to us in order that [it] may be known for what reason is this noise.' Thereupon the woman was brought to them.

Her consort, namely Feidlimid, then said:

> 'What [is] the violent noise that resounds,
> That rages throughout your bellowing womb?

The clamour between your sides – strongly it sounds
It crushes him who hears with ears.
My heart fears
Much terror that wounds severely.'

Thereupon she rushed to Cathbad, for he was a seer:

'Hear handsome Cathbad of the comely face,
A prince, a diadem great [and] mighty,
Who is magnified through the wizardries of druids,
Since I myself have not wise words
With reference to which Feidlimid might obtain
The illumination of knowledge,
Because a woman does not know
Whatever is wont to be in [her] womb,
Though it cried out in my womb's receptacle.'

Then Cathbad said:

'In the receptacle of your womb there cried out
A woman of yellow hair with yellow curls,
With comely, grey-blue irised eyes.
Her purplish-pink cheeks (are like) foxglove;
To the colour of snow I compare
The spotless treasure of her [. . .] teeth.
Lustrous (are) her scarlet-red lips
A woman for whom there will be many slaughters
Among the chariot-fighters of Ulster.
There screams in your womb which bellows
A woman, fair, tall (and) long-haired,
Concerning whom champions will contend,
Concerning whom high kings will ask.
They will be in the west with oppressive bodies of troops
Supported by the province of Conchobor.
Her scarlet-red lips will be
About her pearly teeth
Against whom high queens will be jealous,
Against her matchless, faultless form.'

Cathbad thereafter put his hand on the stomach of the woman so that
the infant resounded under his hand.

'True (it is),' he said, 'that a girl is there, and her name will be Derdriu, and concerning her there will be evil.'

Afterwards the girl was born, and Cathbad said:

'O Derdriu, you will destroy much
If you are comely-faced (and) fair of fame.
The Ulstermen will suffer during your lifetime,
O demure daughter of Feidlimid.

'Even afterwards jealousy will be
Ablaze on your account, O woman.
In your time it is – hear this
(That will be) the exile of the three sons of Uisliu.

'In your time it is that a violent deed
Will be performed then in Emain.
Even afterwards will be repented the destruction
(Done) under the protection of the very mighty Mac Roích.

'O woman with destiny, it is on account of you
(That will be) the exile of Fergus from the Ulstermen
And a deed for which weepings should lament,
The slaughter of Fiachna mac Conchobuir.

'O woman with destiny, it is for your crime
(That will be) the slaying of Gerrce mac Illadain
And a deed, the penalty of which is not less,
The killing of Eóghan mac Durthacht.

'You will perform a horrible, fierce deed
For anger against the king of the noble Ulstermen.
Your little grave will be everywhere.
It will be a famous tale, O Derdriu.'

'Let the girl be slain,' said the warriors.

'By no means,' said Conchobor. 'I shall carry off the girl tomorrow,' Conchobor added, 'and she will be reared according to my own will: and she will be the woman who will be in my company.'

And the Ulstermen did not dare to set him right with respect to it. That, moreover, was done. She was reared by Conchobor until she was by far the most beautiful girl who (ever) had been in Ireland. In a court apart it is that she was brought up, in order that no man of the

Ulstermen might see her up to the time that she should spend the night with Conchobor, and no person ever was allowed into that court except her foster-father and her foster-mother and Leborcham; for the last mentioned one could not be prevented, for she was a female satirist.

Once upon a time, accordingly, the foster-father of the maiden was skinning a weaned calf on snow outside in the winter to cook it for her. She saw a raven drinking the blood on the snow. Then she said to Leborcham:

'Beloved would be the one man on whom might [have] yonder three colours – that is, hair like the raven, and a cheek like blood, and a body like snow.'

'Dignity and fortune to you!' said Leborcham. 'He is not far from you. He is inside near to you, even Noisiu son of Uisliu.'

'I shall, indeed, not be well,' she said, 'until I see him.'

On one occasion, then, the aforementioned Noisiu was alone on the rampart of the earthwork (that is, of Emain) singing in a tenor voice. Melodious, however, was the tenor singing of the Sons of Uisliu. Each cow and each animal that heard (it), two thirds of surplus milk always was milked from them. Each person who heard it always had a sufficient peaceful disposition and musical entertainment. Good also were their arms. Although the (whole) province of the Ulstermen were in one place about them, they might not gain the victory over them on account of the excellence of the parrying and the self-defence, provided that every one of the three of them put his back against the other. As swift as hounds, moreover, they were at hunting. By virtue of (their) swiftness they used to kill the wild animals.

While, therefore, the aforesaid Noisiu was alone outside, she quickly stole out to him as if to go past him, and he did not recognise her.

'Fair,' he said, 'is the heifer that goes past me.'

'Heifers,' she said, 'are bound to be big where bulls are not wont to be.'

'You have the bull of the province,' he said, 'namely, the king of the Ulstermen.'

'I would choose between the two of you,' she said, 'and I would take a young bullock like you.'

'By no means!' he said. 'Even because of Cathbad's prophecy.'

'Do you say that in order to reject me?'

'It assuredly will be for that reason,' he said. Therewith she made a leap to him and grasped both ears on his head.

'These (are) two ears of shame and of derision,' she said, 'unless you take me away with you.'

'Go away from me, O woman,' he said.

'You shall have that,' she said.

Thereupon, his tenor song arose from him. As the Ulstermen yonder heard his tenor song, each man of them arose from the other.

The Sons of Uisliu went out to hinder their brother.

'What ails you?' they said. 'Let not the Ulstermen slay one another for your crime.'

Then he related to them what had been done to him.

'Evil will ensue,' the warriors said. 'Although there may be (evil resulting therefrom), you shall not be under disgrace as long as we shall be alive. We shall go with her into another land. There is not in Ireland a king who will not give welcome to us.'

That was their decision. They set out that night with their hundred and fifty warriors, women, dogs and servants; and among them was Derdriu mingled in with everybody (else).

For a great while they were under protection all around Ireland, and often through the snares and guiles of Conchobor their destruction was attempted from Ess Ruaid southwestwards round about northeastwards again to Benn Etair. The Ulstermen, however, chased them, then, over (the Irish sea) into the territory of Scotland. They settled down there in the desert. After the mountain game failed them, they turned aside upon the cattle of the men of Scotland in order to appropriate it to themselves. The latter went on a single day to destroy them, whereupon they proceeded to the king of Scotland, and he took them into his household following. They assumed mercenary service with him and placed their houses on the green. On account of the maiden the houses were made so that no-one with them might see her in order that they might not be killed with respect to her.

Once upon a time, therefore, early in the morning the steward went and made a circuit about their house. He saw the couple asleep. Afterwards, he went and awakened the king.

'I have not found,' he said, 'a woman equal to you until today. Along with Noisiu son of Uisliu there is a woman worthy of the king of the Western World. Let Noisiu be killed immediately, and let the woman spend the night with you,' the steward added.

'No,' the king said, 'but you shall go every day to beseech her secretly for me.'

That is done. However, what the steward said to her at any time she used to relate, at once, that night to her consort. Since one never could attain anything with respect to her, the Sons of Uisliu often were enjoined to go into dangers, battles and hazards in order that they might be killed. Nevertheless, as regards each slaughter they were doughty so that one never could attain anything with respect to them from these attempts.

After consultation with her regarding it, the men of Scotland were assembled to kill them. She related that to Noisiu.

'Depart hence,' she said. 'Unless you shall have gone away by to-night, you will be killed to-morrow.'

That night they went away until they were on an island of the sea. That was related to the Ulstermen.

'Grievous it is, O Conchobor,' the Ulstermen said, 'for the Sons of Uisliu to fall in hostile lands through the crime of a bad woman. It were better to be lenient with them and to feed them and not to slay them and for them to come to the land than for them to fall at the hands of their foes.'

'Let them come, therefore,' Conchobor said, 'and let sureties go for them.'

That (message) was brought to them.

'We welcome it,' they said. 'We shall go, and let Fergus come for us as surety and Dubthach and Cormac mac Conchobor.' They went and gave them accompaniment from the sea.

With respect to Fergus, however, by the counsel of Conchobor a contention took place to invite him to ale-banquets, for the Sons of Uisliu said that they would not eat (any) food in Ireland except at first the food of Conchobor. Then Fiachu mac Fergusa went with them, and Fergus and Dulathach remained behind. The Sons of Uisliu came until they were on the green of Emain. Then, moreover, Eóghan mac Durthacht, king of Fernmag, came for peace with Conchobor, for he had been at strife with him for a long period. He it is who had been entrusted to kill them, and the mercenaries of Conchobor were about him (Conchobor) in order that they might not come to him.

The Sons of Uisliu were standing in the middle of the green, and the women were in their seats on the rampart of Emain. Eóghan, accordingly, went up to them in his body of troops along the green. The son of Fergus, however, came until he was on one side of Noisiu. Eóghan welcomed them with a thrust of the great spear into Noisiu so that his back broke through it. Therewith, the son of Fergus threw himself and put both arms around Noisiu and brought him under him and cast himself down upon him, and thus it was that Noisiu was struck from above through the son of Fergus. Thereafter, they (the Sons of Uisliu) were killed throughout the green so that none escaped thence, save those who went by point of spear and by edge of sword; and she [Derdriu] was brought over to Conchobor so that she was beside him, and her hands were bound behind her back.

That, then, was related to Fergus and Dubthach and Cormac. They came and performed at once great deeds. Dubthach killed Mane, Conchobor's son, and by a single thrust Fiachna, son of Feidelm, Conchobor's daughter, was dispatched. Fergus slew Traigthren, son of Traiglethan and his brother. With respect to them, Conchobor's honour was outraged, and afterwards battle was joined between them on a single day so that three hundred of the Ulstermen fell among them. Before morning, the maidens of Ulster were put to death by Dubthach, and Emain was burned by Fergus. Thereupon they went to Ailill and to Medb, for they knew that that couple would be able to support them; and for the Ulstermen, moreover, it was not a refuge of love. Three thousand was the number of those exiled. To the end of sixteen years neither weeping nor trembling ceased in Ulster through them, but each single night (there was) weeping and trembling through them.

A year, now, [Derdriu] was with Conchobor, and during that time she did not smile a laughing smile, and she did not partake of her sufficiency of food or of sleep, and she did not raise her head from her knee. Whenever, therefore, they brought the musicians to her, then she recited this following extempore poem:

> Though fair you deem the eager warriors
> Who stride about in Emain after an expedition,
> More nobly used to march to their dwelling
> The three very heroic sons of Uisliu.

> Noisiu with good hazel-mead
> Him I washed at the fire –
> Arddan with a stag or a fine pig,
> A load (was) over Aindle's tall back.

> Though sweet you deem the goodly mead

Which the battle-glorious Mac Nessa drinks,
I had heretofore – ocean over (its) brink –
Frequent refection that was sweeter.

As often as modest Noisiu had spread out
The cooking hearth on the martial plain of the forest,
Sweeter was always than each honeyed food
What the son of Uisliu had contrived.
Though melodious you deem at all times
Pipers and hornblowers,
This is my confession today:
I have heard music that was more melodious.

Melodious used to deem Conchobor, your king,
Pipers and hornblowers;
More melodious I used to deem – fame of hosts
The strain which the Sons of Uisliu used to sing.

Noisiu's voice (was like) the sound of a wave;
To hear him always was (like) melodious music.
The baritone of Arddan was good
The tenor song of Aindle (on his way) to his shieling.
Noisiu – his sepulchral mound has been made.
Sad was the accompaniment.
For him I have poured out – host over a height -
The deadly draught of which he has died.

Beloved (is) the little crop of hair with yellow beauty
Comely (is) the man, even (. . .)
Sorrowful it is (indeed) that I do not expect today
To await the son of Uisliu.

Beloved (is) the desire, steadfast (and) just;
Beloved (is) the warrior, noble (and) very modest.
After a journey beyond the forest's fence,
Beloved (is) the (. . .) in the early morning.

Beloved (is) the grey eye that women used to love;
Fierce it used to be against foes.
After a circuit of the forest – a noble union
Beloved (is) the tenor song through a dark great wood.

I do not sleep now,
And I do not redden my fingernails.
Joy, it comes not into my observation
Since it will not lead hither the son of Tindell.
I do not sleep
Half of the night as I lie.
My reason is agitated about the hosts;
Not only do I not eat, but I do not laugh.

Joy, today, (for it) I have no leisure
In the gathering of Emain (there) nobles are thronged
Nor peace, nor delight, nor ease,
Nor a big house, nor fair adornment.

Whenever Conchobor, moreover, mollified her, then she recited this
following extempore poem:

O Conchobor, what ails you?
For me you have [made] sorrow under weeping.
Yes, indeed, as long as I may abide
My love for you will not be of very great account.
What I deemed most beautiful on earth,
And what was most beloved,
You have carried off from me – great the crime –
So that I shall not see it until my death.

His absence, it grieves me
How the son of Uisliu shows (it) to me:
A jet-black little cairn over a white body;
It was well-known beyond (those of) a multitude of men.

Both purple cheeks (were) fairer than a river meadow,
Red the lips, eyebrows of beetle colour;
The pearly row of shining teeth
(Was) like the noble hue of snow.

Well-known was his bright apparel
Among the warrior bands of the men of Scotland.
Fair (and) purple (was) the mantle – a fitting union
With its border of pure gold.

Of satin (was) the tunic – a treasure with substance
On which there were a hundred gems – a gentle multitude.
To adorn it, clear it is,
(Were) fifty ounces of *findruine* [white-silver].

A sword with a golden pommel (was) in his hand,
Two green spears with a javelin point,
A shield with a rim of yellow gold,
And a boss of silver upon it.

Fair Fergus has committed trespass against us
By bringing us over the great sea.
He has sold his honour for ale.
His great deeds have declined.

Though on the plain might be
The Ulstermen around Conchobor,
I would give them all without concealment
For the companionship of Noisiu son of Uisliu.
Do not break today my heart;
Soon shall I reach my early grave.
Sorrow is stronger than the sea,
If you are wise, O Conchobor.

'What do you see that you hate most?' said Conchobor.
    'You, to be sure,' she said, 'and Eóghan mac Durthacht!'
    'You shall be, indeed, a year with Eóghan,' said Conchobor.
    Thereupon he brought her beside Eóghan. On the following day,
they went to the assembly of Macha. She was behind Eóghan in the
chariot. She had promised that she would not see her two companions
on earth on the same occasion.
    'Well, O Derdriu,' said Conchobor, 'it is a sheep's eye between two
rams that you make between me and Eóghan.'
    There was a great stone boulder in front of her. She dashed her head
against the stone until she had made a mass of fragments of her head so
that she died.

DEATHS

35. The Death of Conchobar Mac Nessa

(Aíðeð Conchobar meíc Nessa)

Translated by Kuno Meyer

There are several versions of this text, all following more or less the same direction, but varying in detail. Most of what follows is from the *Book of Leinster*, but since the ending is missing from this we have added one taken from a MS in Edinburgh University: MS xl. The Christianisation of the story probably covers a far older version, now lost, in which there was another reason for Conchobar's outburst, but the knowledge of the death of Christ expressed by the druid Bacrach is interesting and has given rise to a good deal of speculation as to whether the druids really did know something of the Crucifixion at this time, rather than, as one might suppose, later on when word of it finally reached Ireland via the first monks to reach the Celtic world. It shows a willingness on the part of the clerics to merge the two traditions rather than purging the ancient tales of their original pagan content.

Once upon a time the men of Ulster were greatly intoxicated in Emain Macha. Thence there arise great contentions and comparison of trophies between them, even between Conall and Cú Chulainn and Loegaire. 'Bring me,' said Conall, 'the brain of Mesgegra, so that I may talk to the competing warriors.' At that time it was a custom with the men of Ulster to take the brains out of the head of every warrior whom they slew in single combat, and to mix lime with them, so that they were made into hard balls. And whenever they were in contention or at comparison of trophies, these were brought to them, so that they had them in their hands.

'Well, O Conchobar,' said Conall, 'until the competing warriors perform a deed like this in single combat, they are not capable of comparing trophies with me.'

'That is true,' said Conchobar.

Then the brain was put upon the shelf upon which it was always kept. On the morrow every one went his own way to his sport. Then Cet, the son of Matu, went upon a round of adventures in Ulster. This Cet was the most troublesome pest that was in Ireland. This is the way he went, across the green of Emain, having with him three warriors' heads of the men of Ulster.

While the jesters (of Emain) were at play with the brain of Mesgegra, this is what one jester said to the other. Cet hears that. He snatches the brain out of the hand of one of them, and carries it off; for he knew that it had been foretold of Mesgegra that he would avenge himself after his death. In every battle and in every combat which the men of Connaught had with those of Ulster, Cet used to carry the brain in his girdle to see whether he could compass a famous deed by slaying a man of Ulster with it.

Once then Cet went eastwards until he took a drove of cows from the men of the Rosses. The men of Ulster overtook him in pursuit after him. Then the men of Connaught came up from the other ride to rescue him. A battle is fought between them. Conchobar himself went into the battle. And it was then that the women of Connaught begged Conchobar to come aside so that they might see his shape. For there was not on earth the shape of a human being like the shape of Conchobar, both for beauty and figure and dress, for size and symmetry and proportion, for eye and hair and whiteness, for wisdom and manners and eloquence, for raiment and nobleness and equipment, for weapons and wealth and dignity, for bearing and valour and race. That Conchobar was faultless indeed. However, it was by the advice of Cet that the women importuned Conchobar. Then he went aside alone to be seen by the women.

Cet, however, went until he was in the midst of the women. He adjusts the brain of Mesgegra in the sling, and throws it so that it hit the crown of Conchobar's head, so that two-thirds of it entered his head, [and] he fell upon his head forward to the ground. The men of Ulster ran towards him, and carried him off from Cet. On the brink of the ford of Daire Dá Báeth it was that Conchobar fell. His grave is there where he fell, and a pillar-stone at his head, and another at his feet.

[. . .]

The men of Connaught are then routed to Scé Aird na Con. The men of Ulster are driven eastwards again to the ford of Daire Dá Báeth.

'Let me be carried out of this!' said Conchobar. 'I shall give the kingship of Ulster to anyone who will carry me as far as my house.'

'I will carry thee,' said Cenn Berraide his own attendant. He puts a cord around him, and carries him upon his back to Ardachad of the Fews. The attendant's heart broke within him. Hence is the saying 'Cenn Berraide's kingship over Ulster, to wit, the king upon his back for (only) half the day.'

However, the fight was kept up after the king from one hour of the day to the same hour on the next day, after which the men of Ulster were routed.

In the meantime his physician was brought to Conchobar, even Fingen. 'Tis he who would know from the smoke that arose from a house how many were ill in the house, and every disease that was in it. 'Well,' said Fingen, 'if the stone is taken out of thy head, thou wilt be dead forthwith. If it is not taken out, however, I would heal thee, but it will be a blemish for thee.'

'It is easier for us,' said the men of Ulster, 'to bear the blemish than his death.'

His head was then healed; and it was stitched with thread of gold, for the colour of Conchobar's hair was the same as the colour of gold. And the physician said to Conchobar that he should be on his guard lest anger should come on him, and that he should not mount a horse, that he should not have connexion with a woman, that he should not eat food greedily, and that he should not run.

In that doubtful state, then, he was as long as he lived, even seven years, and he was not capable of action, but remained in his seat only, until he heard that Christ had been crucified by the Jews. At that time a great trembling came over the elements, and the heavens and the earth shook with the enormity of the deed that was then done, even Jesus Christ, the Son of the living God, to be crucified without guilt.

'What is this?' said Conchobar to his druid. 'What great evil is being done on this day?'

'That is true, indeed,' said the druid [who then tells the story of the Crucifixion].

'Awful is that deed,' said Conchobar.

'That man, now,' said the druid, 'was born in the same night in which thou wast born, even on the eighth before the calends of January, though the year was not the same.'

It was then that Conchobar believed. And he was one of the two men that had believed in God in Ireland before the coming of the Faith, Morann being the other man.

Then Conchobor said: 'A thousand armed men shall fall by me in the rescue of Christ.'

Thereupon he sprang towards his two lances and brandished them stoutly so that they broke in his hand; and then he took his sword in his hand and attacked the wood around him so that he made a plain of the wood, even Mag Lhmraige in the land of the men of the Rosses. And he said this: "'Tis thus I should avenge Christ upon the Jews and upon those that crucified him, if I could reach them.'

This is the last thing that Conchobar said, [for] through that fury the brain of Mesgegra sprang out of his head so that his own brains came upon him, so that he died of it. And hence all say: 'A dweller in Heaven is Conchobar for the wish which he has uttered.'

[Afterwards] God revealed the brain of Mesgegra to Buite the son of Bronach, so that at this day it is Buite's pillow; and everyone upon whom the brain of Mesgegra goes as he goes to death is sure of Heaven. And there is a saying that it will be carried southward into Leinster, and that thereafter Leinster will have superiority. So this is the Death of Conchobar as far as that.

36. The Death of
Conn Cetchathach

(Aíðeð Conn Cetchathach)

Translated by Caitlín Matthews

Conn of the Hundred Battles is a legendary king whom the Annals situate in the second century CE. He is the father of Art, whose story we told in *Encyclopaedia of Celtic Wisdom* p. 376 and to Connla whose story appears on p. 385 of the present volume. He has a special role in the history of the Irish kings in that he is the first to hear the prophecy of his lineage from the Lia Faíl, literally 'the Prophetic Stone' known also as the Stone of Destiny. It is he who gives his name to the upper half of Ireland which is known as Leth Cuinn. This story makes much of Conn's unopposed status as High-King, and tells of his defeat and death at the hands of the Ulstermen. Conn's boast underscores what was commonly understood as the benefits of a good kingship: fertility and peace were the outcome of such a reign as his. The Feast of Tara at the time of Samhain was one of those sacred occasions when people laid aside their arms to meet peacefully to arbitrate in disputes and implement governmental decisions, which is why Conn is so under-guarded.

He is given the opportunity by his sister, Aoife, to magically protect himself with the 'mantle of unwisdom,' in the last frame of the story, but he choses not to, since it was not considered manly to use magical or female protections. We find a similar theme in the fourteenth century poem Sir *Gawain and the Green Knight*, where Gawain accepts such a protection from Lady Bercilak. Aoife's mantle may be a form of magical invisibility spell rather than an actual cloak, but we are not told about it. Other supernatural elements come into the story, where Conn's death is prophesied by the same faery woman, Roithniamh or 'Sky-Wheel,' who announced his birth. She stands in the tradition of the family *bean-sídhe* or banshee, whose duty is to announce the imminent departure of the living.

Our translation is from a seventeeth century MS, no. G448 in the National Library of Ireland. Other earlier versions appear in the *Book of Fermoy*. For more background on this text, see Caoimhín Breatnach's edition of this text.

Conn Cetchathach, son of Fedlimid, son of Tuathal was a high-spirited, firm-minded, argumentative but perceptive high-king whose accession to the high-kingship and supreme sovereignty of Ireland, in the time of battle and conflict, caused no dissatisfaction. Between him and Tibraide, son of Mál, son of Rochraidhe, there was conflict over the fact that Conn had killed Tibraide's father, Mál. This happened when an argument arose concerning the division of Ireland between Conn and Eóghan Mór. On the appointed day of battle at Mag Tualaing when the four regional kings of Ireland came against Conn and the Connachtmen, Eóghan Mór sent messengers to Mál, the king of Ulster, pointing out the fact that he might use the coming battle to avenge himself upon Conn. Hearing this, Mál mustered his army from every airt and made ready to leave. But when Conn got wind of the king of Ulster's coming to the Boyne with all his allies, he sent to Conall of Cruachan and all the Connachtmen, advising them to ambush the king of Ulster and his host, so that they couldn't assist the Munstermen.

Hearing these words, Conall and his men marched to where Conn lay at Knowth. Conn was delighted to see them and shared his plans with them. 'Let it be done so,' said Conall of the Connachta, 'because if Ulster and Munster join forces it would be hard to give battle against them.' Conn and all the Connachtmen moved speedily along the easy roads until they came to the Boyne where they came upon the king of Ulster's camp on this side of the river. Upon seeing each other, Conn unfurled his standard and both sides gave battle until the Ulstermen suffered defeat and King Mál had been killed. His son, Tibraide, acceded to the Ultonian kingship after his father's death. Conn kept in hostage some of the king of Ulster's relatives at that time, and Tibraide sent to them, commanding them to betray Conn to him.

It was Art Coirbthe, son of Fiacha Suidhe, whom the hostages sent back to Tibraide to tell him about how he might surprise Conn. Art worked against Conn's interests by telling Tibraide and Ailill Gaibhne to come with a hundred and fifty warriors dressed like women, with white hoods over their head-dresses and with swords hidden under their clothes, and with spears secreted under their chariots. Now Conn was in Tuaithemhair preparing the Feast of Tara, completely unprotected by troops. The pretend women were to say that they were Corb Mhór, daughter of Breasal mac Cearb and the women of Ulster, and that they had come to speak with (Conn's sister) Aoife, daughter of Fedlimid. Corb Mhór was none other than Tibraide's own mother. This was on a Sunday, eleven nights before Samhain, that the Ulstermen came to trick Conn.

Then it was that Roithniamh, daughter of Umhaill Uarchoraigh of the *sídhe* of Ochta Clithigh, stepped on to the grass of Tara. She was a faery woman, a powerful magician, and she chanted this poem, publically prophesying the death of Conn:

> 'Sorrow of the earth, feast of travail,
> gashing of the roast, Tuaith Theamhair;
> the body of Conn is tamed
> by young women from Emhain.

> 'Tara's green places will be laid waste
> because of Conn's death upon Ethne's ground;
> the Boyne river will be without harvest,
> it will be empty, no salmon, no fin.

> 'Taillte will be no shelter for young women
> because of Conn's betrayal, cleared out by a woman;
> wild-boar will tear up the earth so green;
> no horse-racing in pleasant Taillte.

> 'Cnoc Tlachta will be without its beacon
> of the young men on that cold night;
> severing of heads from fair flesh;
> on Samhain eve, ill-fortuned death.

> 'The great gathering of Uisnech without people,
> because of Conn's death, everyone grieving;
> no one will be left seated,
> not one person will remain.

> 'Eochaidh Fionn who made this treachery,
> and Fiacha Suidhe so carefree,
> his family will be tearful
> because of the Ultonian assault.

> 'With the noble young women is my grieving;
> nearer to each of them is the danger;
> although they make merry in hall,
> a more fitting mood would be black sorrow.'

The young men of Tara and the heroes of Meath said that the woman's poem was a false recital. 'It is not false,' said the druid Maol, 'in that it prophesies Conn's death.' And the druid asked her more about it. 'It was I,' she said, 'who recited every particular concerning Conn's birth while he was yet in the womb.' The following recital was one she made about him:

> 'The sun's arising will be forever sunset,
> the moon dark over the smooth lands.
> The hazels will not yield their harvest,
> nor the rivers be full of fish,
> the land will suppress its heavy yield,
> failure of mast and great goods
> will befall the region of Tara
> if contentious Conn is killed.
> The son of generous Mál
> will murder Conn because of an old dispute,
> right in the middle of these bold heroes.
> To the druid Maol it will be evil news,
> the end that resolves this dreadful conflict.'

'What great and dreadful news you bring us, woman!' said the druid Maol. Roithniamh said goodbye but no-one noticed which way she went as she left them.

Tibraide and the Ultonian warriors came to Tulach in Toirléime above Tuaththeamhair and hid there as they had been instructed (by Art). The next morning, Aoife, daughter of Fedlimid, set about shearing her sheep upon the green at Tuaththeamhair along with her women, leaving Conn still in bed, protected by too few warriors.

So it was that Conn of a Hundred Battles arose from his bed shaking off sleep even as the radiant sun arose in the sky from the heavy clods of the earth. Two were the royal, most noble, pre-eminent, warlike ones who rose from their pillows that morning. First was the sun in its rising, as a steadfast, ever-clear shield-boss or like a lively, graceful, sparkling, spherical apple in its motion along the zones of the great Regulator.

Second, but as glorious in appearance, was the high-king rising from his pillow at that time.

This was the appearance of Conn: his face was noble, honourable, very wide, mobile yet settled, clear, pleasant, fair-complexioned, muscularly dynamic and very handsome. Two fair curly locks of hair fell over his forehead. Two fine, slender, dark eyebrows curved in lordly fashion over his searching, brilliant, sea-green eyes, the very same as Fedlimid's. His hair foamed just like the many-shaped, wondrous cotton-grass, fine-braided, fair hair which spilled from under the helmet encircling his royal head. Against his skin he wore a shirt of yellow silk embroidered with white bronze and worked with exquisite gold thread, that fell to his feet. Upon his head, he donned his gold-bordered, brown-coloured helmet to conceal his broad skull from danger. His royal red over-tunic of high-kingship had been prepared for him and he put it on: there were four green eyelets let into it and it fastened with a bright gold brooch. Between his feet and the ground were two broad-toed sandals of bronze, fastened with gold buckles. In his hand was his decorated, gold-hafted sword from the weapon-rack.

The five warriors guarding the king, each man directly responsible to him, also rose and dressed in their chain-link shirts over their expensively-fastened tunics, and over all they wore clean half-cloaks of bright blue, green and yellow, fastening their outer clothes with flexible brooches. Their sharp, ivory-hafted swords they clutched in their right hands. About their necks were blue-backed, shining-sided torques and, for their protection, their strong-headed spears. These five were handsome, curly-haired warriors, continually attendant upon Conn to punish the regional kings who contended together in parochial disputes.

They passed Conn his crimson shield with its five shining circles, and his triumphantly-achieving spear which had humbled many a regional king. 'It was not to exhibit them to maidens or women that my arms were made of gold,' said Conn. 'If everything that is justly mine were taken away, it were as if the Frozen Sea had been made low, or the motion of the universe had been stopped or as if the stars above had been reordered. The man who would dare to bring about my downfall, would be unable to succeed to the sovereignty or enjoy its fruits. Among the seed of Ior, Eibhear or Eireann, my equal has never been seen. And never since my accession to the Kingship of Ireland has Leth Mug refused the cattle-tribute owed to Leth Conn. With the exception of Connal of Cruachan and the Connachtment, none has opposed me in battle. I have defeated Eóghan Mór, son of the poisonous Mog Neit, and overcome the lords of Munster and Leinster in battle. Since I took the kingship, Ireland has enjoyed a hundredfold increase in its harvests. Every lesser chieftain has had a sevenfold increase from the ploughing of their furrows since my reign. Seven bushels of grain tribute come to Tara from each of the long, fair furrows. Each full-leafed oaktree has fattened fifty pigs in my reign. Every river estuary in Ireland has enriched its lands with treasure from the sea. There is no dairy-cow in Ireland whose udders does not fill with seven times the increase of its first milk, and it is a rare thing for the first calf of each cow to lack sufficient nurture for fifty from just one milking.'

And Tibraid mac Cleitach said to him, 'Noble king, do not imagine that your reign is at its end, for corn-yields fall before they increase.'

Then Conn and his five body-guards came to where the women were shearing their sheep, to the south of Tuaitheamhair, and there they remained, for is it not said that there are three places that we cannot avoid – the sod of one's birth, the sod of one's death and the sod of one's burial? Not long afterwards, Conn and his body-guard saw the troop of disguised women comes towards them.

'Who are those women approaching us from the hill?' Conn asked. 'It seems to me that they don't look much like women.' He assumed that they were the maidens from the retinue of the Ulster women.

'Corb Mhór, mother of Tibraide mac Mál, comes with gifts for me this Feast of Tara,' said Aoife, Conn's sister.

But soon they saw that it was warriors coming towards them and that they had taken off their female clothes, emboldened at the sight of Conn so ill-guarded.

'That's no band of women at all,' cried Conn. 'It is the Ulstermen! Art son of Fiacha Suidhe has betrayed me to them.' To his body-guard he said, 'Do your very best in this fix! It is a shame that the heroes of Tara, the men of Odhbha and the champions of Cruachan were not beside me! And I thought that conflict and battle in Ireland had been ended by my killing of Eóghan Mór!'

Then those five, excessively brave warriors who were with Conn, rose up. They were Ailill mac Luchta, Asal mac Forannán of Formhaol, Eanna mac Deadhadh of Leinster, Tibraide mac Clieteach of Tuaithmhidhe and Foitin Fionnabhair mac Fionchon Eachtach. These five swore to serve Conn, to defend him and bring him back safely from the Ultonians.

'Tell me, will I enjoy a long life with you after this, one free of opposition to my reign?'

'You will not,' they said.

'If that is so,' said Conn, 'do not prevail upon me to retreat. If my last day had not dawned, the Ultonians would not have found me so vulnerably guarded as this. Good fellows, show courage on your own account.'

Aoife approached Conn and said, 'Lord king, I have a method of deliverance. The mantle of unwisdom will protect you!'

'That I will not take from you,' said Conn.

Then Tibraide Tíreach and the men of Ulster attached Conn and his bodyguard. Conn of a Hundred Battles showed no weakness, fear or cowardice but confronted the king of Ulster and his men. Tibraide struck him a frenzied blow with his spear and the five body-guards raised their arms and each wounded him. When the Ultonians saw this, they sent fifty warriors against Conn. His five body-guards shielded him as they went forward together into battle but soon they were all killed by the Ultonian forces. When Conn saw that, he uncovered his broad-bladed spear and cast it against the king of Ulster, but Tibraide cast it back at Conn. So it was that the king whom no-one had previously dared to oppose was slain at that place by the king of Ulster and his host. They soon fled the field in case the champions of the people of Tara came against them. And this was how Conn was murdered.

37. The Death of Cú Chulainn

(Brislech mór Maige Muirthemne)

Translated by Whitley Stokes

In spite of the embarrassment of describing the death of Ulster's unconquerable champion, the ancient Irish poets could not resist the drama of his last stand (though of course this was not his last appearance, for he rides again in 'Cú Chulainn's Spirit Chariot') . The result was 'The Great Rout of Muirthemne', *Brislech mór Maige Muirthemne*, generally known as 'The Death of Cú Chulainn'. Composed, probably as early as the eighth century, by a writer of unusual ability, it is one of the most striking pieces of early Irish literature. The closing passage describing Cú Chulainn's death, tied to a pillar so that he can die standing up, is genuinely heroic in conception and in style. Fully conscious that his end is near, Cú Chulainn goes forth to battle despite the omens that warn him; like Conaire in 'The Destruction of Da Derga's Hostel' (pp. 2890–324), he is forced to break the taboos upon which his life depends (that he should not eat dog because he is named after 'the Hound of Culainn' but at the same time could not refuse a feast) and at length falls fighting single-handed against a band of vengeful enemies whose own fathers, in several cases, he had killed in battle. The final moments of the fight, and its aftermath, are astonishingly powerful, even today. Here is a great hero dying by the hand of a cowardly murderer; even the death of his charioteer rises to great heights of poetry. Cú Chulainn's own final moments are something few can forget once they have read them; they are the heart and soul of epic and mythic story-telling.

When Cú Chulainn's foes came for the last time against him, his land was filled with smoke and flame, the weapons fell from their racks, and the day of his death drew nigh. The evil tidings were brought to him, and the maiden Leborcham bade him arise, though he was worn out with fighting in defence of the plain of Muirthemne, and Niam, wife of Conall the Victorious, also spoke to him; so he sprang to his arms, and flung his mantle around him; but the brooch fell and pierced his foot, forewarning him. Then he took his shield and ordered his charioteer Loeg to harness his horse, the Gray of Macha.

'I swear by the gods by whom my people swear,' said Loeg, 'though the men of Conchobar's province were around the Gray of Macha, they could not bring him to the chariot. I never refused thee till today. If thou wilt, come thou, and speak with the Gray himself.'

Cú Chulainn went to him. And thrice did the horse turn his left side to his master. On the night before, the Mórrígu had broken the chariot, for she liked not Cú Chulainn's going to the battle, for she knew that he would not come again to Emain Macha. Then Cú Chulainn reproached his horse, saying that he was not wont to deal thus with his master.

Thereat the Gray of Macha came and let his big round tears of blood fall on Cú Chulainn's feet. And then Cú Chulainn leapt into the chariot, and drove it suddenly southwards along the Road of Midluachar.

And Leborcham met him and besought him not to leave them; and the thrice fifty queens who were in Emain Macha and who loved him cried to him with a great cry. And when he turned his chariot to the right, they gave a scream of wailing and lamentation, and smote their hands, for they knew that he would not come to them again.

The house of his nurse that had fostered him was before him on the road. He used to go to it whenever he went driving past her southwards and from the south. And she kept for him always a vessel with drink therein. Now he drank a drink and fared forth, bidding his nurse farewell. Then he saw three Crones, blind of the left eye, before him on the road. They had cooked on spits of rowantree a dog with poisons and spells. And one of the things that Cú Chulainn was bound not to do was going to a cooking-hearth and consuming the food. And another of the things that he must not do was eating his namesake's [i.e. dog's] flesh. He sped on and was about to pass them, for he knew that they were not there for his good.

Then said a Crone to him: 'Visit us, O Cú Chulainn.'

'I will not visit you in sooth,' said Cú Chulainn.

'The food is only a hound,' said she. 'Were this a great cooking hearth thou wouldst have visited us. But because what is here is little, thou comest not. Unseemly are the great who endure not the little and poor.'

Then he drew nigh to her, and the Crone gave him the shoulder-blade of the hound out of her left hand. And then Cú Chulainn ate it out of his left hand, and put it under his left thigh. The hand that took it and the thigh under which he put it were seized from trunk to end, so that the normal strength abode not in them.

Then he drove along the Road of Midluachar around Sliab Fuait; and his enemy Erc son of Cairbre saw him in his chariot, with his sword shining redly in his hand, and the light of valour hovering over him, and his three-hued hair like strings of golden thread over the edge of the anvil of some cunning craftsman.

'That man is coming towards us, O men of Erin!' said Erc; 'await him.' So they made a fence of their linked shields, and at each corner Erc made them place two of their bravest feigning to fight each other, and a satirist with each of these pairs, and he told the satirists to ask Cú Chulainn for his spear, for the sons of Calatin had prophesied of his spear that a king would be slain by it, unless it were given when demanded. And he made the men of Erin utter a great cry. And Cú Chulainn rushed against them in his chariot, performing his three thunder-feats; and he plied his spear and sword; so that the halves of their heads and skulls and hands and feet and their red bones were scattered broadcast throughout the plain of Muirthemne, in number like to the sands of the sea and stars of heaven and dew drops of May, flakes of snow, hail stones, leaves in the forest, butter cups on Mag Breg, and grass under the hoofs of herds on a day in summer. And grey was the field with their brains after that onslaught and plying of weapons which Cú Chulainn dealt unto them.

Then he saw one of the pairs of warriors contending together, and the satirist called on him to intervene, and Cú Chulainn leaped at them, and with two blows of his fist dashed out their brains.

'That spear to me!' said the satirist.

'I swear what my people swear,' said Cú Chulainn, 'thou dost not need it more than I do. The men of Erin are upon me here and I am attacking them.'

'I will revile thee if thou givest it not,' said the satirist.

'I have never yet been reviled because of my niggardliness or my churlishness.'

With that Cú Chulainn flung the spear at him with its handle foremost, and it passed through his head and killed nine on the other side of him.

And Cú Chulainn drove through the host, but Lugaid son of Cú Roi got the spear.

'What will fall by this spear, O sons of Calatin?' asked Lugaid.

'A king will fall by that spear,' said the sons of Calatin.

Then Lugaid flung the spear at Cú Chulainn's chariot, and it reached the charioteer, Loeg mac Riangabra, and all his bowels came forth on the cushion of the chariot.

Then said Loeg, 'Bitterly have I been wounded, etc.'

Thereafter Cú Chulainn drew out the spear, and Loeg bade him farewell. Then said Cú Chulainn: 'Today I shall be warrior and charioteer also.'

Then he saw the second pair contending, and one of them said it was a shame for him not to intervene. And Cú Chulainn sprang upon them and dashed them into pieces against a rock.

'That spear to me, O Cú Chulainn,' said the satirist.

'I swear what my people swear, thou dost not need the spear more than I do. On my hand and my valour and my weapons it rests today to sweep the four provinces of Erin today from the plain of Muirthemne.'

'I will revile thee,' said the satirist.

'I am not bound to grant more than one request this day, and, moreover, I have already paid for my honour.'

'I will revile Ulster for thy default,' said the satirist.

'Never yet has Ulster been reviled for my refusal nor for my churlishness. Though little of my life remains to me, Ulster shall not be reviled this day.'

Then Cú Chulainn cast his spear at him by the handle and it went through his head and killed nine behind him, and Cú Chulainn drove through the host even as he had done before.

Then Erc son of Cairbre took the spear. 'What shall fall by this spear, O sons of Calatin?' said Erc son of Cairbre

'Not hard to say: a king falls by that spear,' said the sons of Calatin.

'I heard you say that a king would fall by the spear which Lugaid long since cast.'

'And that is true,' said the sons of Calatin. 'Thereby fell the king of the charioteers of Erin, namely Cú Chulainn's charioteer, Loeg mac Riangabra.'

Now Erc cast the spear at Cú Chulainn, and it lighted on his horse, the Gray of Macha. Cú Chulainn snatched out the spear. And each of them bade the other farewell. Thereat the Gray of Macha left him with half the yoke under his neck and went into the Gray's Linn in Sliab Fuait.

Thereupon Cú Chulainn again drove through the host and saw the third pair contending, and he intervened as he had done before, and the satirist demanded his spear and Cú Chulainn at first refused it.

'I will revile thee,' said the satirist.

'I have paid for my honour today. I am not bound to grant more than one request this day.'

'I will revile Ulster for thy fault.'

'I have paid for Ulster's honour,' said Cú Chulainn.

'I will revile thy race,' said the satirist.

'Tidings that I have been defamed shall never reach the land I have not reached. For little there is of my life remaining.'

So Cú Chulainn flung the spear to him, handle foremost, and it went through his head and through thrice nine other men.

''Tis grace with wrath, O Cú Chulainn,' said the satirist.

Then Cú Chulainn for the last time drove through the host, and Lugaid took the spear, and said: 'What will fall by this spear, O sons of Calatin?'

'I heard you say that a king would fall by the spear that Erc cast this morning.'

'That is true,' said they, 'the king of the steeds of Erin fell by it, namely the Gray of Macha.'

Then Lugaid flung the spear and struck Cú Chulainn, and his bowels came forth on the cushion of the chariot, and his only horse, the Black Sainglenn, fled away, with half the yoke hanging to him, and left the chariot and his master, the king of the heroes of Erin, dying alone on the plain.

Then said Cú Chulainn, 'I would fain go as far as that loch to drink a drink thereout.'

'We give thee leave,' said they, 'provided that thou come to us again.'

'I will bid you come for me,' said Cú Chulainn, 'if I cannot come myself.'

Then he gathered his bowels into his breast, and went forth to the loch.

And there he drank his drink, and washed himself, and came forth to die, calling on his foes to come to meet him.

Now a great ring [of stones] went westwards from the loch and his eye lit upon it, and he went to a pillar-stone which is in the plain, and he put his breast-girdle round it that he might not die seated nor lying down, but that he might die standing up. Then came the men all around him, but they durst not go to him, for they thought he was alive.

'It is a shame for you,' said Erc son of Cairbre, 'not to take that man's head in revenge for my father's head which was taken by him.'

Then came the Gray of Macha to Cú Chulainn to protect him so long as his soul was in him and the 'hero's light' out of his forehead remained. And the Gray of Macha wrought three red routs all around him. And fifty fell by his teeth and thirty by each of his hoofs. This is what he slew of the host. And hence is the saying, 'Not keener were the victorious courses of the Gray of Macha after Cú Chulainn's slaughter.'

And then came the battle goddess Mórrígu and her sisters in the form of scald-crows and sat on his shoulder.

'That pillar is not wont to be under birds,' said Erc son of Cairbre.

Then Lugaid arranged Cú Chulainn's hair over his shoulder, and cut off his head. And then fell the sword from Cú Chulainn's hand, and smote off Lugaid's right hand, which fell on the ground. And Cú Chulainn's right hand was cut off in revenge for this. Lugaid and the hosts then marched away, carrying with them Cú Chulainn's head and his right hand, and they came to Tara, and there is the 'Sick-bed' of his head and his right hand, and the full of the cover of his shield of mould.

From Tara they marched southwards to the river Liffey. But meanwhile the hosts of Ulster were hurrying to attack their foes, and Conall the Victorious, driving in front of them, met the Gray of Macha streaming with blood. Then Conall knew that Cú Chulainn had been slain. And he and the Gray of Macha sought Cú Chulainn's body. They saw Cú Chulainn at the pillar-stone. Then went the Gray of Macha and laid his head on Cú Chulainn's breast And Conall said, 'A heavy care to the Gray of Macha is that corpse.'

And Conall followed the hosts meditating vengeance, for he was bound to avenge Cú Chulainn. For there was a comrades' covenant between Cú Chulainn and Conall the Victorious, namely, that whichever of them was first killed should be avenged by the other. 'And if I be the first killed,' Cú Chulainn had said, 'how soon wilt thou avenge me?'

'The day on which thou shalt be slain,' said Conall, 'I will avenge thee before that evening. And if I be slain,' said Conall, 'how soon wilt thou avenge me?'

'Thy blood will not be cold on earth,' said Cú Chulainn, 'before I shall avenge thee.' So Conall pursued Lugaid to the Liffey.

Then was Lugaid bathing. 'Keep a lookout over the plain,' said he to his charioteer, 'that no one come to us without being seen.'

The charioteer looked. 'One horseman is here coming to us,' said he, 'and great are the speed and swiftness with which he comes. Thou wouldst deem that all the ravens of Erin were above him. Thou wouldst deem that flakes of snow were specking the plain before him.'

'Unbeloved is the horseman that comes there,' said Lugaid. 'It is Conall the Victorious, mounted on the Dewy-Red. The birds thou sawest above him are the sods from that horse's hoofs. The snow-flakes thou sawest specking the plain before him are the foam from that horse's lips and from the curbs of his bridle. Look again,' said Lugaid, 'what road is he coming?'

'He is coming to the ford,' said the charioteer, 'the path that the hosts have taken.'

'Let that horse pass us,' said Lugaid. 'We desire not to fight against him.' But when Conall reached the middle of the ford he spied Lugaid and his charioteer and went to them.

'Welcome is a debtor's face!' said Conall. 'He to whom he oweth debts demands them of him. I am thy creditor for the slaying of my comrade Cú Chulainn, and here I am suing thee for this.'

They then agreed to fight on the plain of Argetros, and there Conall wounded Lugaid with his javelin. Thence they went to a place called Ferta Lugdach.

'I wish,' said Lugaid, 'to have the truth of men from thee.'

'What is that?' asked Conall the Victorious.

'That thou shouldst use only one hand against me, for one hand only have I.'

'Thou shalt have it,' said Conall the Victorious.

So Conall's hand was bound to his side with ropes. There for the space between two of the watches of the day they fought, and neither of them prevailed over the other. When Conall found that he prevailed not, he saw his steed the Dewy-Red by Lugaid. And the steed came to Lugaid and tore a piece out of his side.

'Woe is me!' said Lugaid, 'that is not the truth of men, O Conall.'

'I gave it only on my own behalf,' said Conall. 'I gave it not on behalf of savage beasts and senseless things.'

'I know now,' said Lugaid, 'that thou wilt not go till thou takest my head with thee, since we took Cú Chulainn's head from him. So take,' said he, 'my head in addition to thine own, and add my realm to thy realm, and my valour to thy valour. For I prefer that thou shouldst be the best hero in Erin.'

Thereat Conall the Victorious cut off Lugaid's head. And Conall and his Ulstermen then returned to Emain Macha.

That week they entered it not in triumph. But the soul of Cú Chulainn appeared there to the thrice fifty queens who had loved him, and they saw him floating in his phantom chariot over Emain Macha, and they heard him chant a mystic song of the coming of Christ and the Day of Doom.

Appendix: Story List

It would, of course, not be possible to include everything that has survived in any single volume, but we can still look at the names of the stories and reflect on what they might, or do, contain. A number of medieval story-lists have survived, part of the recollection of latter day bards who would once have had to learn these, and more, by heart during their twenty years training. Many of these are now believed lost, others remain untranslated, but they continue to offer a tantalising glimpse into the world of the Celtic myth and legend.

Destructions

The Three Circuits of the House of Lir
The Possession of Burach's House
The Ears-Battle of the House of Dumha
The Difference of Cathbhadh's House
The Destruction of Nechtain's House
The Destruction of the Court of Da Derga
The Destruction of the Court of Bron, the son of Briun
The Destruction of the Court of Ua Duilé
The Destruction of the Court of Da Choca

Cattle Raids

The Cattle Raid of Cuailgne [The Tain]
The Plunder of the Three Cows of Echaidh
The Cattle Raid of Ros
The Cattle Raid of Regaman
The Cattle Raid of Flidais
The Cattle Raid of Freach
The Cattle Raid of Fithir

The Cattle Raid of Failin
The Cattle Raid of Gé
The Cattle Raid of Dairt
The Cattle Raid of Creban

Courtships, or Wooings

The Courtship of Medhbh
The Courtship of Emer
The Courtship of Ailbhe
The Courtship of Etain
The Courtship of Faef
The Courtship of Ferb
The Courtship of Finniné
The Courtship of Grian the Fair haired
The Courtship of Grian the Brown haired
The Courtship of Sadhbh the daughter of Sescenn
The Courtship of Fithirné and Dairiné the two Daughters of Tuathal
The Courtship of the Wife of Crunn
The Courtship of Eithne the Hateful, the Daughter of Crimthann

Battles

The Battle of Magh Tuiredh
The Battle of Tailten
The Battle of Magh Mucruimhé
The Battle of Druim Dolach, in which the Picts were defeated
The Battle of Magh Rath
The Battle of Corann
The Battle of Cláiré
The Battle of Toiden
The Battle of Teamair

Caves (Incidents of)

The Cave of Ainged
The Cave [or Cellar] of the Church of Inchummar

The Cave of Leac Bladha
The Cave of the Road of Cu-glas
The Cave of Magh Uatha
The Cave of Magh Imbolg
The Cave of Benn Edair
The Cave of Loch Lurgan
The Cave of Dearc Ferna
The Plunder of the Cave of Cruach

Voyages

The Navigation of Máel Dúin
The Navigation of the Sons of Ua Corra
The Navigation of the ship of Muircheartach Mac Erca
The Navigation of Brigh Léith
The Navigation of Brecan
The Navigation of Labhraidh
The Navigation of Fothadh

Tragedies (or Deaths)

The Tragical Death of Curoi
The Tragical Death of Cú Chulainnn
The Tragical Death of Ferdiadh
The Tragical Death of Conall
The Tragical Death of Celtchair
The Tragical Death of Bla Briugad
The Tragical Death of Laeghaire
The Tragical Death of Ferghus
The Tragical Death of Conchobhar
The Tragical Death of Fiamai
The Tragical Death of Maelfatharhtaigh son of Ronan
The Tragical Death of Tadgh the son of Cian
The Tragical Death of Mac Samhain

Feasts

The Feast of the House of Forblai
The Feast of the House of Bichar
The Feast of the House of Tulchinn
The Feast of the House of Trichim
The Feast of the House of Li
The Feast of the House of Liné
The Feast of the House of Got
The Feast of the House of Gnarr
The Feast of the House of the Three Sons of Demonchatha
The Feast of the House of Ausclé
The Feast of the House of Melldolaigh
The Feast of Cruachain
The Feast of Emhain
The Feast of Ailenn
The Feast of Temair
The Feast of Dunbolg
The Feast of Dun Buchet

Sieges

The Siege of the Men of Falga
The Siege of Etair
The Siege of Acaill
The Siege of Dun Barc
The Siege of Dun Binné
The Siege of the Men of Fidhgha
The Siege of the Liffey
The Siege of Ladhrann
The Siege of Drom Damhghaire

Adventures

The Adventures of Nera
The Adventures of Fiamain
The Adventures of Curoi

The Adventures of Cú Chulainn
The Adventures of Conall
The Adventures of Conchobhar
The Adventures of Crimhthann Nia Nair
The Adventures of Macha, daughter of Aedh Ruadh
The Adventures of Nechtain son of Alfronn
The Adventures of Ailchinn, son of Amhalgaid
The Adventures of Finn in Dercfearna
The Adventures of Aedhan, son of Gabhran
The Adventures of Maeluma, son of Batthan
The Adventures of Mongán, son of Fiachna

Elopements

The Elopement of Mugain with Fiamain
The Elopement of Deirdre with the Sons of Uisnech
The Elopement of Aife, the daughter of Eoghan, with Mesdead
The Elopement of Naise, the daughter of Fergus, with Nertach, son of Ua Leith
The Elopement of the Wife of Gaia, the son of Dert with Glas, the son of Cimbaeth
The Elopement of Blathnait, the daughter of Pall, Son of Fidhach, with Cú Chulainn
The Elopement of Grainne with Diarmait
The Elopement of Muirn with Dubhruis
The Elopement of Ruithchean with Cuana, the son of Cailcin
The Elopement of Erc, daughter of Loarn, with Muirdéadhach the son of Eoghan
The Elopement of Dighe with Laidcnen
The Elopement of the wife of Ailell, the son of Eoghan, with Fothudh Canann

Slaughters

The Slaughter of Magh Cégala, by the son of Feba
The Slaughter of Ath-hí (Athy)
The Slaughter of Dun Dubhghlaisé
The Slaughter of Din Righ

The Slaughter of Ath Cliath
The Slaughter of Dun Delga
The Slaughter of Conaing's Tower
The Slaughter of Aileach upon Neit, the son of Indai
The Slaughter of Belchu of Breifne
The Slaughter by Cairpré 'Cat-head' of the Nobles of Erinn
The Slaughter by Echadh of his sons
The Slaughter of the Wood of Conall
The Slaughter of St Donnan of Eg
The Slaughter of Mac Datho
The Slaughter of the Sons of Magech
The Slaughter of Sidh Nenta
The Slaughter of Srath Cluada
The Slaughter of Shabh Soilgech
The Slaughter of Rath Righbard
The Slaughter of Rath Rosguill
The Slaughter of Rath Tuaighe
The Slaughter of Rath Tuaisle
The Slaughter of Rath Tobachta
The Slaughter of Rath Timchill
The Slaughter of Rath Cuinge
The Slaughter of Rath Cuillenn
The Slaughter of Rath Crochain
The Slaughter of Cathair Boirche
The Slaughter of Rath Blai
The Slaughter of Rath Gaila
The Slaughter of Rath Uillne
The Slaughter of the Rath of Naa
The Slaughter of the Rath of Binn Cé
The Slaughter of Rdith Granard
The Slaughter of Rdith Buirigh
The Treachery of Scone
The Visitation of [King] Arthur

Irruptions

The Irruption of Loch Echach
The Irruption of Loch Eirne

Visions

The Vision of the Wife of Neimidh
The Vision of Conchobhar (the Tochmarc Feirbe?)
The Vision of Conn, i.e., *Baile an Scail*
The Vision of Fursa

Love

The Love of Caillech Berre for Fothadh Chonann
The Love of Dubhlacha for Mongán
The Love of Gormlaith for Niall

Expeditions

The Expedition of Ugaine Mor to Italy
The Expedition of Dathi to the Alpine Mountains.
The Expedition of Mall, son of Eochaidh, to the Ictian Sea.
The Expedition of Fiachna, the son of Baedan, to Dun Guaire in Britain, and
    the prime Expeditions of Erinn besides

Progresses

The Progress of Partholon to Erinn
The Progress of Neimidh to Erinn
The Progress of the Firbolgs
The Progress of the Tuatha dé Danann
The Progress of Mile (Milesius), son of Bile, to Spain
The Progress of the Sons of Mill (or Milesius) from Spain to Erinn
The Progress of the Cruithneans (Picts) from Thrace to Erinn; and their
    progress from Erinn to Albain
The Progress of the Exile of Fergus out of Ulster
The Progress of the Muscrigians Magh Breagain
The Progress of the Deisi from Temair
The Progress of the Sons of Eochidh Muighmhedhoin out of Meath
The Progress of Tadhg, son of Cian (son of Oilill Oluim) from Cashel into
    Meath

The Progress of the Dail Riada into Scotland. And all that were killed, and wounded, and died.

He is no poet who does not synchronise and harmonise all the stories.

GLOSSARY

Only the more important people and terms mentioned in this collection are included here. A brief pronunciation guide is given in brackets after each name. The stress comes upon the syllable before the apostrophe. Irish has passed through a great number of changes over the last two thousand years: even modern Irish has variants from province to province, so what follows is necessarily a rough guide. Use standard pronunciation where no guide is given. Italicised words can be cross-referenced. Many names have variant spellings.

aes dána (ois daan'a): 'the people of the gift'; the professional artists, specifically, poets.

Aife (eef'a): a female warrior of Alba by whom *Cú Chulainn* had a son, Connia.

Ailill mac Matach (al'yil) mok mat'a): king of Connacht; husband of *Medb*.

Ailill Olom (al'yil ol'um): 'A. Bare-Ear;' king of Munster, father of *Eóghan mac Ailill*.

Aillén mac Eogabál (al'ayn mok yo'gabl): warrior of the *Tuatha dé Danaan*, lover of *Uchtdelb*.

Aillinn (al'yin): daughter of Lugaid of Leinster and lover of *Baile*.

Almu (ol'moo): chief seat of *Fionn mac Cumhail*, now the Hill of Allen north-east of Kildare.

Aine (awn'ye): daughter of *Eogabul*, lover of *Manannán*, raped by *Ailill Olom*.

Ainle (eyen'ly): brother of *Noisiu;* son of *Usnech*.

Alba: Scotland.

Amairgin Glunmar (av'er'gin gloo'ma): poet of the Milesian invaders.

Amergin (av'er-gin): poet, protegé of *Athairne;* his childhood name was *Greth*.

Ana/Anu/Danu: ancestress of the *Tuatha dé Danaan*.

Angus: son of Aed Abrat; brother of Fann; a messenger sent to invite *Cú Chulainn* to the fairy world.

Annwn/Annwfn (an'oon/ an'uvn): lit. 'the in-world', the Welsh Otherworld.

Ardan: brother of *Noisiu;* son of *Usnech*.

Art mac Conn: king of Ireland and father of *Eochaid Mor*.

Athairn/Atherne/Athirne (ath'irn): poet and satirist of Ulster.

Badb (borv): goddess of battles, daughter of Ernmas, sister to *Macha* and *Mórrígan*.

Baile Binnbérlach (baal'ye binn-bayr'la): 'Vision of the Melodious Voice'; lover of *Aillin*.

Balor, son of Net: a king of the Fomorians, overcome by his grandson, *Lugh*.

Banba, goddess of Ireland, daughter of *Ernmas*. Now a poetic name for Ireland.

Bean sí (ban shee): a woman of the fairy-mound.

Becfola (bek'fol-a): wife of Diarmuid of Tara, lover of *Flann.*

Beltane (bel'ten'a): festival heralding the coming of summer, held on 1 May, origin of modern May Day.

Benn Etair: now the Hill of Howth near Dublin.

Blathnat (blaa'net): daughter of Mind and wife of *Cú Roi mac Daire;* lover of *Cú Chulainn.*

Boann (bo'an): mother of *Oengus* of the Brug, and of the three musical strains (see *Uaithne*). The River Boyne takes its name from her.

Bodb Derg (borv darg): a fairy king in Munster; son of the *Dagda.*

Bran or Bendigaidfran (braan/ ben-dig-geyed'vran): 'B. the Blessed;' titantic Welsh god.

Bran mac Febal (brahn mok fay'bl): voyager to the otherworld islands of the west who never returned.

Breccán (brek'awn): grandson of *Niall Nóigiallach* who drowned in Corryvrekin.

brehon: one skilled in the ancient laws and legal institutions of Ireland.

Bres mac Elatha/Elada (bre moc el'a-a): son of *Eriu* and the Fomorian, *Elada;* briefly king of the Tuatha dé, husband of *Brigid.*

Bricriu Nemthenga (brik'roo nayv'enga): Bricriu of the Poison Tongue, son of Carbad, the malicious trouble-maker of Ulster.

Bri Leith: the location of the fairy-mound of Midir, Otherworld lover of Etain; now a hill near Ardagh, Co Longford.

Brian (bree'an): one of *Tuirenn*'s sons who kills *Cian*, *Lugh*'s father.

Brigid (bri'yid): daughter of the Dagda, wife to Bres, goddess of smithcraft, poetry and domestic beasts.

bruiden (broo'yen): a banqueting hall.

Bruiden Da Derga: stronghold on the River Dodder near Dublin.

Brugh na Boinne (broo na boin): fairy-mound; a group of prehistoric mounds and the surrounding district on the River Boyne in modern Leinster.

Buchet (boo'khet): Leinsterman of great hospitality, foster-father of *Ethne Tháebfhota.*

Caer Ibormeith (care yb'or-may): faery woman beloved of *Oengus mac Og.*

Cai Hir (keye heer): one of Arthur's chief followers, later called Sir Kay in Arthurian tradition.

Cailb (kaalb): the many-named seeress who enters *Da Derga*'s Hostel.

Cailleach (kal'yak): literally, old woman. Ancient goddess of the land, associated in Scotland and Ireland with the mountains.

Cailte mac Ronain (cwel'sha mok ro'nawn): One of *Fionn*'s companions.

Caintigerna (ken-tig-ern'a): mother of *Mongán.*

caird: a smith or artificer.

Cairenn (kar'en): daughter of Sachell Balb the Saxon, mother of *Niall.*

Catháir Mór (ca'hoir more): king of Leinster, father of *Ethne Tháebfhota.* Killed by Conn Cet Cathach.

Caswallawn (kas-wahl'lown): son of Beli Mawr; usurper of *Bran or Bendigaidfran*; possessed of a cloak of invisibility.

Cathbad (kath'vad): chief druid of Ulster; according to one tradition, the father of Conchobar.

Celtchair mac Uthechair (kelt'har mok ooh'eha): a distinguished Ulster warrior.

Cessair (kes'er): queen-leader of the first invasion of Ireland, grand-daughter of Noah.

Cet mac Matach (ket mok mat'ar): Connacht warrior who wounds Conchobar with the calcified brain of *Mesgegra*.

Ciabán mac Eochair Imderg (kee'bawn mok eo'her im'derg): Ultonian warrior whose beauty caused such jealousy that *Fionn* expelled him from the *fianna*.

Cian (kee'an): son of Cainte, father of *Lugh,* killed by *Tuirenn's* sons.

Ciarraige Luachra (ker'ry loo'kra): a hilly district between Co Limerick and Co Kerry.

Cigfa (kig'va): wife of *Pryderi*.

Cliodna (klee'na): wife of *Manannán* who drowned. See *Tonn Clidna*.

Cobthach Cóel Breg (ko'vach coil bre): 'C. the Slender of Breg'; became king of Tara by killing many of his relatives, including his brother, *Loegaire Lorc*.

Conaing/Conand (kon'an): Fomorian leader whose tower on Tory Island was made of glass.

Conaire Mór: King of Ireland near the beginning of the Christian era; grandson of *Etain* and son of *Mess Buachalla* by an otherworldly bird-man father, though he is known as *Eterscel's* son.

Conall Cernach (kon'al kyern'akh): 'Conall the Victorious.' A distinguished Ulster warrior; fosterer of *Cú Chulainn*.

Conall Corc (kon'al cor'ec): son of Luigthig; founder of Cashel, seat of the Munster high-kings.

Conchobar (con'o-her) King of Ulster about the beginning of the Christian era.

Conla's Well: source of inspiration, kept by *Nechtain*; probably synonymous with the *Well of Segais*.

Conn Cet-Cathach (kon ket kath'a): Conn of the Hundred-Battles. King of Ireland beginning about 177 CE; son of Fedlimid Rechtmar.

Connacht: the westly province of Ireland, with its capital at *Cruachan*.

Connla: son of Conn Cet Chatach who falls in love with an Otherworldly woman and passes into the Otherworld.

Corc: see *Conall Corc*.

Cormac mac Airt (kor'mak mok art): wisest king of Ireland c. 227–266 CE; grandson of *Conn Cet-Chathach*

Cormac (kor'mak), son of Lactighe: king of Ulster 48 CE; grandfather of *Conaire Mor* and husband of *Etain*.

Cormac Connlonges: son of Conchobar who went into voluntary exile in Connacht after the killing of the sons of Usnech, for whom he was one of the sureties.

Cormac mac Cuilleanáin (kor'mak mok cwil'en'awn): ninth-century abbot-king of Cashel; compiler of Cormac's Glossary.

Craiphtine (kraf'tyn'e): harper to *Labraid Loingsech*.

Crimthann (krif'han): foster-son of Diarmuid of Tara who refused *Becfola's* love because Sunday travel was involved.

Crimthann mac Fidaig (crif'an mok fi'dag): an early king of Munster, uncle to *Conall Corc*.

Cruachan (croo'a-han): Rath Cruachan. Royal seat of Ailill and Medb, now Ratheroghan between Belanagare and Elphin in Co Roscommon.

Crunnchu mac Agnoman (crun'hu mok ag'no-mon): indiscreet husband of *Macha*.

Cualgne (coo'ley): an ancient district probably corresponding roughly to the modern parish of Cooley in Co Louth; the territory especially assigned to the guardianship of *Cú Chulainn*.

Cú Chulainn (koo hull'in): 'The Hound of Culan', originally called Setanta. Son of Deichtire, sister of Conchobar, by the *Tuatha dé Danann* prince *Lug* or by Sualtam (Sualtach); the central hero of the Ulster cycle.

Cú Roi mac Dairi (koo roi mok day'ry): a powerful chieftain in Munster, usually opposed to Ulster but friendly to Connacht. He possessed supernatural powers.

Cuimne (kwiv'na): the cailleach who helps *Mongán* make a fool of a king of Leinster.

Curithir (kur'eer): poet who loved *Liadain*.

Cymru (kum'ree): the Welsh people.

Da Derga: host of a spacious *bruiden* that was destroyed by Conaire Mor's foster brothers.

Dagda (dogh'da): gargantuan leader of the Tuatha dé, also called Eochaid Ollathair 'father of all', and Ruad Rofessa 'Red One of Great Knowledge'.

Deirdre/Deirdriu (dair'dre): the promised bride of *Conchobor* who eloped with *Naoisi*.

Dian Cecht (dee'an hacht): doctor of the *Tuatha dé*.

Diarmuid ui Duibne (jer'mwid o duv'ny): a leading warrior of the fianna, lover of *Grainne*.

Dind Ríg (din ree): 'Fortress of Kings;' one of the chief seats of the Leinster kings.

dindsenchas/dinnshencas (din hen'kus): 'the lore of place'; stories which give derivations of places.

Dubh-Lacha (doov lok'a): wife of *Mongán*.

Dubthach Dóeltenga (doov'tah doil'teng-a): 'Chafer Tongue', the trouble-making Ulster warrior.

Elaha/Elada (el'aha): undersea King of the Fomorians who seduced *Eriu;* father of *Bres*.

Emain Ablach (e'win av'lak): 'encircling of apples'; the otherworldly domain of *Manannán mac Lír,* identified both with the Isle of Man and with Isle of Arran in Scotland; cognate with Welsh Avalon.

Emain Macha (e'win ma'ha): Navan Fort, near Armagh, capital of ancient Ulster.

Emer (ev'er): daughter of Forgall, wife of *Cú Chulainn*.

Eochaid Airem (yo'he er'm): legendary king of *Tara*, marries the metamorphosed *Etain* and sleeps with their daughter, *Etain Og*, thinking her his wife.

Eochaid Feidlioch (yo'he fyel'lyikh): 'E. the Enduring'; an early king of *Tara*.

Eochaid mac Eirc (yo'he mok erk): Fir Bolg king of Ireland when the Tuatha dé arrive.

Eochaid mac Luchta (yo'he mok looh'ta): king of Munster at the time of *Conchobor*.

Eochaid Mugmedón (yoh'he moo'ma-don): 'E. Lord of Slaves'; fourth century king of Ireland, father of *Niall*.

Eogabul mac Durgabul (yo'gabl mok der'gabl): faery king, father of *Aine* and *Fer Fí*.

Eóghan mac Ailill (yo'han mok ay'il): king of Munster who fought his foster-brother, *Lugaid mac Conn*.

Eóghan mac Durthacht (yo'han mok door'okh): king of Fernmag, killer of *Naoisi*.

Eóghan Mór (yo'han mor): also known as Mug Nuadat; king of Munster. His many contentions with *Conn Cet-Chathach* ended with the division of Ireland into two parts. See *Leth Moga*.

Eoghanacht (yo'han-okt): ruling family of Munster, descended from *Eóghan Mór*.

éric (ay'rik): compensation or recompense levied against injuries received by victim upon the perpetrator or his family, most often implemented in cases of homicide; a person's éric was set by law and varied according to gender and position in society.

Eriu (ay'ryu): sister of *Fodla* and *Banba*, the triple sovereignty goddesses of Ireland. Now remembered as Erin, the romantic name for Ireland.

Ernmas: ancient mother of many gods, including the *Mórrígan*.

Essyllt (es'ihlt): wife of King *March*, lover of *Trystan*. She becomes Isolt in later Arthurian tradition.

Etain (ayd'in): wife of *Midir* who metamorphoses into several incarnations of herself.

Etain Og (ayd'in oge): the reincarnated *Etain*'s daughter whom *Eochaid Feidlech* mistakenly marries believing her to be her mother, his lost wife; mother to *Mes Buachalla*.

Eterscel (ed'er'scyal): king of Tara, putative father of *Conaire Mór*.

Ethne/Eithne (en'ya): daughter of *Balor*, wife of *Cian*.

Ethne Tháebfhota (en'ya heye'ot-a): daughter of *Catháir Mór*, fostered by *Buchet*, wife of *Cormac mac Airt*.

Fann/Fand (fawn): faery woman, daughter of Aed Abrat, wife of *Manannán*, lover of *Cú Chulainn*.

Fedelm Láir Derg (Fed'elm loir der'eg): 'F. Red mare'; witch and foster-mother of *Conall Corc*.

Fedelm Noíchrothach (fed'elm noi'ro-akh): 'F. the fresh-hearted'; wife of *Loegaire Buadach*.

Fedlimid mac Criomthan (fel'im'id mok krif'on): ninth-century bishop-king of Munster who visits *Guile*.

Fer Caille (fair cawl'ye): 'man of the wood'; the one-handed, one-footed, one-eyed being who comes to *Da Derga*'s Hostel.

Fer Fí (fair fee): 'man of Yew', son of *Eogabul*.

Fer Rogain (fair ro'gan): treacherous foster-brother of *Conaire Mór* who sacks *Da Derga*'s Hostel with *Ingcel*.

Ferches mac Commán (ferg'us mok com'awn): poet to *Ailill Olom*, killer of *Eogabul*.

Fergus mac Roich (fair'gus mok ro'ih): Ulster hero, foster-father of *Cú Chulainn* who went into exile in Connacht; lover of *Flidais.*

Fiachu Muillethan (fee'hoo mwil'a-han): Fiachu Broad-Crown, son of Eóchaid Mór.

fianna (fee'ana): any band of warriors, or, more specifically, the Fianna, the troops of *Fionn mac Cumhail.*

fianna of Emain: Bres, Nar and Lothar, the sons of Eochaid Feidlioch.

fidchell (feech'yel): lit. 'wood-wisdom', a board-game between two players, similar to chess.

Findabair/Finnabair (fin'a-ver): daughter of *Medb* and *Ailill,* courted by *Froech,* offered to Connacht champions as an incentive during the Táin Bó Cuailgne.

Fingen mac Luchtra (fin'gen mok loo'tra): King of Munster at the time of *Conn Cet-Chathach.*

Finn: see *Fionn mac Cumhail.*

Fintan mac Bochra (fin'tan mok boch'ra): the only survivor of the invasion led by *Cessair,* and guardian of Irish memory.

Fionn mac Cumhail (fin mok cool): also called Demne, as a child, and Fionn ua Baiscne.

Fir Bolg (feer bolg): fourth race of invaders in Ireland.

Fir Domnann (feer dom'nan): early invaders of Ireland.

Flann (flawn): lover of *Becfola.*

Flidais: (fli'dyesh): ancient goddess whose cattle are deer; lover of *Fergus mac Roích.*

Fodla/Fotla (fo'la): goddess of the land of Ireland, sister of *Banba* and *Eriu.*

Fomoiri (fo'voir-ee): race of undersea people.

Froech/Fraech/Fraich (froi'kh): son of Bébhinn, sister of *Boann.*

Garaid (gar'ee): son of *Gol mac Morna,* responsible for burning the wives of *Fionn's* warriors.

geis s.(gesh) pl. **geasa** (gyas'a): a positive or negative injunction binding upon a person who must honourably obey it or suffer loss of face or life.

glám dicinn (glawm dyik'in): a withering satire which cursed the recipient with ill health or social exclusion, delivered while standing on one leg, with one arm behind the back and one eye closed.

Goibniu (gwiv'ne-oo): smith of the Tuatha dé.

Greth (grey): prodigious child who grew up to be Amairgin, a poet and brother in law of *Conchobor,* protegé of *Athairne.*

Gruibne (grwiv'ny): Pictish poet who rescues *Conall Corc.*

Guile (gwil'y): of Atha Loich, client of *Fedlimid* of Munster who receives his king unexpectedly.

Guile Beag (gwil'y beog): the not-so-shy daughter of *Guile.*

Gwalchmai (gwalk'meye): Arthur's nephew; later called Sir Gawain in Arthurian tradition.

Gwawl (gwowl): Otherworldly suitor of *Rhiannon,* overcome by *Pwyll.*

Gwenhwyfar (gwen-hwee'var): wife of Arthur; Guinevere in later Arthurian tradition.

imbas forosna (im'bas for'os-na): 'inspirational illumination': a prophetic skill of poets.

Imbolc (im'olc): festival celebrating the birth of lambs and heralding spring on 1 February, dedicated to *Brigid*.

Ingcél Cáech (ink'ayl coich): one-eyed British pirate who sacks *Da Derga*'s Hostel.

Iuchar (oo'a): one of *Tuirenn*'s sons who kills *Cian*, *Lugh*'s father.

Iucharba (oo'a-ba): one of *Tuirenn*'s sons who kills *Cian*, *Lugh*'s father.

Kicva: see *Cigfa*.

Labraid Loingsech (low'ree long'she): 'L. the Mariner'; also called L. Moen, the dumb; king of Leinster.

Labraid Luath Lambh ar Claidib (low'ree loo'ah laav ar cleev): L. 'Swift Hand on the Sword'; faery king, husband of *Liban*.

Laeg/Loeg mac Riangabra (loig mok reen'gab-re): *Cú Chulainn*'s charioteer and friend.

Leborcham (lay'vor-ham): female messenger of *Conchobor*, nurse to *Deirdre*.

Leinster: the easterly province of Ireland with its capitals at Dún Ailinne and Dind Ríg.

Lendabair (len'ov-ar): daughter of *Eoghan mac Durthacht*, wife of *Conall Cernach*.

Leth Cuinn (lay cwin): the northern half of Ireland under the protection of *Conn Cet Chathach*.

Leth Moga (lay mog'a): the southern half of Ireland under the protection of *Eochaid Mor*.

Liadain (leead'an): poetess of Kerry, lover of *Curithir*.

Liban (lee'vaan): sister of *Fand*.

Lloegr (loi'gre): Welsh name for England.

Lochlann (lokh'lon): Scandinavia or, more specifically, Norway.

Loegaire Buadach (loi'er'a boo'da): 'L. the Triumphant'; son of Connad mac Iliach; Ulster hero.

Loegaire Lorc (loi'ger'a lork): 'L. the Fierce'; king of Tara, killed by *Cobthach Coél Breg*.

Luaine (lwawn-ye): the chosen bride of *Conchobor* who was cursed by *Athairne*.

Lug/Lugh Lamfhada (loogh lav-ada): 'the long-hand', champion of the Tuatha dé, also called Samildanach, or 'many skilled'.

Lugaid mac Conn (loo'gy): leader of the Erainn of Munster, foster-brother to *Eochaid mac Ailill*; briefly King of Tara.

Lugaid Mal (loo'gy mol): also known as Lugaid Laígde, son of Dáire, who sleeps with *Sovereignty*.

Lughnasadh (loo'nas-a): harvest festival celebrated around 1 August, instituted by *Lug*.

Mac an Daimh (mok n dawv): *Mongán*'s servant.

Mac Cecht: 'son of the plough'; Conaire Mór's champion.

Mac Da Cherda (mok de kher'da): 'son of the Two Arts'; the wisest and most foolish poet in Ireland who acted as messenger for *Cuirithir*.

Macha (mokh'a): daughter of Ernmas; with *Badb* and *Mórrígan*, she makes up the triple Mórrígna of battle goddesses.

Macha: wife of *Crunniuc mac Agnomen*, who pronounces the curse of debility in their greatest need upon the Ulstermen due to their treatment of her; foundress of *Emain Macha*.

Maelduin (mile'dooin): voyager to the Otherworldly islands of the west.

Maeve: see *Medb*.

Mag Tuiread (moy too'ra): site of the two battles fought by the Tuatha dé against the *Fir Bolg* and *Fomoire* in N.W. Connacht.

Manannán mac Athgno (man'an-awn mok ag'no): avenger of the sons of *Uisnech*.

Manannán mac Lír (man'an-awn mok leer): God of the sea and the Otherworld, cognate with *Manawyddan*.

March ap Meirchion (mark ap myre'che-on): king of Cornwall, husband of *Essyllt*, uncle of *Trystan*.

Medb/Maeve (mayv): queen of Connacht, protagonist in the *Táin Bó Cuailgne*. Her husband is *Ailill mac Matach*.

Mes/Meas Buachalla (mes booch'all-a): 'Cowherd's Foster-child'; the incestuously-begotten daughter of *Eochaid Airem* and the reincarnated *Etain Og*, his daughter; mother of *Conaire Mor*.

Mesgegra (mes gay're): a king of Leinster, whose brain was made into a ball by *Conall Cernach*; this ball subsequently killed *Conchobor*.

Miach (mee'ak): son of *Diancecht* who healed *Nuadu*'s arm.

Midir (mij'ir): faery king, one of the *Tuatha de Danann*; he married, lost and refound *Etain*.

Mil: leader of the sixth invasion of Ireland.

Mongán (mon'gawn): son of *Caintigerna*, raised by *Manannán mac Lír*.

Mongfinn (mo'vin): daughter of Fidach, wife of *Eochaid Mugedón*.

Morann mac Maine (mor'ann mokmaan'ye): druidic judge to *Conchobor mac Nessa*.

Mórrígan (mor're-gan): shapeshifting daughter of Ernmas, who incites war.

Mórrígna: name for the triple goddesses *Badb*, *Macha* and *Mórrígan*.

Mugain (moo'gawn): tutlary goddess of Munster.

Muirchertach mac Erca (mwir'ket-a mok erk'a): high-king of Ireland, husband of *Sin*.

Munster: the southerly province of Ireland, with its capital at Cashel.

Nechtan (nekh'tun): husband of *Boann*, keeper of Nechtain's or *Conla's Well*.

Némain (nem'awn): war-goddess whose name is often fused with that of *Macha* and *Badb*.

Nemed: Scythian leader of the Nemedians.

Nemedians: third race of invaders in Ireland, forebears of the *Tuatha dé Danann*.

Nemglan (nav'glon): 'Clear-Sky'; bird-man messenger who gives *Conaire Mór* his kingly *geasa*.

Ness/a (nyes'a): originally called 'Assa'; daughter of Eochaid Salbuide, wife of *Cathbad*.

Niall Nóigiallach (neyel noi'gyel-akh): 'N. of the Nine Hostages'; king of Tara, son of *Eochaid Mugmedon;* he sleeps with *Sovereignty*.

Noidiu Nae-mbreathach (noy'dyoo nay mrath'ekh): miraculous child who spoke at birth.

Noisiu/Naoisi (noi'she): son of *Uisnech*, nephew of *Conchobor*, lover of *Deirdre*.

Nuadu Airgetlam (noo'ad-a areg'et-lav): 'Silverhand', King of the Tuatha dé who loses his arm in battle.

Oengus mac Og (an'gus mak oge): son of *Dagda* and *Boann*, one of the Tuatha dé, living at *Brugh na Boinne*.

ogam/ogham (anciently, og'am: modern oh'am): early form of Irish writing; its straight strokes were incised against the edges of pillar stones and on slips of wood.

Ogma: poet-warrior of the Tuatha dé, inventor of *ogham* writing.

Oisín (os'sheen): warrior and poet, son of *Fionn mac Cumhail.*

Olc Aiche (olk ay'ha): 'Drinks the Field', smith-druid, grandfather of *Cormac mac Airt.*

Owain (o-wine'): Arthurian hero, Prince of Rheged, son of Urien Rheged.

Partholon: leader of the second invasion of Ireland.

Pryderi (prud-er'ee): son of *Pwyll* and *Rhiannon,* husband of *Cigfa.*

Pwyll (poo'ilh): prince of Dyfed, Wales; father of *Pryderi.*

Rhiannon (hree-ann'on): horse-goddess, wife of *Pwyll* and then *Manawyddan;* mother of *Pryderi.*

Rhonabwy (hron-ab'wee): Welsh warrior who dreams of Arthur.

Rothniamh (roh'nyeev): 'Wheel Splendour'; faery woman who prophesies to *Fingen mac Luchtra.*

Ruadan (roo'dan): son of *Brigid* and *Bres,* killed by *Goibniu.*

Samhain (sow'an): festival heralding winter's beginning on 1 November, from which Hallowe'en derives.

Scathach (skaw'tha): female warrior living in Scotland; instructor of *Cú Chulainn.*

Sencha mac Ailill (shen'ka mok al'yil): peacemaker among the Ulstermen.

Senchán Torpeist (shen'kaan tor'pesht): sixth century Connacht poet.

sí/síd/sidhe (shee): anciently, the faery-mound; now used for the people of the faery race.

Sin (shin): Otherworldly woman married to *Muirchertach mac Erca.*

Sithchenn (she'hen): druidic smith who arranges a sovereignty test for the sons of *Eochaid Mugmedón.*

Sovereignty: the Irish Goddess of Sovereignty is called Flaitheas (fla'has) or 'Lordship;' she appears to both *Niall* and *Lugaid Mal* in the shape of an ugly hag before assuming a beautiful appearance.

Sreng: Fir Bolg assailant who cuts off Nuadu's arm.

Súaltaim (sooal'ta): father of Cú Chulainn.

Tailltiu (toil'tyo): *Lug*'s foster-mother, clearer of the forests for agriculture. After her death, Lug established funeral games at Teltown, creating the festival of *Lughnasadh.*

Tara: elevated place of assembly in Co Meath, site of the high-or over-kingship of Ireland, where the sacred marriage between the land and king was enacted.

tarbh feis (tar'ev fesh): 'bull-feast;' incubation ritual whereby a druid would sleep in the hide of freshly-flayed bull after eating a broth of its flesh in order to receive prophetic information.

Tibraide mac Mál (tee'bra mok maal):`enemy of *Conn Cet-Chatach.*

tiompán (tyim'pawn): a psaltery-like instrument of strings laid across a sounding board, often played by Otherworldly beings.

Tir Tairngire (cheer taren'ge-a): 'the Land of Promise;' the Otherworld.

Tonn Cliodna (ton klee'na): one of three great waves that struck the Irish shores, named after *Cliodna* who drowned there at Glandore, Co Cork.

Trystan ap Tallwch (tris'tan ap talh'uk): nephew of *March ap Meirchion,* lover of *Essyllt.*

Tuan mac Carill (too'an mok kar'yil): the metamorphised reincarnation of one of *Partholon's* men

Tuatha dé Danann (too'aha day dan'an): the people (descendants) of *Ana,* the fifth invaders of Ireland.

Tuirenn Bicreo/Bigrenn (teer'enn big'cro): son of *Ogma* and Etan. His three sons, Brian, *Iucharba* and *Iuchar,* kill *Cian, Lugh's* father.

Uaithne (ooe'nye): the *Dagda's* harper, father of the three musical strains goltraiges, gentraiges and suantraiges, the laugh-strain, the wail-strain and the sleep-strain.

Uathach (uer'ech): 'Horrible'; the daughter of *Scathach.*

Uisnech/Usnech (ish'na): sacred and ceremonial centre of Ireland; a hill in West Meath where all four provinces meet.

Usnech/Uislech, Sons of: *Noisiu, Ardan* and *Ainle,* who are called so after the place, not a person.

Ulster: the northly province of Ireland, with its capital at *Emain Macha.*

Well of Segais (seg'ash): source of poetic inspiration, source of the Boyne River, where nine hazel trees drop their nuts into the waters, feeding the Salmon of Wisdom.

Bibliography

(Texts with a direct relationship to this collection are marked with *)

Abbreviations for Periodicals are as follows:

BBCS   Bulletin of the Board of Celtic Studies
DIAS   Dublin Institute for Advanced Studies
EC   Etudes Celtiques
MMIS   Medieval and Modern Irish Series
PRIA   Proceedings of the Royal Irish Academy
PMLA   Proceedings of the Modern Language Association
ZCP   Zeitschrift für Celtische Philologie

Texts and Textual Editions

*Bergin, O. and Best, R. L., *Leabhar na hUidre (Book of the Dun Cow)*, Dublin, Early Irish Text Society, 1929

Bergin, O. J., Best, R. L., Byrne, M. E., Meyer, K. and O'Keefe, J. G., eds., *Anecdota from Irish MSS* (5 vols), Dublin, Halle, 1907–13

Best, R. I., 'The Adventures of Art Son of Conn', *Eriu*, III (1907), pp. 149–173

*Best, R. I. and O'Brien, M. A., *The Book of Leinster*, Dublin, Early Irish Text Society, 1954–67

*Byrne, Mary E. & Myles Dillon, *Táin Bó Fraích*, EC. I, 1936, pp. 1–19

Carey, John, *A Tuath Dé Miscellany*, BBCS vol XXXIX, 1992

Connellan, O., ed., *The Proceedings of the Great Bardic Institution*, Dublin, J. O'Daly, 1860

*Corthais, Johan, *Táin Bó Regamna and Táin Bó Flidais*, Hamburg, 1979 (dissertation)

*Cross, Tom Peete & Clark Harris Slover, Ancient Irish Tales, Dublin, Figgis, 1936

*Cross, Tom Peete, 'A Welsh Tristan Episode', *Studies in Philology* 17, 1920

Cross, Tom Peete and A.C.L. Bown 'Fingen's Night Watch', *Romanic Review* vol 9 (1918), pp. 29–47.

Crowe, J.O'Beirne, 'The Adventures of Condla Ruad,' Journal of the *Royal Irish Archaeological Institute*, 4th ser., 111 (1874), pp. 118–133

Crowe, J. O'Beirne, 'The Phantom Chariot of Cú Chulainn', '*Siabur-charpat Con Culaind'*, Journal of the Royal Irish Archaeological Institute, 4th ser., 1 (1871), pp. 371–448.

Dillon, Myles, *Serglige Con Culainn* (MMIS, XIV), Dublin, 1953.

Dillon, Myles, *The Cycles of the Kings*, London, Geoffrey Cumberlege, 1946

BIBLIOGRAPHY   495

* Dillon, Myles, 'The Taboos of the Kings of Ireland', *PRIA*, 1951
* Dobbs, Margaret, 'Cath Cumair,' *RC* 20, 1926, pp. 279–342
* Dobbs, Margaret, 'The Battle of Finchorad', *ZCP* 14, 1923
* Dobbs, Margaret, 'The Story of Noidhiu Nae-mBreathach', *ZCP* XIX, 1907
*Dobbs, Margaret, 'On Táin Bó Flidais' *Eriu* vol 8 (1915), pp. 133–149
Dooley, Ann and Harry Roe, *Tales of the Elders of Ireland*, Oxford, Oxford
     University Press, 1999
*Faraday, L. Winifred, *The Cattle-Raid of Cualnge*, London, David Nutt, 1904
* Fraser, J., 'The First Battle of Moytura', *Eriu* VIII, 1915, pp. 1–63
*Guest, Lady Charlotte, *The Mabinogion*, London, J. M. Dent, 1937
*Gwynn, E.J., 'The Burning of Finn's House,' *Eriu* I, (1904), pp. 12–37
*Gwynn, E. ed. and trans., *The Metrical Dindsenchas, Parts 1–5*, Dublin, Hodges,
     Figgis, 1903–1935
*Hancock, W N., ed., *Senchus Mor: The Ancient Laws of Ireland*, Dublin,
     Alexander Thom; London, Longman Green & Co, 1865
*Henderson, George, *Fled Bricrend*, London, Early Irish Text Society, 1899
*Hennessy, William M., 'The Intoxication of the Ulstermen.' *Mesca Ulad*, Todd
     Lecture Series I., Dublin, 1889
Hennessy, W. M., 'The Cause of the Battle of Cnucha', *RC*, 11 (1873), pp. 86–93
*Henderson, George, *Bricriu's Feast, Fled Bricrend* (ITS, II) Dublin, 1899
*Hull, Eleanor, 'The Cattle Raid of Regamna' in *The Cuchullin Saga*, London,
     1898, pp. 101–107
*Hull, Eleanor, *The Cuchullin Saga in Irish Literature*, London, David Nutt, 1898
*Hull, Eleanor 'The Debility of the Ulstermen' in *The Cuchullin Saga*, London,
     1898, pp. 95–107
Hull, Vernam, 'The Exile of Conall Corc', *PMLA* Vol LVI (1941), pp. 937–950
Hull, Vernam, 'De Gabail in T-Sida (Concerning the Seizure of the Fairy Mound)',
     vol 19, pp. 53–58, 1931–3
* Hull, Vernam, 'The Exile of Conall Corc', *PMLA*, LVI, 1941
*Hull, Vernam, *Longes mac n-Uislenn*, New York, Modern Language Assoc. of
     America, 1949
Jones, G. and Jones, I., trans., *The Mabinogion*, J. M. Dent, 1974
Jones, O., Williams, E. and Pughe, W. O., eds., *The Myvyrian Archaiology of Wales*,
     Thomas Gere, Denbigh, 1870
Joynt, M., *Feis Tighe Conain*, Dublin, Hodges & Figgis, 1936
*Joynt, M. 'Ectra mac Echdach Mugmedoin', *Eriu* IV (1910), pp. 91–111
*Kinsella, T. trans., *The Tain*, Oxford University Press, 1970
* Knott, Eleanor, 'Why Mongán was Deprived of Noble Issue', *Eriu* vol 8, 1916
Leahy, A. H., *Heroic Romances of Ireland*, London, David Nutt, 1906
*Leahy, A. H., 'The Sick-Bed of Cú Chulainn' in *Heroic Romances of Ireland*, I
     (London, 1905), pp. 51–85.
*Leahy, A. H., 'The Exile of the Sons of Usnech' in *Heroic Romances of Ireland*, I
     (London, 1905), pp. 87–109.
*MacAlister, R. A. S., *Lebor Gabála Erenn vols 1–4*, Dublin, Irish Texts Society,
     1939–41
*Macneill, E., *Duanaire Finn*, Irish Texts Society, 1908
Meyer, Kuno, 'The Adventures of Nera', *RC*, X 1889, pp. 212–228; XI; 1890, pp.

210–218

*Meyer, Kuno, Anecdota from the Stow MS. no 992, in *RC*, vol 6, 1883–5

Meyer, K., 'The Boyish Exploits of Finn', *Eriu* 1, pp. 180–190, 1904

Meyer, K., 'The Colloquy of Colum Cille and the Youth at Cam Eolairg', *ZCP* vol 2, pp. 313–317

*Meyer, Kuno, 'The Death of Celtchar mac Uthecair', *Death Tales of the Irish Heroes*, Dublin, 1906, pp. 24–31

*Meyer, Kuno, 'The Death of Conchobar', *Death Tales of the Irish Heroes*, Dublin, 1906, pp. 2–21

*Meyer, Kuno, *Fianaigecht*, Dublin, School of Celtic Studies, 1999

Meyer, K., 'Finn and the Man in the Tree', *RC* XXV, 1904, pp. 344–349

*Meyer, K., [ed. and trans.] *Hibernica Minora*, Oxford, The Clarendon Press, 1894

Meyer, Kuno, 'How Ronan Slew His Son', *RC*, XIII (1892), pp. 368–397

*Meyer, Kuno, *The Instructions of King Cormac mac Airt*, Dublin, Hodges, Figgis & Co, 1909

Meyer, Kuno, *Liadain and Curithir*, London, D. Nutt, 1902

Meyer, Kuno, *Otia Merseiana*, London, D. Nutt,1900

*Meyer, Kuno, *Sanas Cormaic*, Dublin, Halle, 1918

*Meye, Kuno, 'Scel Baili Binnberlaig' *RC*, 13, 1892, pp. 220–227

*Meyer, Kuno, 'The Tragic Death of Connla' *Eriu*, 1, 1904, pp. 113–121

Meyer, Kuno, *The Triads of Ireland*, Dublin, Royal Irish Academy Lecture Series XIII, 1906

Meyer, Kuno, *The Vision of MacConglinne*, D. Nutt, 1892

*Meyer, Kuno, *The Voyage of Bran, son of Febal*, London, D. Nutt, 1895

*Meyer, Kuno, 'The Wooing of Emer', *Archaeological Review*, I,1888 .

*O'Curry, Eugene, 'The Fate of the Children of Tuirenn', *The Atlantis* IV (1863), pp. 157–240

*O'Daly, Máirín, *Cath Maige Mucrama*, Dublin, Irish Texts Society, 1975

O'Donovan, J., Cormac's *Glossary*, edited, with notes and indexes, by Whitley Stokes, Calcutta; Irish Archaeological & Celtic Society, 1868

*O'Donovon, J., *Miscellany of the Celtic Society*, Dublin, Celtic Society, 1849

O'Grady, Standish, 'The Death of Fergus Mac Leide', *Silva Gadelica*, Dublin, 1892

O'Grady, Standish, *The Colloquy of the Elders*, Felinfach, Llanerch Publishers, 2000

O'Grady, Standish, 'The Pursuit of Diarmuid and Grainne', *Transactions of the Ossianic Society*, III (1855/7), pp 40–211

*O'Grady, S., ed. and trans., *Silva Gadelica* (2 vols), Williams & Norgate, 1892

*O'Keeffe, J. G. ed. and trans, *Buile Suibne*, D. Nutt, 1913

O'Looney, B.' The Wooing of Becfola', *Proceedings of the Royal Irish Academy*, I, pt. i (Dublin, 1870), pp. 172–183

*O'Rahilly, Cecile *Táin Bó Cuailgne*, Dublin, Dublin Institute for Advanced Studies, 1976

Skene, W. E, ed. and trans., *The Four Ancient Books of Wales* (2 vols), New York, AMS Press, 1984–5

*Sjoestedt, M. L., 'Seige De Druim Damhgaire', *RC* vol 44, pp. 157–186, 1927

* Stokes, Whitley, 'Acallamh na Senórach', in *Irische Texte* vol iv, Leipzig, 1900

Stokes, Whitley, 'The Adventures of the Sons of Eochaid Mugmedon' in 'The
    Death of Crimthann and the Adventures of Eochaid,' *RC*, XXIV (1903), pp.
    172–207
*Stokes, Whitley, 'Aided Muirchertaig maic Erca Insin', in *RC* XXIII, 1892
Stokes, Whitley, 'The Borama', *RC* 13, pp. 33, 1892, pp. 33–124,
*Stokes, Whitley, *The Calendar of Oengus*, Dublin, Hodges, Fisher and Figgis,
    1880
Stokes, Whitley, 'The Colloquy of the Two Sages', *RC* vol 26, pp. 4–64, 1905
Stokes, Whitley, 'The Death of Cú Chulainn' *RC*, 111 (1887), pp. 175–185.
*Stokes, Whitley, 'The Destruction of Dind Ríg', *ZCP* III, 1901
Stokes, Whitley, 'Find and the Phantoms', *RC* VII, pp. 289–307, 1886
Stokes, Whitley, 'The Prose Tales in the Rennes Dindsenchas', *RC*, XIII, pp.
    124–43
*Stokes, Whitley, 'The Second Battle of Mag Tured', *R.C.* XII 1891, pp. 52–130,
    306–308
*Stokes, Whitley, 'The Siege of Howth', *RC* VIII, pp. 47–64, 1887
*Stokes, Whitley, 'Songs of Buchet's House' *RC* XXV, 1904, pp. 20–39
*Stokes, Whitley, *Togail Bruidne dá Derga*, Paris, Librarie Emile Bouillon, 1902,
*Stokes, Whitley, Tochmarc Luaine, *RC* XXIV, 1903
*Stokes, Whitley, 'The Voyage of Maelduin', *RC* vol IX, (1888), pp. 447–495,
    and X (1889), pp. 50–95
*Stokes, Whitley, 'The Wooing of Luaine' *RC*, XXIV, (1903), pp. 172–285
*Stokes, W. and Windisch, E., 'The Irish Ordeals' and 'The Fitness of Names',
    Irische Texte (3rd Series, vol 1) Leipzig, Verlag von S. Hirzel, 1891
Van Hamel, A. G., *Compert Con Culainn*, Dublin, 1933
Williams, G. J., 'Tri Chof Ynys Brydain', *Llen Cymru* vol 3, pp. 234–239, 1955
Williams, L, Armes Prydein: *The Prophecy of Britain* (English version by Rachel
    Bromwich), the Dublin Institute for Advanced Studies, 1982
*Williams, M., 'An Early Ritual Poem in Welsh', *Speculum* 13, pp. 38–51, 1938

General

Bartrum, P. C., *Early Welsh Genealogical Tracts*, Cardiff, University of Wales Press,
    1966
Bergin, O., *Irish Bardic Poetry*, Dublin Institute for Advanced Studies, 1970
Breatnach, Caoimhín, *Patronage, Politics and Prose*, Maynooth, An Sagart, 1996
Bromwich, R., 'The Character of Early Welsh Tradition', *Studies in Early British
    History*, H. M. Chadwick *et al.*, Cambridge University Press, 1954
Bromwich, R., *The Trioedd Ynys Prydein in Welsh Literature and Scholarship*,
    Cardiff, University of Wales Press, 1969
Bromwich, R. (ed.), 'Trioedd Ynys Prydain: The Myvyrian Third Series',
    Transactions of the Honourable Society of Cymmrodorion, pt 1, pp. 299301,
    1968; pt. 2, pp. 127–56, 1969
Bromwich, Rachel, *Medieval Celtic Literature*, Toronto, University of Toronto
    Press, 1974
Byrne, Francis, *Irish Kings and High Kings*, London, Batsford, 1973

Calder, G., *Auraicept Na N-Eces (The Scholar's Primer)*, Edinburgh, John Grant, 1917

Carmichael, A., *Carmina Gadelica* (5 vols), Edinburgh, Scottish Academic Press, 1928–1972

Camey, J., *Medieval Irish Lyrics with The Irish Bardic Poet*, Portlaoise, The Dolman Press, 1985

Chadwick, H. M., *The Heroic Age*, Cambridge University Press, 1967

Chadwick, H. M., and Chadwick, N. K., *The Growth of Literature* (3 vols), Cambridge University Press, 1932–40

Curtin, J., *Myths and Folk Tales of Ireland*, New York, Dover Publications, 1975

Dictionary of the Irish Language, Dublin, Royal Irish Academy, 1998

Dineen, Patrick, *Foclóir Gaelilge agus Béarla*, Dublin, Early Irish Text Society, 1927

Dillon, M., *The Cycles of the Kings.* Oxford University Press, 1946

Dillon, M., 'Stories from the Law Tracts', *Eriu* XI, pp. 42–65

Gantz, J., *Early Irish Myths and Sagas*, Harmondsworth, Penguin Books, 1981

Gose, E. G., Jr., *The World of the Irish Wonder Tale*, University of Toronto Press, 1985

Green, M., *The Gods of the Celts, Gloucester*, Alan Sutton, 1986

Green, M., *Symbol & Image in Celtic Religious Art*, Routledge, 1989

Jackson, K. H., *The International Popular Tale in Early Welsh Tradition*, Cardiff, University of Wales Press, 1961

Joyce, P. W., *A Social History of Ancient Ireland* (2 vols), Longmans, Green & Co, 1903

Jubainville, H. D., *The Irish Mythological Cycle*, Dublin, O'Donoghue & Co, 1903

Macalister, R. A. S., *The Secret Languages of Ireland*, St Helier, Amorica Book Co. Amsterdam, Philo Press, 1976

Mac Cana, Proinsias, *The Learned Tales of Medieval Ireland*, Dublin, Dublin Institute for Advanced Studies, 1980

MacKillop, James, *Dictionary of Celtic Mythology*, Oxford, Oxford University Press, 1998

McCullough, David Willis, *Wars of the Irish Kings*, New York, Crown, 2000

Maier, Bernhard, *Dictionary of Celtic Religion and Culture*, Woodbridge, Boydell Press, 1997

Martin, M., *A Description of the Western Islands of Scotland 1695*, ed. Macleod, D., Stirling, 1934

Matthews, Caitlín, *Celtic Love: Ten Enchanted Stories*, San Francisco, Harper, 2000

Matthews, Caitlín, *The Celtic Spirit*, San Francisco, Harper, 1999

Matthews, Caitlín, *The Celtic Tradition*, Shaftesbury, Harper Collins, 1989

Matthews, Caitlín, *Celtic Wisdom Sticks: An Ogam Oracle*, London, Connections 2001

Matthews, Caitlín, *King Arthur and the Goddess of the Land*, Rochester, Inner Traditions, 2002

Matthews, Caitlín, *Mabon and the Guardians of Celtic Britain*, Rochester, Inner Traditions, 2002

Matthews, Caitlín and John, *The Encyclopaedia of Celtic Wisdom*, London, Rider,

2001

Matthews, John, *The Bardic Source-Book*, London, Cassell,1999

Matthews, John, *The Celtic Seers Source-Book*, London, Cassell, 2000

Matthews, John, *The Celtic Shaman*, London, Rider, 2001

Matthews, John, *Celtic Totem Animals*, London, Connections, 2002

Matthews, John, *The Druid Source-Book*, London, Cassell, 1997

Matthews, John, *The Song of Taliesin*, Wheaton, Quest Books, 2001

Matthews, John, *Taliesin: Shamanism and the Bardic Tradition in Britain and Ireland*, Rochester, Inner Traditions, 2001

Matthews, John, *Drinking from the Sacred Well*, Harper, San Francisco, 1999

Nagy, Joseph F., *The Wisdom of the Outlaw*, Berkeley, University of California Press, 1985

O'Curry, Eugene, *Lectures on the Manuscript Materials of Ancient Irish History*, Blackrock, Four Courts Press, 1995

O'Driscoll, R., ed., *The Celtic Consciousness*, Edinburgh, Cannongate Publishing; Portlaoise, The Dolmen Press, 1982

O'Hogain, D., *The Hero In Irish Folk History*, Dublin, Gill & Macmillan, 1985

O'Hogain, D., *Fionn mac Cumhail: Images of the Gaelic Hero*, Dublin, Gill & Macmillan, 1988

O'Rahilly, T. R., *Early Irish History and Mythology*, Dublin Institute for Advanced Studies, 1976

Parry, I., *A History of Welsh Literature*, Oxford, The Clarendon Press, 1955

Rees, A. and Rees B., *Celtic Heritage*, Thames & Hudson, 1961

Rhys, J., *Lectures on the Origin and Growth of Religion as Illustrated by Celtic Heathendom*, Williams & Norgate, 1888

Ross, A., *Pagan Celtic Britain*, Cardinal, 1974

Rowland, J., *Early Welsh Saga Poetry*, Cambridge, D. S.Brewer, 1990

Rowlands, R. R, 'Bardic Lore and Education', *The Bulletin of the Board of Celtic Studies* vol 32, pp. 143–155, 1985

Schofield, W H., *Mythic Bards*, Cambridge, Harvard University Press, 1920

Scott, R. D., *The Thumb of Knowledge in Legends of Fionn*, Sigurd and Taliesin, Publications of the Institute of French Studies, Columbia University, New York, 1930

Sjoestedt, M. L., *Gods and Heroes of the Celts*, Berkley, Turtle Island Foundation, 1982

Stephens, M. ed., *The Oxford Companion to the Literature of Wales*, Oxford University Press, 1986

JOHN AND CAITLÍN MATTHEWS

For details of the author's courses, books and events worldwide, see www.hallowquest.org.uk

Alternatively you may write to them at BCM Hallowquest, London WCIN 3XX, UK, sending a $5 US bill for a copy of their recent newsletter.

Index

Achtan 73ff., 238
Adventures of Connla 385–7
Adventure of Eachdach's Sons 379–84
Agnoman 14, 325
Aided Conchobor meic Nessa 457–60
Aided Conn Cetchathach 461–7
Aife 364–5, 484
Ailill mac Matach 71, 83ff., 109–110, 153ff., 192–4, 222, 224, 228–9, 236, 300, 404ff., 417, 450, 484
Ailill Olom 230–2, 239–42, 484
Aillinn 331, 484
Aine 231, 484
Ainle 451, 484
Airmend 48, 58, 484
Airne Fíngein 245–55
Aislinge Oenguso 189–94
Alba 91, 230, 233–5, 258, 270, 360ff., 438, 439ff., 448–9, 484
Amairgin Glunmar 260, 270, 484
Amergin mac Eculsach 260, 484
Ana/Anu/Danu 257, 484
animal sacrifice 222
Ardan 451,484
Art mac Conn 73, 231, 234, 236, 237, 238–9, 385, 387, 461, 484
Athairn/Atherne 260, 281–8, 369–75,484
Arthur 186, 271, 334–9, 340

Badb 28, 31, 32 36, 63, 87, 92,104, 353, 484
Baile Binnbérlach 331–3, 484
Balor 45, 51, 52, 59, 60, 484
Banba 36, 270, 485
Battle of Findchorad 221–9
Battle of Mag Mucrama 72, 230–42
battle-magic 55, 57ff., 318
Beltane 353, 359, 485
birth, delayed 67, 69–71, 72–3
Blathnat 418, 421, 485
Boann 190ff., 245, 356–7, 485

Bodb Derg 32, 36, 191ff., 226, 249, 252, 255, 485
Book of Invasions 11–16
Bran mac Febal 113–122, 485
Brandubh mac Echach, 172–180
Bres mac Elatha/Elada 25–27, 36, 37, 38, 40, 46, 47ff., 56, 59, 61, 485
Bricriu Nemthenga 97, 124, 391–425, 485
    B's feast 391–425
Brigid 58, 246, 257, 485
Brislech mó r Maige Muirthemne 468–75
Brown, A.C.L. 245
Brugh na Boinne 192, 485
Buanann 257
bulls 67, 89, 91, 153, 221–9

Caer Ibormeith 189–93, 485
Cai Hir 334, 335–6, 341, 485
Cailb 290, 304, 485
caill crinmon 257
Cailte mac Ronain 167, 182, 485
Caintigerna 166, 168, 171, 485
Cairenn 379–80, 485
Cairpre Musc 262–3
Cath Findchorad 221–9
Cath Maige Mucrama 72, 230–42
Cath Mag Tuiread 44–64
Cath Mag Tuiread Cong 17–43
Cathbad 67–71, 159ff., 370, 415, 445–6, 447, 486
Cattle Raid of Cuailgne 67, 71, 87, 91–110
Cattle Raid of Flidais 83–86
Ceasacht Inghine Guile 426–34
Celtchair mac Uthechair 347, 373, 374–5, 486
Ces Noínden Ulad 325–8
Cessair 12ff., 486
Cet mac Matach 458, 486
Champion's Portion 391–425
Christianity 3, 457, 459, 475

Cirb 28, 30, 31, 33–4
Cobthach Có el Breg 275–80, 486
Coire Breccain 258
Compert Conchobor 67–71
Compert Cormaic mac Airt 72–6
Compert Con Cú Chulainn 153–165
Compert Noidiu 77–9
Conaing/ Conand 16,17–18, 20ff., 486
Conaire Mor 289–324, 468, 486
Conall Cernach 157ff., 161–2,185, 196,
        197, 199, 205, 229, 236, 281,
        285–8, 313–14, 320, 322, 324, 347,
        352, 360, 361, 366, 367, 373, 391,
        393–4, 395–6, 403, 406–7, 410ff.,
        457, 469, 473–5, 486
Conall Corc 437–43, 486
conception
    by water 69
    prophecy 47, 70–1, 72–3, 78, 120–1,
        253–5, 293, 445–6
Conchobar 84, 102, 154ff., 159ff., 165,
        197, 222, 228, 246, 281, 346, 347,
        351, 358, 360, 361, 392ff., 404,
        409, 415, 422, 444ff., 469, 486
    birth of 67–71
    death of 457–40
    marries Deirdriu 369, 370, 450–5
    woos Luaine 369–75
Conn Cet-Cathach 230, 245, 251, 252,
        253–5, 251, 252–5, 385–7, 486
    death of 461–7
Connla mac Conn Cet Chatach 385–7,
        461, 486
Corc *see* Conall Corc
Cormac Connlonges 229, 307–8, 486
Cormac mac Airt 239, 240, 332, 333, 486
    birth of 72–76, 237
Cormac mac Lactighe 292, 486
Cormac mac Cuilleanáin 256–271, 486
Cormac's Glossary 256–71
Craiphtine 275ff., 486
Credne 36, 45, 52, 56, 58, 264
Crimthann mac Fidaig 439, 486
Crimthan Nia Nair 246, 249, 281
Cross, T.P. 245
Crunnchu mac Agnoman 325–8, 353, 487
Cú Chulainn 87–90, 91–110, 257, 285–8,
        328, 340, 373, 391, 392, 394ff.,
        457, 487
    and the Champion's Portion 391–425
    appearance of 103–4, 106–7
    battle distortion of 104–6

boyhood deeds 153–165
death of 468–75
heals Mórrígan 98–9
naming of 157–9
rescues Conchobor 156–7
sickness of 195–218
training of 361–7
Cu Roi mac Dairi 225, 228, 391, 402,
        417–25, 487
Cuimne 177–180, 487
Culainn 158ff.
Cuscraid Menn 197

Da Derga 289–324, 487
Dagda 17, 30ff., 36, 38, 40–42, 47–8, 53,
        190ff., 252, 257
    cauldron of 45
    harp of 62–3
    union with *Mórrígan* 54–5
Danann 32, 36, 57
Debility of the Ulstermen 325–8
Deirdre/Deirdriu 83, 92, 369ff., 374,
        444–53, 487
Destruction of Da Derga's Hostel 289–324,
        468
Destruction of Dind Rig 275–80
Dian Cecht 32, 36, 38, 45, 52, 54, 56, 58,
        258, 487
dichetal do chennaib 4, 258, 261
Dillon, Myles 7
dindsenchas/dinnshencas 256, 487
divination of luck 160
Dobbs, Mary 7, 78, 221
Dubh-Lacha 167,169ff., 487
Dubthach Dóeltenga 84ff., 107ff., 318,
        322, 347, 416, 421ff., 449, 450, 487

Echtra Connla 385–7
Echtra mac nEchach Muigmedóin 379–84
Emain Macha 101,102, 154ff., 204, 259,
        325, 331, 346ff., 353–5, 359, 360,
        392, 487
Emer 195,197, 204–7, 340, 345, 348–53,
        367–8, 397–8,399–400, 487
Encyclopaedia of Celtic Wisdom 3,77, 258,
        270, 289–90, 385, 461
Eochaid Airem 113, 488
Eochaid Feidlioch 290–2, 395, 487
Eochaid mac Eirc 24, 29, 32, 33ff., 38ff.,
        45, 487
Eochaid mac Luchta 221ff., 282, 488
Eochaid Mugmedón 379–84, 488

Eochu Rígéigeas 184–6
Eogabul mac Durgabul 230–1, 255, 488
Eogan mac Ailill 230–3, 234, 236–9, 488
Eogan mac Durthacht 156, 373, 397, 398, 449, 453, 488
Eogan Mor 72, 462, 466, 488
Eoghanacht 73, 124, 230, 437, 488
éric 437–8, 441, 488
Eriu 36, 270, 488
Ernmas 45, 60, 63, 488
Essyllt 334–9, 488
Etain 167, 289, 488
Etain Og 289, 290–2, 488
Eterscel 292, 293, 488
Ethne/Eithne 52, 488
Ethne Tháebfhota 197, 488
Excuse of Guile's Daughter 426–34
Exile of Conall Corc 437–43
Exile of the Sons of Uisliu 444–53

Fal
    Stone of 45, 83, 461
Fann/Fand 198, 199, 200 ff., 210–8
Fathach 28, 30–1, 35–6
Fedelm Láir Derg 439, 488
Fedelm Noíchrothach 396, 488
Fedlimid mac Criomthan 426–34, 488
Fer Caille 299, 488
Fer Fí 230–2, 240, 247, 250, 255, 488
Fer Rogain 293, 300–1, 305, 489
Ferches mac Commán 231, 241, 488
Ferdia 91, 110, 363
Fergus mac Roich/Róig 67, 83ff., 92, 94, 97, 108ff., 154ff., 196, 228, 229, 347, 352, 393, 396, 404, 409, 416, 422, 423, 449–50, 489
fertility of the land 49–50, 61–2, 295, 466
Fiachna Finn/Lurga 168, 169–171, 489
Fiachu Muillethan 72, 237, 489
fianna 67,68, 489
fidchell 155, 172, 259, 489
Findabair/Finnabair 91, 404–5, 409, 489
Fingen mac Luchtra 245–55, 489
Fingen's Nightwatch 245–55
Fintan mac Bochra 13,17, 18–19, 23, 35, 246, 249, 489
Fionn mac Cumhail 167, 257, 265–7, 489
Fir Bolg 12, 15, 22, 24 ff., 45, 489

Fir Domnann 12, 489
Fled Bricriu 391–425
Flidais 83–86, 246, 489
Fodla/Fotla 36, 270, 489
Fomorians 12, 14,18ff., 36, 45ff., 53, 55ff., 312, 489
Fraser, J. 17

geis/ geas 290, 293, 294ff., 468ff.
gléfisa 1, 8
Goibniu 36, 38, 41, 53, 58, 264–5, 489
Greth 260, 489
Gruibne 437, 439ff., 489
Guile 426–34, 489
Guile Beag 426–34, 489
Gwalchmai 334, 336–8, 489
Gwenhwyfar 340–2, 489

healing 30, 32, 48, 58, 98–9, 101, 459
Henderson, George 391
Hull, Eleanor 325
Hull, Vernam 444

Igraine 166
imbas forosna 4, 261, 290, 490
Imbolc 101, 153, 359, 490
Imram Brainn mac Febal 113–22
Imram Máel Dúin 123–150
Ingcél Cáech 296, 300ff., 305ff., 490
Ireland
    division of 22–3
Isle of Man 46, 267–70, 318–9

kennings 350–9
Knott, Eleanor 166, 168

Labraid Loingsech 275–80, 490
Labraid Luath Lambh ar Claidib 199ff., 204ff., 207, 490
Laeg/Loeg mac Riangabra 88, 95ff., 198, 201ff., 345, 348, 353–9, 404ff., 413, 469, 471, 490
    description of 102
    visits the sí 208–213
Land of Women 117, 121, 123, 141–4
Leahy, A.H. 195
Lebor Gabála Erenn 11–16
Leborcham 197, 370, 447, 469, 490
Lendabair 397, 398–9, 490
Leth Cuinn 437, 461, 465, 490
Leth Moga 437, 465, 490
Liban, 198, 199, 200ff., 212ff., 490

Lóch 91,93–8
Lochlann 51,169ff., 491
Loeg *see* Laeg mac Riangabra
Loegaire Buadach 205–6, 347, 360, 361,
    366, 367, 391, 393–4, 395–6, 398,
    402–3, 405–6, 410ff., 457, 491
Loegaire Lorc 275 ff., 491
Lomna 265–7, 316
Longes Chonaill Corc 437–43
Longes mac nUislenn 444–53
Luaine 369–75, 491
Luchta/Lucraid/Luchtine 36, 38, 57, 58,
    264, 491
Lug/Lugh Lamfhada 17, 44, 54, 56ff., 92,
    358, 491
  coming of 51–3
  heals Cú Chulainn 99–102
  spear of 45
Lugaid mac Conn 72, 74ff., 230–242,
    491
Lughnasadh 359, 490

Mabinogion 113, 167
Macalister, R.A.S. 5, 11
Mac an Daimh 173ff., 490
Mac Cecht 297,302, 303, 310–1, 312,
    321–4, 490
Macha, daughter of Ernmas 28, 32, 36, 60,
    87, 490
Macha, wife of Crunniuc mac Agnomen,
    259, 325–7, 353–4, 490
Maelduin 123–150, 167, 491
Maeve *see* Medb
Mag Tuiread *see* Moytura
Manannán mac Athgno 369, 371–2, 491
Manannán mac Lí r 61, 113, 117–121,
    166, 169, 172,174, 195, 200,
    216–8, 246, 263–4, 371, 491
March ap Meirchion 334–9, 491
Matthews, Caitlín, 72, 83, 91, 123, 153,
    167, 195, 230, 256, 340, 385, 426,
    437, 461
Matthews, John 340, 385
Medb/Maeve 67, 71, 83ff., 91, 93ff.,
    109ff., 153ff., 192–4, 222, 224,
    228–9, 236, 300, 325, 404ff., 417,
    450, 491
Mesgegra 281, 283–8, 457–8, 460, 491
Mes/Meas Buachalla 292–3, 491
Meyer, Kuno 7, 67,113, 166, 168, 331,
    345
Miach 48, 58, 491

Midir 32, 252, 491
Mil 29, 250, 491
Mongán 113, 117, 120–1, 166–186, 271,
    491
  antagonises Forgoll 180–82
  birth of 168–9
  childlessness of 184–86
  death of 120–1, 186
  gives alms 182–3
  rescues Dubh-Lacha 173–80
  vision of 183–4
Mongfinn 379ff., 492
Morann mac Maine 77, 261–2, 491
Moriath 277ff.
Mórrígan 28, 32, 36, 55, 60, 63–4, 93,
    97–9, 249, 257, 350, 356, 491
  Mórrigan's Cattle Raid 87–90
Moytura
  First Battle of 12, 17–42
  Second Battle of 12, 43–64
Mugain 395, 491
myth 2–3

Naoisi/Noisiu 84, 92, 444–53, 491
Nechtan 245–6, 247, 356, 491
Némain 91, 99, 492
Nemed 12, 14ff.,18 ff., 25, 356, 491
Nemedians 12, 14 ff., 18, 18ff., 39, 325,
    491
Nemglan 294, 491
Ness/a 67–71, 264–5, 491
Niall Nóigiallach 258, 379–84, 491
Noah 3, 11,13, 246
Noidiu Nae-mbreathach 77–9, 491
Noisiu/Naoisi 369ff., 491
Nuadu Airgetlam 17,27, 29, 35, 36–38,41,
    43, 45, 46, 53ff., 60, 357, 358, 492
  healing of 49
  sword of, 45

Odyssey 113, 124
Oengus mac Og 48, 189–194, 252, 325,
    356, 492
ogam/ogham 492
Ogma 32 ff., 36,38, 47, 49, 52, 53, 60, 62,
    492
Olc Aiche 72,73ff., 237, 492
Orgain Denna Rig 275–80
otherworld
  names of 113
Partholon 12 ff. 492
poetic

circuit 268, 282, 288
cursing 283, 369–70, 372
curriculum 4–5
incubation 5–6
spirit 267–70
Pwyll 113, 167, 438, 492

Rhiannon 167, 492
Rothniamh 245–255, 461, 463–4
Ruadan 58, 492

Sadb 231, 241–2, 493
Samhain 54, 55, 101, 153, 193, 196, 199,
    231, 247, 332, 359, 366, 461, 492
Sanas Cormaic 256–71
Scathach 70, 91, 346, 360ff., 492
Scel Baili Binnberlaig 331–3
Scoriath 277ff.
Sencha mac Ailill 196, 317–8, 322, 351,
    373, 393, 398, 410, 416, 444, 492
Senchán Torpeist 267–70, 492
Serglige con Cú Chulainn 195–218
sí/síd/sidhe: 18, 92, 189, 195 ff., 231–2,
    296, 492
  land of 208–10
  sinlessness of 113, 115
  treasures of 182–3, 246–55
  warriors 320–1
  women of 226, 245–55, 325, 385–7
Sickbed of Cú Chulainn 113,195–218,
    325
Siege of Howth 281–8
Sithchenn 380ff., 492
Sovereignty 382ff., 492
Sreng 25–28, 34, 37–8 ,40,42, 43, 45,
    492
Stokes, Whitley 7, 44, 45, 123, 230, 275,
    281, 289, 369, 379, 468

Tailltiu 52, 493
Táin Bó Cuailgne 6, 84, 87, 91–110, 153,
    194, 221, 325
Táin Bó Flidais 83–6, 391
Táin Bó Regamma 87–90
Taliesin 77, 260
Talland Etair 281–8
Tara 75, 240, 247, 252, 294, 296, 333,
    350, 379, 382, 383, 461ff., 492

tarbh feis 222, 290, 293–4, 492
teinm laegda 4, 261, 263, 266–7
three musical strains 232, 275, 277–8
Tibraide mac Mál 462–7, 492
tiompán 189, 190, 231, 232, 493
Tir Tairngire 104, 493
Tochmarc Emer 345–68
Tochmarc Luaine agus Aidedh Aithairne
    Andso 369–75
Togail Bruidne da Derga 270, 289–324
Tonn Cliodna 224, 315, 493
Torna Eces 380
Tory Island 15
triplicity 270–1
Trystan ap Tallwch 334–9, 493
Tuan mac Carill 12, 14, 167, 493
Tuatha dé Danann 24ff., 44ff., 251, 257,
    350, 431, 493
  skills of the 51–8
  treasures of 44, 45
Tuirenn Bicreo/Bigrenn 36, 45, 246, 493

Uaithne 62–3, 493
Uathach 363–4, 493
Uisnech/Usnech 183, 247, 254, 463,
    493
Urard mac Coise 3–4
Uther Pendragon 166

Voyage of Bran, Son of Febal 113–122
Voyage of Brendan 113
Voyage of Maelduin 123–150

waters
  dried up 54
  inundations of 245–6
Well
  of Healing (Slane) 30, 32, 58, 59
  of Segais 493
wolves 74–5
Wooing of Emer 345–68
Wooing of Luaine and the Death of
    Athirne 369–75

Y Melwas 340–2, 491
Ystori Tryston 334–39